Also by LeeAnna Keith

The Colfax Massacre: The Untold Story of Black Power, White Terror, and the Death of Reconstruction

WHEN
IT
WAS
GRAND

WHEN IT WAS GRAND

The Radical
Republican History
of the
Civil War

LeeAnna Keith

HILL AND WANG

A division of Farrar, Straus and Giroux   New York

Hill and Wang
A division of Farrar, Straus and Giroux
120 Broadway, New York 10271

Library of Congress Cataloging-in-Publication Data
Names: Keith, LeeAnna, author.
Title: When it was grand : the radical Republican history of the Civil War /
    LeeAnna Keith.
Description: First edition. | New York : Hill and Wang, a division of
    Farrar, Straus and Giroux, 2020. | Includes bibliographical references and index. |
    Summary: "A history of antiracist and abolitionist activism in the Civil War–era
    Republican Party"—Provided by publisher.
Identifiers: LCCN 2019028465 | ISBN 9780809080311 (hardcover)
Subjects: LCSH: Republican Party (U.S. : 1854–)—History—19th century. |
    Political parties—United States—History—19th century. | Antislavery
    movements—United States—History—19th century. | Radicalism—United States—
    History—19th century. | African Americans—Politics and government—19th century. |
    African Americans—Civil rights—History—19th century. | United States—Politics and
    government—1849–1877. | United States—History—Civil War, 1861–1865.
Classification: LCC JK2356 .K45 2020 | DDC 973.7/1—dc23
LC record available at https://lccn.loc.gov/2019028465

Designed by Abby Kagan

Our books may be purchased in bulk for promotional, educational, or business use. Please
contact your local bookseller or the Macmillan Corporate and Premium Sales Department at
1-800-221-7945, extension 5442, or by e-mail at MacmillanSpecialMarkets@macmillan.com.

www.fsgbooks.com
www.twitter.com/fsgbooks • www.facebook.com/fsgbooks

1 3 5 7 9 10 8 6 4 2

To My Three Dads—

Sam, Buck, and Don

CONTENTS

WHEN
IT
WAS
GRAND

EHE
_____

PROLOGUE: GREAT OLD PARTY

he Republican Party was born in a blast that destroyed what historians came to call the second political party system in 1854. Its
most ardent faction, the Radical Republicans, helped to destroy
slavery and used the conflagration of the Civil War to initiate a revolution
in race relations. The first era of Republican supremacy in government,
from 1861 to the mid-1870s, produced an ashy aftertaste that has lingered
in the politics of the U.S. South for more than 150 years. The daring of the
Radicals became notorious, reviled by the now defunct White Supremacy
Democrats (1854–1964) and never celebrated by what came to call itself
the Grand Old Party.

When it was grand, the Republican movement asked the most important questions and demanded the most extreme sacrifices of its partisans.
Beginning as a tiny minority, antislavery Republicans came to command
the creative destruction and Reconstruction of the most politically and
economically powerful interest group in American history. Its coalition
brought together men and women, whites and blacks, poets, philosophers,
captains of industry, and humanitarians of many political stripes. The
Radical Republicans dominated their party and transformed the nature of
government to achieve their goals.

Radical Republicans of the Civil War era subscribed to a comprehensive conspiracy theory about the plotting of proslavery activists to control

government and extend the practice of slavery into Free States and beyond the borders of the United States. They had excellent evidence in support of their claims. More important, they made note of the blueprint of the Slave Power Conspiracy as a model for their own hostile takeover of government.

They dominated the Republican Party, constantly conspiring against coalition partners such as more moderate Republicans, and they thrived as wily conventioneers and parliamentarians. Radicals talked tough—for states' rights, for the local nullification of proslavery federal laws, and in favor of the dissolution of the union. They stockpiled armaments, carried weapons on their persons, and used their bodies as weapons. They reveled in war talk, and their militant actions helped to drive the country toward the most destructive war in its history.

The Radicals were culture warriors, committed to a nearly mystical vision of representative government based on free labor. Prizing equal opportunity and expansion, they championed government spending for education and transportation infrastructure, and they celebrated the self-made men and women in their ranks, such as Abraham Lincoln and Frederick Douglass. These Republicans appealed to populism without demonizing capital, being mostly disunited on economic policy questions such as tariffs versus free trade. Most shared the mainstream Republicans' respect for property rights, and even partisans of humble origins expected to grow rich amid general prosperity. Wealthy industrialists figured prominently among the Radicals, putting their personal means at the service of armed colonization, slave rescues, and the militant John Brown conspiracy. In wartime they would contribute their organizational expertise, machinery, and capital to both Union victory and racial uplift, demonstrating by war's end that their theory about the superiority of free labor had been true.

Radical Republicans aimed to restore what partisans considered the true history of the American Revolution, including the subverted antislavery intentions of the founding generation. An antislavery interpretation of the Declaration of Independence and the Constitution animated the work of party lawyers and their followers. Historical treatises appeared as landmarks of the Radical ascendancy: Salmon Chase's 1842 legal brief on behalf of the slave Matilda, Charles Sumner's 1845 speech "The True Grandeur of Nations," and the Cooper Union address delivered by Abraham Lincoln early in 1860. Their authors would make America great by restoring the originally intended course of slavery toward its ultimate extinction.

Lawyers such as Lincoln, Sumner, Chase, William Seward, and Thaddeus Stevens led the party in an era of open conflict between state courts and federal law enforcement. Republican-affiliated judges employed writs of habeas corpus to secure the persons and derail the prosecution of detained antislavery activists in an increasing number of cases arising from fugitive slave renditions. Legal aid societies operated formally and informally to assist accused fugitives and those who risked their lives and liberty in antirendition activities. Proslavery pronouncements in the federal courts—particularly the notorious outcome of *Dred Scott v. Sandford* (1857)—inspired conspiracy theories and official proclamations of noncompliance with Supreme Court rulings by state legislatures. During the Civil War, the Lincoln administration packed the federal courts with Radical judges and agitated to establish operating federal judicial districts in occupied territories. Afterward, Radicals in the Ulysses S. Grant administration fielded an army of race-conscious U.S. attorneys in the newly established Department of Justice.

Radical Republicanism was also a religious and philosophical movement that arose from the evangelical and intellectual boom of the antebellum era. Participants were overwhelmingly Protestant or members of the Unitarian Universalist church. Advocacy for the enslaved stimulated a variety of Christian impulses, as churches and ministers became centers of political and humanitarian agency. Gripped by the plight of fugitives and the violent expansion of slavery to new territories, the "Transcendentalist" American philosophers Ralph Waldo Emerson and Henry David Thoreau reflected on and reinforced the political work of Radicals. The incredible emotional and physical costs of the Civil War brought existential anguish into the everyday in a way that deeply reinforced religious and philosophical beliefs. Awe, horror, leaps of faith, and religious ecstasy inspired the physical and policy acts of Radical Republicans as well as their interior lives.

Though men predominated and maintained exclusive rights to hold office, women found greater opportunity for participation during the Radical ascendancy than in any previous political moment. The most "radical" of Republican Radicals were woman suffrage activists of both sexes, while even more mainstream participants supported limited voting rights for women in local elections and in frontier territories. Women speakers and political organizers enjoyed the respect of many men in the Republican Party.

The Civil War Radicals were more racially inclusive than their twenty-first-century counterparts. Even in its earliest months, the Republican Party made room for black men in the movement, seeking their support in Northern states that offered full or qualified voting rights to black men. The early Republican Lewis Hayden in Massachusetts gained a patronage post in the state legislature controlled by Republicans in the 1850s, while John Mercer Langston was the first to hold an elected office, in Oberlin, Ohio. Radicals active in national politics made repeated overtures to Frederick Douglass, who would not commit to the party until 1863 but who later became a Republican for life. The war years introduced a host of active black Republicans into public service in the army, Freedmen's Bureau, and missionary agencies, including many who gained election to local and national offices during Reconstruction. Although it did not last, a short-lived program of federal voter registration and election monitoring extended the franchise to the black masses, North and South, producing black-majority districts, black candidates, and responsive white officials in the 1870s.

Radicals exploited the advanced media opportunities of the nineteenth century to gain advantage over their political enemies. As publishers, editors, and investor-owners of news organizations, the Radicals hammered out their messages about the moral hazards of slavery and its extension and advocated for the citizenship rights of African Americans in the North as well as the South. They participated in and reported on their own conferences, rallies, and committee meetings in publications with national circulation and subscriptions, and they sponsored grand events promoting antislavery music, satire, and charitable giving.

Radicals transformed the federal government into a leviathan during the Civil War, empowered physically by the largest armies and fleets of ships ever assembled on the continent and legally and philosophically by what historians have called a new birth of freedom. Their attention to the problem of race relations in American life made the Radical Republicans the most courageous elected officials in our history. The first generation, considered in the pages that follow, knew more scorn than success for their work, and they endured imprisonment, the loss of property by auction, assassination and assault, steep federal fines, and ignominy among their neighbors and their distant critics. In wartime, along with others, they would sleep on the ground, sacrifice limbs, and overcome their mortal terror in the service of a just cause. Before ending their campaign—and even before victory in the Civil War had been secured—Radicals wrote into the Constitution, where they could not be easily reversed by changing times, protections for the civil equality and voting rights of all.

That truth kept marching on, even as the nation and the Grand Old Party looked away.

PART I

Warriors Before the War

1

FILIBUSTERING IN KANSAS

The founding father of the Republican Party hailed from Illinois and stood just over five feet tall with his boots on. His name was Stephen Douglas, and by 1854 the so-called Little Giant of the United States Senate was the country's most prominent Democrat, surpassing even the sitting president, Franklin Pierce, as a party operator and philosopher. So great was his influence that by a single legislative initiative, the Kansas-Nebraska bill, Douglas accidentally ballooned into existence an opposition movement that formed almost immediately as a potent new political party.

Kansas-Nebraska, which churned toward becoming law in the winter and spring of that year, represented the "Democracy," as the party used to be known, at its most revolutionary: it overturned the twenty-four-year-old Missouri Compromise, opening the remaining unincorporated parts of the Louisiana Territory to the possibility of slavery at the insistence of the Democratic Party's fervent proslavery wing. "Thunderstruck and stunned," as Abraham Lincoln later described them, Republicans came into the world bearing the mark of the radical circumstances of the party's birth.

In the decades leading up to 1854, the country had divided into hostile parties, though no one had known yet what to call them. The Kansas-Nebraska Act completed the transformation of the Democratic Party into the tool of white supremacy, an identity that it would need more than a

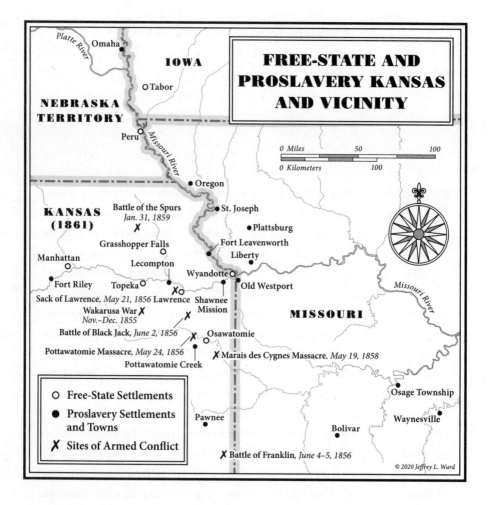

FREE-STATE AND PROSLAVERY KANSAS AND VICINITY

Platte River

Omaha

IOWA

Tabor

NEBRASKA TERRITORY

Peru

Missouri River

0 Miles   50   100
0 Kilometers   100

Oregon

KANSAS (1861)

Battle of the Spurs
Jan. 31, 1859
X

St. Joseph

Plattsburg

Grasshopper Falls

Fort Leavenworth
Liberty

Manhattan

Lecompton

Fort Riley

Topeka

Wyandotte

Old Westport

Sack of Lawrence, May 21, 1856   Lawrence   Shawnee
Wakarusa War X   Mission
Nov.–Dec. 1855   X

Missouri River

Battle of Black Jack, June 2, 1856   Osawatomie

MISSOURI

Pottawatomie Massacre, May 24, 1856
Pottawatomie Creek   X Marais des Cygnes Massacre, May 19, 1858

Osage Township

O   Free-State Settlements
●   Proslavery Settlements
    and Towns
X   Sites of Armed Conflict

Pawnee

Waynesville

Bolivar

X Battle of Franklin, June 4–5, 1856

© 2020 Jeffrey L. Ward

century to shake. The first Republicans, meanwhile, represented opposition to slavery, even as their commitment to that goal existed on a spectrum. Radicals in the avant-garde carried enough weight in the founding generation to steer the party toward total abolitionism (1854 to 1863), and even briefly (1864 to 1875) toward a broader antiracist agenda.

Republicanism emerged from a series of meetings of outraged officials in the fall of 1853 and the spring and summer of 1854 in locations such as Ripon, Wisconsin, Exeter, New Hampshire, and Jackson, Michigan. The origins of the Republican Party featured the defection of prominent officeholders, drawn from the ranks of new "Independent Democrats" and from the collapse of the ailing Whigs. Senator Salmon Chase of Ohio—a dissident Democrat—denounced the Kansas-Nebraska legislation as "a gross violation of a sacred pledge" and "part and parcel of an atrocious plot to . . . convert [the Nebraska Territory] into a dreary region of despotism." Senator William Seward—an antislavery Whig—condemned the Democrats' apocalyptic partisanship. "To ravage, to slaughter, to usurp under false titles, they call empire," Seward insisted, quoting Tacitus in Latin in a Senate speech: "and where they make a desert, they call it peace."

In his bill, Douglas had proposed that slavery in Kansas and Nebraska be allowed if a majority of settlers voted for it at some later date—the doctrine of "popular sovereignty." To the surprise of the Democratic leader, opponents of the measure objected to the idea of sacrificing any portion of the territory to the Slave Power. Led by the Free-Soil Party—an antislavery coalition that included members of Congress from both parties—officeholders actively campaigned against the bill, moving directly to sever the ties that most Free-Soilers had maintained to the mainstream parties. In a series of manifestos, speeches, and office discussions, the major players rapidly aligned themselves in a single-issue "Anti-Nebraska" coalition.[1]

While congressional and party officials contemplated legislative and electoral responses, a second tier of activists took the Kansas-Nebraska matter into their own hands. Legislatures in nine Free States passed condemnation resolutions, the first in a series of official rebukes of federal policy in the years leading up to the Civil War. Party organizers and abolitionist groups moved to take up the gauntlet (as William Seward had described it) and contest neighboring Missourians for control of the lower "Kansas" portion of the territory, still sometimes spelled "Kanzas" in 1854. Citizen migrants who could populate the zone roused themselves for relocation, hoping to swing the outcome of any future slavery referendum. In an innovation, dealmakers in the private sector moved to organize antislavery migration to Kansas for both patriotic and profit-minded reasons.

The face of the campaign to win settlers for a Free Kansas was Eli Thayer, a member of the Massachusetts legislature, a feminist and founder of a women's college in Worcester, the Oread Institute. Thayer became famous nationwide in 1854 as a promoter of organized colonization. While Kansas-Nebraska was still only a bill, Thayer obtained a charter and sold shares in a joint stock company he named the Massachusetts Emigrant Aid Company. Its business model was to resist the expansion of slavery into Kansas while making a profit by providing the goods and services that emigrants required.

Once the Free State had been secured, Thayer forecast, his company could demonstrate the superiority of Yankee ingenuity and free labor in underdeveloped territories elsewhere. "We shall beat you like a threshing floor," he warned Southerners, "filling the land with the portents of your general doom."[2]

Thayer directed his program to the attention of genuinely antislavery white people, though he also hinted at organized black migration to the territory. His organization—incorporated early in 1854 and active by midsummer—aimed "to fill up that vast and fertile Territory with free men—men who hate slavery, and will drive the hideous thing from the broad and beautiful plains where they go to raise their free homes." The company was also marketed to potential shareholders and the public as a commercial advancement in the rapidly expanding field of Westward Movement. Massachusetts Emigrant Aid would specialize in developing transportation routes to Kansas and later to such other areas of settlement as became available to industrious Northerners. They could hope to turn a profit by charging fees, and by operating facilities and useful enterprises to assist in the migration.

In promotional materials and Thayer's speeches, the entrepreneurial aspects of the project received more emphasis than the humanitarian intent. In its opening report, for example, the subject of "philanthropy" did not appear until the thirtieth page. Thayer noted the burgeoning population of the

Atlantic States, buoyed by new arrivals from Europe—four hundred thousand in 1853. "Especially will it prove an advantage to Massachusetts"—the most industrialized part of the New World at that time—"to supply first the necessities to inhabitants—and [then to] open, in the outset, communications between their homes and her ports and factories."[3]

Though Thayer predicted the sale of $5 million in company shares, the directors of Massachusetts Emigrant Aid were mostly political and antislavery. Alongside Thayer in the published list stood Samuel E. Sewall, a soon-to-be Republican colleague of Thayer's in the legislature; Francis W. Bird and Samuel Gridley Howe, Massachusetts Free-Soilers and philanthropists; Anson Burlingame, a state senator soon to be elected to the Congress; and Moses Kimball, a future Republican, museum owner, and associate of P. T. Barnum (himself a future Republican office-seeker). Within a year of its first stock offering, in fact, the directors would reorganize the company as a traditional nonprofit philanthropic organization.[4]

Emigrant Aid was a private company operated by Republicans to promote the fundamental cause of the party, although a key donor and supporter—the industrialist Amos A. Lawrence—would identify himself as a Whig long after the party ceased to function. Seeking action, Lawrence cast his lot with Republicans and transitory figures such as Thayer himself, who later became famous as a conservative. The founder of the company would speak out bitterly against class and racial protest in the decades after the Civil War, but the fluid 1850s saw Thayer occupy the vanguard of vanguards, in Kansas and elsewhere. As an officeholding Republican, elected to Congress in 1856, he drove his party hell-bent into what became an armed struggle on the western frontier.

Thayer promoted Kansas as a first-rate agricultural region, blessed with fertile soil, a favorable climate, and ample supplies of water and timber, citing the observations of a Massachusetts doctor and adventurer, Charles S. Robinson, who had made extensive notes about the area when he passed through en route to California in 1849. Robinson was the first to join the company payroll, charged with organizing transportation by steam and rail to Iowa, hiring wagons and teamsters, and scouting out appropriate areas for settlement. The company had yet to make arrangements to build boardinghouses, sawmills, and other amenities for travelers, but all of these and more were intended as the program reached maturity. For the comfort of its subscribers and to underscore the superiority of the free labor system, Emigrant Aid promised to re-create the sophistication of New England on the Kansas plains by establishing newspapers, lecture halls, and schools.

The prospective printing presses and newspapers in Kansas were deemed especially important, both as a means of advertising the success of the venture and as an expression of the movement's Free-State, antislavery, and ultimately Republican ideals. A hopeful rumor in the early weeks proposed that the activist and editor Frederick Douglass would lead the company-sponsored masthead, a prospect that promoters celebrated as "Douglass versus Douglas."[5]

For those "self-sacrificing" migrants who were willing to brave the initial rough conditions, the Emigrant Aid Company offered passengers an 1854 discount. The special offer of the summer was for tickets "at half the usual rate," as well as the assistance of an agent of the company in every stage of transit to the new territory.[6]

July and August were disastrous months to relocate to unsettled territory, unfortunately—too late for crop planting and too close to the onset of the deadly plains winter. Unanswered questions—Was Kansas a desert or a watered plain? Was it temperate or tropical?—would be resolved in disappointing ways.

Charged with constructing the boardinghouses and other essential facilities in the name of the company, Robinson and his cohort struggled to put together even basic housing for themselves and the other migrants. An Emigrant Aid party led by James B. Abbott, formerly of Hampton, Connecticut, arrived in October to find the future Governor Robinson and his household living in a tent.

By the end of 1854 the company had sent 450 settlers, including many families, to their outpost at Lawrence and scattered destinations. All were left to squabble among themselves and with outsiders over company assets: grist and sawmill equipment, tools, food supplies, and even the tents, which had been designated to change hands as more permanent housing was obtained. They fought over claims and proximities, struggling to reach terms with squatters and new claimants from Missouri and Iowa. Theft and attacks on property proliferated, particularly along the lines of transportation into the territory. Within weeks of the first arrivals—and while, in fact, new parties straggled in as late as December—rival emigrants began to challenge the New Englanders on the Kansas plains. Proslavery settlers and joyriders from Missouri, scorned by the Free-Soilers as "Border Ruffians," made it clear that they would not surrender Kansas without a fight.

Before the physical assaults had come the threats. In late July, a group advertised in an Iowa paper a reward of $200 "for the apprehension and safe delivery into the hands of the squatters of Kansas territory one Eli Thayer."[7] On the ground in the West, the company agents encountered direct and personal threats against their safety and the security of their claims.

By October, these disputes resulted in the first round of gunplay between the two sides, as well as an exchange of hostile notes. "Dr. Robinson," demanded a James Baldwin in a missive datelined "Kanzas Territory, Oct. 6th," "Yourself and friends have one half hour to move the tent which you have on my undisputed claim." Robinson's response—"If you molest our property, you do it at your peril"—was delivered by an armed contingent of thirty Yankees.[8] Bloodshed averted, the scramble for land claims continued with the planting of a second New England Emigrant Aid town, Topeka, and a missionary outpost in Osawatomie, to the west and south of the original settlement, named for the investor Amos Lawrence.

The menace of a series of harsh winters first showed its face on November 11, when an unexpected snowstorm caught Kansas settlers by surprise. With many residing in tents, the so-called town of Lawrence, at the junction of the Kansas and Wakarusa Rivers, made emergency provisions for housing. The grandly named meetinghouse and hotel provided by the company were in fact A-frame lean-tos, roofed with thatch and surrounded on all sides by stacks of sod.[9] Within these walls and a scattering of other dens, those migrants who did not contrive to leave waited out the winter months in uncomfortable proximity to one another. Their dreaming and scheming did not cease, however, as they sketched out visions of their model town, designating a donated plot of land as the future home of the University of Kansas.

By springtime, Kansas partisans had broadened their appeal for support in the East, making a special plea for weaponry and finding allies more than ready to provide it:

The Philadelphia Ledger states that [the Unitarian minister and abolition-ist] Theodore Parker told them in his antislavery address in that city, last week, that 200 of Sharp's [sic] rifles had been sent from Boston in boxes labeled "books," to arm as many of the New England settlers in Kansas ter-ritory against the attacks of Missourian incursionists.[10]

The demand for rifles among antislavery Kansas pioneers surged in spring 1855 and accelerated virtually without pause for the next two years. A key motivation was the violence of proslavery incursions, sponsored mostly from Missouri, where a fire-eating U.S. senator, David Atchison, rallied resi-dents to "shoot, burn & hang" until antislavery settlers abandoned the field. By the end of the year, the conflict over slavery in Kansas had resulted in two hundred deaths and some $2 million in damages—mostly inflicted by the antislavery side.[11] The Massachusetts Emigrant Aid Company sponsored eastern tours of company officials for fund-raising and political awareness, while a National Kansas Committee functioned as a kind of war depart-ment in exile for an emerging antislavery army.

In Manhattan, the rough-and-ready James B. Abbott met at Astor House with the editor Horace Greeley and other antislavery activists in the city. Among the New Yorkers recruited for the defense of Free Kansas was the landscape architect Frederick Law Olmsted, then at work on the construc-tion of Central Park. A longtime abolitionist, Olmsted was among those who came to embrace violent solutions to the slavery problem. Within weeks of the meeting, Olmsted would personally supervise the shipment to Abbott in Kansas of a howitzer cannon and a supply of shell and canister ammunition.

Olmsted's cannon was not just for show. "One discharge of it at mus-ket range is considered equally effective with the simultaneous fire of one hundred muskets," the park designer reported, speculating that its effect on disorganized Missouri militants would be profound. "If you can use it prop-erly, as I doubt not you will," he wrote, "it is worth a dozen field pieces."[12]

The Free-Staters would require all the firepower that friends in the East could provide that autumn. Militant Republicans—including Radical organizers Martin Stowell of Worcester, Massachusetts, and the English journalist Richard Hinton—took the lead in organizing a constitutional convention that met in Topeka on October 23, 1855.[13] One measure of the movement's success was its ability to attract delegates from a broad political range. While devoted to Free Kansas, the forty-seven participants included Democrats, Whigs, Free-Staters, Free-Soilers, and Independents, as well as a handful who already called themselves Republicans. Free-Statism did not overlap neatly with antislavery and humanitarian impulses. Many participants manifested an open disdain for African Americans as neighbors in the frontier districts.

At Topeka, they were quick to agree on language prohibiting slavery or indentured servitude in the proposed state. More radical measures failed to win a majority, including a bid to strike the word "white" from militia and voting requirements. Seven of the delegates, however, led by the New England Aid Company's Dr. Robinson, identified themselves as champions of a Kansas constitution blind to color.[14]

As Theodore Parker understood it, the Topeka Movement embodied the emergence of a new party system, and indeed a new society. "Just now there are two great ideas in the consciousness of the people, that of Slavery and that of Freedom," he wrote on the opening day of the convention. The Slavery Party was entrenched, empowered, and frankly out of contact with the wellsprings of patriotism. "The second party," he admitted, "exists in the young woods and mills on the rivers of Kansas, hardly more." The Party of Freedom lacked experience, organizers, offices, even a platform for action, "but it is exceedingly powerful through [its] ideas," and in the courage and integrity of its adherents, Parker argued. "All the genius of America is on that side, all the womanly women."[15]

Meanwhile, the nascent party in the "young woods" of Kansas hastily suspended its constitutional proceedings in late November 1855. A dispute over claims had resulted in bloodshed in the vicinity of Lawrence. Inflamed by arrests and the successful rescue of a Free-State prisoner, both Free-State and Pro-Slave partisans set aside their peaceful enterprises to prepare for battle. The Free-Stater and future senator James H. Lane moved as president of the convention to suspend discussions. Lane himself, along with Dr. Robinson and "Major" Abbott, assumed command of hastily assembled militia units. They dug trenches in the streets of Lawrence, including four embankments on central Massachusetts Street. Forts appeared on Vermont, New Hampshire, and Rhode Island Streets. Somewhere amid the fortifications, Abbott placed the massive howitzer recently shipped from New York.

The siege of Lawrence (called the Wakarusa War of 1855 by antislavery partisans) heightened the profile of the Kansas Troubles, attracting more than a thousand proslavery militants from out of state and also winning the support of new antislavery radicals.[16]

Among the Free-State cadres mobilized for the fight was a new arrival, still unknown and undistinguished at the opening of Bleeding Kansas. John Brown was a moral purist who despised the Republican Party until his death. While he had been a fervent antislavery activist all his life, he had come to Kansas that winter only to assist his grown sons and a cousin who had settled in the Free-State town of Osawatomie. Introduced at Wakarusa, Brown would rise among the ranks of Free-State militants to become the protégé and idol of Republican Radicals.

Back east, Thayer arranged for the Emigrant Aid Company to deliver a thousand rifles to Lawrence. Out west, the Free-Staters reconvened in Topeka and scheduled elections on the basis of the new constitution. The vote—on January 15, 1856—resulted in a landslide for Kansas Radicals, not least because proslavery voters refused to participate. The Emigrant Aid Company's top officer, Dr. Charles L. Robinson, emerged as governor. To the U.S. Senate, Free Kansas elevated another company man, Samuel C. Pomeroy, and Topeka Convention president James H. Lane. These men held office in a theoretical sense only, since Congress refused to admit Kansas or its representatives under the Topeka document. Led by President Pierce, Democrats rejected the movement emphatically, favoring a proslavery government based in the town of Lecompton, elected by what Free-Staters claimed to be a majority of nonresidents from across the Missouri border. Pierce pushed Congress to recognize the Lecompton Constitution and admit Kansas as a slave state, denouncing the Lawrence, Kansas, government as "a mere party in the territory" and its election as "revolutionary."[17]

If Topeka, Kansas, was the scene of revolution in 1856, the East Coast Republicans were its committees of correspondence. They prepared a warm welcome for Free-State fund-raisers on winter tours, arranging meetings with potential supporters of every antislavery stripe. The Massachusetts Emigrant Aid Company also merged with a New York–based agency and renamed itself the New England Emigrant Aid Company. Eli Thayer's new partner, John C. Underwood, was a Northern abolitionist married to a Southern woman, the sponsor of a network of free-labor farms in Virginia. Underwood's plan called for northern migration to the border regions, starting with Kansas and Virginia and ultimately expanding into Texas and Arkansas. From the beginning, the colonization scheme hinted at land grabbing and potential violence. It was aligned from the outset with Republicans like Thayer and Underwood, who used their party contacts to raise money and build support for the movement in Boston and New York City.[18]

The most famous minister in the United States, the Reverend Henry Ward Beecher, weighed in in favor of the resort to force in early February. Hosting Kansas freedom fighters at his Plymouth Church in Brooklyn— the largest and most politically active congregation in the New York area— Beecher raised more than $30,000. He praised the use of force by Free-State pioneers: in the context of the Kansas fight, he said, "the Sharpe [sic] Rifle was a truly moral agency."[19] Border Ruffians would not be moved by moral suasion, said Beecher: "You might just as well read the Bible to Buffaloes." Being immoral but not stupid, he suggested, such men "have a supreme respect for the logic that is embodied in Sharp's [sic] rifles." Beecher admired the sturdy resistance of New Englanders in Kansas and recognized their historical antecedents. "The Puritans used to carry their Bibles and their muskets to church," the minister insisted, "the one for inside work, and the other for outside work!"[20] In a church ceremony, Beecher distributed rifles to migrants with an equal number of Bibles stamped with the motto "Be ye steadfast and immovable."[21]

Reverend Parker shared Beecher's enthusiasm (having carried a loaded pistol on his person since 1850) but was less inclined to align guns and godly work. He did not pack guns and Bibles together or use crates labeled "Bibles" to disguise his shipments, preferring merely to call them books.[22] The book label served as both a subterfuge and an inside joke among the Free-Staters, a way of satirizing the supposed lack of sophistication of the Border Ruffians. Vegetarians associated with the Transcendentalist Bronson Alcott's movement, for example, reported that their enemies had seized their wagons and all their freight while they were crossing into Kansas from Missouri. Upon discovering that the boxes held books instead of weapons or whiskey, however, the ruffians had abandoned the lot undamaged, to be joyfully reclaimed.[23]

In April 1856, Parker cheered a group of pioneers departing from the train station and expanded the book metaphor. "There were twenty copies of 'Sharp's [sic] Rights of the People'" in their hands, "of the new and improved edition, and divers Colt's six-shooters also." The settlers' parting hymn was apropos: "When I Can Read My Title Clear."[24]

Washington witnessed the parliamentary version of drilling and presenting arms, as the Kansas Crisis made its way home to Congress. Senator Henry Wilson, a Massachusetts Know-Nothing turned Republican, serving as junior senator alongside the abolitionist Charles Sumner, anticipated trouble even in the halls of government. "The next Congress will be the most violent one in our history," Wilson had written on July 23, 1855; "and if violence and bloodshed come, let us not falter, but do our duty, even if we fall upon the floors of Congress."[25]

In the spring of 1856, Wilson took the floor, despite his lack of seniority, to assail members of Congress and the Franklin Pierce administration. The problem in Kansas, as he saw it, was that proslavery had recruited Border Ruffians, mercenaries, and even the U.S. Army post in Leavenworth to subvert self-government in Kansas, while Free-State settlers appeared virtually defenseless. Wilson saw the repeated "invasions" of the territory as part of a Washington conspiracy, citing the offer of a Democratic representative from South Carolina, Preston Brooks, to pay $100 to any man from his district willing to travel to Kansas. Free-State Kansas needed more guns and cannons to confront the challenge, while people of conscience in the Senate and elsewhere needed to recognize the nature of the game. "We accept your issue," Wilson taunted proslavery senators, using language borrowed from the ritual of dueling. "Nominate some one of your scarred veterans." In what Wilson called "the battle of 1856," this champion might prevail, but "he will not come out of it without scars."[26]

Politicos awaited with anticipation the remarks of Charles Sumner—the handsome, combative, and outrageously erudite senior senator from Massachusetts. "Pardon me for the expression of an earnest wish to hear from you soon upon the Kansas Freedom Question," wrote a constituent. Sumner should hit them fast and hit them hard, another advised: "Bold deeds and bold language," said a man who had apparently found Henry Wilson's speech too mild; "I have always felt humiliated by the tone our men have taken in Congress, yielding everything, and never daring to assert their rights or to exercise their true power to crush these fellows into submission."[27]

Sumner reciprocated warmly: "I shall pronounce the most thorough philippic ever uttered in a legislative body," he told Parker.[28] He would employ "argument, scorn and denunciation" on both "crime and criminals": the repression in Kansas and its authors and abettors among Sumner's colleagues in the U.S. Senate. "The whole arsenal of God is ours," he wrote, "and I will not renounce one of its weapons,—not one."[29]

In the space of three days in 1856, Sumner's speech and its aftermath, along with a pair of violent events in Kansas, put the country on what seemed like a war footing.

Sumner's speech was extraordinarily long even by the standards of the nineteenth century, and its author presented it over the course of two full days of the session. He had enjoyed himself too much in the writing of it, indulging his waspish sense of humor, bons mots delivered in foreign languages, and ad hominem attacks. Stephen Douglas had bad breath, Sumner said; he was "noisome, squat." Butler of South Carolina (a stroke victim) gurgled when he spoke. South Carolina, Sumner stated, in elaborate language, was populated by lushes and dimwits, achieving less in its two hundred years of existence than the industrious Yankees in Kansas had accomplished already.[30]

Sumner got personal, while simultaneously, Border Ruffians in Kansas unleashed their own barrage of personal attacks against Free-Staters in what became known as the Sack of Lawrence. Attackers injured no one, but they destroyed the printing presses and scattered the type to disrupt the publication of two newspapers in the antislavery town, burning the Free State Hotel to the ground after failing to destroy it with cannon fire and gunpowder. A number of prominent Free-Staters were taken captive, including Henry Lane (who escaped) and "Governor" Charles Robinson and his wife, Sara Lawrence Robinson.

Like many women in Lawrence, Mrs. Robinson had been active in the city's defense. She was scarcely the only woman to be personally assaulted or threatened during the raid.[31] The would-be governor's wife was part of a more or less official women's unit for self-defense, said to have studied marksmanship as well as less traditional defenses. In the buildup to Lawrence, for example, one woman had deterred a man attacking her home by dousing him with hot water from the stove.[32] The wife of James B. Abbott, the Free-State "major," distributed rifles from her home during the height of the attack on Lawrence.[33]

Neither the women's vigilance nor the stockpile of arms from back east could prevent the antislavery team from being routed, however. Humiliated and terrorized, the Robinsons and other victims were imprisoned at Leavenworth, where a proslavery prosecutor prepared to try them on the capital charge of treason against the United States.

Offended Southerners also mobilized a direct response to Sumner's incendiary speech. His remarks (and Henry Wilson's) seemed calculated to escalate tensions into physical conflict, Democrats believed. Stephen Douglas—accused by Sumner, in a new round of rhetoric days after the original speech, of "switch[ing] out from his tongue the perpetual stench of offensive personality"—said publicly that he thought Sumner meant "to provoke some of us to kick him as we would a dog in the street, that he might get sympathy upon the just chastisement."[34]

Sumner's friends were quick to offer physical protection but were rebuffed. "None of that, Wilson," he had said when his colleague offered to serve as bodyguard. Rumors circulated about Congressman Brooks, a relative of the maligned Butler of South Carolina, but Sumner was not afraid.[35] Amid sweltering heat on May 23, Brooks surprised Sumner at his desk in the Senate, beat him mercilessly upon the head with a heavy cane, and left him bleeding and unconscious.

The dual assaults on Sumner and Lawrence mobilized a profoundly militant antislavery response. The most dramatic of these fell outside the purview of Republican activism, as the antipolitical John Brown and some followers hacked to death with broadswords five proslavery Kansans in a settlement on Pottawatomie Creek.

The Pottawatomie Massacre hurt the cause of Free Kansas in public opinion, and created a dilemma for Republican sponsors of the Kansas militants. Though Brown was not working directly with Republicans, many proved all too ready to justify the crime or to accept his naked claim that he had not killed the men with his own hand. As the Massachusetts abolitionist the Reverend Thomas Wentworth Higginson explained later in the year in a speech transcribed by a newspaper, as a Christian "he had great faith in the general efficacy of returning good for evil . . . but he believed there were exceptional cases when it would not only be right, but a duty, to take the sword and rifle." In "every such case," Higginson insisted, "he thought the end would justify the means."[36]

Radical Republicans also embraced violence as a rhetorical device and organizational initiative. Addressing the American Antislavery Society in New York, Theodore Parker advocated resistance with such zeal that the feminist Lucretia Mott took the podium to remind him that the society was "opposed to the use of carnal weapons" and that he should not imagine "for a moment that it was right to use physical force." Parker had brought Lucy Stone and Senator William H. Seward of New York to the speakers' rostrum to advocate for the Republican Party (and for Seward the presidential candidate, as Parker's choice). Warming to Parker's message, the assembly resolved "that all constitutional liberty has ceased in this country," that Pierce "was no longer the legitimate President of the United States," and that "we are in the midst of a revolution." In the face of this emergency, the nation's most venerable antislavery group resolved "that we shall neither give nor ask for any quarter; but our motto is, Victory or Death!"[37]

On the following Sunday, Parker delivered a surprisingly cold-blooded sermon on the subject of the attack on Sumner, which he claimed to see as no surprise. Visionaries had always been subject to scorn, he reminded parishioners:

> In all those dark days behind us, there have been found faithful men who risked their political prospects, the desires of honorable ambition, their social standing, [and] the esteem of their nearest relatives, and were faithful to truth and justice. What treatment have they met in the parlor, in the forum, in the market, in the church? One day their history must be writ; and some names now hated will appear like those which were the watchwords of the revolution.

Parker said that he expected people of goodwill to follow in Sumner's example, and if he died, to make his cause the object of a struggle to the death. "There is a war before us worse than Russian," he insisted, referring to the horrors of the recent conflict in Crimea.

> It has already begun: when would it end? "Not till slavery has put freedom down," say your masters at the South; "Not till freedom has driven slavery from the continent," let us say and determine."[38]

Listening in the pews was Richard Hinton, who resolved that day to go back to Kansas, believing, as he later wrote, that "it was the road to South Carolina!"[39] Hinton, like others in the movement, enrolled in an organized antislavery militia. That summer they would venture into filibustering, a piratical new nation-building technique that they aimed to transplant from its roots in Central America and the Caribbean to the Kansas plains. Filibusters used armed force and phony electoral districts to stage coups d'état and establish governments dominated by Americans, often proslavery Southerners, in neighboring Latin American districts. The king of filibustering was William Walker, a proslavery gunslinger with a record of attacks on civil government in California, Mexico, and Nicaragua, where he had been recognized by Franklin Pierce as head of state the same week that conservatives sacked Lawrence and caned Sumner. Free Kansas had long accused Missourians and allies of employing Walker's filibuster tricks against settlers in Kansas: the recruitment of mercenaries, the establishment of bogus towns and polling places, terrorization and diversionary violence, and the early recognition of the bogus government by the avidly proslavery Pierce. The antislavery National Kansas Committee now aimed to appropriate the tactics for their own use, staging a new political bid using military power in Kansas.

The roots of the NKC lay in Boston and in New York City, where co-chairman Thaddeus Hyatt lived and marketed his best invention, glass sidewalk tiles as a source of lighting for basement spaces. Hyatt was a lapsed antislavery Democrat, a minor officer in a recent New York City convention in which the visiting Benjamin Butler of Massachusetts and a number of other prominent officeholders publicly defected from their party to endorse the Republicans.[40] To fulfill his local responsibilities to the movement, Hyatt culled the Democratic city's modest ranks of Republican activists for Kansas adventurers.

In the end the New York recruits fell short of a state contingent, but the experience of young New Yorkers answering the call casts a light on the culture of Free Kansas filibustering. Future president Chester Alan Arthur and some of his aristocratic friends enlisted, departing after posing for a jaunty souvenir photograph in which three of them embraced facing the camera. Arthur also outfitted himself with a gray suit and matching military cap. The future president bought land near Leavenworth and considered opening a Kansas practice with his partner, Henry Gardiner, who had accompanied Arthur and companions from New York. Meeting with Charles Robinson and attending political rallies at the very least, Arthur probably also took part in a series of so-called battles in August and September 1856. He found Kansas rough going, hard living. In response to an imploring letter from his fiancée, the young lawyer packed up his shingle and returned to New York after a few months.[41]

Massachusetts dispatched three full companies, surpassing the New York branch of the committee by virtue of the state's radical politics and the relative prestige of the Boston organizer, "Chevalier" Dr. Samuel G. Howe, a noted philanthropist and Republican. The first group departed in July under the direction of Calvin Cutter, a forty-nine-year-old medical doctor. Cutter was an experienced Kansas hand, having run rifles for the National Kansas Committee and commanded a military company during the violence that spring. Cutter's party of sixty settlers followed the river transit route from St. Louis through Missouri, but was stopped by armed men just inside the border of Kansas.[42] Its members were disarmed and briefly held prisoner. When a second Massachusetts party also failed to find safe passage into the territory, a sense of outrage spread across the state. Amid talk of accumulating military force to break the impasse, a third Massachusetts company began to coalesce among the most radical of the Radical Republicans.

At its head was Martin Stowell, a strongman of antislavery agitation from Worcester, Massachusetts. Stowell recruited the toughest men he knew, including the young Englishman Richard Hinton. They were—a partisan later recalled—"the finest set of men for physique I ever encountered and not bad at heart."⁴³ To project a plausible identity as settlers, the Stowell group also solicited the participation of activist women and families. All were prepared for the worst as they moved toward Kansas in August 1856.

Both Stowell and Hinton were veterans of the Kansas movement, credited with helping to organize the Topeka constitutional convention and early efforts at self-defense. So-called Border Ruffians and recruits from the Southern states had already come to know both of them by sight. During a scouting mission early in the summer, Hinton had been captured and tortured with a rope; he had attended the Republican convention in June with noose marks still visible around his neck.⁴⁴ For his part, Stowell carried a price tag on his head. By 1856, he had already abandoned the idea of homesteading in Kansas and instead purchased farmland nearby in Peru, Nebraska. They would lead the mission even as men of higher rank in the movement—Higginson, Hyatt, and Dr. Howe—accompanied the group to Chicago and then launched the company as an armed expeditionary force.

Since river transport had proven vulnerable to attack, the group crossed the entire state of Iowa overland, with teams and wagons stretched out in a single line. Arriving at Tabor, Iowa, near the borders with Nebraska and Missouri, the Massachusetts party made a rendezvous with travelers from other National Kansas Committee companies: one from Indiana, one from Ohio, two each from Wisconsin and Illinois, and three from Iowa, partially recruited en route. In this company, comprising two or three hundred, the Free-Staters hoped to find safety in numbers. Before entering the territory, after traveling seven hundred miles by wagon train, the Stowell migrants met up with the militia commander Colonel James H. Lane.

Lane had also been traveling overland. His group got under way in Buffalo with supplies and encouragement from a group calling itself the National Convention of Friends of Freedom in Kansas. Accompanied by a marching band, the Lane party functioned as the political and fund-raising arm of the summer missions. In major stops at Chicago and Detroit, Lane had delivered speeches in a style that one viewer compared to "lava from Vesuvius."⁴⁵ Lane was a former member of Congress from Indiana, the claim to fame that he had leveraged to win appointment to the Senate from the aspiring Topeka legislature. Lane had been a Democrat, a supporter of the Kansas-Nebraska Act, and a sponsor of legislation at Topeka to ban African Americans from the Kansas Territory. Now, however, he spoke as a fire-breathing Radical Republican and, most of all, as a general in the antislavery war for control of Kansas.

The atmosphere in Tabor was ebullient, its pioneers punch-drunk. "One particularly jolly fellow asked us over and over if we had enough Beecher's Bibles," remembered a young woman traveling from Michigan with her father and sister. "He said he would be happy to supply . . . 'a rifle for every rifleman.'" Asked if he meant to include the women, the Free-Stater said, "You betcha, little sister," to the great amusement of the ladies.[46] Pamphlets on woman suffrage, spiritual healing, and Free Kansas circulated among the campsites, including one that invited audiences to hourly lectures by representatives of the National Kansas Committee. The band played, strident singing filled the air, and everyone seemed to regard everyone else with an air of wonder. Even the women were drilling, and the thrill of holding weapons and camping on the plains suffuses every surviving account.[47]

On August 7, 1856, the Kansas Filibusters surged forward from Tabor to the strains of martial music. Immediately across the Kansas line, they encamped and declared that their encampment was a town, a technique of William Walker–style banana republic filibusterism. Hastily elected town officers made a survey of the eligible voters for use in future electioneering; Conestoga wagons circled for self-defense; and the men of the expedition assembled for the purpose of drilling and forming ranks.

One of the militants had devised a clever salute to allow antislavery militiamen to recognize their friends. It was initiated on the scene by an enormous, stentorian drillmaster, an escaped army prisoner from Fort Leavenworth named Aaron Stevens (at the time using the alias Colonel Whipple), who would later die with John Brown at Harpers Ferry. "Present arms!" shouted Whipple. Seeing guns, he boomed out, "What are you doing here?" *"Holding town meeting,"* the militiamen would reply. "Where is your ballot box?" *"Here!"* was the response, as three hundred hands struck the stock ends of three hundred rifles, a resounding charge.

The leading men among the militants assembled to make strategy: Jim Lane and the Republicans Stowell, Hinton, and James Abbott; Aaron Stevens and the wizened, bloody-minded John Brown. They agreed upon immediate departure from the first encampment, now called Plymouth, and the settlement of two new towns in which the process of establishing electoral districts and military drills would be repeated. Martin Stowell, elected president of a town calling itself Lexington, made haste to leave behind a token of the founders' intentions—an antislavery fort, constructed of logs and pointed sticks—before rushing to settle the next town.[48]

As a matter of filibustering for control of the interior of the territory, the summer 1856 exercises offered little to the cause of Free Kansas. Despite all, Missourians staged repeated advances on the genuine and established Kansas towns in August and September, terrorizing Topeka and Grasshopper Falls and defeating John Brown's allies and killing one of his sons in what both sides called the Battle of Osawatomie. Congress and the Pierce administration held their ground. Instead, the overland crossings served as an exercise in cultural and political unity, in which Yankees mobilized their most sacred institutions, resources, and drives for the cause. Their sacrifices on the march and in camp anticipated the hardships of the looming war.

2

THE ANTISLAVERY RESISTANCE

O nly abnormal politics could produce the extremism of the Kansas project, and the 1850s stood on the brink of the greatest disaster in American history. The Constitution had bestowed immense power on slaveholders and the states where they resided, and, paired with fate, geography, and local cultural practices, these advantages gave them disproportionate control of the presidency, congressional committees, the Supreme Court, and federal bureaucracies, including the bare-bones armed services divisions, the army and navy. The emergence of abolitionism as a force in the 1830s and afterward inflamed Southern opinion just at the moment when the value of cotton exports overtook manufacturing and grain as the single most valuable U.S. commodity.

Reinforced by tradition, supercharged by their burgeoning wealth, and led by ambitious legal theorists and public intellectuals, "fire-eating" proslavery Southerners had initiated the ultimate era of scorched-earth politics. Congress and the executive branch employed gag rules and mail censorship in order to counter abolitionist initiatives. "The right to seize and retake fugitive slaves, and the duty to deliver them up, in whatever State of the Union they may be found," pronounced the court, in 1842's *Prigg v. Pennsylvania*, "is . . . recognized as an absolute positive right and duty pervading the whole Union with an equal and supreme force uncontrolled and uncontrollable by state sovereignty or state legislation." Upon the foundations of this victory, the Slave Power in Congress erected the Fugitive Slave Act of 1850. No other legislative act of the nineteenth century did more to swell the coercive power of the central state.

Blame the matter on California—or, more specifically, upon the lust for gold that drove U.S. nationals shovel-over-fist to the edge of the continent in 1849. The Californians' hasty bid for statehood and federal legal protections raised the specter of a race for congressional representation throughout the new territories in the Southwest in which Free-State partisans had secured the early bid. Taking a holistic view of the crisis, Great Compromisers in the Senate, acting in the final stages of their party system, had secured California's admission as a Free State by engineering an agreement of parts, with a grand victory and smaller satisfactory outcomes for each side. Antislavery could have California, plus a ban on slave auctions in the federal district—a nod to the "Freedom National" antislavery agenda, to exercise regulatory power in Washington. The Slave Power would settle for a pronouncement, heavy with significance for the Kansas-Nebraska debacle, that popular sovereignty would determine the loyalty of other candidates for statehood in the Mexican Cession. The extra sweetener in their portion of the Compromise of 1850 was the law requiring the return of fugitives from bondage, which created a powerful new federal bureaucracy that reached into every community in the North.

The Fugitive Slave Act of 1850 created the first new categories of federal crimes since the annulled Alien and Sedition Acts of 1798, naming penalties for persons who impeded or who failed to assist in the recapture of alleged slaves. Accused persons of color were denied the right of representation and discovery in court, and U.S. marshals and commissioners—equipped with all the legal and material resources of the federal courts—obtained better pay when they acted to remand persons into slavery. The number of persons recaptured or kidnapped as slaves in the Northern states increased by a factor of ten.

The outcry over the Fugitive Slave Act in Northern states initiated the crack-up of the Whig Party, wrecking the career of the compromiser Daniel Webster (d. 1852), whom New Englanders had revered and others respected. Percolating outside the party structure for a time (and without the sanction of nonviolent Garrisonians), Fugitive Slave Act resistance eventually found

a home in the Radical wing of the new Republican Party. Prior to its establishment, future Republican Radicals participated in a series of successful
efforts to disrupt the federal process. Alongside others with mixed political views, Radicals participated in hundreds of rescues across the Northern
states.[1]

The first African American Republican, Lewis Hayden of Boston, organized the liberation of Shadrach Minkins from a federal commission in
February 1851. Using arms inside the courtroom, Hayden's exclusively African American crew secured the fugitive within a safe house, Hayden's own,
rigged with barrels of explosives to facilitate suicide bombing in the case
of attempted recapture. A mixed crowd of Quakers, free blacks, and other
fugitives rescued four men in Christiana, Pennsylvania, killing two white
men who claimed them as slaves, in September that year. Within weeks,
an antislavery crowd including the (future) Kansas desperado Martin Stowell (white) and the Reverend Jeremy Loguen (an African American fugitive
from Tennessee) set at liberty William "Jerry" McHenry in Syracuse. A Boston Vigilance Committee led by the Reverend Theodore Parker helped to
shelter a fugitive couple united by marriage in Parker's church, John and
Ellen Craft.

The early successes of the Fugitive Slave Act resistance movement—
swollen to greater significance by the success of the runaway drama *Uncle
Tom's Cabin* in 1852—produced a backlash that coincided with the political party crisis unleashed by the Kansas-Nebraska Act. Simultaneous with
the alarm about congressional power grabbing in the territories, a surge of
judiciary intervention with executive support inflamed dissidents on the
fugitive slave issue. The sense of outrage upon outrage made its mark on
the character of the emerging Republican Party, in which Radicals already
enjoyed organizational advantages. The party became sharper, looser, and
more cynical as its partisans confronted proslavery law enforcement.

Racine, Wisconsin, was a western outpost on the shores of Lake Michigan that had shed its frontier image and acquired some polish by 1854.
Settled by Yankees from New England, and recently home to an influx of
liberal-minded German and Danish immigrants, the town included the now
defunct Racine College, Wisconsin's first high school, established in 1852, a
newspaper, city directory, and waterfront lighthouse. Its small community of

fugitives from slavery had felt comfortable, poised as they were to escape by water into Canada at any sign of danger.

The likelihood of such an escape preoccupied the U.S. marshal affiliated with Wisconsin's federal court, Stephen Van Rensselaer Ableman. Ableman was a career militia officer and a physical giant, appointed by President Franklin Pierce to Wisconsin's federal judicial district in 1853.

The Fugitive Slave Act had immensely augmented the responsibilities of court officers such as Ableman. Because there had been few federal criminal statutes, marshals traditionally supported the work of federal judges by delivering subpoenas, managing the courtroom budget, and conducting the census when it fell within their four-year term. Now they faced the distasteful and often dangerous tasks associated with seizing suspected fugitive slaves—while drawing extra pay from the government's accounts.

Ableman laid careful plans for the capture of Joshua Glover, for whom a St. Louis white man had filed papers with U.S. District Court judge Andrew G. Miller. Dispatching a deputy marshal, and obtaining the complicity of another black man, the federals surprised Glover at a card game and whisked him to a Milwaukee jail on March 10, 1854.[2]

Fortunately for Joshua Glover, his abduction coincided with the birth of the Republican Party in Wisconsin. Less than two weeks before the fateful visit of Stephen Ableman to Racine, progressive men of the city had convened in inland Ripon to organize a new political party—an early example of the fallout from the pending Kansas-Nebraska bill. Though the party was new, the networks of associations among leading antislavery and political activists were well established. Spreading the news of Glover's capture in Racine, the local population quickly organized a crowd one hundred strong and arranged transportation by water to Milwaukee. To prepare that city for a rescue riot, the antislavery mayor of Racine sent a telegram to a friend from the Ripon Republican convention, Sherman Booth.

Booth had the biggest and blackest beard in town-dwelling Wisconsin— long before that look became the nineteenth-century standard. He was physically awkward and morally unsteady, soon to be unmasked as a sexual predator and enjoying the last days of his acceptance in polite society. His abolitionist fervor burned pure, however, having its origins in his days as a Yale undergraduate, when he happened to be appointed to teach English to the imprisoned crew of the slave ship *Amistad*. As a journalist, organizer, and true believer, Booth had been an energetic presence at the Ripon Republican Party convention, and he worked in partnership with the leading political men in Wisconsin. His newspaper, the *American Freeman*, was the leading antislavery sheet in the state.

Booth's role in the Glover rescue illustrates the mix of legal and extralegal resistance on the fugitive's behalf—as well as the prominence of the parliamentary procedures associated with political parties. At nine a.m. on March 11, the editor presented himself in the courtroom of District Judge Miller, asking to see an arrest warrant and demanding that the alleged fugitive receive the benefit of counsel. When Miller refused—and upon hearing that the captive had arrived at the jailhouse bloodied and bruised—Sherman Booth printed a handbill and mounted a horse to spread the word, urging citizens to ring the church bells to assemble a crowd. By two p.m., a crowd of more than one thousand convened as a formal meeting and elected to preside Dr. E. B. Wolcott, a surgeon, philanthropist, and future Union general. Booth addressed the crowd, reporting that a similar meeting in Racine had called on Milwaukee County and Wisconsin judges to intervene in the federal process and try Joshua Glover before a jury of his peers.

Next arrived a sheriff from Racine, bearing a state court warrant for the arrest of the deputy marshal and accompanied by a formal delegation of a hundred men. When Judge Miller dismissed them, the meeting and delegation quickly degenerated into a mob. They used a twenty-foot beam to smash open the courthouse door, seized the prisoner, and fought the marshal and his deputies with their fists until the wounded Glover had been removed from the town.

Never mind that the driver of the getaway vehicle was a Democrat—overcome by the emotion of the moment, but distressed and embarrassed by his choice once he confronted the difficulty of spiriting the fugitive along late-winter roads. Local conservatives understood the rescue to be the work of political Radicals. At a rally in Milwaukee four days afterward, Democrats burned an effigy of Sherman Booth, even as the U.S. marshal, Stephen Ableman, took the editor into custody and presented him before a fugitive slave commission, where U.S. Commissioner Andrew Miller (a Polk appointee) detained Booth on a $2,000 bond.

Judge Miller, reflecting after the Civil War on the events of 1854, admitted that "twenty years had modified his opinion of slave-holding and slave-hunting." In the heat of the moment, however, the judge remembered, "mere loyalty to party was often stronger than [his] love for the right." Sherman Booth and the Republicans, in contrast, acted with the righteous conviction that their advocacy served the greater good. When ordinary governmental processes failed them, they readily embraced extraordinary—indeed revolutionary—tactics. The practice fused itself into the genetic code of the party that would free the slaves and upend traditional relationships in the Reconstruction South. Booth and his network would use any means necessary to resist injustice, starting with his refusal to recognize the U.S. slave commission as a legal venue.

Booth also disputed the charge that he had participated in disorder, yet defended the action on the grounds that the Fugitive Slave Act was unjust:

> I am frank to say—and the prosecution may make the most of it—that I sympathize with the rescuers of Glover, and rejoice at his escape. I rejoice that, in the first attempt of the slave-hunters to convert our jail into a slave pen, and our citizens into slave-catchers, they have been signally foiled, and it has been decided by the spontaneous uprising and sovereign voice of the people, that no human being can be dragged into bondage from Milwaukee.

With the commissioner, Winfield Smith, already banging his gavel to silence the crowd, Sherman Booth began to shout:

> *I am bold to say that rather than have the great Constitutional rights and safeguards of the people—the writ of Habeas Corpus and the right of trial by jury—stricken down by this Fugitive Slave Law,* I WOULD PREFER TO SEE EVERY FEDERAL OFFICER IN WISCONSIN HANGED ON A GALLOWS FIFTY FEET HIGHER THAN HAMAN'S.

Booth's speech set a new standard for the confrontation between antislavery forces and the national government. He spoke, he said, for "all who would die on the battle-field or on the gibbet, rather than sacrifice their conscience."[3]

Fast on the heels of what became known as *Ableman v. Booth*, a case destined for the Supreme Court of the United States, a rescue drama roiled the city of Boston, home to some of the most important and most Radical of the emerging Republicans.

The mood in Boston was sour on both sides, with fugitive slave law-and-order advocates and federal appointees exhausted by the nonstop agitation of the Boston Vigilance Committee, and antislavery organizers, for their part, embittered by their alienation from the national state. The city suffered especially from the estrangement of political elites from the masses and their Democratic representatives, who had built a majority political machine on the strength of working-class politics and appeals to Catholics and immigrants.

Boston Brahmins, in contrast, were conspicuously Protestant or Unitarian. They shared ties to Harvard College and a handful of associated institutions, and all read the same dozen or more progressive newspapers and magazines. Their pantheon of antislavery locals included the biggest names in abolitionism, William Lloyd Garrison and Wendell Phillips, both of whom would ultimately join with the Republicans—however much, in 1854, they still claimed to despair of politics.

Many men and women active in the Concord, Massachusetts, literary and philosophical circle circulated freely among Boston and suburban events, facilitated by the nation's first commuter rail network. A core of successful industrialists—magnates of the paper mills and pipe factories among the interconnected municipalities—brought ingenuity and capital into the reform movements of their time.

A Boston steering committee had brokered much of the intraparty infrastructure of the Free-Soil faction in Congress—and later served the Republican Party's Radical faction. Meeting at the Parker House Hotel every Saturday as the Bird Club, hosted by antislavery political organizer Frank Bird, this group stood ready to align with the emerging Republicans. As eyewitnesses and participants in the fugitive drama of May and June of that year, Bird Clubbers and other Massachusetts Radicals embraced the revolutionary means and values that left their mark on the party organization.

Anthony Burns was no Bostonian, being newly arrived in the city at the time of his arrest on May 24, 1854. As a stranger, Burns's identity as a fugitive slave was mostly unknown. News of his capture spread instantly, however, because vigilance committee members had made a practice of tailing the U.S. marshal and his deputies around town. A prominent abolitionist attorney observed Deputy Marshal Asa O. Butman carrying Burns into the federal courthouse. Within moments, antislavery Bostonians were seeking to orchestrate the fugitive's release.

The Reverend Theodore Parker—self-proclaimed minister at large to Boston's fugitive slaves—quickly arranged for the circulation of a handbill to organize a mass meeting at Faneuil Hall. In the lead-up to the meeting, however, the Boston Vigilance Committee failed to agree upon a course of action. A faction led by Thomas Wentworth Higginson, Martin Stowell, and Lewis Hayden argued for storming the courthouse to remove the fugitive by force, while others urged a more cautious response. Confusion prevailed at the public meeting, where Parker and others denounced the fugitive law but were not certain whether to mobilize the crowd in an attack on the courthouse, only four blocks from Faneuil Hall at 26 Court Street.

While the speakers hesitated, Hayden, Stowell, and Higginson mounted their attack, hammering the courthouse doors with a beam lifted from a nearby construction site and using axes. A phalanx of armed special deputies stood inside, armed mostly with swords. A shot rang and a deputy named James Batchelder fell mortally wounded, but the rescuers were unable to penetrate to the interior. The would-be rescue fell flat, with the crowd from Faneuil Hall arriving late and the prisoner still secured in an upstairs room.

During an uncomfortable interlude, antislavery agitators milled around the courthouse while police assembled and began to arrest suspected participants. Having angered Bostonians during previous attempted slave rescues, municipal officials determined to keep their law enforcement at a perfunctory level during the Burns rescue clean-up. They removed suspects one at a time, leaving time for escape, and their failure to search those in custody meant that either Hayden or Stowell, chief suspects in the shooting of Batchelder, went to jail with the murder weapon cooling in his pocket. In the end a mixed docket of white and African American defendants—minus the canny Lewis Hayden—was indicted by a federal grand jury on charges of violating the Fugitive Slave Act.[4] A federal military escort costing more than $10,000 spirited Burns out of Boston. He later obtained his freedom with help from Northern friends and enrolled in Oberlin College before succumbing to tuberculosis.

While *United States v. Martin Stowell* made its way to court in the summer and fall of 1854, U.S. attorneys appointed by the Pierce administration set out to make an additional example of the leaders of the Boston Vigilance Committee. Much as Sherman Booth in the Glover rescue had drawn attention to his role by printing flyers to raise a crowd (for which Booth, a newspaper publisher, had set the type with his own hands), Theodore Parker had left a paper trail regarding his authorship of the broadside headlined in massive letters with the words A MAN KIDNAPPED! In November, the minister and other leaders faced charges of incitement for their printed and spoken words in the hours surrounding the failed Burns rescue. Also in the docket stood Thomas Wentworth Higginson, not charged in the first round, Martin Stowell, the subject of two simultaneous criminal trials, and the antislavery orator Wendell Phillips, who had taken the podium during the Faneuil Hall rally. Even indirect encouragement of actions intended to thwart the fugitive process, Judge Benjamin Curtis said in his charge to the grand jury, could be considered evidence of obstruction and criminal interference.

The slow decline of religiosity in America after the Civil War has diminished the historical standing of clerical Transcendentalists such as Parker, but to his contemporaries, Parker ranked alongside Ralph Waldo Emerson as one of the great thinkers of the time. While his body of work lacked the topical breadth and universalism of that of Emerson and Henry Thoreau, Theodore Parker more than matched his famous counterparts in reaching audiences. The weekly sermon regimen kept Parker's views constantly before the public, with more than two thousand people in attendance at the Sunday services of his 28th Congregationalist Society, which hired out the entertainment venue Tremont Temple to accommodate the crowds. Thousands more read printed versions of his talks that circulated in pamphlets and newspaper accounts. The Concord, Massachusetts, purists (who lived so close to Boston that the Transcendentalist educator Bronson Alcott helped to coordinate the Burns rally by traveling from Concord to Worcester and Boston in one day) insisted frequently that they preferred not to engage in the burdensome responsibilities of politics. Parker, by contrast, maintained an avid correspondence with leading political figures of the day, setting up meetings and writing letters of introduction. He self-consciously functioned as a Free-Soil and Republican Party organizer. In the grip of the proslavery Democratic federal state as a Burns defendant, Parker seized the opportunity to articulate the political dimensions of the prosecution.

Parker was arrested in his study on November 29, 1854. "You must not suppose that I did not expect this," he told the chagrined process server. Indeed, antislavery and Republican strategists in Massachusetts had come to see the pending trial as a great opportunity for winning support. "I am glad you have been indicted—pardon me," wrote Charles Sumner, eighteen months before the attack by Preston Brooks: "Of course you will defend yourself . . . face to face." The excitement mounted with the detention of Wendell Phillips on December 15: "Hancock was also once arrested," Parker trumpeted to Sumner. "A chance to be heard!"

Herein was the prosecution's dilemma, a discomfort that also extended to Benjamin Curtis, the judge. As William Lloyd Garrison described it in an editorial for the (local) *Liberator*:

> Political prosecutions are almost always blunders . . . The Circuit Court cannot reasonably expect to shut Mr. Parker's mouth; he will probably continue to say what he thinks; while his auditors and admirers will grow more numerous and warmer at every successive indictment. It is out of the power of His Honor or of Mr. Attorney to stop preaching and pamphleteering, unless the Fugitive Slave Law is amended by the introduction of a special clause against Faneuil Hall, and against the presses and printing-offices of Boston.

Curtis was already the bête noire of antislavery Boston for his own and his brother's contributions to the smooth operation of the Fugitive Law process in local courts (George Ticknor Curtis having been the U.S. commissioner who remanded Thomas Sims to slavery in 1851). Now he found himself unfavorably juxtaposed against a favorite son of the city.

Parker, for his part, began preparing and publicizing an extended brief for himself and the other Burns prisoners: Stowell, Higginson, Phillips, and three African American participants, John Morrison, Samuel T. Proudman, and John C. Cluer. He scribbled furiously to Republican friends, including New York's William Seward and Salmon Chase of Ohio as well as Sumner. It was the great honor of his life, he told his congregation, to impart a vivid lesson of the times.[5]

Represented by the best lawyers in the commonwealth, but prepared to speak in his own defense, Parker assembled a manuscript of more than two hundred pages. Before he had the chance to take the stand, however, the judge dismissed the case as a matter of *nolle prosequi*—in which the prosecution failed to present or withdrew a legitimate criminal charge. The aborted indictment saved the Curtis court and U.S. attorney from the likely termination of their work in the more common form of Northern courtroom nullification in the 1850s, in which juries refused to convict antislavery peers.

In any case, the judge himself was silently aligned with the liberators. "Organized disobedience is rebellion, and if force is used, insurrection or revolution," Curtis had written to a friend, shortly after the Fugitive Act went into effect. "I wish these Unitarian ministers would sit down calmly and measure . . . the place where that step must carry us."

> I would like to see somebody come manfully up to the point, and attempt to show that the moral duty which we owe to the fugitive slave, when in conflict with the moral duty we owe to our country and its laws, is so plainly superior thereto, that we may and ought to engage in a revolution on account of it.

In his memoirs, Curtis objected to Parker's characterization of the dismissal as the work of the defense attorneys, and to the sensationalized version of the case that the minister published as *The Trials of Theodore Parker* some months later. He remained silent on the subject in 1855, however, intent on advancing his career and perhaps hopeful (like the Radical Republicans) that he could make a difference by pushing for change within the system. His example invoked the spirit of Thoreau's 1849 essay *Civil Disobedience*: "When the subject has refused allegiance, and the officer has resigned his office, then the revolution is accomplished."[6]

Parker's published brief fused his scholarly, religious, and political convictions with the dilemma presented by the fugitive slave emergency. As a

Unitarian and Transcendentalist, he spoke with authority on the spiritual dimension of political life, particularly as interpreted by the New England philosophy. Parker's politics—what he called transcendental politics—was idealistic in the sense that a perceived ideal of truth and justice was seen to bear upon material events. The transcendental in politics "starts not from experience alone, but from consciousness; not merely from human history but also from human nature." Conscience allowed men and women to recognize "natural justice, natural right; absolute justice, absolute right" in the world, and to act in accordance with conscience to make the world right with God.

It was easy for Parker to demonstrate the slow emergence of the ideal in the signal events of history. He saw a dialectical progression in which the friction of opposing forces had inexorably generated forward pressure. The tyranny of King John had produced the Magna Carta, and amid the chaos of 1789 the Declaration of the Rights of Man had been delivered to the world. In his own age, Parker saw the "tendency towards Democracy or Despotism" as locked in a mortal embrace.

"Gentlemen of the Jury," he was to have said in his address, "the Party of Slavery has long been the conqueror in the field of Federal politics." The Circuit Court was an instrument of the Slave Power to punish and suppress the transcendent politics of antislavery. "Slavery is the Plaintiff in this case; Freedom Defendant."[7] The weapons and cruelty of slavery were well known; less well understood, and yet more important for understanding the forward trajectory of politics, he said, was the Party of Freedom.

True democracy drew its strength from four great principles, as Parker saw it. First, "respect for labor": Parker saw such recognition as the foundation of egalitarianism and meritocracy. As laborers in one form or another, women and men, free and unfree workers, whites and blacks, could meet on common ground. On such a footing fully participatory democracy could be established. Second, "government over all," as he wrote in his brief, fulfilled the fundamental requirement of liberal politics, equality before the law. Third, government "by all" embraced the ideal of full political participation, including by women and African Americans. In a reversal of the current form, in which the federal government embraced the moral and political evils of proslavery, Parker finally predicted the emergence of government "for all." *Of the people, by the people, for the people*, he averred, in a phrase that Parker would repeat for the six remaining years of his life, "is what I call the American idea."[8]

The enemies of freedom believed that history had stopped moving forward, he said. They denied that the principles of the Declaration of Independence exerted any claim upon the present. As a proud son of New England, Parker would not dismiss the achievements of the founding generation so readily. The Declaration had posited a transcendent truth—that governments existed to secure the natural rights of humankind:

> The American Revolution, and American history since, is an attempt to prove by experience this transcendental proposition, to organize the transcendental idea of politics. The idea demands for its organization, a democracy—a government by natural justice, by . . . legislation that enacts law representing a fact of the universe, a resolution of God.

Everywhere in 1855, the Party of Despotism appeared "in admirable order and discipline," while "the Party of Freedom is not yet well organized." Yet "these two parties are continually at war and attended with various successes."

The prosecution could dismiss its charges, but Parker's audience could not afford to shrink from the confrontation, he wrote. "In transcendental politics the question of expediency is always subordinate to the question of natural right"; its agent "asks not merely about the cost of a war, but its natural justice."

> It aims to organize the ideals of man's moral and social nature into political institutions; to have a government which shall completely represent the facts of man's social consciousness so far as his nature is now developed.[9]

Whatever the obstacles, Parker was sanguine about the outcome. "The arc [of the moral universe] is a long one," he had written in a sermon of 1852. "And from what I see I am sure that it bends toward justice."[10]

3

TRANSCENDENTAL POLITICS

The quotable Theodore Parker had observed the arc of the moral universe bending toward justice. How to hasten its trajectory, if indeed such progress could be facilitated by human action? Here was the existential question facing nineteenth-century progressives of all kinds.

Parker and the Radicals imagined a fully politicized transition to a better world, in which the timetable of change responded to nominations, balloting, and government policy. They recognized the tremendous latent power of the state, increasingly mobilized in the 1850s to serve the interests of slaveholding. Such power, they believed, could be seized and used to accelerate the bend toward justice in American life.

The Radicals did not disavow the possibility, indeed the certainty, that their hoped-for capture of the system would result in violence. Led by Parker, who sprinkled his sermons and speeches with bloody imagery, Republicans at the extreme imagined politics by extreme means. The minister was fated to die of tuberculosis in 1860, but he would have heartily approved the massive application of political power to the problem of slavery during the Civil War and afterward, despite the huge material and human costs. The Radical Reconstruction of the postwar South made vivid Parker's sense of how a government "of the people" could act as midwife to "natural justice."

In the 1850s, however, Parker's Republican political views occupied merely the Radical fringe of the still marginalized abolitionist minority.

Competing visions of the end of slavery held much more sway in the North and commanded much more notoriety in the South than any political agenda. First, the recognized dean of the antislavery movement was not Parker or any elected official but William Lloyd Garrison, who denounced the politics of his day as immoral. Second, outflanking Parker in the field of political philosophy were his fellow Transcendentalists Henry Thoreau and Ralph Waldo Emerson, who offered a vision of personal independence that seemed at odds with compromise and partisanship. Already in the 1850s the destructive energy of the Civil War was brought to bear upon both Garrisonian and Transcendentalist idealism, neither of which would survive the war unchanged. Radical Republicans advanced in part by striving to incorporate the purity and drive of their progressive counterparts.

Imagined as lines plotted against the timeline of the universe, Garrison's moral arc rose and fell at a steeper angle than Reverend Parker's. The pursuit of justice in the nineteenth century, as he saw it, encompassed a multivalent and complete reorganization of human values and relationships, in which committed individuals held themselves up as models of a new way of living in the world. Garrisonians embraced nearly all of the progressive causes: abolition, women's rights, and nonviolence, including physical passive resistance for individuals and antiwar activism at the societal level. Many practiced temperance, and others interpreted nonviolence to preclude the consumption of animal flesh. Garrisonians invested thousands and even millions of hours in the work of *moral suasion*—seeking to build a consensus against slavery and other forms of oppression by reasoning and inspiration. They wrote and read pamphlets and newspapers, including Garrison's *Liberator*, circulated petitions, encouraged one another and built social networks through correspondence, and attended hours of topical presentations at antislavery conventions, symposia, and lecture series. Their hard work aimed to overthrow oppression by way of a seismic moral shift, suddenly and completely.

Garrisonians used Christian imagery and songs, focusing with special relish on the promise of Apocalypse. Perceiving a crisis of the old order, they

urged full disassociation with the corrupt institutions—some going so far as
to eschew the wearing of cotton clothing or the consumption of sugar raised
by the enslaved. Garrisonians considered participation in politics as a way
of fortifying the Slave Power and they repudiated all compromises including
the Constitutional Union itself. The slogan "No union with slaveholders"—
part of the *Liberator* masthead—favored secession over what the Garrisonian orator Wendell Phillips called "that 'compromise' which was made
between slavery and freedom, in 1787," i.e. the U.S. Constitution.[1]

The disunionists refused to celebrate the national tradition by honoring
its sacred documents and founding anniversary. Since 1829, when Garrison
had declared himself to be ashamed of his country in a holiday address, a
countercultural antislavery Fourth of July movement had marked the day for
mourning rather than for celebration. Antislavery Massachusetts, in many
ways the epicenter of Garrisonianism, nurtured an alternative tradition of pic-
nicking at "the Grove" in Framingham, a natural amphitheater on a lake and
near a train station. The Massachusetts Antislavery Association—a chapter
of the national group led by Garrison himself—printed advertisements and
organized transportation to the venue, inviting like-minded people "there to
pass the day in no idle glorying in our country's liberty, but in deep humilia-
tion for her Disgrace and Shame."

On the platform for the Framingham Grove ceremonies on July 4, 1854,
hung an American flag, inverted *union down* with its stars on the bottom
and edged with black.

For the conscientious anti-picnickers, it had already been a spring and
summer of meeting after meeting, as the Kansas-Nebraska Act and the Anthony Burns slave commission roiled local opinion. Natick, Framingham,
Worcester, Concord, and Worcester again: every week presented a new set of
conventions and speeches, often in uncomfortably hot weather.

The pace was made bearable only by the intensity of the excitement and
the presence of antislavery women in the railway cars and at the more avant-
garde events. Louisa May Alcott, flushed from the publication of her first
book that summer, *Flower Fables*, told everyone how she had seen the face
of Anthony Burns and noticed a scar on his face on the day he was hauled
out of Boston by federal troops. The papers had reported that Abby Fol-
som had been arrested while making a speech on the courthouse grounds

on the Saturday of Burns's rendition. The old lady had employed full-body nonresistance and had to be carried from the scene. Reverend Higginson's mother, Mary Higginson, housebound like his wife, was not present, but she made it known that she was proud of her boy and in no need of sympathy about his legal troubles. Nearly everyone was talking about the way Lydian Emerson had draped the Emerson house in Concord in black crepe for the Fourth of July.[2]

"To-day, we are called to celebrate the seventy-eighth anniversary of American Independence. In what spirit?" Garrison began, when he took the podium. "With what purpose? to what end?" He did not pass judgment on the Declaration of Independence with the same certainty with which he denounced the Constitution. However much its lofty language failed to square with the realities of 1776, its proclamation was "the greatest political event in the annals of time," as Garrison saw it. But, he continued, "where can our Declaration be proclaimed, and faithfully applied to men and governments, without subjecting the enforcer of it to ridicule, odium, persecution, imprisonment, martyrdom, or lynch law?"

The outrages of 1854 had accentuated Garrison's old complaints about government under the Constitution—"the most bloody and heaven-daring arrangement ever made." At Framingham, the editor kept his speech short but doubled down on the anger that he and many in attendance were feeling. In a stunt that became famous, Garrison held up a series of documents, announcing their titles to the crowd: the Fugitive Slave Act of 1850; the commissioner's ruling in the Anthony Burns rendition; the Martin Stowell indictment; and finally a printed Constitution. Striking a match, he burned each document to ashes while demanding the approval of the crowd. "Amen," shouted people in attendance, "amen, amen." Garrison condemned the Constitution as "a covenant with death, and an agreement with hell" before consigning it to flames. "So perish all compromises with slavery!" he declared.[3]

Garrison was not the only speaker at Framingham to manifest his severe disapproval of government. Whereas Garrison had focused on the perfidy of the national authorities, the philosopher Henry Thoreau took the podium to denounce state officials in his speech, "Slavery in Massachusetts."

Prior to the Mexican-American War of 1846–48, Transcendentalists had avoided political themes, preferring to contemplate nature, the sacred, and the place of the individual in society. The early stages of the movement, which had origins in Concord and Harvard in the 1820s, took aim at institutionalization and dogma, and as the philosophy matured under the leadership of Ralph Waldo Emerson, it prized individualism and the spirit of self-reliance. Seeking the divine in ordinary human emotions and experiences, Transcendentalists found little fascination in the sordid workings of government. The Fugitive Slave Act stirred Emerson and Thoreau to denounce the new law as the undoing of American civilization, a tragedy that Emerson firmly interpreted as a disaster for white people. "The absence of moral feeling in the whiteman [sic] is the very calamity I deplore," he wrote in 1851, acknowledging that "the captivity of a thousand negroes is nothing to me," so long as their plight did not depend on the actions of elite New Englanders such as himself.[4]

Even as the portents of civil war appeared on the horizon, the philosophers' professed reluctance to turn their attention to current events. Thoreau's appearance at Framingham, however—and the pointedly partisan nature of his speech—advanced a final stage of Transcendentalist thought, in which the growing slavery emergency elicited an outpouring of political ideas.

Henry Thoreau was not a Republican—and to guard against being represented as a partisan of any unauthorized organization he had issued a blanket disavowal in his great 1849 essay *Civil Disobedience*: "I, Henry Thoreau, do not wish to be regarded as a member of any incorporated society which I have not joined."[5] In fact Thoreau was not a joiner. *Civil Disobedience* had explored the proper orientation of an individual to the state in an era of the Mexican War, and Thoreau had advocated radical personal separation rather than even passive political participation. In advocating this stance, Thoreau aligned his philosophy with the Garrisonian "non-citizen" and "non-resistant" postures.

More than the pacifists, however, Thoreau also contemplated the subversion and transformation of the state, both in *Civil Disobedience* and in the text he delivered at the Framingham picnic. His essay vividly depicted the political events and personalities of his day, calling out Democrats and the emerging

Republicans by name, and in the process sketching out a revolutionary political vision.

July 4 was not an incidental holiday on Thoreau's calendar. For a son of Concord, the date of the Declaration of Independence was second only to the anniversary of Patriots' Day, April 19, when the village had mobilized in the first fighting of the Revolutionary War. Thoreau had chosen July 4, 1845, to begin housekeeping at Walden, in the experiment that had produced his greatest book. The events of 1854 had roused him from the final round of editing for *Walden; or, Life in the Woods*, which would be published on August 9 of that year.

Walden Pond represented the antithesis of the national and geopolitical struggles surrounding Kansas and the Boston courthouse, a place to contemplate the minute, eternal, and cyclical patterns in nature. It was a source of frustration to the author to turn his attention from divinity to the bitter political demonstrations of his day. "What signifies the beauty of nature when men are base?" he asked his audience on the shores of the Framingham lake.

Disunionism and noncitizenship would not suffice as a response to the encroachments of the Slave Power. The problem with Garrisonianism, as Thoreau depicted it, was its refusal to accept responsibility for the fate of the nation as a whole. "Suppose you have a small library, with pictures to adorn the walls—a garden laid out all around—and contemplate scientific and literary pursuits," Thoreau said, sketching out a particular dream of many in his Victorian audience, epitomized by a famous woodcut of the study of Theodore Parker. Suppose that you "discover all at once that your villa, with all its contents is located in hell, and that the justice of the peace has a cloven foot and forked tail." Such was the fate of Massachusetts in the era of the Fugitive Slave Act: "to me morally covered with volcanic scoriae and cinders, such as Milton describes in the infernal regions."

Governments had been devised to add value, not detract, to provide safety and not to imperil it, Thoreau said. He archly remarked on the degree to which the national state and the government of Massachusetts had strayed from their intended functions when understood as having responsibility for slaves, fugitives, and allies in the antislavery movement. The governor of Massachusetts, Emory Washburn, had not moved to uphold the Massachusetts personal liberty law, which prohibited the participation of state officials in slave renditions. He had also bypassed the opportunity to enforce a legal writ of habeas corpus—a summons to a sympathetic judge's courtroom—on Burns's behalf. To rely on state laws that conformed to conscience instead of immoral federal laws seemed to Thoreau to be a minimum standard for leadership and personal integrity.

"If to be Governor requires to subject one's self to so much ignominy without remedy, if it is to put a restraint upon my manhood," he quipped, with wry acknowledgment of his own bohemianism, "I shall take care never to be Governor of Massachusetts."

Thoreau also called out the judges in the Burns rendition by name and scolded them as lawbreakers. They had failed to obey "that eternal and only just CONSTITUTION, which [God], and not any Jefferson or Adams, has written in [their] being." The demand was a direct citation of Republican Party dogma—the "higher law" doctrine associated since 1850 with New York senator William Seward, which identified the operation of natural law as superior to the Constitution and federal statutes.[6] "The law will never make men free," said Thoreau; "it is men who have got to make the law free." Those who refused cooperation with laws codifying slavery did their part as "lovers of law and order who observe the law when the government breaks it."

Unelaborated in Thoreau's text, but latent in the same logic, was the possibility that concrete positive acts could also aid in the transformation of the state. The philosopher offered a few recommended courses of action. "Among measures to be adopted, I would suggest to make as earnest and vigorous assault upon the press as has already been made upon the church," he said, referencing the emergence of antislavery and humanitarian congregations in New England and the North. His larger program urged a wholesale disassociation with the state until Massachusetts officials gained resolve to resist the oppressiveness of the federal government.

Political parties need not congratulate themselves on their fitness. "The fate of the country does not depend on how you vote at the polls," he pronounced. "It does not depend on what kind of paper you drop into the ballot-box once a year, but on what kind of man you drop from your chamber into the street every morning."

A call to duty sounded for all who would have justice, to address the moral emergency of slavery regardless of age, gender, or standing. As for the cost: "I need not say what match I would touch, what system endeavor to blow up; but as I love my life, I would side with the right, and let the dark earth roll from under me, calling my mother and my brother to follow." Thoreau perceived that quiet times had passed and gone. His vision of generational sacrifice prefigured the impending crisis of the Civil War.

In the spirit of the Fourth of July, Thoreau managed a word of cheer for the would-be rescuers of Anthony Burns. Just because they had not succeeded, he said, did not mean that the revolution had not begun.[7]

Emerson himself participated in the summer's whirl of activity. Along with his wife, Lydian, Cynthia Dunbar Thoreau, the thinker's mother, and other citizens of Concord, the author of *Nature* and *Self-Reliance* joined a Concord discussion group that resolved to "aid and assist all in our power to help the fleeing bondsman to obtain his God-given rights."[8]

Emerson thought more than usual about politics and compromise that summer, composing a poem of sorts in his journals that he dedicated "*To the Whigs*":

> These men meant well, but they
> allowed the Missouri Compromise;
> meant well, but allowed Texas;
> meant well, but allowed the Mexican War;
> meant well, but allowed the Fugitive Slave Law.
> They resisted Nebraska, *but it is too late.*[9]

He also attended a meeting on June 22, 1854, in Concord in the company of Henry Thoreau. Henry was appalled to find that the subject of the meeting was the Kansas-Nebraska Act—a matter he considered secondary to "slavery in Massachusetts." Waldo entertained a broader view of the crisis, however, and signed his name to a circular calling for a national discussion of the territorial issue. The petitioners called themselves members of the Massachusetts People's Party and the Freedom Party in the same document, but in fact their caucus was a stalking horse for the emerging Republicans.

Like his younger friend, Emerson perceived a crisis at hand in the body politic, but unlike Thoreau he aimed not to strike a match but to work within the nation's institutions to achieve peace. The nation as a whole must atone, he declared, in a winter 1855 address entitled "American Slavery." He proposed compensated emancipation to eradicate slaveholding—a position commonly held among moderate Republicans—insisting that no price the slaveholders could name would be too much. Americans must sell off their public lands, delay their public works, and sacrifice their luxuries in order to obtain a treasure great enough to buy the nation out of its slavery conundrum. "The needlewomen will give," he predicted. "Children will have cent societies . . . Every man in the land would give a week's work to dig away this accursed mountain of sorrow once and forever out of the world." The example of the Kansas pioneers, he argued, foretold the hardships of the final reckoning that all virtuous Americans must share.

The sacrifices loomed uncomfortably for the Sage of Concord, who entered into a period of mental and physical decline during the Civil War or shortly afterward. Henry Thoreau's days were also numbered. During the Civil War, as people of his generation acted to destroy the system of oppression he had despised, the younger philosopher turned away from society and conflict, choosing to spend the months leading up to his premature death from tuberculosis editing and organizing his written work. He died in 1862 without acknowledging that an Age of Transcendence had begun.

Republicans stood to inherit the zeal of Garrisonian antislavery—and the support of Garrison himself, who moved steadily into the party embrace. They would also embody the sacrifices and self-reliance prized by Transcendentalists, giving their lives to the pursuit of justice in the revolutionary 1850s and 1860s.

4

FREE SOIL, FREE MEN, FREMONT

Galvanized by current events and elevated by the philosophical debate, the Republicans made their national electoral debut in 1856. Radicals committed to the most direct assaults on slavery expansion and fugitive rendition leaned hard on the new party apparatus. Escalating violence heightened the urgency of the Radical appeal as new runaway dramas and the onset of Bleeding Kansas roiled emotions in the North.

The West—which was bigger in the nineteenth century, encompassing the Old Northwest Territory Free States of Ohio, Indiana, Illinois, Michigan, and Wisconsin along with California, Iowa, and the unorganized territories—played a powerful role in the formation of the Republican Party, including its Radical faction. Westerners had been the first to adopt the name Republican Party—at Ripon, Wisconsin, in February 1854; the first to hold party conventions—in Michigan and Wisconsin in July; and the first to win elections under the partisan banner, sweeping every office they contested for in Michigan. In the 1854 elections, "Anti-Nebraska" candidates claimed 120 of 142 open Northern seats in Congress on the wave of regional outrage.[1] Republicans in eastern strongholds such as Massachusetts and New York State shared their gains with the insurgent anti-immigrant parties in 1854 and 1855, led by the Know-Nothing/Americans, while westerners laid claim as governors and other high officials to the party leadership.

The heartland of western Republicanism was Ohio, where Radicals commanded statewide and national prestige, led by Senator and soon-to-be Governor Salmon P. Chase.

Chase was an idea jockey and legal theorist in a party that was born ideological. His most sweeping vision was the "Freedom National" interpretation of the Constitution of the United States, the core of which insisted that slavery was a local, not a national, institution, deprived of the protection of any but local government. The interpretation suggested a number of legal strategies for containing and reversing slavery, including a ban on slavery in the federally managed District of Columbia and in the territories, a ban on interstate traffic in slaves, and an active naval presence to combat international slave trading. Chase had been an architect of the Free-Soil interparty coalition, casting his lots with the Democrats until the Nebraska Act betrayed his trust. He was an author of the "Appeal of the Independent Democrats," the declaration that initiated the Republicanization of Free-Soilers in Congress early in 1854. Reelected as a Free-Soil senator that year, Chase would win as a Republican in the Ohio gubernatorial election in 1855. As a leading face of the Radicals, however, he would encounter a crisis that reshaped his relationship to the party's left wing.

Blame it on winter. Between January 1855 and February 1856, historic cold resulted in a deep freeze on the Ohio River, the western border between slavery and freedom. Enslaved persons in Kentucky and elsewhere seized the opportunity to venture on foot or by conveyance across the river to the Free States. Life imitated art as real individuals acted out the icy crossing scene in *Uncle Tom's Cabin*—pure imagination in 1852, when Harriet Beecher Stowe published the book.[2]

Thousands were thought to have escaped, an estimated 175 through Cincinnati, Ohio, alone. Amid the surge, the Cincinnati case of Margaret Garner and her young children produced the most tragic and politically explosive results.

Garner had escaped with her family by sleigh, but opportunistic slave catchers had observed them and pursued them across the river to a safe house where she and her family were expected. "Mother, before my children are taken back into Kentucky I will kill every one of them," she declared as captors approached. While her husband shot and wounded a deputy marshal, Garner cut the throat of her two-year-old daughter, bludgeoned her baby with a shovel, and stabbed her other children and herself until she was overpowered.[3] Imprisoned by state authorities as a murderer, Margaret Garner quickly attracted the support of abolitionists and Radical Republicans in Cincinnati and across the North.

According to abolitionists, Garner stood more in jeopardy of state law than of the fugitive slave process, having murdered and attempted the murder of her own children. Though an Ohio judge issued a writ of habeas corpus, seeking her arraignment in his courtroom on state charges, the tragic mother remained in the custody of federal authorities. In a shocking summation on the fourth day, the attorney arguing against the writ denounced the intervention of abolitionist agitators in what should have been a straightforward slave rendition, citing an incident in which the activist Lucy Stone had proposed to deliver a knife to Margaret Garner in her jail cell. After the ruling in their favor, the U.S. marshal and his associates became drunk and disorderly, threatening the life of a reporter in a late-night steamboat encounter. The friends of Garner, in contrast, responded to the denial by remaining silent in their seats in the courtroom, convening a citizens' meeting in which the slaveholder in question as well as his lawyer politely awaited remarks by Lucy Stone.

With the defense attorney acting as the chair and Garner's purported owner and his attorneys present, "the lady mounted to the judge's desk." "I had a right to put a dagger in her hand," Stone declared, revealing that she had also advised Garner on a suicide technique that did not require a weapon. Margaret Garner's attack on her children and herself was a political act, Stone insisted, and her own participation was justified: "I exercised the same right as those who distributed weapons to the combatants on Bunker Hill." Given the stakes, the cause of freedom for the slave was more properly revolutionary, Stone said, than the patriots' objections to "a paltry tax on tea."[4] Stone herself, she said, would resist the Fugitive Slave Law by any means necessary.

Stone wore a dress—a fact reported in full detail because of her recent appearances in short hair and the reformist Bloomer costume. Asked how she wished to be addressed in light of her recent marriage to Henry Blackwell, the feminist replied politely but firmly: "I call myself *Mrs.* Lucy Stone," she said. Despite this preference, conservative newspaper accounts gave her name as "Mrs. Blackwell."[5]

If Stone's stature was enhanced by her ghastly advocacy, the tragedy of Margaret Garner proved a setback for the career of Salmon Chase. Chase had campaigned for the center in the 1855 election, trying to hold a local reputation as a moderate even as he bid for stature as one of the highest-ranking Radicals in the new party. Chase proceeded to alienate abolitionists by neglecting to support a new state bid for habeas corpus over Margaret Garner, refusing to provoke a states' rights conflict on her behalf.

The Fugitive Slave Commission convened in March did not permit Garner or her friends to speak in her defense and quickly remanded her to slavery. In federal custody, Garner boarded a steamer going south without abandoning her revolutionary suicidal aims. She threw herself into the Ohio River holding a child, whom she drowned. She was rescued, sold, and held in bondage in New Orleans and Mississippi until her death from unknown causes the following year. She was later immortalized as the central character of Toni Morrison's novel *Beloved*.[6]

Chase would feel the aftereffects of the tragedy longer, and would live to regret his compliance with the federal law. Theodore Parker spoke for many in a letter to Chase, which the fastidious governor preserved in his personal archive despite its sting. "I would have thought the antislavery Governor of Ohio would get possession of that noble woman," Parker said, "either by the *Hocus Pocus* of some legal technicality . . . or else by the *red right arm of Ohio*."[7]

His hesitation would cost Chase as the party moved toward the presidential nomination of 1856. In February, self-described "Friends of the Republican Movement" convened in the first-ever national Republican convention in Pittsburgh, a prelude to the nominating convention scheduled for the summer in Philadelphia. Westerners took prominent roles as party organizers and leading men: Joshua R. Giddings, an Ohio representative in the House; Representative Owen Lovejoy of Illinois; George Bingham and Zachariah Chandler of Michigan; and a handful with ties to Kansas, including Wyman Spooner of Wisconsin and the Englishman James Redpath, representing Missouri. Though many were Radicals—in the case of Redpath, extreme enough to ride with John Brown in Kansas—moderates dominated the convention, which chose the slaveholding Republican, Senator Francis P. Blair of Maryland, to preside. It was only after hours that genuinely radical precepts were heard. A mass meeting on the evening of February 23, for example, gave voice to "those who feel determined to use every means" on behalf of Free Kansas. Zachariah Chandler claimed "he believed with Mr. [Horace] Greeley [also a delegate] that the Sharp's [sic] rifles were very great peacemakers, and that there was not much danger of introducing too many into Kansas."[8]

On June 18, less than four weeks after the Sack of Lawrence and the assault on Sumner, the Republicans opened their first national convention in Philadelphia. They would not be the only party to that year's presidential contest to seek to maximize the sense of outrage over Kansas violence. Indeed, the Know-Nothing American Party, holding its last national convention, also in Philadelphia, had been the first to introduce the catchphrase "Bleeding Kansas" only days before.[9] The Republicans complained in their platform that the constitutional rights of Free-State settlers were under attack, including their right to keep and bear arms. They called for the immediate admission of Kansas as a Free State and the recognition of Charles Robinson, James H. Lane, and the others as officeholders under the Topeka Constitution.

This time Radicals dominated the floor sessions, issuing repeated calls for speeches from such favorites as Henry Wilson and the Pennsylvania congressman Thaddeus Stevens. Making common cause with moderates in the elevation of a relative outsider, the Californian John C. Fremont, the Parker and Ohio cliques laid claim to key passages of the party platform. Its opening claim, for example, held as sacred the assurance of equality in the Declaration of Independence.[10] Delegates saluted the armed colonization of Kansas and predicted escalations. If things went well in 1856, said E. Rockwood Hoar of Massachusetts, the Republicans might hold their next convention in Virginia or Maryland. Indeed, delegates from three states in the Upper South attended the convention, including the associate of Eli Thayer John C. Underwood, who lobbied tirelessly on behalf of his plan to build a network of free labor colonies in Virginia, his own adopted home.[11]

As if to answer the stridency of the Republican convention, the Democratic Pierce administration moved on July 4 to terminate the proceedings of the Topeka legislature. Dispatching artillery and troops under the commander of Fort Leavenworth, Colonel Edwin V. Sumner of the Massachusetts Sumners, the proslavery Kansas contingent savored an ironic victory against the backdrop of the national holiday.[12] Undaunted, Topeka legislators under armed guards led the crowd in cheers for Fremont.[13]

The Republican offensive moved forward on two fronts. The mainstream and officeholders pushed the presidential and congressional tickets, headed by a man whose views on slavery remained undefined in the public mind. Speakers delivered variations on the tiresome slogan "Free Soil, Free Labor, Free Men, and Fremont" and defended the candidate against accusations of foreign birth and Catholicism, a hazard of the explorer's partial French Canadian patrimony. Responding to complaints that a Catholic priest had married Fremont to Jessie Benton, the daughter of Senator Thomas Hart Benton of Missouri, for example, the Reverend Henry Ward Beecher commented almost lasciviously on the charms of the celebrity bride. "Like a true lover and a gallant man, Colonel Fremont has said that he didn't care *who* did it, [just] so long as it was done quick and strong," he reported. "Had we been in Col. Fremont's place we would have been married if it required us to walk through a row of priests and bishops as long as from Washington to Rome, winding up with the Pope himself."[14]

Indeed, Jessie Benton Fremont was as attractive as her husband as a standard-bearer for the new party. The great career of her father traced a trajectory from the slaveholding mainstream of the Democratic Party to a moral abhorrence for slavery and finally to a role as an éminence grise of the antislavery opposition in the Senate. Her own abolitionist credentials were sterling, and yet her status as a daughter of slaveholding Missouri inoculated her against charges of Radicalism. Except for her adventurous spirit, Jessie Fremont was not like her taciturn and ultimately disappointing husband: she was well educated, engaged in a network of constructive correspondence, principled, confident as a writer and speaker, skeptical of balderdash, resourceful, and oozing with charisma. "Fremont and Jessie" was a slogan of the campaign, a wink at the truth of the strengths of the candidate's wife. John C. Fremont as a strong, silent type navigated the difficult events of the summer and fall of 1856, putting a no-comment policy to good effect. In a better world their names would have been reversed upon the standard.

Extremism on both sides escalated as Election Day approached. Martin Stowell fled Kansas under threat of lynching, and the wife of John C. Underwood was threatened by her neighbors for displaying a Fremont flag on her Virginia farm. Mr. Underwood received official notice that he had been banished from Clarke County.

Republicans, meanwhile, wore their most militant expressions. The moderate Republican New Yorker William Seward hit the stump in the Empire State to recommend that black voting be expanded and that black men vote for Fremont. Immense crowds came out to cheer radical speeches—twenty thousand, fifty thousand, and, at a speech attended by Charles Francis Adams, Sr., what appeared to be every eligible voter in Philadelphia. Adams said that all he heard from the podium was one third Kansas-Nebraska Act, another third Kansas atrocities, and the last third pure Radical demagoguery.[15]

On the strength of its Radical platform and its Radical campaign tactics, the ticket headed by John C. Fremont garnered 45 percent of the national popular vote against a majority of Democrats united behind the pro-Southern Pennsylvanian James Buchanan.

Still subordinated to a national government controlled by the Slave Power, American Radicals would react to the electoral victory of their enemies by conspiring to subvert government, starting with a consideration of whether to dissolve the Union and proceeding to a direct assault—colonizing and filibustering as necessary—upon the slave states themselves.

5

DRED SCOTT NULLIFICATION

The Supreme Court's decision in *Dred and Harriett Scott v. Sandford* had officially invalidated the Republican Party: so said the *Charleston Mercury* in a sunny editorial from March 14, 1857. *Dred* had left "nothing vital in [R]epublicanism," while elevating the Democrats "beyond and above all competition as the constitutional, national, Union party of the country." The recently inaugurated Democratic president, James Buchanan, said the *Mercury*, "takes the helm under these auspicious circumstances, and his acts thus far give token of a successful and prosperous administration."[1]

Democrats and Southerners were wrong about Buchanan, who would be remembered as one of the most disastrous chief executives in American history, but their claims about the constitutional crisis confronting their Republican rivals could scarcely be denied.

Dred Scott was a case initiated in 1846 with the approval of antislavery activists, who encouraged the Scotts in hopes of securing the freedom of enslaved persons taken into territories and states where slavery was banned. Their hopes proved ill founded in light of the extreme conservatism of the 1850s' judiciary, especially in Chief Justice Roger Taney's Supreme Court. Taney wrote the opinion explaining the decision to deny the Scotts' petition, earning lasting infamy for his conclusion that blacks "had no rights which the white man was bound to respect." More significant for partisan politics was the chief justice's insistence (offered after his dismissal of the plaintiffs' lack of standing in a breach of standard practice) that the defunct Missouri Compromise had been unconstitutional because Congress lacked the power to ban slavery in the territories where the Scotts had resided. Such claims hurt Republicans, since the raison d'être of the party was the Free-Soil commitment, the only principle upon which all Republicans agreed. It weighed especially heavy on the small number of black Republicans, now deemed to be noncitizens without hope of attaining basic American protections.

In fact Republicans had had little to gain from the invitation of the judiciary branch into the debates about slavery in the territories. Democrats had been the chief advocates of a judicial resolution of the overall slavery problem, arguing that the resistance to popular sovereignty in Kansas demonstrated the futility of congressional solutions to the dilemma. A Supreme Court stacked with current and former slaveholders—and elevated to nearly co-equal status with the other branches by the nationalist jurisprudence of the early nineteenth century—could be counted on to validate the proslavery argument about expansion. In combination with the perpetuation of the anti-antislavery executive under James Buchanan, such a victory might put an end to the whole antislavery and Republican rebellion.[2]

Democrats assumed the burden of the apparent total victory of proslavery, condemning their party for the rest of the century to participation in the most backward-looking trends in U.S. society. Stephen Douglas in particular had been left to answer whether his party could offer any check upon rampaging slavery expansion.[3]

The decision laid bare to the general public the fundamental constitutional debates that had already divided the ranks of antislavery activists, bolstering the Garrisonian argument that the government was irredeemably proslavery. In the minority in Congress and state legislatures, denied access to the presidency and governors' seats in the contests of 1856, and now chastened by the high court, Republicans chafed under the total victory of their enemies. They complained about the partisanship of Chief Justice Taney, who had deliberately sought to terminate the slavery debate in his opinion in a way that aimed to shut down Republican and antislavery agitation.

Noting his dismissal of the case on the grounds of Dred Scott's citizenship status, many denounced his statements on the merits of the case's territorial and property claims as obiter dicta, that is, as nonbinding expressions of the judge's personal opinion.

A Republican member of Congress from western Massachusetts experienced a career-ending setback when news broke that the decision made Dred and Harriet Scott officially his property by virtue of marriage to the widow of the original owner, though he quickly organized their manumission.[4]

Republicans struck back, starting in the black caucus. An African American oyster dealer from Rhode Island, George T. Downing, published the first legal brief in favor of black citizenship, citing an opinion of Supreme Court justice Joseph Story as well as numerous examples of the exercise of voting rights and of U.S. passports issued to persons of color.[5] Seeking to turn the legal setback to their advantage, perhaps in jest, a group of four black men in Chicago accused of theft pleaded for their release on the grounds that "under the decision of the Supreme Court in the famous Dred Scott case they were merely chattels and not persons as alleged in the indictment."[6]

Others despaired, with many among the Radical Republicans deepening their commitment to extralegal action. Secession from the Union was already a well-established goal of antislavery partisans. Even before *Dred Scott*, disunionists had attempted to align Republican officeholders and organizers with their cause. At a disunion convention staged in Worcester in January, for example, the outrageous Thomas Wentworth Higginson had invited "Republicans and Garrisonians" to discuss the wisdom of a rupture. A few endorsed the call, with Congressman Joshua Giddings of Ohio offering the most explicit encouragement.

"I hesitate not to declare that this Federal government has been destructive of the ends for which it was instituted," Giddings wrote, citing from the Declaration of Independence, "and the people now hold the clear and indisputable right to alter or abolish it, and replace it with a new one."[7] A veteran of the Anthony Burns debacle and party organizer, Frank Bird, agreed to preside over the conference but made it clear that he was willing to discuss but not endorse secessionist threats.

Theodore Parker, for one, wrote that he was "glad to hear of any sign of manhood in the North," but he declined to attend the disunion conference in person. "I think a fire in the rear of some of our Republican members of Congress will do them no harm," Parker told Higginson. He liked the idea of turning tables on the South, which had "so long cried Wolf! Wolf!" with its own threats of disunion. Let them have "a glimpse of the real animal, and see how the South will like his looks." For himself, however, Parker would not condone "backing out of the Union" while slavery persisted and enlarged its sphere.

"I used to think that this terrible question of freedom or slavery in America would be settled without bloodshed," he told Higginson, using the same words that John Brown delivered on the way to the gallows two years afterward. Now Parker welcomed the prospect of a fight, and he calculated that the North held every important advantage in a military conflict. Northerners held the upper hand in numbers, geographic distribution, and technology and manufacturing, he wrote, while slaves and poor whites made "the Southern animal exceedingly weak in the whole hind-quarters." North versus South, Parker thought, "there is no doubt which goes into the ditch."[8]

Republican legitimists—committed to reforming the system by electoral politics—also redoubled their work in the aftermath of *Dred Scott*. New York State lodged the first formal complaint against the action of the Supreme Court, denouncing with special bitterness the pronouncements against black citizenship and calling for the reorganization of the high court to allow for more representation from the Free States.[9] The blistering report of the special state committee to consider *Dred Scott* included a series of defiant resolutions, all of which were confirmed by a large majority of assembly: (1) "Resolved, that this State will not allow slavery within its borders, in any form, or . . . for any time, however short," a statement of noncompliance with the Fugitive Slave Act; and (2) a vote of no confidence in the Supreme Court.[10] In making these resolutions, the committee expounded, the assembly "place[d] the Empire State on the Republican [nullification] doctrines of 1798, known as the 'Virginia Resolutions,' which were acquiesced in by the great Republican Party of that day."[11]

Radicals exhorted New Yorkers to do more. Speaking at a special convention of the American Anti-Slavery Society in New York City, Lucy Stone called on state governments to erect a bulwark of liberty against the power of the central state. "The Dred Scott decision is more dreadful to me than all the Sharp's [*sic*] rifles that can be made," Stone told the audience. "I must raise you to the level of disobeying what the country says is law." Stone invoked the "one word that anti-slavery Americans dare not speak." As it was with abolitionists, Stone said, "So it is with the Republican party; every one holds his hand over that hidden consciousness that this is a revolution."[12]

The abolitionist Gerrit Smith—heir to part of the Jacob Astor fur trade and a real estate fortune, who used his wealth to ease suffering and champion justice—publicly taunted New York Republicans in the New York State Assembly about their weakness in the face of *Dred*. Smith was the captain of the most vigorous remaining portion of the Liberty Party, which had represented the most uncompromising antislavery politics since its establishment in 1840 and which had become something of a New York State movement sustained by his generosity. Unlike all-white Free-Soilers and mostly white Republicans, the Liberty Party (and its successor, the Radical Abolition Party) openly celebrated racial equality and African American participants, counting Frederick Douglass, James McCune Smith, and other black luminaries in its ranks. Gerrit Smith saw the Supreme Court decision and electoral defeats as a moment of reckoning for Republicans, whom he considered both as rivals and as potential recruits to higher standards. "Great and frequent events are crowding the Republican party to choose its future," Smith wrote in a public letter to the Speaker of the New York assembly DeWitt Clinton Littlejohn. "Will it remain upon its present low and false ground, and perish speedily and disgracefully?—or will it rise into an Abolition party; expel slavery from the land; and live forever in the grateful hearts of the wise and good?"[13]

Led by the Speaker, in fact, Empire State Republicans sought to elevate their party by discreetly integrating African American interests into the party agenda. A push for black voting rights was the most striking part of the plan. Critics of the *Dred Scott* decision, such as George Downing, cited the right of black citizens to vote in several states including New York as one of the most important contradictions to Chief Justice Taney's nonrecognition of black citizenship precedents. To reinforce their objection to the court's effort to deny black citizens' rights, New York State acted quickly to enlarge the sphere of black political participation. Within two weeks of the ruling, Speaker Littlejohn introduced a bill to amend the state constitution to remove the residency and property requirements that applied only to blacks, seeking to establish universal manhood suffrage in the state. The legislation offered the added benefit of enlisting new Republican voters in New York City and other precincts currently controlled by the already well-established Democratic Party political machine at Tammany Hall.

Republicans in Albany scarcely subjected the matter to debate. The Republican newspaper in the capital sourly described black New Yorkers as "better qualified to vote than the mass of ignorant foreigners who have no knowledge of, or regard for, the institutions of this country," a jab at Irish-American Democrats. An amendment to the state constitution submitted within two weeks of the *Dred Scott* decision removed the residency and property requirements for African Americans seeking to register to vote. The bill passed the lower house without discussion by a vote of 75 to 27, and in the Senate, 21 to 5. Party unanimity reflected the shared desire to stick it to the Democrats: it multiplied the number of black voters by a factor of five, creating thousands of grateful new Republicans. Their silent work in the legislature also betokened their desire not to go on record as advocates of racial equality.[14]

Among those who remained off the record on expanded black suffrage was Senator William Seward. Though he had called for expanded black voting in New York as early as the 1830s, the push of Radical legislation in the New York Assembly after *Dred Scott* did not inspire any commentary on his part. Speaker Littlejohn maintained the closest of political friendships with both the senator and his friend and sponsor Thurlow Weed, publisher of the *Albany Evening Post*. Seward had little to say about slavery or race relations in the aftermath of *Dred Scott*. His only speech of the period, about Kansas, mentioned *Dred* only in passing and in the context of remarks on the larger Slave Power Conspiracy. As the godfather of New York State's nullification and suffrage drives, however, he stood to gain the respect of Radicals without saying a word. Among those won to Seward's fan club by the events of the spring was the Reverend Theodore Parker, who wrote to obtain an interview with the senator with his eye on the 1860 presidential race.[15]

Democrats were quick to denounce the self-serving nature of the Republican bid for black suffrage. Their amendment would "add ten thousand voters to the ranks of Black Republicans in the state, to assist them in their failing fortunes," complained a newspaper report. "It is to recruit a Black Regiment, which shall march through the breach in the State Constitution!" "Black Republicans" emerged as an epithet for more than just Republicans of color such as those the new amendment sought to add. The Black Republicans, according to language that swept through newspapers across the country in 1857 and 1858, were Radical race egalitarians, operating outside the boundaries of decency and law and order.

The stealth of Speaker Littlejohn's campaign in opposition to the *Dred Scott* doctrine kept much of the revolutionary content of new legislation out of view. Everyone knew about the pending state reorganization of the New York City government and police department, for example—an initiative intended to contain the rising Tammany politician Fernando Wood, the incoming mayor. Only people *in the know*, however, understood the potential for assisting fugitives by use of well-disposed police officers. The Metropolitan Police Act, passed that spring and rapidly vetted and approved by New York courts, replaced all municipal police positions with new officers appointed by a Republican-dominated board. Metropolitans coordinated their activities, when appropriate, with the work of newly created Harbor Wardens, also appointed upstate. Working together, such a force could hope to build an effective network to serve fugitives passing through the nation's busiest port.

The texture of these extremely clandestine arrangements survives in a fragment of debate for a Supply Bill amendment that made its way into Thurlow Weed's *Albany Evening Post*:

$175 to Rev. Dr. [James W. C.] Pennington, for releasing two colored seamen from prison, was proposed by Mr. CULYER. He stated that the gentleman had been employed—

Mr. SICKLES:—to run the underground railroad. [Laughter]

Mr. CULYER: Knowing the colored citizens were in prison—to procure their release. How could the money of the state be more wisely appropriated?

Mr. WADSWORTH: Was opposed to recognize the Under-ground Rail Road as a state institution.

Mr. CULYER: at some length opposed the institution of slavery, and favored the adoption of the amendment [which passed without further discussion].[16]

Pennington, himself a former fugitive from Maryland, was a chief operative of New York City's Vigilance Committee, a man with personal experience of the hardships that prevailed in the era of Democratic Party dominance. In 1854, the self-educated minister had lost his two nephews to a Fugitive Slave Act capture and commission hearing in the city, a signal of the weakness of the local operations of the Underground Railroad. The takeover of local policing allowed officers to place arriving fugitives in protective custody and to bail them out to agents such as James Pennington. Boosted by the Republican-dominated legislature, New York City could hope to become a gateway for freedom.[17]

Democrats from all parts of the country denounced the legislature's naked bid for control of the nation's biggest city, even if they failed to recognize the subversive antislavery subtext of the police reforms. "Some gentlemen have even paraded the bugbear 'Revolution' before the people," Littlejohn noted, during published remarks in May. "I love the word. Interpenetrating it, and wrapped up in it, is the word, 'Liberty.'"[18]

As if to underscore the tenor of the times, the legislature openly played host to a fugitive slave, receiving an unnamed passenger on the Underground Railroad in the vestibule of the state capitol. An "act to secure liberty to all persons within this State," passed in mid-May, affirmed that African Americans were citizens of New York regardless of the recent stipulations of the Taney court. All black people in New York would be free, and any person seeking to hold them as slaves within the borders of the state would be subject to a penalty of as much as ten years in prison at hard labor.[19]

For activists in the New York African American community such as Pennington, the legislative offensive rewarded their emerging alliance with Republicans. The first in a series of such victories had been marked just before the *Dred Scott* ruling, in a celebration of the second anniversary of the case *Elizabeth Jennings v. Third Avenue Rail.* Thanks to the work of future president Chester Arthur and his partners—and to a sympathetic hearing in a Brooklyn court—a case arising from the mistreatment of a black woman by a streetcar driver had resulted in a formal ban on segregation in New York City's streetcars. To extend compliance across the city's various lines, each a separate corporate entity, became the object of an extended civil rights campaign under the leadership of the all-black Legal Rights Association.

In February 1857 the Ladies' Auxiliary of the Legal Rights Association sponsored a "grand entertainment" to celebrate the anniversary of the *Jennings* victory, with speeches and a seated dinner starting late on Monday night and lasting into the early morning hours of Tuesday—practical timing in light of the fact that many of the active members worked nights in the food service industry. Neither Elizabeth Jennings nor her activist father took part in the official ceremonies; their contribution, however, was "justly considered as a great triumph for the colored inhabitants of the city" as well as "a strong point gained by the community toward the ultimate recognition of the full measure of their equal rights."[20]

The push to extend streetcar access required participants to put their bodies on the line, much as Elizabeth Jennings had done. Her resistance to being forcibly expelled had resulted in her dress being torn from her body during the scuffle with the streetcar driver. Afterward, Reverend Pennington suffered injuries while being removed from a car on the Sixth Avenue line. With help from Culver and Arthur, he filed suit against the company for his personal damages, and the case was still unresolved at the time of the dinner. Only months before the event, the treasurer of the Legal Rights Association, Peter S. Porter, had been beaten and thrown from a car along with five activist women. Pressing his own lawsuit, Porter argued before the Superior Court that it was a burden on the whole city when blacks "had to wait six or seven times as long as others in order to ride."

Porter was applauded when he said he was "astonished when he thought of the physical force of the colored population, that they did not rise en masse, and strike down their tyrannical oppressors." The campaign had encountered setbacks and yet made progress, he said, keeping pressure on individual lines and seeking the support of judges and elected officials.[21]

The traveling public seemed evenly disposed toward black passengers, reported Reverend Pennington, but managers of lines could not be trusted to do what was right, and in fact might "charge [integrationists] with being revolutionary" and take steps to "gain notoriety and create confusion." As a practical measure, "therefore," said Pennington, "not only the encouraging but the adverse circumstances must be kept in mind."

While some made physical sacrifices, others were encouraged to give money. Thomas Downing, chef-owner of the famous whites-only Downing Oyster House on Wall Street, reminded the audience at the Jennings dinner that too often, New York blacks allowed the wealthy few among them to shoulder the burden for all. Downing believed in the power of the courts—his son George Thomas Downing having penned the well-regarded colored man's rebuttal to the *Dred Scott* decision—and yet he saw more potential in the power of the purse. To get more judges and legislators on their side, African Americans in New York needed allies in state and local government. If they pooled their resources, he suggested, contributing even a dollar apiece, they could hope to raise a large sum, "which, if it had been sent to Albany, and put into the right hands in the Legislature . . . they would have secured them their franchise long ago." The "liberal use of money" was the fastest avenue to political success in the New York legislature, said Downing. Blacks should not forget that in Albany, "money will do anything."[22]

At least, noted Peter Porter, who spoke sometime after midnight, "since the decision of Judge Rockwell, the five cents of the colored man were as good as those of a white man."[23] Porter cut his remarks short, urging the crowd to proceed to the dinner hosted by the caterer Tunis Campbell, famous as the author of a guide to business etiquette in the food service industry and destined to play an outsized role as a Republican agent and elected official in post–Civil War Georgia. Like the featured speakers, Campbell advocated for the practical. Regarding differences of class and status, Campbell had written in a version of his famous guide, "both parties must feel their identity," and "thus a mutual good feeling can be established."[24] His accommodating attitude, widely shared by African Americans of the Civil War era, fit the circumstances of the unequal partnership between blacks and Black Republicans in the 1850s.

One measure of cooperation between black New Yorkers and the Republican Party was the low volume of black commentary on the historic policies adopted by the post–*Dred Scott* state legislature. Just as assemblymen and senators allowed their landmarks to pass without debate, African Americans refrained from public celebrations of their advances. Even on the matter of expanded suffrage—the object of a long campaign and dozens of recent petitions and speeches—leaders among the African Americans kept their thoughts within the community or in records that did not survive. One explanation for the lack of colored conventions or letters to the editor in April and May 1857 may have been the urging of strategic politicians such as Littlejohn to avoid inflaming public emotions on the subject. Another consideration, in light of the tension surrounding city government and police jurisdiction in the city that spring, was the need to avoid creating targets for white reprisals. In an illustration of the risks, gang members aligned with Tammany and Fernando Wood, including the famous Five Points–area Dead Rabbits, attacked a black dance hall and other properties in June 1857, beating patrons and burning several buildings to the ground.[25]

Frederick Douglass, for one, would not be silenced either by force or by the persuasion of Republican benefactors. The editor, orator, and black organizer held aloof from compromising Republicans, but not on the same grounds as Garrisonians, a faction he had publicly denounced when he joined forces with the Liberty Party in the 1840s. As an officer of the original antislavery party—and its 1856 vice presidential candidate—Douglass pushed Republicans to hold to a higher standard, particularly in his adopted home state. As for his assessment of the post–*Dred Scott* era, Douglass remained optimistic, even as he denounced the decision as "the judicial embodiment of wolfishness" and Taney as a "miserable scamp." Appearing in New York City in an amicable debate with the Garrisonian Charles Remond, Douglass insisted that "the Constitution must not be rendered in accordance with the acts of any set of men; but in accordance with the plain meaning of the language used in its construction." The revulsion produced by Taney's reckless opinion—stacked alongside the depredations of Democrats in Congress and the White House in the Kansas difficulties, he said—had produced what Douglass saw as a golden era for antislavery in the United States.[26]

Douglass loved the Constitution, but he also endorsed the agency of downtrodden people to rise up in pursuit of their own liberty. Commenting on the outcome of the recent elections and *Dred Scott*, he noted cheerfully a proliferation of slave rebellions in the South and held up as an example an unidentified leader who had died after receiving 750 lashes with a whip. In

August, he lectured that "if there is no struggle there is no progress" and warned "those who favor freedom and yet deprecate agitation" that they could not have "rain without thunder" or "the ocean without the awful roar." He anticipated bloodshed as a prerequisite to any major change. "If we ever get free from the oppressions and wrongs heaped upon us," said Douglass, "we must pay for their removal. We must do this by labor, by suffering, by sacrifice, and if needs be, by our lives and the lives of others."

Douglass was one of two black New Yorkers to work closely with John Brown as he transferred his operations from Kansas to the heartland of slavery. In 1857, Douglass played host to Brown's hired drillmaster, Hugh Forbes, at his home in Rochester. Early in 1858, the editor gave Brown the use of an upstairs bedroom in his home, in which the militant plotted his future attack on Virginia and drew up a constitution for a postrevolutionary state.[27] Brown also relied on the Brooklyn minister James N. Gloucester to manage New York fund-raising and recruiting for what he called his "secret service." Gloucester offered money and helped Brown solicit donations of key texts—Plutarch's *Lives* and Irving's *Life of Washington*—for the edification of poor recruits.[28] As for black New Yorkers willing to participate in Brown's emerging scheme to invade the South, however, neither Gloucester nor the Legal Rights crew chose to cast their lot with the old man.

Black activists of the 1850s regarded the likelihood of elevating their race by violence with great skepticism. Many acknowledged a similar ambivalence about white antislavery allies. Brown's army had yet to develop a critical mass of black participants, despite his association with Gloucester and Frederick Douglass. A public rupture between black leaders and white antislavery activists emerged in March. It proved particularly embarrassing for Theodore Parker and his Republican brand of racial solidarity.

In a racist era, it was hard for even the most sympathetic whites to avoid giving offense to their black counterparts. Parker's trend toward talking tough, threatening war and revolution, had introduced a line of reasoning in his speeches and letters that seemed to rebuke African Americans held in bondage for their lack of action on their own behalf. Parker's spring lecture circuit speech opened with a riff on the character of the race in which he described black Americans as "docile, pliant . . . always prone to mercy . . . easy, indolent, confiding, and so little warlike."[29] The prominent African

American attorney John S. Rock of Boston chose the occasion of the anniversary of the Boston Massacre one week after the *Dred Scott* ruling to take Parker to task for his aspersions.

Rock disputed Parker's assertion that "a stroke of the axe" was all that was needed but that black men were hesitant to act. The claim was typical, said Rock, of the way "white Americans have always taken great pains to prove we are cowards." Parker's remarks had done "a great injustice," however earnest his sympathy for the enslaved. "The white man contradicts himself who says, that if he was in our situation, he would throw off the yoke," said Rock.[30]

Dr. Rock—a medical doctor and a dentist, soon to be recognized as a groundbreaking lawyer—did not intend to taunt Parker for his physical weakness. Everyone in Massachusetts knew about the minister's failing health, the subject of a public call for prayers issued by the 28th Congregational Society that winter. Rock himself was hardly stronger, and he prefaced by noting that his own health was "too poor to allow me to indulge much in speech-making." Parker's error lay in his tendency to romanticize the militant and crusading aspects of the struggle, said Rock. African Americans—North and South—could scarcely afford to follow suit. "For a man to resist where he knows that it will destroy him, shows more fool-hardiness than courage." Black men would judge when and how best to overcome their hardships without the oversight of whites.

"Whenever the colored man is elevated, it will be by his own exertions," Rock said. Such progress would be achieved not by violence, but "by dint of perseverance and industry." In contrast to the bombast of antislavery revolutionaries, Rock outlined a pragmatic vision of racial uplift. "In this country, where money is the great sympathetic nerve which ramifies society," he argued, "a man is respected in proportion to his success in business." Black people would remain oppressed "until we have our educated and wealthy men, who can wield a power which cannot be misunderstood."

Rock's positions underscored an avant-garde tendency in black politics of the antebellum era, anticipating not only Booker T. Washington–style accommodationism but also the Black Is Beautiful movement of future ages. "I would have you know, that I not only love my race, but am pleased with my color," he said, proud of his black identity, "by feelings and by blood."

Given the results of self-improvement and expanding civil rights, he predicted, the mainstream of society would come to agree that "black will be a very pretty color."

Reverend Parker, who took the podium immediately after Rock's speech, made apologies and tried to correct himself as best he could. "I make no doubt [the black man] will fight," Parker said, adding conspiratorially, "I do not care how soon he has the opportunity." Indeed, "slavery would not be extinguished with one blow, [but would] take a great many blows, and I hope the black man will do his part." He knew stories of African American heroism from Kansas and elsewhere and from the testimony of fugitive slaves of both sexes. Parker would hasten the day when African Americans would confirm their valor, "by rising and achieving their freedom"—

> by the only method which the world thoroughly and heartily ACCEPTS, AND THAT IS, BY DRAWING THE SWORD AND CLEAVING THE OPPRESSOR FROM HIS CROWN TO HIS GROIN, UNTIL ONE HALF FALLS TO THE RIGHT, AND THE OTHER HALF FALLS TO THE LEFT. (LOUD APPLAUSE.) [capitalization in original]

Parker spoke of parchment—the kind employed in constitutional governments, and also the "parchment of the drum-head."[31]

6

JOHN BROWNISM

George L. Stearns looked the part of the most Radical Republican in America, with fervent eyes and an unusually lustrous long beard, which curled across his chest like the black locks of a woman's hair. On doctor's orders, Stearns was doing his best to comfort and protect his ailing chest with the distinctive whiskers. As a hands-on industrialist who made his fortune perfecting a type of lead pipe, he had sucked in enough toxins to permanently damage his lungs. His mind was clear, however, united with that of his wife, Mary Stearns, in passionate devotion to antislavery and other philanthropic causes.

The Stearnses had caught the Kansas Fever in the congregation of Theodore Parker. George became the number-one gun man in the Kansas program, buying Connecticut-made Sharps rifles and a smaller number of Colt pistols for settlers and paid heavies. Making deliveries, occasionally in person, and advising militant leaders in face-to-face meetings and in writing, he functioned as an unofficial war secretary for a conflict that was only beginning—recruiting, promoting, and strategizing for Free Kansas and the broader cause. Alongside these extralegal initiatives, Stearns played a major role as a Republican Party operative behind closed doors. Recruiting young men from the Kansas paramilitaries into patronage positions and elected offices, he helped to build a generation of Wild West Republicans for political and military service.

Kansas militants escalated their defiance of the outgoing Pierce administration's territorial policies in 1857, acting to liberate the Topeka Convention delegates and their wives held on treason charges in a federal prison in Tecumseh. The agent of their liberation was John Kagi, a correspondent of a District of Columbia Republican newspaper, the *National Era*, who shot a U.S. district judge in the groin and took a bullet in his own abdomen. Kagi was camping near Tecumseh in the company of John Brown and a motley group of armed desperadoes and displaced Ottawa and Pottawatomie Indians. By March the band of outlaws had succeeded in springing the Republican detainees and discouraging federal officials from persisting in their prosecution.[1]

George Stearns and the National Kansas Committee sponsored another East Coast tour of Kansas gunslingers, inviting Richard Hinton and other hard-cores to solicit for donations in a series of speaking engagements. A highlight for Hinton was the endorsement of the Republican fighting Quaker and poet John Greenleaf Whittier, who quaintly instructed the younger man that "if thee must fight for freedom, fight well and to the end." Stearns himself accompanied a shipment of armaments to Kansas, meeting Brown for the first time and persuading the old man to come to Boston for the fund-raising campaign. In what would soon be deemed a revolutionary act, the Massachusetts legislature hosted Brown, asking him to testify on Kansas matters at the statehouse.[2]

John Brown found little to his liking in Boston's high-toned abolition parlors, and he departed after only a handful of appearances. He delivered a letter of complaint to Reverend Parker, scolding Bostonians for their meager financial and personal contributions to the struggle. While Bostonians and Republicans dithered in their carpeted rooms, he objected, true patriots and Christians in his band were "hunted like wolves" and "sustained and cared for in part by Indians" in Kansas. The moral posturing of the "Plymouth Rocks, Bunker Hill Monuments, Charter Oakes, and Uncle Thom's Cabins," as he called them, filled the craggy militant with revulsion.[3]

More disappointing still was the lack of responsiveness among black leaders, in Boston and elsewhere. Coequal with the never-ending campaign to raise funds was Brown's recruitment effort. He needed fighting men, and by 1857 and 1858 his vision had already become broader than Kansas. The

Boston Vigilance Committee's Lewis Hayden was beyond the age of military service (like Brown himself), but if he would lend his prestige to John Brown's emerging scheme for confronting slavery in the South, Hayden could deliver large numbers of recruits and other resources. No one would dispute that he was a Radical; that he and his wife defended their safe house with barrels of gunpowder was common knowledge along Boston's Underground Railroad. But like his counterparts in black New York, Hayden held aloof from John Brown's efforts to recruit him and his circle.[4] He had set his sights on a government job in the Commonwealth and had no time for illegal schemes.

The hero of Osawatomie (never acknowledged as the murderer at Pottawatomie among Radical Republicans in those days) also reached out without success to the black activist and future Republican Martin Delany. Rather than take part in an invasion of the South, Delany chose to leave the country for Africa, departing to Liberia in April 1858 to initiate an organized emigration.

Brown also contacted Harriet Tubman, the renowned slave rescuer, now living among black refugees in Canada. Tubman claimed to have seen Old Brown in one of her prescient dreams, and she offered her fervent encouragement.[5] The woman known in Brown's circles as the General was fully briefed on the conspiracy and its network of safe names and way stations, but she never made her way to Brown's camp or sent an emissary. Her nonparticipation proved especially grievous to Brown in light of his early hopes. He considered her, rightly, as "one of the bravest persons on this continent."[6]

Republicans met Tubman on the same ground as Brown: Radicals among them would make common cause with any dedicated to immediate action and personal commitment. The General was a longtime protégé of William Seward, the senator and unacknowledged guiding spirit of that spring's New York legislative initiatives. Seward helped Tubman maintain a small farm near his home in Auburn, offering her work when she was not on missions and keeping an eye out for the well-being of her aged parents. Through Brown she became associated with party Radicals such as Hayden and Franklin Sanborn, and more indirectly Parker, Higginson, and Howe. Unlike Brown, Tubman would survive to see the transcendent Republicans of the Civil War and Reconstruction, and she would cast her lot with the party on a permanent but low-profile basis. It was not her fight (before the Civil War) to require the party that embraced her race to also campaign for the political rights of her gender.

Another Republican woman, Lucy Stone, had found the personal dimensions of her political advocacy to be daunting by the spring of 1858. The State of New Jersey put her worldly goods up for auction in April as a result of her refusal to pay taxes to a government that did not acknowledge her right to vote. At the same time, Stone became dangerously sick.[7] During her recovery, Stone apparently resolved to increase her dedication to the task of mothering (her infant daughter's cradle had been among the items auctioned in the public sale). For a long hiatus, the woman most often identified as a partisan Republican in the 1850s became inactive. In her absence, Republican partisans did not desert her cause.

In fact, the spring of 1858 presented the first Radical Republican woman suffrage campaign, a breakthrough suitably aligned with the militants in Kansas. Free-Staters—officially a wing of the Republican Party since the Big Spring convention of 1856—initiated the latest of the territory's string of constitutional conventions in the military town of Leavenworth near the end of March. From the outset, Radical proposals dominated the floor. Among those that did not succeed was a woman suffrage proposal. Reporting to Higginson, the Kansas activist Samuel F. Tappan observed that the movement might have succeeded if prominent women in the territory had presented a petition as expected; apparently women did not yet see political participation as a duty of their citizenship, as he did. "The men are in advance of them on the question of women voting," offered Tappan, and yet the vote "to strike out the word male stood 25 yeas to 50 nays." And more would have voted in favor, had not "the necessity of union among Free State men" outweighed the urgency of woman suffrage.[8] Even without it, Tappan thought the Leavenworth document to be "the best constitution in the country." The same group that had overridden woman suffrage had voted to remove the word "white" from voting and militia service requirements by a large majority, and also endorsed the racial integration of schools.[9]

Higginson remained dedicated to woman suffrage and other feminist campaigns in 1858 and all his life, and women reciprocated the minister's attentions. A correspondent, Maria Felt, wrote to tell him that he had been the subject of a number of her conversations after she arrived in Kansas that spring. Using her connection to Higginson to make introductions, Felt had met a number of interesting young Republicans around the territory, including Richard Hinton, James Redpath, and Samuel Tappan himself, whom Felt found "certainly less gray-headed than I had expected." They did not compare with Higginson, perhaps, flush that season with the admiration of readers of his new *Atlantic Monthly* article on fitness, "Saints, and Their Bodies." After making a number of flirtatious comments, the lady concluded the letter with lines that Higginson later saw fit to cross out.[10]

As for the cause of Free Kansas and racial equality, Higginson was all in, participating actively in the last rounds of violence between the factions. Increasingly this work aligned the East Coast sponsors and conspirators with Jim Lane, the would-be Kansas senator and paramilitary chief, instead of the more moderate Free-State "governor" Charles Robinson. At the head of the political curve, the contested territory offered an early glimpse of the split between the Radicals and others in the party—a vision complicated by the active militancy and nascent mania of Jim Lane himself, a future suicide. Nearly all were heavily invested in Kansas Territory railroad speculation, a liability that Reverend Parker noted in a letter to Charles Sumner on May 6. "The Land Fever is more contagious than the Presidential Fever," he complained, "and equally fatal to the moral powers."[11]

In fact, the weaknesses of Kansas leadership became more pressing as the era of Kansas troubles started to ebb. A key breakthrough was the establishment of a federal military outpost at Fort Scott near the scene of conflict on the borders of Missouri and the slaveholding Cherokee Nation. The arrival of an antislavery military commander, Nathaniel Lyon, on May 30, 1858, effected the transformation of Fort Scott from an adjunct of the Democratic Party to a Radical Republican stronghold. Within months of his appointment, territorial Kansas ceased to bleed—though it remained excluded from the community of states, thanks to James Buchanan and Democrats in Congress.[12]

Captain John Brown retained his war footing, staging his first direct assault on slavery. On December 20, 1858, Brown intervened to assist a Missouri slave named Jim Daniels in preventing the imminent breakup of his family by sale. "I am sure that Brown, in his mind, was just waiting for something to turn up," remembered a participant, of Jim Daniels's arrival in camp, "or, in his way of thinking, was expecting or hoping that God would provide him a basis of action."[13] Now he would test out the role of liberator in company with Radical Republicans.

Brown accompanied Daniels across the border to his master's estate, while a group led by the charismatic Aaron Stevens, also known as Captain Whipple, attacked a neighboring property. Riding backup were a Free-State militant and political activist, James Montgomery, and dozens of jayhawkers under his command, veterans of a deadly recent standoff in the vicinity of Fort Scott. The term "jayhawkers," first reported in national newspapers in January 1859, referred to armed antislavery bands such as Brown's and Montgomery's that took the offensive against Missourians and proslavery settlers in the territory. Jayhawkers went into battle that winter and never completely stopped fighting until after the end of the Civil War.[14]

Brown's raiders seized movable property as well as enslaved persons, including horses, a wagon and oxen, farm implements, and supplies for a journey. Brown saw these effects "as being owned by the slaves, having surely been bought with their labor." He gave notice to the so-called master, awakening the household before light to report the raid through a closed window shutter. "We have come after your slaves and their property," said Brown, introducing himself. "Will you surrender or fight?"

The Stevens party, taking control of "the contraband 'Jane,'" let their actions do the talking, shooting a white man to death while his children cowered at his feet.[15]

Eleven people liberated from slavery, including two women great with child, accompanied Brown to a safe house in Kansas, the Moneka home of Augustus Wattles. Wattles and his brother, John, were active in politics—formerly contributors to the Free-State *Herald of Freedom* and delegates to the Topeka Constitutional Convention. Since 1857 they had numbered themselves among the territory's Radical faction, having parted ways with Governor Charles Robinson on the rectitude of participating in elections sponsored by the proslavery government in Lecompton. Now the Wattleses rode the swell of an emerging rupture between Brown and politically engaged militants in Kansas.

Augustus Wattles offered shelter to the refugees but scolded Brown on the propriety of seizing them and inflaming the conflict along the border with Missouri. He deplored the killing and the brazen robbery. Joined by Captain Montgomery, who was equally unnerved by the escalation, Wattles convinced Brown that Kansas settlers needed peace instead of more war. The brothers helped to place the refugees in sympathetic households around Moneka (including the home of the Republican physician and future major general James G. Blount). With Montgomery, they extracted a promise from Brown that he would not use Kansas as a base for the invasion of the slave states. Brown, Montgomery, and Wattles signed an itemized list of guarantees, while the old man sketched out what he saw as parallels between his own actions and the depredations of the proslavery party.[16]

The jayhawkers also debated the best course for protecting the fugitives from being recaptured. Montgomery was on record advocating for the settlement of refugees from slavery among Free-State farmsteads in Kansas, a strategy he saw as cost-effective and morally upright. He chafed against instructions from the Radical benefactors back east that all fugitives be transported to Canada. Unlike the Boston Republicans, Frances Bird and George L. Stearns, Montgomery thought the best guarantee of safety lay with his own band of mobile and well-armed freedom fighters. "If Mr. Bird were here he would be disposed to take back what he said to me our first meeting; and agree that fugitives may be protected in Kansas," he had written to Stearns. The fervently religious Montgomery cited the Bible to justify the policy of integrating former slaves into their own communities: "Thou shalt not deliver unto his master the servant which is escaped from his master unto thee; he shall dwell among you, even within thy gates, in a good place where it liketh him best."[17]

Brown's raid was so inflammatory, however, that to accommodate the eleven in proximity to Missouri was to invite a civil war. Despite the inconvenient timing—set against the backdrop of another winter of historic cold—the conspirators resolved to move the party on to Canada at the earliest possible date. "I have considered the matter well," Brown decided. "You will have no more attacks from Missouri; I shall now leave Kansas; probably you will never see me again; I consider it my duty to draw the scene of the excitement to some other part of the country."[18]

Amid the darkness of winter, Jim Daniels's wife had her baby, and Brown delayed his party's departure to accommodate her convalescence. When it finally got moving on January 20, 1859, the rescue mission included twelve fugitives, one foot soldier, and John Brown himself. They would make their way across Kansas and the plains in a covered wagon, stopping first in Lawrence to gather support from what remained of the militant faction of the Free-State Party.

In Lawrence, Brown encountered more resistance from the Republican peace party. William A. Phillips had been a Brown protégé, a reporter for the *New York Tribune*, and an outspoken Free-Stater, who had once been dragged off to Missouri, tarred, and feathered.[19] Meeting with the old man in January, Phillips made the case for a political solution to the slavery crisis, asking Brown to lay down his weapons and vote Republican. Republicans were cowards, Brown objected: "They have compromised so long that they think the principles of right and wrong have no more any power on this earth." Brown kissed Phillips on the cheek, wiping away tears, and said goodbye. "I never saw him again," Phillips later recalled.[20]

Other Republicans aided Brown that winter without registering complaints. John B. Abbott and his wife, veterans of the Wakarusa Wars and National Kansas Committee, offered food, shelter, and clothing to Brown's refugees. Crossing out of the territory, Brown took refuge with Burns Rescue organizer Martin Stowell at his farm in Peru, Nebraska. Brown asked for donations and permitted Stowell's friends to peek inside the covered wagon and to judge for themselves if the mission was justified.[21]

While still among friends, Brown learned that the governor of Missouri was offering $3,000 for his capture and that President Buchanan had added a federal bounty of $250. He responded in kind, offering $2.50 to anyone who would lock up James Buchanan and taunting would-be captors. "It is perfectly well-known that I will not be taken alive," Brown said.[22]

Brown was not the only antislavery activist making jokes about James Buchanan in January 1859. Thaddeus Stevens of Pennsylvania—soon to be sworn in to Congress as the Radical Republican representative from Buchanan's home district—quipped that if the president were to stop advocating the Southern cause in Washington, the South could always get him back under the terms of the Fugitive Slave Act.[23]

John Brown—fearing neither courts nor men—continued his trek across the frozen Northwest with the twelve fugitives from Missouri.[24] Before dawn on March 11, 1859, his party arrived in Chicago, one of the last U.S. way stations of the Underground Railroad. They were aided in the final stages of their flight by a Radical Republican, Allan Pinkerton, already a famous detective, destined to become one of the great conservatives of the late nineteenth century.

Brown knocked on the door of Pinkerton's house on Adams Street at 4:30 a.m. in the company of Aaron Stevens and the journalist and militant John Kagi. Brown and the detective, who answered with a pistol in his hand, embraced "like brothers." Pinkerton served breakfast and set about finding local accommodations for the crew. The fugitives were secreted at Pinkerton's and in the home of a black Chicago Underground Railroad operative, H. O. Wagoner. An African American couple, John and Mary Jones, took in the white men in Brown's entourage over the objections of Mrs. Jones.

The Joneses were highly educated and opinionated about politics, but their opinions mattered little in antebellum Illinois, which was a bastion of white supremacy as well as patriarchy. John Jones would eventually align himself with the Republicans, presenting a written testament in 1865 on civil rights abuses in Illinois just as the party took control of the legislature for the first time. In 1859 the standing of a man like Jones relied entirely on the mutual respect he cultivated with civic leaders such as Pinkerton. Cooperation of this kind on the Underground Railroad and with Brown laid the foundation for the short-lived interracial Republican Party in Illinois and elsewhere in the Reconstruction North.

John Brown was dangerous company, company that would not be taken alive. "Four or five of the roughest looking men I ever saw," Mary Jones later remembered: Stevens enormous and boisterous, Kagi masked by a dreadful beard, and all of the company ragged and filthy from months living as fugitives and outlaws. Brown himself was clad in rags and boots so tattered that the Joneses purchased him a set of clothes.

John Jones resisted John Brown's effort to recruit him for his secret service (in the presence of two men other than Brown who would die at Harpers Ferry). The suit that Jones, a clothier, contributed would have to suffice as his contribution to the plan. Death was hovering, imparting every aspect of the party's passage through Chicago with an air of ceremony. "I guess John Brown was hung in these same clothes," said Mary Jones.[25]

Back at Pinkerton's, a second baby was born, bringing the total number of fugitives to thirteen. The detective, meanwhile, set out to raise money to facilitate the final passage of the company by rail. He directed his appeal to the Republican Party—though later, after Pinkerton's disappointments as a military spy and his alignment with General George B. McClellan, a Democrat, he would falsely identify his coconspirators as Democrats. Republicans were meeting that week to discuss a recent verdict in *Ableman v. [Sherman] Booth*, the Wisconsin slave rescue case that had inflamed states' rights tensions across the North. Calling themselves the Chicago Judiciary Convention, a body of lawyers and Republicans were preparing formal resolutions on behalf of defendant Sherman Booth when Alan Pinkerton interrupted their work with his urgent business. Pinkerton could count on a number of respectable men in the room to assist in his cause.

> Gentlemen, I have one thing to do and I intend to do it in a hurry. John Brown is in this city at the present time with a number of men, women and children. I require aid, and substantial aid I must have. I am ready and willing to leave this meeting if I get this money; if not, I have to say this. I will bring John Brown to this meeting and if any United States Marshal dare lay a hand on him he must take the consequence. I am determined to do this or have the money.[26]

No one in Chicago wanted to be in the same room with John Brown. Pinkerton raised $600 and gained the assistance of the superintendent of the Michigan Central Railway, who secured a boxcar and provisions for the journey to Detroit. Pinkerton accompanied Brown to the railroad station as he traveled ahead of his party to arrange for the ferry to Canada. "Friends," said Brown, "lay in your tobacco, sugar, and cotton, because I intend to raise the prices."[27]

After delivering the fugitives to safety, John Brown stopped in Cleveland, looking for money and recruits among participants in a recent slave rescue in Oberlin, Ohio. He plotted with a future African American Republican,

George DeBaptiste, who recommended setting off simultaneous explosions in fifteen Southern churches on a designated Sunday—a proposal that Brown rejected as immoral. He saw his family briefly and visited his benefactor Gerrit Smith in New York State, who gave him $400. He endured a number of fruitless interviews with his good friend Frederick Douglass, who could not be persuaded of the wisdom of escalation. Through it all, he labored under the symptoms of malaria, saved his money, and issued orders to his scattered cadres.

Brown dogged the Republicans and "Plymouth Rocks" of Massachusetts one last time. On May 8 he appeared in the Town Hall in Concord, speaking about Kansas but alluding to a wider war. "Our best people listen to his words," wrote Bronson Alcott, "Emerson, Thoreau, Judge [Ebenezer] Hoar [of the state senate and Massachusetts Supreme Court], my wife." Though the penniless Alcotts could not, many Concord residents opened up their wallets for Brown's campaign—"without asking particulars," as Alcott put it. "The Captain leaves us much in the dark concerning his destination and designs for the coming months." The effect was conspiratorial and thrilling. He was "the manliest man I ever saw," said Alcott, using the same phrase his famous daughter had employed to describe Henry Thoreau.[28]

From Concord, Brown made a quick commute into the heart of Republican Radicalism. Boston was a Democratic town with an especially influential Radical fringe, many of whom had been drawn into the Brown conspiracy by May 1859. Among his closest collaborators—later called the Secret Six—no fewer than four lived in the metropolitan area, and all of those were also active in party politics. George L. Stearns, Franklin Sanborn, and Thomas Wentworth Higginson learned the specifics of what became the Harpers Ferry plot in a series of meetings in Brown's room at the United States Hotel and in the medical office of Burns rescuer Dr. Samuel Gridley Howe. Reverend Parker—one of the Six—had recently left Boston for the Caribbean in a doomed effort to restore his health.

Many important details of the Harpers Ferry raid remained undecided in the spring of 1859: the training site and staging area; weapons caches, including Brown's order for a thousand iron pikes (to be used as weapons by rebelling slaves) and its past-due bill (to be paid by George L. Stearns); the estimated number of likely fighters; and of course the timing of the attack.

The choice of Harpers Ferry as a target was not open to debate, however much Frederick Douglass and other insiders believed that it would be a strategic mistake.

Above all, Brown called on his Massachusetts allies to raise money. Brown needed money for weapons, rent, mounts, and equipment for his raiders. He needed money to pay salaries, having narrowly escaped the hazards of not paying when Hugh Forbes, the disgruntled drillmaster, had revealed details of his plan to Senator Henry Wilson and others the previous year.[29] He needed money to sustain his own wife and his nine surviving children, some of whom had also volunteered their lives to the fight. These demands were a pittance, Brown maintained, when juxtaposed against the magnitude of property in slaves, which accounted for more wealth than all of the bank assets, stock shares, railroads, and manufacturing capacity and inventory in the country combined, and which had insinuated itself into every institution of the Northern economy.[30] Northern capitalists must be willing to gamble from their own stacks if they were sincere about their intentions to eradicate the national scourge. And yet everywhere Brown saw them reveling in fine clothing and eating the best foods in the most comfortable rooms.

Even the most dedicated of the Massachusetts Radicals existed in a state of opulence entirely unknown in the personal experience of John Brown and his large family. Brown had tried and failed to make his way as an entrepreneur and a farmer, and since he had dedicated himself in entirety to the antislavery cause years before he had subsisted meanly and only by constant solicitation. His experience stood in marked contrast to that of his chief backers George Luther and Mary Preston Stearns. Since his religious epiphany of 1854, George Luther Stearns had proven to be the most dedicated and most resourceful of the Boston reformers. Stearns and his equally militant wife had each raised tens of thousands of dollars for Free Kansas and John Brown—the husband through his network of pipe fitters and abolitionists, and Mary Stearns in company with women reformers of the Boston metropolitan area.

The Stearnses personally contributed a thousand dollars in the spring of 1859 and would have given more had Mr. Stearns agreed to Mary's proposition that they sell their home and give their all for Brown's "sublime purpose."[31] Instead they kept their stately Medford mansion, Evergreens, and dedicated their tremendous energies to organizing and fund-raising.

During his stay in Boston in the final year of his life, John Brown made arrangements to honor George Stearns for his efforts in a way that would educate men of Stearns's social milieu. To do so, the old revolutionary invited his friend to meet him at the Parker House hotel at a weekly gathering of Boston's rich and powerful Republican club.

Parker House was a marvel of modern refinement, newly relocated to a splendid marble edifice erected in 1855 and richly appointed. Its chefs had already pioneered some classic American recipes, including the signature Parker House rolls, Boston cream pie, and lemon meringue pie. Parker House was the place to be, as Stearns later explained to a committee of Congress: "If a literary club wish to dine, they go to the Parker House; if a political club wish to dine, they go to the Parker House."[32] Brown declined to seat himself at its opulent tables, "excusing himself by saying that he must eat sparingly and fare hard, as became a soldier."[33] He had come to tap the pocketbooks of Boston's political elite and to leverage his local popularity to elevate the standing of his ally Stearns in their midst. It was the May 28, 1859, meeting of the so-called Bird Club, the Republican gathering named for its host, the Walpole paper factory magnate Frank W. Bird.

Brown had arrived in the company of Dr. Howe, a regular participant in Bird Club functions since the early 1850s. Before Stearns arrived, the old man tangled with United States senator Henry Wilson, another regular. Introduced to Wilson, Brown immediately began to complain about Wilson's public denunciations of Brown after the disclosure of his plans by the unfaithful lieutenant Hugh Forbes. "Senator Wilson," he said stiffly, "I understand you do not approve my course." The senator was unapologetic, reproving Brown for his plotting and specifically criticizing the recent slave raid in Missouri. "I am opposed to all violations of law, and to violence," said Wilson, insisting that such actions "lay a burden on the anti-slavery cause." As Wilson remembered it later, Brown scolded him for his compromising attitude. "He responded with some positiveness and no little emphasis: 'I do not agree with you, sir.'"[34]

Stearns arrived at the Bird Club late in the afternoon, after the dishes had been cleared and the men had settled in to smoke ("Oh, if I could have the money that is *smoked away* during a single day in Boston," Brown had said in 1857, "I could strike a blow which would make slavery totter from its foundations!").[35] Brown greeted him warmly, allowed twenty minutes or so for the typically shy manufacturer to make acquaintances, then departed very publicly in company with Stearns and Howe. The conspirators retired to Brown's room for a final meeting, after which the captain reached into his boot and presented Stearns with a pearl-handled Bowie knife that he had seized from a Missouri opponent.

"I am going on a dangerous errand and may never see you again," said Brown; "I wish you to keep this bowie as a token of my respect."[36]

George Stearns and others in the Harpers Ferry conspiracy had nurtured a civil war before the Civil War, starting in Kansas and moving headlong toward the captain's final destination. To the extent that Republican donors such as Bronson Alcott or Ralph Waldo Emerson, party organizers such as Stearns, whose career behind the scenes was still in its beginning stages, and partisan organizations such as the Chicago Judiciary Convention played a role, the plot was partially a Republican Party initiative. So long as the conspiracy remained a secret, Radicals could enjoy the thrill of participation without paying a political price.

7

HOUSE DIVIDED

Allan Pinkerton's Illinois was scorched earth in the winter of 1858–59, the site of the epic political confrontation between Stephen A. Douglas and Abraham Lincoln. John Brown had not passed through Springfield or solicited from Lincoln in his final campaign. Had Lincoln met him, he would not have liked either the Harpers Ferry conspiracy or John Brown himself, a man without a sense of humor. Setting aside his personal distaste, moreover, Lincoln would have judged Brown's mission as a danger to the Republican Party—a cause that the future president had adopted with the same sense of mission that was motivating Brown.

Moreover, Lincoln's Republicanism was just the kind that sickened Brown most. While moralizing on the subject of expansion, Lincoln prayed before the flawed godhead of the U.S. Constitution, recognized property in slaves, and freely floated racist epithets and stereotypes in private and in public remarks. Indeed, the party as Lincoln represented it offered little to nothing to people of color apart from a long-term strategy for surrounding slave states and harassing the institution of slavery to extinction. It was not a party of civil rights for African Americans or voting rights for African American men. Its rapid transformation in the war years and afterward would have astounded the audiences of the Lincoln-Douglas debates of 1858. Like Lincoln, who grew as a humanitarian during the war, the Republican Party became less racist and temporarily antiracist amid the national crisis.[1]

Like most things that Abraham Lincoln did, his bid to unseat Stephen Douglas had a funny side. It was funny that the tall country lawyer had made a habit of following the diminutive senator when Douglas made appearances or speeches in Illinois. The two looked funny standing next to each other or shaking hands, and when Lincoln had a chance to speak—whenever he could find an audience—he inevitably had funny things to say about Douglas and the Democrats. But the subject was in deadly earnest, and the taller man became grave when speaking of the existential threat posed to the nation by the opposition party.

Illinois Republicans recognized Lincoln's insurgent candidacy for the Senate by making him the official nominee to challenge Douglas on June 16, 1858. Lincoln accepted—and immediately made statements that ensured the defeat of Illinois Republicanism by aligning his candidacy with Radicals in a conservative state.

The controversy arose from Lincoln's use of the metaphor of the house divided to explain the tension over slavery within the political system. "A house divided against itself cannot stand," he had pronounced, predicting that "this government cannot endure, permanently half slave and half free." For all its earthiness, the comparison struck many as militant. After all, in predicting that the house "would cease to be divided," Lincoln anticipated a final reckoning and dedicated himself to the "ultimate extinction" of the slave system. Furthermore, he bet heavily on the success of antislavery in the coming crisis. "The result is not doubtful," Lincoln projected. "Wise counsels may accelerate, or mistakes delay it, but sooner or later, the victory is sure to come."[2]

Lincoln described Douglas as a tool of the Slave Power Conspiracy—the Stephen who, along with "Roger, Franklin, and James" (Taney, Pierce, and Buchanan), was reconstructing national institutions. He predicted this cabal would succeed in making slavery "alike lawful in all the states" by means of a decision in pending jurisprudence. "We shall lie down pleasantly dreaming that the people of Missouri are on the verge of making their State free," said Lincoln, "and we shall awake to the reality, instead that the Supreme Court has made Illinois a slave State." What force might contrive to counter such momentum, Lincoln did not say.

Lincoln had circulated an advance copy of the speech to a number of

Republican friends—all of whom deplored it. Indeed, its tone was revolutionary, a point that became a mainstay of Douglas's campaign. The most famous of his antebellum statements, House Divided nonetheless stood out for Radicalism against a backdrop of caution and attention to the vox populi in Lincoln's career. He may have acted in a bid for national and Radical Republican consideration.[3] If so, his speech may be judged a resounding success.

Among those riveted by Lincoln's participation in the famous debates of that summer, few were more intrigued than party boss Theodore Parker. Parker relished "the noble speeches" in which he heard Lincoln appeal to the morality of slavery. He urged Lincoln's friend William Herndon to help Lincoln remember that Douglas was "more dangerous than the wolf."[4] When Lincoln seemed to waffle on antislavery principles, Parker was unforgiving. Douglas had asked "the most radical questions," cutting right "to the heart of the question, before the people," Parker complained, in a letter to Herndon, but Lincoln "did not meet the issue" and "dodged them." "That is not the way to fight the battle of freedom," he told Herndon, predicting that William Seward of New York, coordinator of the Littlejohn Revolution in the Empire State, would lead the party in 1860.[5]

Parker also entered into deep discussions with Ohio governor Salmon P. Chase. Chase and Parker had bad blood between them in the aftermath of the Margaret Garner rendition, but the governor moved to improve their relationship. Chase paid a Sunday morning call at the 28th Congregational Society, though he did not succeed in pressing the flesh with Parker amid the after-service crush. Chase recognized in Lincoln a threat to his own standing as a leading man of the West. Lincoln as a speaker and letter writer paid due diligence to the ideas that Chase had developed in his decades of antislavery legal argument, and yet he tended not to credit his rival by name. The Illinoisan also laid claim to the antislavery credentials that Chase hoped to command as an 1860 Republican contender for the presidency. By inventing the House Divided metaphor, Lincoln had brilliantly encapsulated the premises dearest to the far left of the Republican Party.

With his unworldly capacity for cogent speech, Lincoln, a part-timer in politics, sketched out a vision of the Slave Power Conspiracy, as he called it, that incorporated worst-case scenarios for *Dred Scott, The People of New*

York v. Lemmon, a slave transit case, the Fugitive Slave Act, and Kansas. His forward motion left Salmon Chase, Seward, and other Radicals of national reputation in the rear.

Radicalism had momentum as the 1858 elections came into view. Ohio and Vermont passed *Dred Scott* nullification resolutions in the early fall, and Vermont's legislature claimed the right to interpose its authority between citizens and the operations of the federal Fugitive Slave Act. "Resolved," the motion read, "that whenever the government or the judiciary of the United States refuses or neglects to protect the citizens of each State in their lives or liberty . . . it becomes the duty of the sovereign and independent States of this Union to protect their own citizens at whatever cost."[6]

Most important, the party rocked the midterm elections that November, sending to Congress a number of notorious names. Just past the fourth anniversary of its establishment, the Republican Party captured a narrow majority of seats in the House of Representatives and gained six seats in the United States Senate. Among the Radicals winning for the first time were James N. Ashley of Ohio (future steward of the Thirteenth Amendment), Owen Lovejoy of Illinois (brother of a martyred abolitionist), and Thaddeus Stevens of Pennsylvania (a wisecracking lawyer said to be secretly married to his black housekeeper). Radicals achieved an outsized influence in the party by virtue of the broad consensus that Democrats had become the party of extremists, which pushed Republican moderates into closer collaboration with their own party's more extreme wing.[7]

Stephen Douglas was reelected to the Senate in a Pyrrhic victory over Abraham Lincoln, having deepened the connections between Democrats and white supremacy. Ironically, Douglas's statements during the debate in Freeport also put him on record as open to the possibility of admitting new Free States in the West, permanently damaging his standing with the fire-eating Southern wing of the Democratic Party. Controversy arising from what became known as the "Freeport Doctrine" foretold the temporary breakup of the Democrats that began with the 1860 elections.

Did black leaders rejoice at the rally of antislavery Northerners? That was harder in the aftermath of the New York State enfranchisement debacle. In September, a state employee confessed to having missed a necessary deadline for publishing the proposed black suffrage amendment ahead of

Election Day and thereby doomed the Littlejohn racial democracy initiative as ineligible for balloting in 1858. Black New York men would not have another chance so favorable until 1869 and in fact would not achieve greater access until the passage of the Fifteenth Amendment. Most remained ineligible as the 1860 contest loomed.

"When had the Republicans ever done anything for the black man?" complained a delegate to the State Convention of Colored People in Cincinnati. Only voters could participate as partisans, however much the experience of radical enclaves in Oberlin and Boston suggested the contrary. The speaker, P. H. Clark, "had about made up his mind never to petition for a right again," he announced, "but if he could seize it, he would do so."[8]

Despite the objection, the Cincinnati convention could only celebrate the surging fortunes of America's antislavery party and the spirit of opposition to the national Slave Power. "We rejoice at the declension of the Democratic party at the North, and hope that its defeat presages the downfall of slavery, of which accursed system it has been a firm supporter." They would leave no means of advance untested, "believing that by united and concentrated action on our part, we can do much toward securing the immediate and unconditional abolition of American slavery, and the removal of the legal and social liabilities under which we suffer in the State of Ohio and in the United States."[9]

Unbeknownst to participants, Ohio stood poised to be the next theater of confrontation between antislavery and the oppressive power of the federal state.

The victim's name was John Price, and he had thought that he had made his home among friends in the village of Oberlin after his escape from slavery in 1856. Oberlin was an experimental community established in 1832 around the liberal-minded college that shared its name. Led by feminists and antislavery activists, the college accepted women and blacks and charged no tuition, and its students and professors frequently assisted in the activities of the Underground Railroad, which made use of the town's proximity to Lake Erie escape routes.

On that day in September 1858, however, Price did not get any kind of acknowledgment from the pedestrians he identified as students when he called to them that he was a fugitive slave and had been taken captive. The students kept their heads down as they passed the wagon that carried Price, a U.S. marshal, and a pair of bounty hunters toward the train station in a nearby town. Only after the wagon moved out of sight did the young men sprint toward campus to organize a rescue party.[10]

Rescuers quickly staged a raid on nearby Wellington, where the marshal and his posse aimed to catch the evening train: students, professors, and townspeople representing all classes and both races. All were men: even at Oberlin, alma mater of Lucy Stone and other gender pioneers, women thought it best not to participate in a fight. A fortnight earlier, Professor Henry Peck, a philosopher and Congregationalist minister, had hosted Governor Chase and Michigan governor John Bingham at an event to honor Oberlin's women graduates.[11] Now Peck, known to be a Sharps rifle man and Free Kansas stalwart, made sure to get his own gun into the hands of someone who would use it if necessary to free John Price.[12]

Peck was head of the coop for antislavery students, Republican townspeople, and Underground Railroad participants in Oberlin, black as well as white. The professor and his fellow liberators had worked the Ohio angles for the support of Brown, Lane, and other Kansas freedom fighters. They loved guns as much as any of the eastern Radicals and were known to appear with Republican candidates that year bristling with hardware, a display Peck called the Filibuster Platform.[13] In dozens of smaller operations, participants had defied the Fugitive Slave Law and brandished weaponry in defense of refugees without attracting unfavorable attention.

Slave rescuing was work for respectable men in Oberlin, and in Oberlin, of all places in America, the bar for respectability did not recognize the color line. The African American owner of a grocery store, John Watson, was the first to arrive at the Wellington boardinghouse where Price was held; he worked to direct the crowd of more than five hundred surrounding the building. John A. Copeland, a black Oberlin student who would later die at Harpers Ferry in Virginia, scaled a balcony to hold a marshal at gunpoint while the crowd looked on. Another black man, Charles Langston, initiated negotiations with one of the captors, a white citizen of Oberlin whom Langston knew well. "I did say to Mr. Lowe what I honestly believed to be the truth," Langston later remembered, "that the crowd were very much excited . . . bent upon a rescue at all hazards; and that he, being an old acquaintance and friend of mine, I was anxious to extricate him from the dangerous position he occupied, and therefore advised that he urge [the U.S. marshal] to give the boy up."[14]

Only in Oberlin could a black man negotiate with a slave catcher from a position of strength and call him friend. In this community—as in perhaps no other—Langston could speak earnestly as a neighbor without regard to race. Indeed, Langston's brother—the only African American elected official in America, a Republican and town clerk, John Mercer Langston—lived on the same six-block street as Professor Peck and two other prominent participants in the Oberlin-Wellington fugitive rescue, one white and one black.[15] In the end it was a gentlemen's agreement, without Boston-style bloodshed, that resolved the crisis and restored John Price to his freedom (en route to Canada). Oberlin was for Radicals, and the Slave Power would approach the town and its citizens of color at its own peril.

The satisfaction of the Oberlin rescuers ended in January 1859, when two men brandishing guns arrested a teacher who had participated, William Lincoln, in his rural Ohio classroom. Told that the teacher was a bad man, a crying girl objected: "There is more goodness in his little finger than in your whole carcase." Lincoln was an Oberlin/Wellington rescuer, a violator of the Fugitive Slave Act, and his captors were deputies to U.S. Marshal Matthew Johnson assisting in a new federal indictment.

The teacher tried to reassure his students: "Come next Monday to school," he said; "I should be back by that time." Dragged in handcuffs from the classroom to a Cleveland jail, Lincoln learned that one of the deputies had been present in Wellington during the rescue of John Price and held a grudge. "You d—d fanatical fool," said the man, "do you think the N[orth] and the S[outh] are such fools as to cut each other over the d—d [Negro]?" William Lincoln responded with pious conviction: "God wd. smite N. & S. unless the slaves were freed."[16]

Miles away in Oberlin, the schoolteacher's Republican friends had been provoking their enemies, and Lincoln's fate served as a kind of comeuppance. Two days before his arrest, on January 11, 1859, his coconspirators in the Wellington case had celebrated their own release from jail with an interracial festival they nicknamed Felon's Feast. Ralph Plumb, an indicted Oberlin lawyer and member of the Ohio legislature, presiding, had offered only defiance in the face of the state's prosecution: "Call it treason if you like and the courts may punish me if they will," he declared. "They may drag me to prison, and from prison to death, yea, let me die a felon's death, but let me die a man."[17] John Mercer Langston, the fiercely partisan brother of the indicted Charles Langston, agreed that "we must make sacrifices—go to prison, or, if necessary, go out onto the battle-field to meet the Slave Oligarchy."[18]

The Rescuers had plotted legal strategy at their cheeky feast and also read aloud a letter from John Brown, Jr., who advocated a more concrete response. Sometime after the event, the younger Brown called on John Langston in person to recruit him to the secret service. "My father is John Brown of Osawatomie, who proposes to strike at an early day a blow which shall shake and destroy American slavery itself," said the man, who had introduced himself to Langston using a pseudonym. "For this purpose we need, and I seek to secure, men of nerve and courage."[19] Despite Langston's respectable credentials as an elected official and Republican, the Browns recognized the black man as a kindred spirit. Like other prominent African Americans, however, Langston refused to join in John Brown's illegal scheme.

Just as the Oberlin-Wellington prosecution hit the docket in Ohio, the Supreme Court in Washington issued a new verdict in *Ableman v. Booth*— denying to state courts the writ of habeas corpus in cases arising under the Fugitive Act. The ruling had direct bearing on the new case, *U.S. v. Simeon Bushnell et al.*, which got under way in April 1858 with the prosecution of Bushnell, an Oberlin printer who had driven the buggy that carried John Price to freedom after the rescue. In company with the other thirty-six indicted men, Bushnell traveled to Cleveland, appearing on his own recognizance. The federal prosecutor—condemning what he called "Oberlin Higher Law"—presented a straightforward application of the terms of the Fugitive Slave Act. A federal judge also approved the relocation of the trial to Cleveland, remote from the radical precincts surrounding Oberlin College, hoping to avoid the upheavals surrounding the abortive trials in the Booth and Anthony Burns rescue cases.

The defense tried to cast doubt on the technical merits of the case, summoning one of the African American defendants, Orindatus Simon Bolivar Wall, to challenge a description of the fugitive. Wall's highly differentiated account of the varieties and names for African American skin tones prompted laughter in the courtroom but failed to persuade the jury, said to be comprised entirely of Democrats. While on the subject of technicalities, Wall pointed out that the indictment misspelled his own highly idiosyncratic first name, an error that ultimately resulted in the dismissal of all charges against him.[20] Bushnell was not so lucky. It took the jury only minutes to convict him of the federal offense.

The judge called for the immediate consideration of the case of Charles Langston. Lawyers for the accused objected that Langston could not have a fair trial before the same jury that had just rapidly convicted Bushnell. In the ensuing controversy, all thirty-seven Oberlin-Wellington defendants (including both Wall and Bushnell) were remanded to police custody.

Before entering the Cleveland jail en masse on Sunday, April 17, the thirty-seven Rescuers posed for a photograph (in which O.S.B. Wall, destined to be a late–Civil War army captain, appeared conspicuously in a stovepipe hat). A crowd of four hundred listened to a sermon by Professor Peck delivered from the jailhouse door. Observing from a corner of the prison yard was John Brown, back from Canada and again on the hunt for people "of nerve and courage" to participate in his ongoing campaign.[21] To gain the assistance of the Oberlin-Wellington men, however, the righteous outlaw would have to wait out their extended incarceration by federal authorities.

Put on trial before a new jury the following week, Charles Langston presented an indictment of the Fugitive Slave Act. The law created an atmosphere of terror among free African Americans like himself as well as fugitives, he testified. As an example, Langston cited the case of one of his own former students, a free girl born to free parents in Columbus who was languishing in prison on the false accusation that she was a fugitive slave. "Langston claimed that by the very nature of the case he could not have, and had not had, a fair trial," reported *The New York Times.* The judge and jury— indeed, all white people—were prejudiced against all African Americans. "Langston said that this prejudice was owing to the fact that his race submitted to being held in bondage," he said. He himself would not submit—"*and if that is a crime, [I am] guilty, and for such guilt [I am] willing to submit, if needs be, to the extreme penalty of the law.*"[22] Charles's brother John Mercer Langston also demonstrated the kind of spunk that Radicals appreciated in his own courtroom remarks, declaring that "he hated the Fugitive Slave Law as he did the Democratic Party, with a deep, unalterable hatred."[23]

Despite the remonstrations of a crowd of six thousand that rallied in Cleveland, an Ohio court struck down the Rescuers' appeal for habeas corpus. Antislavery Ohio looked to Governor Salmon Chase, who disappointed his allies again by making an appeal for supporting the rule of law. The state's Republican congressional delegation offered a more satisfying response. Calling it an "hour of trial," Senator Benjamin Wade insisted that the time had come to take the "sword in hand" to reclaim the defendants from prison. Wade quoted with approval from a letter by Joshua Giddings, whom Republican moderates had just replaced as the 16th District's representative in Congress. In his letter, Giddings had publicly wished the Rescuers had *executed the slave-catchers promptly [which] would have taught the [Buchanan] Administration a lesson not soon forgotten.*"[24]

The officeholders' remarks conveyed the general tone of the state Republican convention, which opened on June 2 in Cleveland. The position of the Ohio Republicans on the Fugitive Slave Act was the only issue under consideration and served as the litmus test for all candidates for the gubernatorial nomination. Salmon Chase, with his eyes on the Senate and the presidency, did not stand for office as his term as governor expired. The delegates nominated William Dennison, Jr., a railroad entrepreneur and antislavery activist, who promised to do everything in his power as governor to thwart the enforcement of the Fugitive Slave Act.

Putting words into policy, the Ashtabula County prosecutor pressed charges against the federal marshal and his deputies in direct defiance of the *Prigg v. Pennsylvania* and *Ableman* legal doctrines. In the end, they struck a deal with federal officials to suspend the charges in the thirty-four Oberlin cases not yet tried. Nullification prevailed, as the prisoners obtained a transfer into the custody of the state.

Shortly after July 4, 1859, the State of Ohio dismissed all charges against the Oberlin-Wellington defendants, who returned home to a tremendous picnic celebration. Giddings made a congratulatory speech, and the crowd also heard from Ralph Plumb, Professor Peck, and John Mercer Langston, speaking on behalf of his absent brother. The theme was gratitude—for the kindness of the jailers, for the wisdom of the judicial officers, and especially for the sacrifices of the Rescuers and their families. John Mercer Langston said it best: "He thanked them in his character as a negro—as a white man—as one in whom the blood of both races joined—as a *man*—and as an American citizen," noted *The Liberator*. Its reporter futuristically wished "that the whole world could have seen him standing there, pouring forth in clarion notes his noble, man-like, and Godlike thoughts."[25]

Civil disobedience and judicial obstruction in Ohio tipped the balance toward Radical politics in the national Republican Party and yet also exposed the weaknesses of Chase, one of the most important Radical contenders for the 1860 presidential nomination. Moving quickly to seize the advantage was Abraham Lincoln, who cautioned, in an echo of Chase's own caution in the Oberlin case, that Republicans would do well to avoid public celebration and commentary of any kind on extralegal antislavery resistance.

Lincoln had not retired from politics after his defeat by Stephen Douglas, but rather had remade his image by painstaking means, looking to undo the damage of the House Divided metaphor debacle. He had gone so far to establish credentials as a moderate during the 1858 debates that he left himself open to charges of racism, uttering disparagements that would never be forgotten. In 1859 he urged the same centrist course for every Republican. In a series of letters to the leaders of statehouse protests, Lincoln denounced personal liberty bill initiatives and *Dred Scott* and Fugitive Act interposition statements such as those passed by New York, Ohio, Wisconsin, and Massachusetts. He complained of grandstanding, such as that by the Supreme Court of Wisconsin, still smarting over *Ableman v. Booth*, which pronounced the Fugitive Slave Act void within the state.[26]

Lincoln had his eyes on winning elections—not the scattered contests of 1859 but the presidential contest of 1860. He endeavored to pass on the hard-won wisdom of his own House Divided misstep: that radical declarations might damage the antislavery cause. "My main object in such conversation[s]," he wrote to Schuyler Colfax, a rising Republican star, "would be to hedge against divisions in the Republican ranks generally, and particularly for the contest of 1860." Candidates and state organizations must learn to "look beyond their noses," Lincoln wrote.[27] The point was not to determine what was right—for example, the constitutionality of the Fugitive Slave Law—but to acquire the political power to change things.[28]

At the same time he counseled against overtly radical politics, Lincoln rejected current overtures to build alliances among Republicans and moderate or Southern voters. "If the rotten democracy shall be beaten in 1860," he wrote to a former Whig, "it has to be done by the North; no human intervention can deprive them of the South."[29] When he took to the hustings for Republican candidates in September and October 1859, Lincoln emphasized the moral purity of the Republican movement regardless of the necessity of compromise.

Rather than tactical engagements, Lincoln advocated a broader, philosophical kind of Radicalism. To an Ohio audience bristling with resentment over the Oberlin case, Lincoln adapted an 1857 speech on black equality, in which he had movingly identified with an allegorical black woman, changing only the pronouns. "In the right to eat the bread . . . which his own hand earns," said Lincoln, in the more conventional 1859 address, *"he is my equal and the equal of Judge Douglas and the equal of every living man."*

He reviewed the fiery predictions of his own House Divided speech and William Seward's autumn 1858 statement that "an irrepressible conflict" divided North from South, and he positioned himself as the Radicals' candidate: "I do not believe that Gov. Seward uttered that sentiment because I had done so before, but because he reflected upon this subject and saw the truth of it."[30] Invoking Seward, Lincoln moved against another rival on the Left.

The Republican Party would not shrink from the irrepressible conflict. "Its underlying principle is hatred to the institution of slavery; hatred to it in all its aspects, moral, social, and political," Lincoln said in Beloit, Wisconsin. He described the party's fundamental purpose as conservative, in that it aimed to preserve the compromises that had permitted the establishment of the Union in spite of slavery. But this inheritance was only a part of the revolutionary vision of a government established on the principle that all people were equal, he explained. "The orator went on to prove the identity of Republican principles with those of the Fathers of the Republic," wrote an observer in Janesville, Wisconsin. In Lincoln's reasoning, it was the Democratic Party that expressed heretical views: "Mr. Lincoln said that he had failed to find a man who five years ago had expressed it his belief that the declaration of independence [*sic*] did not embrace the colored man."[31]

Republicans would hate slavery as their forebears had, Lincoln told Wisconsinites, citing for the first time Stephen Douglas's assertion that "Our fathers, when they formed this government under which we live, understood [the slavery] question just as well, and even better, than we do now," a phrase that Lincoln would later make the centerpiece of his famous Cooper Union speech. Republicans would act—as Washington, Jefferson, and Madison had acted, by Lincoln's reading of the texts—to put the practice on the road to natural extinction.

Returning to Springfield by mid-October, the western politician addressed his friends on "the recent glorious victories achieved by the Republicans in Ohio and other States as clearly indicative that the good old doctrines of the fathers of the Republic would yet again prevail, and become the rule of action of the Government."

Lincoln's arguments pealed with humor and with truth, a participant reported in the papers, "which again and again brought down the crowd."[32]

8

HARPERS FERRY

Republicans surged in the scattered elections of the autumn of 1859, claiming huge majorities in the New England states that Lincoln had visited, securing William Dennison, Jr., as governor of Ohio, and making a clean sweep of every office in Iowa.

Radicals experienced somewhat less success than their moderate counterparts. The divide among Kansas Republicans remained intense, the result in part of the refusal of the Democrat-controlled U.S. Senate to admit Kansas as a state, which denied credibility to any of the officials recognized by the competing state constitutions. In territorial Nebraska, the veteran activist Martin Stowell found himself shut out of party politics when antislavery candidates seized control of Republican organizations. While protesting that he "heartily endorse[d] most of the principles of the Republican party" and considered it "the party in the States [that] is the nearest right," Stowell watched his third-party bid for a position in the territorial legislature come up bust.[1]

Like Stowell, other Republicans endeavored to outflank the emerging moderate line by activism outside the party line. The philosopher Ralph Waldo Emerson, Republican, was one of many notable Northerners collecting money for the ongoing John Brown conspiracy, no questions asked. On October 11, 1859, Emerson accepted $5 for the John Brown fund from Henry Thoreau. In fact the money was not from the cheerfully poor writer and thinker, but from his mother and sister, who earned money by operating a boardinghouse in the family home and who had contributed steadily from their slim accounts to the John Brown movement.

Forward-looking men within the party would have recognized the Thoreau women as respected fellow travelers. Writing home from Europe that October, for example, the Reverend Theodore Parker asked a friend to "remember me to the virtuous Republicans—both genders of them." The Radicals were making revolution, after all, and God himself was no "respecter of persons"—a fragment of King James biblical multiculturalism that validated innovative nineteenth-century ideas.[2] Like so much that Parker wrote, the phrase was soon to gain prominence when it was invoked in association with the martyrdom of John Brown.

John Brown launched his invasion of the South on October 16, attacking the federal arsenal at Harpers Ferry, Virginia. The men in his company were mostly antipolitical, like Brown himself. Only John Kagi, who wrote for Republican newspapers, and Francis Merriam, a young white associate of Lewis Hayden in Boston, might be said to have any ties to the party establishment. In a fundamental way, the raid endeavored to transcend the limits of the political system in favor of the Higher Law. The possibility of success hinged upon what Brown believed to be the general will of the enslaved population to overthrow the system that enslaved them. Alerted to the arrival of champions from out of state, Brown imagined, the enslaved would seize the iron pikes he had provided and retreat into the mountains to begin a sustained antislavery insurgency.

But bondsmen in Virginia did not assert their right of revolution, despite Brown's efforts. The power of the state rapidly overwhelmed John Brown and his raiders, killing ten, including John Copeland and Shields Green of Oberlin, Aaron Stevens of Kansas and the 1858 slave liberation, and two of Brown's sons. Militia led by the future Confederate general Robert E. Lee injured or captured nearly everyone else who remained alive.

The Radical Republicans bore responsibility for Harpers Ferry insofar as the partisans Stearns, Higginson, Sanborn, Parker, and Howe had participated in the planning, and a broader spectrum of Republicans such as Emerson, Bronson Alcott, and others had funded and encouraged it. They did not need to shed blood themselves to show their colors as revolutionists.

Radicals would also take part—voluntarily and against their will—in the explosive aftermath of Brown's attack.

The names of Republicans figured prominently in a number of schemes to rescue John Brown from the jailhouse in Charles Town, Virginia. The aged Emerson hosted a meeting in his home in which citizens of Concord discussed the possibility of staging a jailbreak. Reverend Higginson plotted with militants including the Republican and future army captain J. W. Le-Barnes to storm the prison with hand grenades and "Orsini bombs" such as those used in 1858 in an attempt on the life of Napoleon III. Allan Pinkerton dispatched undercover agents from Chicago to report to the detective on the likelihood of a successful rescue. Samuel C. Pomeroy, the future U.S. senator from Kansas, traveled to Charles Town intent on capture and gained admission to John Brown's cell. Only old Dr. Howe seemed content to surrender the captain to the state. The best way to help Brown's movement, Howe told LeBarnes and other plotters, was to let him be a martyr to his cause.[3]

Brown was grateful for the support. "In prison ye came unto me," he said to Pomeroy, quoting from the New Testament. But he quickly made known that he agreed with Howe. "I am worth now infinitely more to die than to live," he told Pomeroy.[4] Brown had made a promise to his jailer, whom the old man had enlisted in his final campaign for Northern support. John Brown's body was wounded, expendable, but the truth of his message could not be stopped.

Relieved of the responsibility to rescue Brown, the Radicals did what they could to protect the Harpers Ferry coconspirators amid a surge of alarm and calls for reprisals. The first and most vulnerable of Brown's friends to be targeted was Frederick Douglass—still not a Republican—who was saved by an obscure Philadelphia telegraph clerk, who held up the delivery of a U.S. attorney's orders for his arrest on October 17.[5] The former fugitive was on the lam again, taking steps to secure incriminating documents before catching the ferry to Canada and on to England. Douglass's only crime was friendship: he had loved and supported John Brown, but he had refused to participate in the old man's militant scheme. In the era of the *Dred Scott* decision, however, Douglass rightly feared that he could not get a fair hearing in a court of law, a forum in which individuals of his race had recently been deemed to have no standing.

Even hardened conspirators with recognized civil rights feared to con-
front the burgeoning federal and Virginia dragnet. Parker was already
abroad and did not take a stand on whether he would have surrendered to
investigators or evaded arrest, but others in the Secret Six sought sanctuary
in the tense weeks after Harpers Ferry. The most outspoken was young Frank
Sanborn, who had played perhaps the biggest role in connecting Brown to
his network of East Coast supporters. Sanborn anticipated "treason trials,
bloody threats, and some bloodshed." With his letters "in the hands of Buchanan" and his name in all the papers, the schoolteacher and Republican
feared that his illicit acts "would ruin my worldly prospects for years to
come."[6] By his own account, Sanborn had channeled $4,000 to Brown in the
buildup to Harpers Ferry—"at least thirty-eight hundred dollars [of which
was] given with a clear knowledge of the use to which it would be put."[7]

After consulting with future Massachusetts governor John Andrew and
with the Garrisonian orator Wendell Phillips, Sanborn burned his John
Brown letters and made haste for Canada in late October. Stearns and Howe
did likewise; only Higginson elected to flout federal authority and remain
visible. Higginson continued to plot with LeBarnes and other militants,
inquiring into the cost of renting steamboats and transporting a cannon
in the vicinity of western Virginia, and dispatching a Republican lawyer,
George Hoyt, to the prison house in Charles Town as a kind of decoy. Scorn-
ing the caution of his erstwhile colleagues, the minister signed his letters
with his full name and a postscript: "T. W. Higginson. There is no need of
burning this."[8]

Many Radical Republicans found the record of their own incendiary
language inconvenient amid the uproar about Northern conspiracy. Southerners and Democrats were quick to revisit statements such as that of Joshua
Giddings, who had claimed to look forward to the outbreak of servile insurrection, or of the presidential front-runner William H. Seward about irrepressible conflict. Conservative newspapers seized on John Brown's cache of
letters to incriminate Radicals who had kept their distance from the Harpers Ferry plot.

Others mocked the sensationalism of Democratic claims. "Dear Brown,"
wrote a purported Henry Wilson in a published satire, "I will be on hand
with Governor Banks and the Massachusetts militia."

Dear Sir: I will be at Harper's [*sic*] Ferry with 20,000 Republicans in time to carry our plan. Senator Wade will shoot the president, and Grow will blow up the Capitol. It's all right.—Mum's the word.—Yours, J. R. G[iddings][9]

For Seward (said to offer up a company of Zouaves, militiamen attired brightly in the style of French fighters in North Africa), the John Brown raid was no laughing matter. The invasion "has thrown us, who were in a splendid position, into a defensive position," complained Senator Wilson on behalf of Republican office-seekers. "If we are defeated next year we shall owe it to that foolish and insane movement of Brown's."[10] Salmon Chase's commentary encapsulated the main points of the Republican denial: "how rash," he wrote on October 29, "how mad, how criminal."[11] Even the antipoliticals described it as *The Liberator* did: "misguided, wild, apparently insane."[12]

Brown's enemies could hardly say enough about the man and his dreadful work, but his friends dared scarcely speak his name. When Henry Thoreau delivered letters to his neighbors inviting them to hear his thoughts about John Brown on October 30 in the Town Hall, Concord's Republican Committee was quick to counsel that the time was not ripe for discussing such a controversial topic.

"I did not send to you for advice," Thoreau replied, "but to announce that I am to speak."[13] In fact, Thoreau's address, entitled "A Plea for Captain John Brown," was a summons to Republicans—even though the Concord selectmen refused to ring the bell to assemble the townspeople for the speech, leaving it to Henry to climb the steps and pull the rope himself. Those who came would hear the thinker and outdoorsman denounce them for their cowardice and lack of vision. Thoreau was bothered by what he heard Republicans saying about John Brown—Republican officeholders, editors, and voters. They had more in common with John Brown than any of them dared to admit, he said. For example, "I should say that he was an old-fashioned man in respect for the Constitution, and his faith in the permanence of this Union," Thoreau declared. Like Republicans, Brown deemed slavery "wholly opposed to these" and committed himself to its extinction. Did not most of them "think much as the present speaker does about Brown and his enterprise"? Were not the friends of John Brown "an important and growing party"?

"The Republican party does not perceive how many his failure will make to vote more correctly than they would have them," said Thoreau, in a reference to Radicalism. "What though [Brown] did not belong to your clique!" Thoreau would not join them either, though he would admit to finding the Democrats and their accounts of Brown "not human enough to affect me at all." Brown was magnanimous—"Would you [Republicans] not like to claim kinship with him in that"?

"You do not know your testament when you see it," said Thoreau. To illustrate the blindness of pretended authorities, the speaker cited passages from Brown's courtroom statement of his beliefs. "I want you to understand that I respect the rights of the poorest and the weakest colored people, oppressed by the slave power, just as much as I do those of the most wealthy and powerful," Brown had said. Republicans and their disgruntled fellow travelers should admit that all people were created equal, and that governments were constituted to defend their rights. "I wish to say furthermore," Brown had said, "that you had better, all you people at the South, prepare yourselves for a settlement of that question, that must come up for settlement sooner than you are prepared for it." Republicans (and disgruntled fellow travelers such as Brown and Thoreau) would terminate the threat that slavery posed to righteousness and the survival of the American Republic. They would make war—were already making war—and they would win.

Brown had shown them the way. Thoreau perceived that the old man's captivity "advertises me that there is such a fact as death." Brown would die for his cause, while Thoreau himself was left merely "here to plead his cause with you": "I plead not for his life, but for his character,—his immortal life; and so it becomes your cause wholly, and is not his in the least." Thoreau and his countrymen must dedicate their lives to the pursuit of what was right just as John Brown and his militants had done—even at the pain of death. "These men, in teaching us how to die, have at the same time taught us how to live."[14]

On the day after Thoreau's speech, a handful of stalwarts (at least one of whom had been present in the Town Hall the previous night) signed their names to a newspaper solicitation for the relief of Brown's family: T. W.

Higginson, Samuel Gridley Howe, and Ralph Waldo Emerson.[15] On November 2, Higginson undertook a journey to remote North Elba, New York, to comfort the family and to bring John Brown's wife to Boston. Emerson, speaking on the theme of courage in Boston on November 8, echoed Thoreau's call to service and complaint. "See what white lips they have!" the philosopher complained of his fellow Republicans. "Why do we not say, in reference to the evil of the times, that we are Abolitionists of the most absolute abolition?" Emerson thrilled his audience by calling Brown a saint and anticipating that his death "would make the gallows as glorious as a cross."[16]

Thoreau had the opportunity to repeat his John Brown address a few days later when he filled in for the exiled Frederick Douglass in the Parker Fraternity lecture series sponsored by the radical minister's admirers in Boston. It was an atypical marker of success for him, as he had often found audiences indifferent to his uniquely strident style of presentation and writing. He could thank his Republican friends for the endorsement—strongly recommended by Emerson, and approved by the associates of the absent party manager and Radical Republican theorist Theodore Parker. The Republican state assemblyman Charles W. Slack introduced the speaker, who proceeded to reiterate his fierce denunciation of the party and of politics in general.

Among a handful of small revisions to his original "Plea," Thoreau included a statement that paraphrased a well-known Republican motto as a call for John Brown heroism: "There is hardly a house but is divided against itself," said Thoreau, "for our foe is the want of vitality in man, whence are begotten fear, sloth, superstition, persecution, slavery of all kinds."[17]

Massachusetts Radicals took note. In mid-November, John A. Andrew—the abolitionist attorney and Bird Club favorite—presided over a meeting to raise money for the families of John Brown and his men. His speech opened with a stark assessment of the stakes:

> There is an irrepressible conflict (great applause) between Freedom and Slavery, as old and as immortal as the irrepressible conflict between right and wrong. [John Brown and his companions at Harpers Ferry] are among the martyrs of that conflict.

Andrew was soliciting donations and offering items for sale to raise money for the families of Harpers Ferry men: a poster-sized reprint of Brown's speech in the Virginia courtroom; a signature; and a carte de visite photograph prepared by Thaddeus Hyatt of New York. Andrew introduced Emerson, who took the podium "leaning on the arm" of Assemblyman Slack. Emerson said,

> [Brown] believes in two articles—two instruments, shall I say—the Golden Rule and the Declaration of Independence; and he used this expression in conversation here [in Massachusetts], "Better that a whole generation of men, women, and children should pass away by a violent death, than that one word of either should be violated in this country."

"There is a Unionist," shouted Emerson to a roar of applause, "there is a strict constructionist for you!"[18]

Expressions of solidarity with the Harpers Ferry raiders proved irresistible to the radical fringe but perilous for elected officials. At a meeting in Natick, Massachusetts, organized by the extremist but not yet Republican Henry C. Wright, Senator Henry Wilson took a risk merely by being in the audience. When the crowd affirmed a resolution by voice—"That it is the right and duty of the slaves to resist their masters, and the right and duty of the people of the North to incite them to resistance, and to aid them in it"—and the senator did not indicate his disapproval, Wilson seemed to be endorsing aiding slave rebellions.

Wright thought so, and he wrote with satisfaction to John Brown in prison that Wilson and "a United States Postmaster" had offered a tacit endorsement. Wright told Brown that though Virginia and the national government would "kill your body," they would not succeed in terminating his mission: "John Brown, the MAN, the defender of liberty, the assailant of slavery, and the friend of the slave, will live and be with us, to inspire us, to incite us, to spur us up and lead us on to a still closer and more resolute and deadly assault upon slaveholding."[19]

Wilson, interrogated in Congress on his participation, could only offer lamely that he had attended the Natick Resolution assembly out of curiosity.

The facts suggested otherwise. After Harpers Ferry, Wilson and the other Republicans would begin their Saturday Bird Club dinners at the Parker House by raising their glasses to Frank Bird's new standard toast: "To the next slave rebellion!"[20]

Theodore Parker—aroused from his diminution by the Harpers Ferry excitement—wrote from Europe in the same spirit. "If you were attacked by a wolf," he insisted in a letter to the abolitionist Francis Jackson, "I should not only have a *right* to aid you in getting rid of that enemy, but it would be my DUTY to help you in proportion to my power." Slave rebellions "will continue as long as Slavery lasts, and will increase, both in frequency and in power." White heroes such as Brown would find allies in the black population, as "the negroes will take their defence into their own hands, especially if they can find white men to lead them." As for Brown, he would be dead before Jackson received Parker's letter, he predicted, but his mission would endure forever:

> Virginia may hang John Brown and all that family, but she cannot hang the HUMAN RACE; and until that is done, noble men will rejoice in the motto of that once magnanimous State—"*Sic semper Tyrannis!*" "Let such be the end of every oppressor."

Republicans would be found in the vanguard, he maintained:

> So, first, the wise and just men of the party will sympathize with such as seek to liberate the slaves ... next, they will declare their opinions in public; and finally, the whole body of the party will ... before long control the Federal Government, and will exercise its Constitutional Rights, and perform its Constitutional Duty, and "guarantee a Republican form of Government to every State in the Union."

There will be blood, said Parker, a veritable Red Sea, and it would begin with Brown's. "Let the American State hang his body, and the American Church damn his soul; still, the blessing of such as are ready to perish will fall on him, and the universal justice of the Infinitely Perfect God will take him welcome home."[21]

The most outspoken of the "wise and just men of the party" met in Concord on December 2 to mark the death by hanging of John Brown in Charles Town: Waldo Emerson, Bronson Alcott, Franklin Sanborn, and George L. Stearns. Mary Stearns carried a letter that John Brown wrote her in the final days of his life, in which he expressed his wish that he be "spared from having . . . any hypocritical prayers made over me when I am *publicly murdered*." Instead, Brown insisted in his letter, he wanted to be accompanied to the gallows in the company of a population he had only lately seen in person for the first time: the *"poor little dirty, ragged bareheaded & bare-footed Slave Boys and Girls"* of the benighted South, "led by some old *grayheaded Slave Mother*."[22]

Concord partisans had planned to ring the town bells for one hour in commemoration of the execution, but they had backed down in consideration of a threat by anti-Brown citizens to rebuke such a display with violence and with the hanging of an effigy of Brown. Instead their service was sedate and featured a reading of poetry by Henry Thoreau. Thoreau offered his own translation of a Greek text from Tacitus as an example of the way that "almost any noble verse may be read, either as his elegy or eulogy":

> Whatever of Agricola we have loved, whatever we have admired, remains, and will remain, in the minds of men and the records of history, through the eternity of ages. For oblivion will overtake many of the ancients, as if they were inglorious and ignoble: Agricola, described and transmitted to posterity, will survive.

Louisa May Alcott, in the audience, contemplated the idea—soon to be encapsulated in a poem—that there was "No eulogy like [Brown's] own words."[23]

Republicans and their friends may have venerated Brown, but the old man had never returned the compliment. The Harpers Ferry hearings in Congress delivered a posthumous rebuke from Brown in January 1860 with the testimony of William F. N. Arny, a dyed-in-the-wool political partisan with a long history of association with the militant leader in Kansas. "As to the Republicans," said Arny, "Brown thought they were of no account, for they were opposed to carrying the war into Africa," using one of Brown's favorite phrases, an adaptation of a fragment from the classics. Arny insisted that Brown had repeatedly expressed "dislike" of the party, claiming it had refused to assist him. He had dismissed both Republicans and Garrisonian abolitionists as "cravens."[24]

Republicans in Congress faced ongoing scrutiny nonetheless. The Harpers Ferry investigation doomed the prospects for rehabilitating the career of Joshua Giddings, whose correspondence with Brown turned up in the Harpers Ferry document cache. Henry Wilson of Massachusetts issued so many denials about his approval of the Natick Resolution that he finally provoked a public denunciation from Henry C. Wright, who published a letter to Wilson in February that indicted both the senator and the Republican Party as a whole as closet militants. Wright's letter to Wilson—titled "What Is Well Known to Hon. Henry Wilson and the Republican Party"—unfolded as a series of accusations satirizing Wilson's claim that "Wright knew" that he did not approve of the call for slave rebellions at Natick.

"You know," said Wright, setting the theme of his critique, and mimicking the language of the *Dred Scott* decision, that slaveholders

"have no right that any man, black or white, enslaved or free, is bound to respect."

"You know" that, in this "irrepressible conflict" between the enslaved and their enslavers, it is the sacred duty of the people and States of the North to side with slaves . . .

Henry Wilson! "You know" . . . that, in the death-struggle between the enslaved and their enslavers, which must come, sooner or later (and the SOONER THE BETTER), you will be struggling with the former and against the latter. In that conflict, you will embody liberty, and your slogan will be—DEATH TO SLAVERY! . . .

"You know" that it is the duty of the people and States of the North to invade slaveholding states to free the slaves, and to annihilate the power that enslaves them . . .

I do you no wrong, but simple justice, when I say, that you do approve of invasion, of *armed* invasion of the slaveholding States . . .[25]

Wright referred to *The Impending Crisis*—an inflammatory antislavery book written by a native of North Carolina, Hinton R. Helper—invoking a second scandal that was polarizing Congress in the winter of 1860. Democrats in the House had promised to deny the office of Speaker to Republicans who had signed their names to a recommendation for a reprint of the book, saying that such displays of support were akin to John Brownism. In fact, the main thrust of Helper's threat was not revolutionary but electoral. He had won the support of Republicans because his book predicted the rise of the antislavery party in the politics of the South.

Meanwhile, the Republican most deeply implicated in the John Brown plot took the stand to testify on Capitol Hill. Despite his obvious culpability, the manufacturer and philanthropist George L. Stearns did not face charges in Virginia or elsewhere. He appeared in Washington unincarcerated and (as usual) traveling on his own dime. His testimony stuck close to the facts—weapons caches, coconspirators, and his lack of detailed knowledge of Brown's plans. Stearns did not denounce slaveholding or indicate his intentions to upset the institution by collaboration with a second hero, and his strategy of full disclosure tended to disarm his questioners. Years later, Emerson would say of Stearns's testimony that the transcript stood as "a chapter well worth reading, as a shining example of the manner in which a truth-speaker baffles all statecraft, and extorts at last a reluctant homage from the bitterest adversaries."[26] In fact it made for dull reading, and it passed virtually unreported in the press.

The Mason Committee of Congress—charged with investigating the Harpers Ferry raid—had been firing blanks all season in its efforts to identify and punish the unindicted coconspirators of John Brown. In March they moved against the handful of witnesses who had so far refused their summons to testify, drawing up warrants for the arrest of Thaddeus Hyatt and Franklin B. Sanborn. Hyatt, the New York glass tile industrialist and Free Kansas activist, did his best to stall the committee with letters and legal maneuvers. When confronted with his arrest warrant on March 3, Hyatt accompanied the deputy sergeant-at-arms at his own expense to Washington but refused to answer questions. The committee responded by seizing Hyatt and incarcerating him in a D.C. jail.

Educated by Hyatt's example—and fearful that he would be charged and hanged in Virginia if he appeared at the capital—Frank Sanborn kept vigilant against the possibility of his own arrest. When a deputy sergeant-at-arms of the Senate came to Concord on April 4, accompanied by four U.S. marshals and bearing an arrest warrant signed by Vice President John C. Breckinridge, Sanborn and his neighbors were (barely) ready to resist.

Sanborn answered the door in his pajamas, without boots, shortly after nine o'clock that evening. Seeing strangers, he called for his sister to get help. Sarah Sanborn managed to shoot past the men at the front door and run to a neighbor's house, shouting. She ran back to find her brother (tall and strong at six feet four) using his arms and feet to prevent being shoved into a carriage. Sarah whipped the horses, creating enough confusion to allow the first of the arriving neighbors, Ann Whiting, to climb into the other side of the carriage. Whiting was still dressed. She braced her hips and spread her hoopskirts against Sanborn's body, straining to keep him out of the carriage. While one of the captors tried to talk the lady out of the carriage, threatening to rip her clothes, the elderly Colonel Whiting, Ann's father, began beating the horses with his cane. Sarah Sanborn grappled with the men holding her brother, while Frank, his wrists in handcuffs, swung wildly, making contact.

The town bells rang, more citizens arrived on the scene, and Radical Republicans came to the rescue. Accompanied by Waldo Emerson, Judge Rockwood Hoar of the Massachusetts Supreme Court produced a document written in haste, a writ of habeas corpus. After a brief standoff during which the citizens of Concord formed a human wall around the carriage, the deputy and his marshals withdrew. Frank spent the night with a friend, while Henry Thoreau agreed to sleep beside the door to keep the Sanborn house safe from further disturbances.[27]

The Concord intervention had merely delayed the danger to Sanborn, who had to face the deputy and his marshals the following day in Judge Hoar's courtroom for the habeas corpus hearing. Pending the outcome of the case, the U.S. officials hoped to carry Sanborn back to Washington for questioning before the Mason Committee.

The teacher's friends had prepared a contingency plan spearheaded by Charles Thayer and William Eldridge, partners in a fledgling publishing house with ties to the Republican establishment. For weeks, the publishers had been stockpiling weapons in their printshop and recruiting participants in a clandestine group that called itself the Black Strings, named for an identifying badge worn under the clothes. A small squad of Black Strings attended the hearing with instructions to seize Sanborn and hustle him out of the courtroom at the appropriate moment. In their company were Thayer, Eldridge, the radical lawyer J. W. LeBarnes, and both of Thayer and Eldridge's current authors, the Kansas veteran James Redpath, commissioned to write a campaign biography of William Seward, and the poet Walt Whitman, who was publishing an edition of *Leaves of Grass* with Thayer and Eldridge that year, working in their shop on the design and type.

Sanborn later remembered taking note of Whitman, wearing a workman's apron and scanning the room suspiciously. The poet tensed when a deputy sergeant-at-arms brandished a Mason Committee summons for Redpath as well, Sanborn remembered. The showdown between federal and state authority ended peacefully, however, when Judge Hoar and the others ruled in Sanborn's favor on a technicality, citing the fact that the warrant named the sergeant-at-arms and not his deputy, who had no authority to detain either Sanborn or Redpath. Hoar said that Sanborn, a teacher, would also face charges of assault stemming from his violent resistance to arrest, a protective charge that would require his presence in the Concord police jurisdiction for many weeks.

The Black Strings would remain on the alert, resolving, as Thayer wrote to Higginson, "that none but *fighters* are eligible," and that all were "willing to shoot or be shot at at five minutes notice in the case of the United States versus Sanborn or Redpath or any other man who represents a principle of right."[28] Sanborn returned home to Concord to the firing of cannons and a round of tart speeches. He told the crowd assembled in the Town Hall that the deputy and marshals "ought to have been killed," and he resolved to kill or be killed before he would surrender to federal authority.[29]

The "Spirit of 1775" pervaded the whole town, and Bronson Alcott said that "he considered April 4 as the [Lexington and Concord anniversary April] 19th in the new calendar."[30] Ladies of Boston sent a bouquet of flowers to Sarah Sanborn, and a local group presented her with an "elegant revolver." The skirt wielder Ann Whiting had to make do with Louisa May Alcott's judgment that she had "immortalized herself" by her display of courage in the Sanborn fight. Louisa regretted that she had not been present, but she signed on to the Vigilance Committee in order to "have [her] share of future combats."[31]

They were under attack but fighting back. Accused of being revolutionaries at the outset of the presidential election calendar, Republicans looked to their candidates for an answer to Democratic and abolitionist charges. "Irrepressible Conflict" Seward managed to remove himself from the scene of controversy by touring abroad; Chase, out of office, turned down speaking engagements and did his best to keep his name out of the papers. And Abraham Lincoln, who had worked behind the scenes to tamp down the nullification and civil disobedience wing of the party in advance of Harpers Ferry, was emphasizing party unity above all, with all eyes directed to the Democrats and their own subversive tendencies and ideological fissures. All through the autumn he had been working with audiences and with texts to develop a comprehensive statement of Republican beliefs. On February 27, 1860, Lincoln presented the fruits of his researches to a New York City audience in the Great Hall of the new Cooper Union, an experimental free educational institution committed to uplifting students without regard to color, gender, or class.

Here was a radical setting, with a strong showing of local and regional Republican Radicals in attendance, including Theodore Tilton, an editor and protégé of Henry Ward Beecher who had recently distinguished himself as being more of an extremist than the famous antislavery preacher. The Harpers Ferry raid and executions had galvanized the young man, an unsuccessful candidate for the state assembly in 1859. Tilton had traveled to Philadelphia to participate in the delivery of John Brown's body from the South to its final resting place in North Elba, New York. Having covertly brought the body into Brooklyn, Tilton was the first man in the city to view the open casket. He found that the face was blackened, and that the noose and tattered clothing still hung around the neck. "I shall never forget the face of the sleeper," he later remembered, "for he did not seem dead."[32]

Emboldened, Tilton had brought one of Brown's Sharps rifles to a church meeting in January, advocating the withdrawal of missionaries from Indian tribes that practiced slavery.[33] Early in February, he had brought to the attention of the Plymouth Church (where he was superintendent of the Sunday school) the plight of nine-year-old Pinky, a slave, whom senior Plymouth minister Henry Ward Beecher then arranged to manumit with the proceeds of a church donation.[34] Tilton occupied the platform on the night of Lincoln's speech, one of the few dignitaries who looked the part of a member of the hosting organization, the Young Men's Central Republican Union.[35]

Tilton and the other New York Radicals may have strained their ears listening to Lincoln and still not caught a whisper of the far-left agenda. Lincoln offered nothing in the Cooper Union speech to Republicans who would nullify the Fugitive Slave Act and *Dred Scott*, abolish slavery in the District of Columbia, or filibuster in the South. The only Radical dimension of the address was its central theme, that the Constitution did not sanctify property in slaves and that the document and its framers were in aggregate opposed to slavery and committed to putting the practice on the road to extinction.[36] In its dialectics and complexity, Lincoln's argument disdained the particulars of Radicalism in favor of a more sweeping vision of the role of Republicans in the crisis of the state.

Democrats and Southerners had accused Republicans of insurrectionism. "We deny it," said Lincoln. "John Brown was no Republican," and his actions had been "peculiar" and "absurd." But an irrepressible momentum had motivated Brown's actions and Republican politics alike:

> How much would it avail you, if you could, by the use of John Brown, Helper's book, and the like, break up the Republican organization? Human action can be modified to some extent, but human nature cannot. There is a judgment and a feeling against slavery in this country that cast a million and a half of votes [in 1856]. You cannot destroy that judgment and feeling by breaking up the political organization that rallies around it ... but if you could, how much would you gain by forcing the sentiment which created it out of the peaceful channel of the ballot-box into some other channel?

What would that other channel probably be? Would the number of John
Browns be lessened or enlarged by the operation?[37]

Brown and the Republicans, Lincoln implied, were brothers under the skin.
And yet the Southern firebrands and secessionists were the more genuine
outlaws. Republicans—conservatives in Lincoln's logic—were the true heirs
of the American Revolution. Lincoln cited anguished antislavery statements
and acts on the part of the founding generation, returning again and again
to Stephen Douglas's less precise claim that the framers of the Constitution
"understood this question just as well, and even better, than we do now."
Republicans were revolutionaries—not as part of an antislavery war of races
such as John Brown and Henry Wright envisioned, but in keeping with the
patriotic Spirit of 1776.

To uphold that trust, Lincoln argued, Republicans must cast aside the
spirit of compromise that had enabled the Constitution but had also permitted the cancer of slavery to grow. The party must be wary of "contrivances
such as groping for some middle ground between the right and the wrong."
The proslavery advocates had grown more and more insistent as the decades
passed and had finally arrived at policies "beseeching true Union men to yield
to Disunionists, reversing the divine rule, and calling, not the sinners, but the
righteous to repentance." They would not be satisfied by any gesture less than
to "cease to call slavery wrong, and join them in calling it right." Republicans
should refuse the Southerners' "invocations to [George] Washington, imploring men to unsay what Washington said and undo what Washington did."

Lincoln's speech managed to outflank party Radicals, bypassing their
ad hoc confrontations with the Slave Power to present a more fundamental
challenge. Its breadth and antithetical construction served mostly to obscure the speaker's real-world intentions, in an early manifestation of the
artful indirection Lincoln used to shape public opinion during the war. Tilton and his like may have understood him as conservative, but Lincoln's
version of conservatism reverberated with a threat. The call to arms was
made explicit in the closing sentence, which Lincoln transcribed for poster-
ity in capital letters: "LET US HAVE FAITH THAT RIGHT MAKES MIGHT, AND
IN THAT FAITH, LET US DARE TO DO OUR DUTY AS WE UNDERSTAND IT."[38]

Among 30 million Americans in 1860, only John Brown and his band at Harpers Ferry and a scattering of Kansas jayhawkers had dared to do their duty at the utmost hazard. The Old Captain had advertised that there was such a thing as a noble death. Lincoln, too, would hazard his life on the theory that right makes might, bringing a generation in his wake.

9

WIDE AWAKE

As Lincoln understood it, the duty of Republicans was to win elections, and therefore he departed from New York immediately after the Cooper Union address to campaign for the party ticket in New Hampshire and Connecticut, where the first 1860 elections were scheduled.

The excitement generated by his speech preceded Lincoln and complicated his speechmaking by requiring something fresh for audiences already informed about his new ideas. Some of what he added sharpened the Radical thrust of his arguments. In Exeter, New Hampshire, for example, he returned to the theme of the House Divided with its stark prognostication of looming conflict. Speaking in Hartford, Lincoln invoked the Declaration of Independence. He not only dared to say directly that he thought "negroes were created equal," but he also dared any Democrats in the audience (and by implication, all Republicans) to say that they were not. He endorsed Hinton Helper's idea that the Republican Party would become established in the South—without, of course, invoking the book or the author by name. He predicted that in spite of the violent suppression of dissent by the slave oligarchy, Republicans "would get votes in [that] section this very year." Lincoln talked about the Irrepressible Conflict, making sure to remind his listeners that his rival William Seward had said it, but acknowledging that also "Jefferson said it; Washington said it [and] before Seward said it, the same statement was made by [Roger] Pryor of Virginia," an outspoken Southern congressman.[1]

New England audiences thronged and cheered. They had listened intently in Dover, New Hampshire, one eyewitness reported, and they would have kept on listening and cheering if Lincoln "had spoken all night." In Hartford, Lincoln's visit heightened the excitement generated by an epic gubernatorial election. The "Wide Awakes"—an organization established one week before Lincoln's speech to salute a speech by the Kentucky abolitionist and Republican Cassius Marcellus Clay—provided an escort for the speaker in military style.[2]

Republican Wide Awake Clubs sprang into existence all over Connecticut in March, and by the end of the month, opposition newspapers were reporting the particulars of their demonstrations. Wide Awakes marched in military formation; they wore black oilcloth slouch caps and capes; they carried medieval-style staves and lanterns that could be detached from long poles also used as clubs; their most striking banners featured a single open eye, and they also carried slogans on banners and lighted transparencies. They were conspicuously ready to fight, and to Democrats and Southerners they seemed like "evidence of the caliber of the army that was said some time since to have in contemplation the rescuing of Old John Brown from the Virginia authorities." Indeed, the name of Brown was invoked repeatedly in the New England contests, and not always with derision as Lincoln employed it. Indeed, a Connecticut speaker called Brown "a good man and true friend of his race" at a Wide Awake rally, saying he was "one of the best specimens of a hero that the world had looked upon this century."[3]

The Republican counteroffensive prompted a renewed volley from the opposition, this time making use of legal instruments to curb the Radicals. The State of Virginia sued the State of New York through an appeal of the New York court's antislavery verdict in the case *Lemmon v. the People of New York*. The sovereignty of states was at issue in the case, which was argued by the young lawyer Chester Arthur and his senior partner, William Evarts. Could Southerners bring the enslaved in transit through New York City and other Free State locations? The state of New York had thought not. Evarts bolstered the brief with a flurry of appearances in city and Republican forums, and he solicited petitions from well-placed "friends of the court." In the end the *Lemmon* verdict stood fast in New York and was certified for the consideration of the Supreme Court of the United States.[4] Advantage: Radicals.

Federal officials in Wisconsin moved unexpectedly to rearrest the antislavery editor Sherman Booth, the beneficiary of the clemency of Wisconsin courts, who had been indicted on federal charges but at large since 1855. On March 1, 1860, a federal judge issued a warrant for Booth's arrest, citing Justice Taney's opinion in *Ableman v. Booth* that denied Wisconsin habeas corpus in the process. A U.S. marshal seized Booth and detained him in the U.S. Customs House in Milwaukee. Dismayed by the allegation that Booth had attempted to rape a fourteen-year-old babysitter the previous month, Wisconsin Republicans hesitated this time to speak out in Booth's defense.[5] Advantage: Opposition.

Some fought against Congress, and others fought within its hallowed walls. On April 5, Representative Owen Lovejoy took the floor to deliver a bitter antislavery diatribe. After weeks of wrangling over the appointment of a Speaker, Republicans were raw and ready to test the strength of their slim majority. Lovejoy opened with a comparison of slaveholding to Mormon polygamy, called the practice the "sum of all villainy," and called Democratic Party philosophy the "doctrine of devils," venturing into the Democratic side of the House with his fists clenched. Pryor of Virginia sprang to his feet, confronting Lovejoy so menacingly that some nearby Republicans came to his defense. Before order was restored, the Republican John F. Potter of Wisconsin had treated Pryor to a number of sturdy punches.

Lovejoy went on to praise Helper and John Brown; "I would I have no more hesitation in helping a fugitive slave than I have in snatching a lamb from the jaws of a wolf," he said.

> It is simply a question whether it will pay to go down into the den where the wolf is. [Laughter.] If you would only go into your lair, and crunch the bones and tear the flesh of your victims, we might let you alone; but you will not. You claim the right to go with this flesh in your teeth all over our Territories. We deny it.

Lovejoy invoked the legacy of his brother Elijah Lovejoy, the abolitionist martyr murdered by a mob back in 1837. He continued to speak, despite constant interruptions, insults, and threats, about "the lesson which the slave States ought to have learned, from John Brown and from all these events." The congressman's conclusion was abrupt, as indicated in a transcript:

> MR. MARTIN, OF VIRGINIA: And if you come among us we will do with you as we did with John Brown—hang you up as high as Haman. I say that as a Virginian.
> MR. LOVEJOY: I have no doubt of it.
> [Here the hammer fell.][6]

The closing of the Lovejoy speech was no end to the controversy it produced. Within days of the melee, Pryor of Virginia challenged Potter of Wisconsin to a duel, to which the Northerner replied with unanticipated alacrity. Potter announced that he would meet his colleague with Bowie knives at four feet, inside or out of doors. Pryor declined, calling the use of knives "barbarous."

Praise for "Bowie Knife" Potter swept the North.[7]

The owner of John Brown's own Bowie knife—George L. Stearns—took the fight back to Kansas late in April 1860, taking Frank Bird with him but leaving behind a regretful Dr. Howe, who was too sick to travel. Their mission was not Free Kansas, an objective that was already attained despite the ongoing refusal of Congress to admit it as a state. Instead, the Boston Radicals took aim at neighboring states. Stearns could think of no more fitting tribute to John Brown than to continue his work, and he and Bird had come to organize an army and initiate a plan. "Colonel" James Montgomery was "a splendid man," Stearns wrote his wife, and he promised "lots of stories about him when I get home." With his leadership, they could help to bring John Brown's project back to life. "I now feel confident," Stearns wrote, "that we can make the whole of Kansas a refuge for the 'panting fugitive,' and *that* done, Missouri, Arkansas, and Indian Territory can be cleared of slaves."[8]

The Civil War had already begun, but only Stearns, Montgomery, and a handful of militants knew that. On their way home from Kansas, Stearns and Bird stopped in Chicago to attend the 1860 Republican Convention.

Republicans in Chicago hosted the greatest political convention in American history, a gathering unrivaled for exuberance, suspense, and portentous outcome. Like most of the Radicals in attendance, Stearns arrived intending to support William Seward of New York, though he was not distressed when his candidate encountered trouble from a vocal anti-Seward segment led by Frank P. Blair. Blair, a conservative, was what one journalistic wag called "one of two delegates from Missouri," a slave state with a slim Republican foothold. The other Show-Me State "delegate" was a six-foot model of a Bowie knife, inscribed on one side as a gift for Representative John F. Potter from Missouri Republicans and on the other with the motto ALWAYS MEET A PRYOR ENGAGEMENT.[9]

The Radicals proved ready to lend their support to Abraham Lincoln, and for the most part they were willing to hold by Lincoln's maxims of 1859 and 1860, that the party should seek to maintain unity by keeping its most divisive factions out of view. The one exception was the insistence of Joshua Giddings that the party maintain its endorsement of the Declaration of Independence from the 1856 platform. When the delegates declined, Giddings left the "Wigwam" in disgust, and his allies scolded the convention for its lack of courage. After some debate, the delegates agreed to acknowledge once again that their party believed all men to be created equal.[10]

Conventioneers wowed the town with an illuminated parade of two thousand Wide Awakes, and yet an unseen tug of tragedy lay below the surface of the Chicago celebrations. Owing to the delay of transatlantic communications, none among them knew that their party godfather, Theodore Parker, had passed away in Rome the week before. Worse still, the passage from Chicago into war—the showdown that the minister anticipated all the final days of his life—was shorter and more direct than any of the living had imagined.

For antislavery Republicans detained by the federal government, the war had already begun. Even though the sheriff had warned that West Indian Emancipation Day, August 1, might be a date when abolitionists would seek to rescue Fugitive Slave Act violator Sherman Booth, officials at the U.S. Customs House in Milwaukee decided to go out to lunch anyway, leaving their star prisoner in the hands of a single deputy. At twelve-thirty, a dozen armed men entered the building and mounted the stairs. They overwhelmed the guard, used his keys to open the door to Booth's room, then placed the jailer inside while spiriting the antislavery editor to a waiting carriage.

Booth was free. "Keep an eye on the little girls," an opposition newspaper warned.[11]

The Booth rescuers—led by the Republican state geologist and Ripon College professor Edward Daniels—were no less put off by the prisoner's sordid personal life than the others. Practically everybody in Wisconsin believed the allegation that Booth had climbed into the bed of a young teenager and then offered her father money not to press criminal charges. But for Daniels and the others, the matter of the Booth incarceration was bigger than Booth the man. As Booth himself had put it in his Fourth of July address—which he had advertised by newspaper and by posters but was ultimately not permitted to deliver in person from the jailhouse window—the abuse of federal power was the rub.

> There is one more decision of the Supreme Court in reserve [the *Lemmon* case], giving the master power to hold his chattels in every state of our Union. If this fails to awaken us, the spirit of our fathers has departed from our government, the torpor of death has fastened upon our body politic, and the crack of doom could not break our slumbers.[12]

Wisconsin citizens would resist such usurpations or confess to terminal inertia.

Daniels and his fellows in the rescue, in contrast, were Wide Awake—figuratively in their willingness to act and literally in the sense that they were acting to promote the interests of the Republican Party in the 1860 presidential election. During his months of incarceration, Booth (like the unlucky Thaddeus Hyatt, whose jail stay ended only when the Senate and the Harpers Ferry investigating committee adjourned in late June) had become a symbol of the conflict between the proslavery national government under James Buchanan and the antislavery citizenry of the Free States. Booth's liberation signified that Republicans would not submit—a message that he underscored in person in a series of campaign appearances that began immediately after his release.

Wearing a pistol and protected by Daniels and a series of local Wide Awake clubs acting as his bodyguard, the outlaw editor offered a Radical counterpart to the overall tone of moderation in the national Republican

ticket. Booth would roil the hard-core antislavery districts in Ripon, Osh-
kosh, and Racine, Wisconsin, reaching out to the John Brown or Garrisonian purists who could scarcely bear to vote Republican. His message
emphasized the imperative to fight: *fight* for the rights of free citizens versus
the Slave Power; *fight* to rescue and to liberate the slaves; *fight* and cheer and
fight some more for Lincoln and Hamlin, Lincoln and Hamlin.

Lincoln and vice presidential nominee Hannibal Hamlin—for the
record—neither condemned nor endorsed the Booth jailbreak or anything
that Booth and his allies said or did on the campaign trail. They were officially silent on all matters political, refusing speaking engagements and
responding to requests for clarification with a form letter explaining their
policy of avoiding the issues.[13] Though enemies and skeptics deplored it,
the campaign strategy of "masterly inactivity" proved ideally suited to the
task of mobilizing the broad and unwieldy Republican Party coalition. All
politics was local in the 1860 Lincoln campaign. The candidates would not
be bothered to authorize supporters or to avow or disavow their political
tactics. If a speaker chose to fire a gun onstage or to brandish a pistol and
call it his "habeas corpus," as Booth did, then it went without saying that
his opinions did not reflect the views of the Lincoln ticket or the Republican
establishment.[14]

The Wide Awakes, for that matter, maintained their own vows of silence
during most of the election calendar in Wisconsin and elsewhere. The Wide
Awake display of marching without songs or speeches in taciturn military
formations helped to create the movement's mystique. Their banners and
illuminated transparencies provided the only commentary in Wide Awake
demonstrations, insisting mutely that THE UNION SHALL AND MUST BE
PRESERVED (a reference to Andrew Jackson) and that UNCLE SAM IS RICH
ENOUGH TO GIVE US ALL A FARM (the title of a song by the antislavery
Hutchinson Family Singers).[15] The image of the open eye—the most common and arresting of the Wide Awake icons—said nearly all that needed
to be said about the new organizations: they were watching, standing by.
Mostly Wide Awakes let actions speak for themselves, as when, in Wisconsin, several dozen took the stage to defend Sherman Booth and punched and
stabbed a U.S. marshal until he had to be carried from the hall.[16]

Other Republican Radicals participated full-throated in the presidential canvassing all summer and fall. Some, like Martin Stowell in Nebraska, ran as candidates for office or for reelection. Others attempted to build bridges to nonpolitical extremists in appearances such as Booth's before the Fourier Utopians in Ceresco, Wisconsin, or in a series of pro-Republican addresses by British Islanders James Redpath and Richard Hinton at Garrisonian conventions. The most prestigious speakers chastened mainstream Republican audiences with calls for more vigorous engagement in antislavery politics. On his feet after an extended convalescence, and appearing at the Cooper Union in July, Senator Charles Sumner enjoined Republicans repeatedly to "Prostrate the Slave Oligarchy" and restore the nation to its intended glory.[17] Rough-and-ready Colonel Jim Lane of Kansas campaigned actively, calling Lincoln his friend, and even Frederick Douglass, who refused to align himself with the party that year, expressed satisfaction with the fact that Lincoln was "a radical Republican" who was "fully committed to the doctrine of 'irrepressible conflict.'"[18]

Douglass was hardly the only abolitionist to withhold his support for the Republican ticket, and yet the resonance between the major strains of antislavery had never been greater. Abbey Kelley Foster and her husband, Stephen Foster, Worcester, Massachusetts, hard-cores, still warned that Republicans' conditional commitment to the cause had the capacity to deceive the faithful and that it therefore represented a more direct threat than the Democrats to genuine antislavery. William Lloyd Garrison, still smarting from his friends' outraged responses to his statement back in 1859 that his "hope" was "in the great Republican party," kept his distance. Thomas Wentworth Higginson—on again and off again on politics—made enthusiastic statements about John A. Andrew, running for governor of Massachusetts on the Bird Club slate, and alternatively endorsed and denied or withdrew his endorsement for Lincoln and Hamlin for much of the season.

An unlikely series of connections, meanwhile, extended the reach of Lincoln/Hamlin into the realm of literature and bohemia. The publishers Thayer and Eldridge had been caught short by the Republican convention, for which they had commissioned Richard Hinton to write a campaign biography of William Seward. Hinton followed with a hastily assembled Lincoln book that became available late in the summer of 1860. An advertisement for the Lincoln book appeared on the back cover of a new edition of Whitman's *Leaves of Grass*. Whitman did not object, even though in other ways he had asserted firm control over the design of the book, including the typ-setting and the self-portrait with butterfly featured on the front cover. For what it was worth, the poet was at that time an active Radical Republican, the author of an idiosyncratic and unhelpful pro-Fremont speech of 1856 vintage in which he had predicted the coming presidency of a "healthy-bodied, middle-aged, beard-faced" workingman such as Lincoln.[19]

Thayer and Eldridge contracted to publish what became another classic during the 1860 election, signing Harriet Jacobs under the pen name Linda Brent. The publishers arranged for an introduction to the autobiographi-cal Jacobs book—*Incidents in the Life of a Slave Girl*—by the feminist Lydia Maria Child. Child did not consider herself a Republican, but in 1860 she confessed to be won over by Lincoln as a personality. She remembered the Radical passages in Lincoln's 1857 and 1858 speeches, particularly "she is my equal," his reference to the dignity of African American labor.[20] Child and Jacobs would be disappointed with the firm of Thayer and Eldridge, which went bankrupt later that year without publishing the pioneering narra-tive of Jacobs's seven years in hiding in the attic of her own home, a blistering indictment of the sexual exploitation of slaves.

Other American feminists were less conflicted than Child in their sup-port of Lincoln. The suffragist Elizabeth Cady Stanton helped to organize a Women's Wide Awake Auxiliary in her hometown of Seneca Falls, New York. Addressing the club, she described herself as "a full-blooded Republi-can," whose husband, Henry B. Stanton, had been a delegate to the Chicago convention.[21] Stanton and her collaborator Susan B. Anthony had worked successfully with New York Republicans to pass the 1860 Married Women's Property Act, a feminist landmark. Anthony was not married, and during 1860 she spent several months living in the Stanton home in Seneca Falls, helping Elizabeth work by sharing responsibility for the family's seven children, as the partners collaborated to take their women's rights campaign into additional states.

During one of these sojourns in September, Susan Anthony and both of the Stantons addressed a torchlight parade of Wide Awakes who had come to serenade them and solicit speeches. Elizabeth Cady Stanton delivered "a *splendid banner speech*" and Susan Anthony "told them she hoped they'd not only keep *Wide awake* to the inauguration of Abram [*sic*] Lincoln but also to go to the aid of the *Slave*, in the case of an insurrection, or another John Brown invasion in Virginia." Breaking their silence, the Wide Awakes offered three cheers for Susan B. Anthony, three for each of the Stantons, cheers for all seven of the "little Stantons," and "three for *Old Abe*."[22]

Seneca Falls Wide Awakes and organizations from Connecticut, New Jersey, and the New England states convened on New York City on October 3 to stage what was at that time thought to be the largest political demonstration in U.S. history. Their silent muster at Twenty-Third Street filled Broadway for a distance of five miles.[23] A yet larger display took place in Boston on October 16, featuring ten thousand torches. A highlight of the parade was the appearance of the nation's only African American Wide Awake company, the West Boston Wide Awakes, led by Lewis Hayden. Hayden and the West Boston group provided the most notable support that year for the Republican presidential ticket, marching under the banner GOD NEVER MADE A TYRANT OR A SLAVE. Among those thrilled by the sight of black men marching in military formation was William Lloyd Garrison, who called the parade the "most brilliant and imposing political demonstration" that Boston had ever seen. The music as well as the pageantry moved Garrison, who admitted it was "hard not to tap one's feet" to the campaign song "Ain't You Glad You Joined the Republicans."[24]

The Wide Awakes presented as Radical—striking Southerners particularly as a silent show of solidarity with John Brown—but in fact incorporated the full spectrum of Republican politics. In St. Louis, for example, the so-called Blair Rifles militia—a Wide Awake club—arrayed itself under the direction of Frank Preston Blair, Jr., a member of an influential family of slave-state Republicans. The Blairs (including Frank Sr. and the editor and lawyer Montgomery Blair) confirmed Hinton Helper's and John C. Underwood's predictions that the party would find ready adherents in the South, but the Missouri faction tacked to the conservative side in 1860 and afterward. St. Louis Wide Awakes also benefited from the military drill instruction of the mostly apolitical Ulysses S. Grant, whose antislavery instincts were gaining but who did not commit to the Lincoln/Hamlin ticket. The social aspects of Wide Awake activity proved as appealing to many recruits as the political message. Buoyed by enthusiasm for the uniform and drill, the ranks of Wide Awakes burgeoned toward half a million as the election approached.

While Republicans rallied, the Democratic Party fell into disarray as Southerners refused to accept the candidacy of Stephen Douglas. The fire-eaters nominated John C. Breckinridge, vice president under Buchanan, who later became the Confederate secretary of war. John Bell, a senator, sought to revive the banner of the Whig Party of the South, calling himself a Constitutional Unionist but later hastening the secession of Tennessee.

The misfortunes of the opposition emboldened Republican extremism. On the Saturday before Election Day, Wide Awakes gave a signal of the degree to which the party Radicals fit into the broader Republican message when they executed an elaborate salute to Medford ultra-Radical George L. Stearns. Meeting Stearns on his way home from the Bird Club (which he attended religiously every weekend after his appointment there with John Brown), Wide Awakes performed a silent drill that resulted in the formation of a square procession to escort him to a torchlit parade ground near the Bunker Hill monument. Called upon for a speech, the usually reticent Stearns mounted a wooden box and cleared his throat to speak. "I can see him now standing there with his long beard against the dark sky," remembered his son, "surrounded by the flaring torches, his face full of earnestness and determination." Said Stearns, "I consider this to be the most important election that has ever taken place in our country. On Tuesday next it is going to be decided whether we are a nation of free men, or [one] to be ruled by an oligarchy of slaveholders, as we have been for the past twenty five years." It was a battle, he said, gesturing, "as important as that . . . fought over there by our grandfathers." Stearns praised Senator Wilson and predicted success for John A. Andrew, who he declared would be "the best governor that has ever sat at the state-house in Boston, and I do not except [John] Hancock and [John] Adams."[25]

Election Day passed in the guise of normalcy. Stearns kept company with his Bird Club friends, not returning home until after eleven that night. Frederick Douglass spent the whole day at the polls in Rochester, New York, campaigning not for Lincoln but for a revised version of the 1857 state constitutional amendment to expand black suffrage. And Lincoln himself retired late, informed of his victory but disturbed by an optical illusion in a wardrobe mirror, which showed two versions of his face that reportedly remained visible no matter how much he adjusted his position. For the superstitious Lincoln and his wife, Mary, the apparition of the second, paler version of his face seemed to foretell his death in office during a second term.[26] No less plausibly, the double image symbolized the apparent and potential Lincoln presidencies: the pale face of Lincoln's supposed moderation juxtaposed with the sanguine revolutionary not yet seen.

PART II

The War Years

10

MILITARY EMANCIPATION

incoln's election sparked secession and other remarkable events. The onset of war with the attack on Fort Sumter in April 1861 inspired what turned out to be a one-time-only surge of cooperation among Radical Republicans, who followed the tacit lead of the incoming executive in avoiding an excess of public grandstanding. Lincoln's unspoken message (as he remained almost silent in public, in keeping with his campaign policy) was to hold firm against proposed compromises such as the peace programs and draft constitutional amendments circulating in Congress. Radicals in Washington offered no compromises and no comment, forming a common flank with all Republicans. Former antipolitical outliers also found themselves in support of the Lincoln administration and the Union they had once despised. The editor William Lloyd Garrison, for example, who had appeared before an upside-down American flag in 1854, now mounted a flagpole and displayed the Stars and Stripes in proper alignment outside the *Liberator* offices.

A different flag had become the obsession of "General" and (at last officially) Senator Jim Lane, whose home territory of Kansas finally achieved statehood in early 1861 and who now resided temporarily in the White House at the head of a hastily organized "Frontier Guard" providing security during the transition. Bivouacking in the East Wing, Lane defied propriety with his unkempt appearance and reputation for profanity. The proximity of so many enemies in the federal district and its slaveholding surroundings had also set the jayhawker's trigger finger on alert. On April 29, 1861, Lincoln's secretary, John Hay, encountered Lane and his colleague in the Senate, the German-born Carl Schurz, in the upstairs bedroom of John George Nicolay:

> Jim was at the window, filling his soul with gall by steady telescopic contemplation of a Secession flag impudently flaunting over a roof in Alexandria [wrote Hay]. "Let me tell you," he said to the elegant Teuton, "we have got to whip these scoundrels like hell, C. Schurz. They did a good thing stoning our men at Baltimore and shooting away the flag at Sumter. It has set the great North a-howling for blood, and they'll have it."[1]

Secessionists were taking aim at the capital, moving troops and weaponry into position for an invasion, and one did not have to be medically paranoid (as Jim Lane may have been) to recognize that the government was in peril.

Lane, for one, would have his or die trying. Taking two of the Frontier Guards in tow, he went in pursuit of the Confederate flag, ripped it down, and took it back to the White House as a trophy. "The General relates the story with great glee," observed the *New York Herald*. "He says he doesn't believe in the southern chivalry."[2]

Lane's company, which also included Kansas's other Radical Republican senator, Samuel C. Pomeroy, acted as a bodyguard for Lincoln (taking over from the detective Allan Pinkerton, who had protected the president-elect en route to Washington the month before in one of his last and most important acts as a Republican). The Frontier Guard afforded protection during the tense days before the arrival of the first available regiments from Massachusetts and New York—the first states to achieve a state of readiness. The movement of troops through slaveholding Maryland had proved more difficult than the Northerners had foreseen. A secessionist mob had interrupted the transport of Northern troops from one railway station to another, pelting soldiers with paving stones and other objects, which resulted in the death of four Massachusetts militiamen. All Washington considered the likelihood of Maryland's secession and the imminent capture of the capital by the rebels.

During these tense days, Hay encountered the "gaunt, tattered, un-combed, and unshorn" Jim Lane stalking the White House in his under-shirt and pants without suspenders. Asked about conditions in Baltimore, the Kansas militant predicted that the crisis would pass within a day or two. If not, the senator predicted, "Baltimore will be laid in ashes" even if he had to burn it himself.[3]

As it happened, another Radical would resolve the Maryland crisis—without resorting to destruction. Benjamin Butler was still a Democrat in 1861, but one accustomed to building bridges between political movements. Despite his prominence within the Massachusetts opposition, Butler had been careful to maintain links to abolitionists, Free-Soilers, and others. He'd made Fremont speeches in 1856 while (notoriously) sponsoring Mis-sissippi's Jefferson Davis for the Democratic presidential nomination in 1860 in a desperate bid to prevent the dissolution of his party into sectional rivalries. On the strength of his connections, Butler had wangled a com-mission as a brigadier general of Massachusetts militia, placed in command of New York and Massachusetts troops transported by sea into the port at Annapolis, Maryland. He was appalled to be met on shore by the mayor of the town and the governor of the state, who explained that local railroads could not be used to cover the thirty-mile distance to Washington and that local merchants and landowners would refuse to supply troops with food or to accommodate encampments.

Butler, a lawyer, was not intimidated. Acting on instinct and making use of his knowledge of the law, he confiscated the railways and their roll-ing stock in the name of eminent domain, finding technicians in his troops to run the engines. As for provisions, he counseled cooperation, reminding the mayor that "a thousand hungry, armed men have other means of getting what they want to eat besides buying it."[4]

Baltimore would find itself similarly helpless when confronted with armed force. Under cover of darkness on May 13, marking the first full month of the war, Butler positioned twelve hundred troops and artillery on high ground in the city, displayed a flag, and announced to the citizens that he would not interfere with ordinary business but would detain without charge those deemed to aiding the enemy. Confederate flags and other em-blems of disloyalty were prohibited.[5] Incensed by the resulting controversy, the elderly commanding general of U.S. forces, Winfield Scott, recalled Butler to Washington and relieved him of command. President Lincoln saw matters differently and promoted Butler to major general of volunteers. Responding to a serenade by citizens of Washington outside his hotel on May 16, Butler was unrepentant. War was hell, he told the well-wishers, and "Woe, woe to them who have made the necessity."[6]

Major General Butler had obtained a premier strategic assignment: to reinforce the garrison at Fortress Monroe in Hampton Roads, Virginia. At the head of New York and Massachusetts troops, Butler bloodlessly assured Union control of the Chesapeake. Within days of his arrival, moreover, the soon-to-be Republican Butler weighed in on the central political issue of the war.

At issue was the fate of three men held as slaves, whose master, a Confederate captain, had employed them on the construction of a new earthworks opposite Monroe. On May 25, 1861, the men applied to Butler's troops for sanctuary, and their commander insisted on protecting them behind Union lines when the captain came to demand their return the following day. Butler did not defend his actions on moral grounds, but in terms of legality. Employed on the enemy front, the slaves were *contraband of war*, and as such were as subject to confiscation as food stores or munitions.

Reporting on the following day, May 26, one of the many journalists who followed the rising political general to Virginia described the outcome of Butler's new policy as "uproarious." By May 27, the correspondent counted "some $60,000 of this sort of property in camp, and the stock is hourly increasing."

The subject is becoming of very great moment [wrote the *Boston Journal* correspondent]. As long as property contraband of war—that is to say, negroes adapted for or about to be employed in military movement—came into our possession, the question was comparatively simple; it was simply military. But when women and children come, as they have by the score, it became a humanitarian question . . . The Massachusetts stores have—by order of the General in command—been taken to feed these panting fugitives. For the present, and until advised by Gen. Scott or President Lincoln or somebody else, I understand that the General has decided to retain all negroes who come.[7]

"We had heard it since last fall," said a "contraband," interviewed by the reporter, "that if Lincoln was elected, you would come down and set us free." In fact Lincoln approved of Ben Butler's legal maneuvers against slavery, sending instructions through Secretary of War Simon Cameron to continue to receive the fugitives and to provide as necessary for their care.[8]

Butler found himself drawn into Radical Republican circles, attracted by their enthusiasm and recruited in person by George L. Stearns, who visited the general at his headquarters in June and reported on their comity of views.[9] Though he had run for governor of Massachusetts against John Andrew in 1860, the Lowell-based attorney and factory owner turned commander was quick to pursue Republican Party associations, appointing young Edward L. Pierce of the Bird Club Pierces to be his special assistant for the management of contrabands at Fortress Monroe and enjoying his new status as an especially resourceful representative of the Lincoln administration.

The fighting had not even started—except in Kansas and Missouri, where old enemies continued to jostle amid escalating stakes. While Butler was making his name among eastern Radicals in May with his knowledge and instincts, an established antislavery player, Nathaniel Lyon, was winning the field by military prowess. Lyon was the Regular Army hero of the Free Kansas fight, an idiosyncratic son of Connecticut with first-hand knowledge of proslavery politics in Missouri. He could plainly see the machinations of Governor Claiborne F. Jackson to deliver Missouri to the Confederacy. There as elsewhere, the Union cause suffered for lack of a substantial standing army. While pro-Confederates converged upon the outskirts of St. Louis, Lyon took steps to augment his own troops by recruiting the services of the city's well-developed Wide Awake organization. In the Battle of Fort Jackson—May 10, 1861—Lyon and his partisans stormed the rebel encampment named after the disloyal governor. In the contested aftermath, his irregulars fired on citizens trying to prevent the incarceration of Missouri rebels, killing twenty-eight. Along with Frank Blair, soon to be commissioned as a general in the volunteer army, General Lyon won accolades for helping to maintain Missouri as a force for the Union.

Kansas, meanwhile, again hosted the peripatetic George Stearns, now dedicated to enlisting the new state's filibuster armies into the armed forces of the United States. Stearns continued his support for undercover operations, writing to Mary Stearns about various "B[rown] movements" in progress, which were swelling the number of African Americans in Lawrence and other Kansas settlements to record proportions.[10]

The fighting moved east in July, with the first major battle in the ground war, at Bull Run (or Manassas), Virginia. Many in the North greeted the defeat of the Union troops with great distress. Not so George Luther Stearns and other Radicals, who were counting on a hard war to achieve their revolutionary goals. "It is the first step toward the emancipation," Stearns told his family. "If we had won a decisive victory, in less than six months the rebellious state would be back in the union, the [Republican] government would be out-voted in Congress, and we should have all our work to do over again."[11]

Stearns, Phillips, and others in the hard-war school were counting on the exigencies of war to build support for emancipation as a war measure. De facto emancipation such as that offered in Benjamin Butler's conditional contraband arrangements did not suffice, particularly the limitation to zones of military conflict. A prolonged confrontation would permit nonbelievers in the North to recognize the role of slavery in sustaining the Southern insurgency and to contemplate the benefits of uprooting the sources of Southern rebelliousness. The war ultras did not anticipate that an ambitious commander might seize upon emancipation as a lever for personal advancement, or that a policy of so much weight might be introduced impulsively. Even insiders were not prepared, therefore, for the first Emancipation Proclamation of the war, issued from the headquarters of General John C. Fremont in the summer of 1861.

Fremont remained largely one-dimensional as an explorer and famous name at the outset of the war. In an era when candidates for president did not participate in campaigns, the party knew as little about him at the end of 1856 as it did at the beginning of its first presidential election season. In those days, Republicans had valued him for what he was not—not nativist, not protectionist, not proslavery, not abolitionist, and yet not simply ordinary, a man who had made a name for himself in remote regions not well known. That Fremont did not become president preserved the essential mysteries of his politics, particularly since the candidate did not remain active in the party but instead dedicated himself to the world of business, investing not in New England or New York but in exotic California and Europe. His return to government work at the outset of the war was not a foregone conclusion, but instead reflected a genuine patriotism. It was also true that his mining enterprises were not faring well. He returned from Europe—without undue haste—and assumed command of the Western Army with the dual conviction that the war could not be won without his leadership, and that his own career could not advance without a share of military glory. He had never made a proper speech when suddenly he issued orders liberating all the slaves of rebels in Missouri.

General Fremont did not act without the advice of true believers. One among his advisers was the Radical Republican congressman Owen Lovejoy. Lovejoy was one of several elected officials to join the armed services, North and South, while Congress was out of session in 1861. His enlistment on the staff of General Fremont passed under the radar of most observers, even in Lovejoy's home district. He had been goaded into action by the failure of his bill to enlarge the scope of General Butler's contraband policy by relieving the army of responsibility to return fugitive slaves, and friends and foes alike had inspired him to throw his shoulder against the wheel of the Union military effort. "The slave question is the war question," insisted the abolitionist Gerrit Smith in a private letter to Lovejoy. "The war began in Slavery and it will end but in slavery."[12]

More pointed was the view expressed in the conservative *Vanity Fair*, which excoriated Lovejoy about his obsession with what the author referred to impolitely by the N-word:

> Simply, the best thing that Mr. Lovejoy can do, in the present juncture, is to resign his seat, take his [Negro] out of the House, and find a position in the army. If he will devote half as much exertion and zeal to putting down

Rebellion as he has heretofore devoted to boring Congressmen and stirring up ill-blood, he will be an invaluable soldier.[13]

Though he never wrote about his reasoning, the congressman apparently took the suggestion to heart. He took a commission as an army major and found his way on to the staff of General Fremont—an officer by no means insensible to the dignity of having a member of House of Representatives as his subordinate. In St. Louis, Lovejoy would dedicate himself with all vigor to the achievement of his lifelong goal. He was supported in this effort by the most influential of Fremont's inner-circle advisers, Jessie Benton Fremont, the general's wife.

Jessie Fremont grew up in politics as the daughter of Missouri's legendary first senator, Thomas Hart Benton. From an early age she had chafed under the restrictions that kept women and girls on the sidelines of public life, cutting her hair short to protest her enrollment in a Washington, D.C., girls' academy and insisting that her father educate her himself in his office and the Library of Congress.[14] After marrying Fremont at the age of seventeen, she had developed a reputation as an independent political actor.[15] While her husband's views were opaque, Jessie openly advocated abolition, convinced that the slavery crisis had cast a shadow on her father's legacy as an advocate of expanding the Union and believing that she had had a supernatural vision of herself as a liberator.

Making a political statement in her home décor, Jessie Fremont had created an abolitionist tableau, complete with an engraving of a slave auction, in her home atop San Francisco's Golden Gate, built when the site was still a glorious wilderness. At Black Point, as she called her house, she cultivated a salon of antislavery, Republican, and literary Californians, including the writer Bret Harte and an antislavery minister, newly arrived from Boston, Thomas Starr King. She and her three children lived mostly separate from Fremont, whose work in the mining districts and solicitations for European investors kept him away from home for months at a time.[16] Maintaining an independent public profile in her husband's absence, Jessie Fremont enjoyed favorable press on personal as well as political subjects, and a wide circle of influential correspondents.

John Fremont's commission as a major general brought the couple back together in the summer of 1861—he by a circuitous route through European capitals, where he purchased arms without advance orders from the War Department, and she by steamer and train across the Central American isthmus to New York, then overland by train to St. Louis, her part-time hometown. Through her family connections, the Fremonts leased a fine mansion to use as their headquarters, and he assembled an idiosyncratic staff of officers and bodyguards.

In addition to Owen Lovejoy, Fremont maintained another abolitionist member of Congress, John A. Gurley, as his chief of staff. Like Lovejoy, Gurley had been ridiculed as a coward in the papers—in his case, accused of having visited the Bull Run battlefield as a spectator, and having run away so fast that he beat his horse and carriage back to Washington.[17] Fremont also commissioned a number of distinguished men he met in Europe, including a dashing Hungarian major, Poles, and German immigrants and veterans of the 1848 revolutionary uprisings.

Jessie Fremont participated actively in the command, writing letters in his name—sometimes with the proviso that the letters were "not absolutely from dictation."[18] As a model of military administration, the Fremont headquarters was profoundly unconventional in its openness to politicians and foreigners and especially to Mrs. Fremont. In keeping with its revolutionary composition, headquarters quickly found itself at odds with the military and political establishment.

Jessie Fremont saw disarray in the army supply and communications infrastructure in St. Louis and immediately suspected sabotage by political rivals of her husband. The slave state Missouri was too important, its loyal status still to tenuous, as she saw it, to permit delays in the delivery of weapons and instructions from the capital. Making use of her family connection to the Missouri Blairs, she tried to open a side channel of communication with the Lincoln administration in correspondence with Postmaster Montgomery Blair, her cousin by marriage. Her opening complaint addressed the War Department's failure to deliver the weapons her husband had purchased in Europe:

His English arms he says were bought for himself & begs that you will not allow them to be intercepted. His battery rifles & pistols might save the

State—but it looks now as if it was intended to let [Missouri] slide (that's my own).

It is also my own [opinion] to say that I don't like this neglect & I look to you and the President to see that it has not a fatal effect.[19]

A letter to the postmaster on July 31 was written in Jessie's hand and purported to transmit "unshaped sentences" based on the general's oral statements. Fremont was angry—at Missouri rebels and also at officials of the Lincoln administration. Complaining that a Treasury Department official had not permitted him to take funds for paying soldiers, the letter made what seemed to be a garbled threat but may have actually hinted at Fremont's intention to unleash a public relations war on Washington: "If any more sub-treasurers stand in the way of necessary work for safety you may look to see secession newspaper columns dressed in mourning for my bloodthirsty acts." And again, "I don't care for my commission—I am determined not to risk my character here for want of means within my reach, and what is needed I will take." The letter was signed "Yours truly J. C. Fremont (by J. B. F.)."[20] "You understand I am a faithful reporter when he has not time to dictate," she said to Blair in a subsequent letter.

On August 5, Jessie Benton Fremont wrote directly to Lincoln, justifying her husband's strategies in light of a critical letter forwarded with the president's endorsement. She signed her letter "Head Quarters Western Division."[21] Amid the upheavals of war, Jessie Fremont recognized an opportunity to transcend a woman's traditional role. "The restraints of ordinary times do not apply now," she told her husband. All month at headquarters, she worked with Fremont's other advisers on a pair of programs destined to have an immense impact on public opinion and the war. She also struggled to protect her husband from increasingly outspoken accusations of corruption and military ineptitude.

The first to call attention to the mismanagement of public funds in the Western Division was the Radical Republican secretary of the treasury, Salmon Chase. Chase was loath to make an enemy, and indeed he presented himself as an advocate of giving Fremont a bigger role in the war, perhaps command of armies in more critical theaters back east or even making Fremont secretary of war. He had provided the money that Fremont demanded to pay troops, he said, and also acted to speed the processing in customs of Fremont's supplies of European arms. Chase urged Fremont not "to withdraw your attention from the expenditures of the army under your command and in your department." The war would be costly, Chase explained, and "already the disgust created by fraud or exorbitance in contracts, and by the improvidence of Quartermasters and Commissaries, is beginning to show itself." Fremont's opulent headquarters and uniformed bodyguards made him a conspicuous target, and Chase would have him know that he was a friend but that he had his own concerns. The treasury secretary maintained an absolute public silence on the topic, filing his copy of the letter in the Special Correspondence file he kept for sensitive communications.[22] A number of Fremont's enemies, however, had already caught the scent.

Fremont took to the field in early August, looking to rout rebel strongholds in the southern portions of the state. He immediately encountered a disaster with military and political dimensions. The need to police against internal insurgents as well as Confederate armies left the western divisions with a shortage of manpower, and Fremont's plans for the operation recognized the necessity of taking action without hope of reinforcements. General Nathaniel Lyon—the hero of Fort Jackson—was said to have chafed under his instructions to fall back in the event of heavy losses. In the Battle of Wilson's Creek on August 10, the abolitionist officer insisted on pressing the fight in the face of a superior rebel force. Lyon took two bullets, his horse was shot dead, and yet he continued to rally the troops. "Come, my brave boys, I will lead you," he shouted, then he fell with a shot to the heart. He was the first general to die in battle, and his death occasioned an outpouring of public grief.

The peculiar horror of Lyon's death derived not only from his position and his romantic personal history but also from its testament to the terrible power of Civil War weaponry. The minié ball that pierced his chest and exited his back created a wound so cavernous that embalmers were hard pressed to make the body suitable for public display.[23] And his was not the only flesh to yield to the new technology of soft bullets. Thirteen hundred Union soldiers and officers were killed at Wilson's Creek, and thousands more survived the battle with appalling wounds. More than seven hundred found their way to the three hospitals in St. Louis, more than two hundred miles from the scene of the fighting.

Though his body was intact, John C. Fremont retreated from the loss at Wilson's Creek with significant political wounds, and the effects were lingering. Lyon's body—repaired, dressed, and shipped east for burial in Ashford, Connecticut—made a cross-country voyage attended by mourning parties and newspaper headlines in various cities and towns. At every juncture, the questions *how* and *why* directed unfavorable attention to General Fremont. The Blair family, of whom Lyon had been a protégé, considered the tragedy the latest manifestation of Fremont's incompetence, and they began campaigning publicly against him.

Wounded soldiers, meanwhile, continued to arrive in St. Louis by rail and wagon. The influx overwhelmed medical facilities and doctors, taxed the army's capacity to provide food and clean clothing, and mounted toward a humanitarian disaster. The substantial disloyal population in St. Louis vigorously derided the U.S. command as usurping and ineffective.

General Fremont lashed back with a declaration of martial law in St. Louis. All through August, he tried to bring his enemies to heel, arresting the police commissioner, searching homes and businesses for weapons, closing newspapers, and arresting and interrogating journalists. Still looking for money to pay his troops and officers, the commander levied a huge sum—$250,000—from St. Louis banks.[24] Confederates pressed their advantages, claiming large swaths of territory in southern Missouri without much opposition by Union forces.[25]

Distressed and embarrassed, the commander retreated from potential critics. His headquarters soon resembled a European court—both in the proliferation of foreign-born staff officers and in the difficulty of obtaining an interview with the master of the house. Influential officers noted the strangeness of their surroundings at Fremont's headquarters. For one thing, the fine furnishings at Brant Mansion stood in sharp contrast to the appearance of headquarters in the field. His Body Guard, in resplendent uniforms, received guests coldly—particularly when officers on duty did not speak English, as one officer reported. Admitted to the next suite of rooms, visitors had to parley with Fremont's aides-de-camp. When finally received in the general's offices, Carl Schurz—like Lovejoy and Gurley, another member of Congress serving temporarily in the armed forces—found Fremont friendly and unassuming. Another said that the general had refused to look him in the eye or address him directly, but had exchanged smirks and comments with a staff officer in the room.[26]

General William Tecumseh Sherman reported memorably that he had encountered a uniformed sentry parading with drawn sword outside Fremont's headquarters before dawn. "Is the General up?" asked Sherman. When the sentry answered that he did not know, Sherman pulled rank, demanding "in a sharp, emphatic voice, 'Then find out!'" Like Schurz, General Sherman found Fremont pleasant and businesslike in person, but such behavior created a wave of unfavorable publicity. Even President Lincoln had to struggle to get the general's attention. "Do you receive these answers?" Lincoln telegraphed on August 15. "Have you received these messages? Answer immediately."[27]

While her husband spiraled, Jessie Benton Fremont took the lead. Most urgently, she acted to address the crisis of caring for wounded soldiers and loyal refugees from Confederate-controlled areas. Her allies in this enterprise were the establishment philanthropists of old St. Louis, particularly William Greenleaf Eliot, grandfather of the poet T. S. Eliot, a New England Unitarian minister who had made himself one of the most respected citizens of the western capital. Eliot was a Republican (his brother Thomas Dawes Eliot served in Congress as a representative of Massachusetts), but in the divided society of St. Louis, he tried to be discreet about it. In the aftermath of the Wilson's Creek defeat, Eliot began visiting the train stations, assisting in the unloading of wounded men, many of whom still wore the bloodied clothing they were wearing when they were shot. He was appalled to learn that some had unextracted bullets in their bodies three weeks after the battle.[28] Rallying his church and the students and patrons of Washington University—an institution he had helped to found—Eliot began ministering to the soldiers' needs, collecting clothing and supplies, organizing food preparation and laundry, and scouring the area for buildings in which to house and care for the wounded. It was not for nothing that Ralph Waldo Emerson had called him "the Saint of the West" in a previous visit.

Jessie Fremont aided in the most urgent part of the relief effort, the search for qualified doctors and nurses. She and Eliot conferred for hours at a time, and she made the most of her continent-spanning address book of connections. She reached out to the philanthropist Dorothea Dix, whose efforts to provide for wounded soldiers in the eastern theater of the war had made her a celebrity of sorts by summer 1861, and secured her agreement to visit St. Louis to advise the emerging caregiving network there. With help from Eliot, Jessie Fremont prepared the city to embrace the still controversial idea that women should serve as professional nurses in army hospitals, writing to a local newspaper that Dix was the "Florence Nightingale of America" and that the system she was pioneering was the best hope for wounded American men. "Amateur or indiscriminate nursing is not enough for the stern realities that war has forced upon us," she wrote, recommending the adoption of "a modern system of female nurses."[29]

Dix served as a model for Jessie Fremont and her St. Louis collaborators in her ability to formalize her role within the federal bureaucracy. By the summer of 1861, Dix had secured recognition as the army's superintendent of nursing, a position that gave her formal authority over hospital procedures and an unofficial rank equivalent to army major.[30] Dix's friends from Massachusetts—Senator Sumner and Dr. Samuel Gridley Howe—had offered their assistance in securing the position. Dix recommended that Eliot and his colleagues secure the same kind of formal recognition from the army, a goal to which Jessie Fremont applied her special effort. The key was to gain the approval of the army medical superintendent in St. Louis, the besieged Dr. Samuel De Camp. "I have written to ask Mr. De Camp to come see me & I can have him on our side," she wrote to Eliot on August 27. "His signature is needed I think."[31]

Jessie Fremont also advised her husband on his burgeoning military and public relations problems. On August 28 she conferred with Fremont, Lovejoy, and Gurley on a new proposal intended to address the two biggest concerns facing the Western Division command: the persistence of pro-Confederate subversion in Missouri and the chorus of criticism of Fremont and his management of the crisis. The imposition of martial law in St. Louis had not done enough to stem the insurgency, Jessie thought. The new proposal would extend military administration to the entire state, with enhanced powers for the commander of the district. "All persons who shall be taken with arms in their hands within these lines," read the proposed order, "shall be tried by court-martial, and if found guilty, will be shot." The property of such men "is declared confiscated to public use, and their slaves, if any they have, are hereby declared free men."

After considering the matter for two days, the Fremonts sought the opinion of Edward M. Davis, a longtime friend who had described Jessie as "a real heroine" back in 1856. With Davis's approval, and with the encouragement of Congressmen Lovejoy and Gurley, General Fremont issued his Emancipation Order on August 30, 1861.[32]

Fremont's order initiated quick action to liberate enslaved individuals. His office issued manumission papers for more than two dozen held in bondage in the first days of September, including domestics employed in the home of an ally of the disgraced former governor Claiborne Jackson. The declaration also prompted an immediate rebuke from President Lincoln:

> Two points in your proclamation of August 30 give me some anxiety. First, should you shoot a man, according to the proclamation, the Confederates would very certainly shoot our best man in their hands in retaliation; and so, man for man, indefinitely. It is therefore my order that you allow no man to be shot, under the proclamation, without first having my approbation or consent.
>
> Secondly, I think there is great danger that the closing paragraph, in relation to the confiscation of property, and the liberating slaves of traitorous owners, will alarm our Southern Union friends [including slaveholders], and turn them against us—perhaps ruin our rather fair prospect for Kentucky. Allow me therefore to ask, that you will as of your own motion, modify that paragraph so as to conform to the first and fourth sections of the act of Congress, entitled, "An act to confiscate property used for insurrectionary purposes," approved August 6th, 1861, and a copy of which act I herewith send you.

Lincoln assured Fremont that he meant no harm, labeling the letter "Private and Confidential" and noting that "This letter is written in a spirit of caution and not of censure." He also took precautions against Fremont's familiar elusiveness, saying, "I send it by a special messenger, in order that it may certainly and speedily reach you."[33]

All summer Jessie Fremont had been pestering her husband to allow her to travel to Washington so she could make the case for her husband's military and political choices. In a letter to her distant cousin Elizabeth Blair (the sister of the prominent conservative Republicans Frank and Montgomery Blair), she had even joked about running away to Washington, D.C. "I will obey a higher law than my dear chief's and open out the view to the [Mississippi]," she wrote. "It seems to stop now at the Potomac." Now that the president had "asked" Fremont to countermand his order, "General Jessie," as the Blairs had come to call her without her knowledge, finally got her wish. On September 8, equipped with a long letter from Fremont to President Lincoln, she set out for Washington to make the case for emancipation in Missouri and Fremont's martial law.

An ordinary person might have hesitated to open a dialogue with Abraham Lincoln in the aftermath of his unambiguous instructions of September 2. But Jessie Benton Fremont was not an ordinary person. The president had sent his letter by special messenger and Fremont had done likewise, endowing his courier with plenipotentiary authority to answer any questions the president might have. Lincoln might have charge of the Oval Office, but Mrs. Fremont saw herself as representing a political constituency that must be heard and a political tradition that must be acknowledged. "All my life I had been at home in the President's House—received as well there as in the family circle," she wrote in a memorandum of her interview, "and with the old confidence of the past I went forward now."[34]

Thus the Radical Republicans, hearts throbbing, moved to join the cause of emancipation to the horrible momentum of the war. Their moves produced controversy, inviting the charge that the war to preserve the Union was being sidelined in favor of a war to abolish slavery. Lincoln showed his impatience with Fremont's excesses, summoning Jessie Fremont to his office before she had time to wash and rest from her journey, objecting to her pose as a "female politician" and summarily overturning Fremont's order of emancipation under his own signature. Within six weeks of Jessie's visit, General Fremont was relieved of duty in the Department of the West, as Lincoln sought to reassure the public that the war effort had not been joined to abolitionism.

11

WOLF KILLERS

My opinion is this," William Lloyd Garrison quoted before a New York audience, three months after Jessie Fremont's interview with Lincoln. "There is a war because there was a Republican Party. There was a Republican Party because there was an Abolition Party. There was an Abolition Party because there was Slavery."

Republicans were not guilty, he cried in his own voice, to the approval of the audience. Then, continuing to read from the letter of young Theodore Tilton—sitting just behind Garrison on the podium with other dignitaries—Garrison repeated Tilton's mockery of both Democratic and Copperhead critics of Republicans and the too-righteous antipolitical antislavery purists who criticized Garrison and Tilton for casting their lot with the government:

> Now, to charge the war upon Republicanism is to blame the lamb that stood in the brook. To charge it upon Abolitionism is to blame the sheep for being the lamb's mother. (Laughter.) But to charge it upon Slavery is to lay the crime flat at the door of the wolf, where it belongs. (Laughter.) To end the trouble, kill the wolf. (Renewed laughter.) I belong to the party of wolf-killers. (Applause and merriment.)

It was true that abolitionists and their political allies had used harsh language against the South, said Garrison. And yet to say that they were the aggressors was to say too much. "I would rather a man would hurl a hard epithet at my head than the softest cannon or shell that can be found in the army of the North," said Garrison, setting aside the Tilton text. "It is said again, 'There was no trouble in the land until the Abolitionists appeared.' Well, the more is the pity!" The abolitionists—"They are very few; comparatively a mere handful," however much they may have "overturned the Government," a fact that Garrison did not deny—could not bear responsibility for the scourge of war that had overwhelmed the country. "No, my friends, this is not of man; it is of Heaven. The war is a judgment. As we have sowed, we are reaping."[1] Tilton, Garrison, the lot of them: they were not acting as Republicans or abolitionists but in keeping with the will of God.

At the outset of 1862 only abolitionists and Radicals were talking about war as judgment and pressing for the hard war. Their past decades of work to publicize the suffering of slaves and, since 1850, their experience with fugitive rescue violence and persecution had quickened their sensitivity to mass suffering, bloodshed, pathos, rage, horror, and heroic sacrifice. They felt it well before such awareness came to dominate mainstream American households as the Civil War progressed. Antislavery had been long in contemplation of the wolf.

More presciently than any of their contemporaries, North and South, Garrisonians and Radicals understood the war to be a fight unto the death. They would press for total victory, perceiving, as the late Reverend Parker had written, that the Southern animal ran on a vulnerable undercarriage, divided loyalties within the pack.

Also savvy to the stakes were Kansas freebooters and vigilantes. Incursions into the Free State by the Confederate commander Sterling Price had sought to take advantage of the relative scarcity of troops in the Union's Western Command. The resistance of the Kansas antislavery paramilitaries, led by veterans such as James Montgomery, James A. Abbott, and Charles Bluejacket, a Shawnee chief and Methodist minister, carried the day using the accustomed lawless tactics that had made Kansas bleed.[2]

Apart from the participation of Native Americans, scenes such as those enacted by Bluejacket and Abbott were textbook illustrations of Kansas jayhawking. Jayhawkers violated all military proprieties, not least those associated with property in slaves. In keeping with nearly a decade of upheaval

The Kansas and Fugitive Slave Act Emergencies

Kansas stalwarts circa 1865 (The New York Public Library)

James H. Lane, jayhawker and senator
(The Library of Congress)

Sherman Booth: antislavery journalist,
fugitive rescuer, sex offender
(Wisconsin Historical Society)

Eminent antislavery men (The New York Public Library)

Margaret Garner confronted (The New York Public Library)

Lucy Stone with daughter (The Library of Congress)

The Oberlin Rescuers: Orindatus Simon Bolivar Wall, second from left, wearing hat; Charles Langston, ninth from right, holding hat against chest; schoolteacher William Lincoln, third from right; professor Henry Peck, second from right (The Library of Congress)

Salmon Chase (National Archives and Records Administration)

Future president Chester Arthur, outfitted for
Kansas in 1856 (Courtesy of the author)

The Harpers Ferry Conspiracy and Glorifying John Brown

GEORGE L. STEARNS

GERRIT SMITH

FRANK B. SANBORN

T. W. HIGGINSON

THEODORE PARKER

SAMUEL G. HOWE

JOHN BROWN'S NORTHERN SUPPORTERS

The Secret Six: John Brown's Northern supporters
(West Virginia Archives and History)

THE WAR COMMENCED.—JOHN BROWN RECEIVING RIFLES FOR "HIS KANSAS WORK." Page 1.

John Brownism illustrated (The New York Public Library)

HARPER'S FERRY INSURRECTION—BRINGING THE PRISONERS OUT OF THE ENGINE-HOUSE.—FROM A SKETCH BY OUR SPECIAL ARTIST.

The rout at Harpers Ferry (The New York Public Library)

Henry David Thoreau
(The Library of Congress)

Warren.   *Cambridgeport.*

Bust of John Brown commissioned by
Mary Stearns and George L. Stearns
(The New York Public Library)

War and Emancipation

Wide Awakes in New York City, 1860 (The New York Public Library)

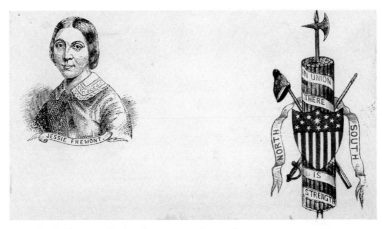

Jessie Fremont depicted on a campaign mailer (Joseph H. Treyz Collection,
Binghamton University Libraries, Binghamton University, State University of New York)

Three Antislavery Generals

— ❧❦ —

General John C. Fremont and his European-style bodyguard
(The Library of Congress)

General David Hunter
(The New York Public Library)

MAJ. GEN. B. F. BUTLER.
Statesman and Patriot.

General Benjamin Butler, "the Bluebeard of New Orleans" and author of the contraband policy (The New York Public Library)

United States Colored Troops

Black officers of the 54th Massachusetts Volunteers,
with Stephen A. Swails at bottom left

(Florida Memory / State Archives of Florida)

ADDRESSING THE COLORED TROOPS AT NASHVILLE, TENN., 1864.

John Mercer Langston addressing black troops, 1864 (The New York Public Library)

Adjutant General Lorenzo Thomas,
recruiter of more than seventy thousand
black troops (The Library of Congress)

Fort Pillow, a no-quarter military engagement for black troops
(The Beinecke Library / Yale University)

Butler Medal from the 1864 James River Campaign
(The New York Public Library)

Harriet Tubman, Union scout (The Library of Congress)

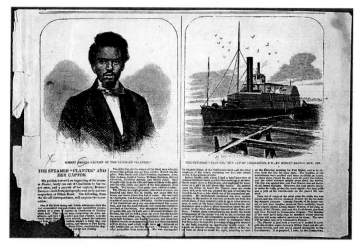

Robert Smalls, captain of the USS *Planter* (The New York Public Library)

John S. Rock: "Black will be a very pretty color."
(The New York Public Library)

Monument to James D. Lynch, a minister, educator, and
black Republican (Courtesy of Tom Rankin)

on the Kansas frontier, Civil War–era operations perpetuated old outrages under cover of legitimate military operations. During raids against Missourians around Christmas 1861, for example, fighters led by the namesake of all jayhawkers, Dr. Charles Jennison, the "Gay Yorker" from New York City, had liberated, looted, murdered, and destroyed, shooting in cold blood a pair of brothers seeking to hide a slave woman from the liberators. By early 1862, Jennison's irregulars had been integrated into the U.S. armed forces, officially renamed the Seventh Kansas Cavalry.[3]

It was bad enough in the eyes of critics that the War Department did nothing to stop the frontier abuses; unbeknownst to the public, President Lincoln had given the Kansas operations his personal seal of approval.

Dirty Jim Lane had returned to Mary Lincoln's White House, boarding there during the winter session of the Senate. He had finally been commissioned to raise a unit of Kansas volunteers—a call to arms long delayed by the efforts of Kansas moderates who despaired to think of their outlandish nemesis wearing a general's star. The Price campaign had elevated Kansas to emergency status and compelled the army to dispense with existing procedures for raising troops. Fortunately for the Union, the new state was already home to a half dozen or more active military units sustained by the philanthropy of George L. Stearns. The problem was to integrate these notorious units into the standard, and with any luck legal, operations of the U.S. Army.

Meeting with the president, Lane was quick to defend the racial politics of the Kansas militants: Indians must be allowed to enlist, he pleaded, and the policy of seizing the slaves of disloyal households must continue. Lincoln acceded to the first point, agreeing to appoint Native Americans as enlisted soldiers and officers, a policy that eventually resulted in a captain's commission for Charles Bluejacket. On the seizure of slaves he expressed misgivings, but not about the legality of piecemeal emancipation. Lincoln cautioned Lane against continuing the current policy of some Kansas commanders of returning enslaved persons, guaranteeing freedom only to those held by rebels.

"The only difference between you and me is that you are willing to surrender fugitives to loyal owners," said Lincoln on January 17, "while I do not believe the United States government has any right to give them up in any case." If it could, he added, he guessed that "the people would not permit us to exercise it." Thus President Lincoln showed himself to the left of the notoriously Radical Kansas senator and militant on the issue of ad hoc emancipation.[4]

Executions and theft were other matters, however. Dr. Jennison was to be disciplined and, soon enough, dismissed from the army.[5]

On his way back to Kansas, Lane checked in with the supreme commander of U.S. forces, George McClellan—a man as fastidious and conservative as Lane was wild and rough. Lane described his plan of operations: to march south from Kansas until he reached the Gulf of Mexico, starting by eliminating disloyal persons in Missouri, Arkansas, and Indian territory. "Sir," said Lane, "I will kill off the white traitors and give their lands to the loyal black men!"

The declaration produced what must have been McClellan's only recorded belly laugh during the war. "You must work out your own plans," he said. "Go your own way, and see to it that no rebel sets his foot in Kansas."[6]

Back in Kansas, Lane initiated one of the first campaigns to enlist black soldiers in the U.S. Army—an outgrowth and complement to the jayhawking and John Brown tradition and the recruitment of Native Americans, including tribes with enslaved and affiliated African Americans. Until 1861, Republican Radicalism had championed emancipation—and in certain isolated cases such as New York's streetcar and voting rights initiatives, a measure of support for Northern free blacks. The campaign for black enlistment led by partisans like Lane and also by African American agitators emerged as the latest Radical Republican political initiative.

Black enlistment furthered the military interests of the United States, particularly in areas with a scarcity of Union personnel—in frontier Kansas, for example, or along the lower stretch of the Atlantic states, where the U.S. Navy laid claim to coastal islands late in 1861. Black and political advocates of inducting black troops also hoped to use military service as a springboard to the advancement of the population.

Outside the South, black enlistment promised to boost the claim of participants to the full rights of citizens, despite the prohibitions theoretically imposed by the *Dred Scott* doctrine. In occupied parts of the Confederacy, starting with the Sea Islands and gaining ground with Union victories in the western theater, the drive to enlist black men against their former masters took on profound momentum, enlarging the sphere of wartime emancipation and rapidly elevating the standing in society of former slaves.

The drive to incorporate black men into the armed forces of the United States originated in the U.S. Navy and traced its origins to the long-standing tradition of racial and cultural mixing on seafaring ships. In an era when sailors were subject to corporal and capital punishment without trial, in addition to scurvy, dysentery, shipboard epidemics, piracy, shipwrecks, and enemy bombardment, naval commanders could not afford to be selective about personnel. This branch of the service also opened the first territory in the South, where the proximity to people held in bondage created a natural military affinity.

The Navy had achieved the first major victory of the war with the capture of Port Royal, South Carolina, a spit of land amid a clustering of large islands and tidal estuaries, in November 1861. Delivering a force of thirteen thousand Union soldiers, the fleet initiated the rapid conquest of neighboring waterways and landmasses, including Hilton Head and Phillips Islands, home to vanquished fortifications defending the port. Troops and armaments under the command of Flag Officer Samuel Du Pont reached north over the coming weeks to Beaufort, Lady's, and St. Helena Islands, and the waterways below the city of Charleston. They moved south, to Tybee Island, Georgia, and to Fernandina and St. Augustine in coastal Florida. The Sea Islands—as they were known collectively in the war era—became home to the first Union army outpost, named the Department of the South. Not incidentally, they were also the site of the largest early encounter between the North and its armies and the population that Confederates had held in bondage.

A key player in the Sea Islands enlistment drama was Major General David Hunter, a career officer who became a friend of Abraham Lincoln during the presidential campaign. Hunter's reassignment to head the army's Department of the South in March 1862 gave new life to a vision of conquest and racial liberation that he had previously proposed as the temporary commander of the Department of the West. Hunter hoped to take Savannah by land in April 1862—and to initiate a fiery revolution among the dense population of Low Country blacks. The early failure of his military assault did not mean a defeat for Hunter's political goals, as the movement of his armies in itself had accelerated a process already initiated by the arrival of gunboats. As white owners and overseers retreated from the area, large numbers of newly independent African Americans fell within the lines of the United States or made their way to safety by their own devices.

Black army regiments occupied a central place in Hunter's scheme, and the general faced two challenges in bringing his plan into practice. To begin, he needed to slow the enrollment of eligible freedmen into the Navy in order to secure sufficient men and talent for his own regiments. More daunting, Hunter also had to overcome the racial constraints on enlistment that governed the army, imposed by a 1792 prohibition on black enlistment. Though irregular and state militia forces had been known to be integrated—most famously the troops directed by General Andrew Jackson in the Battle of New Orleans—the army had been lily-white since the era of George Washington. Hunter acted to alter army policy in April 1862 with what he saw as authorization from Abraham Lincoln's War Department.

Secretary of War Edwin Stanton had served in James Buchanan's cabinet as a Democrat; his defection to the Lincoln administration early in 1862 indicated the ongoing dissolution of the party in the North during the Civil War years. Stanton's emergence as a Radical coincided almost exactly with his assumption of his new duties, signaled first in the text of an editorial suggestion that Stanton offered his friend Simon Cameron, Lincoln's first secretary of war. Cameron was unwise enough to incorporate Stanton's language into a War Department report for publication: "It is as clearly a right of the Government to arm slaves, when it may become necessary, as it is to use gunpowder taken from the enemy," Cameron wrote, dedicating a short paragraph to the topic. As it turned out, the overreaching on black troops was the final breach of trust between the president and Cameron, who had long worked under a cloud of corruption charges. Seeking his replacement, Lincoln happened to select the lawyer and intriguer who had proposed the offending text.[7]

Stanton not only advocated arming black soldiers, but also had particular ideas about their deployment, dress, and drill. In conversations with Cameron he had expressed an interest in the use of scarlet pantaloons to distinguish colored troops. The idea was practical as well as fun, making use of the large War Department stock of red pants acquired during the short-lived Zouave uniform craze of 1861. Zouaves, who wore distinctive "oriental" headgear and jackets in addition to their pantaloons, proved more vulnerable than soldiers in regulation dress to the advanced weaponry of the Civil War. Few white troops were willing to accept the red requisitions by the spring of 1862. Perhaps the same idea had occurred to David Hunter by some coincidence; as it happened, in any case, Hunter's Sea Islands requisition was for fifty thousand pairs of scarlet pantaloons.

"Please let me have my way on the subject of slavery," he had written to Stanton from the West back in January: "The Administration will not be responsible. I alone will bear the blame; you can censure me, arrest me, dismiss me, hang me if you will, but permit me to make my mark in such a way as to be remembered by friend and foe." Hunter's plan was to offer a test case for military emancipation, an initiative that gained the tacit approval of the War Department and the president.[8]

Hunter's instructions, as he later described them, were to enroll "such loyal men as I can find in the country" (a population that could scarcely be thought to include fifty thousand whites willing to serve in the Union Army). He quoted from official War Department orders authorizing him to establish "squads, companies, or otherwise" at his discretion. Opening recruitment in mid-April, Hunter had amassed enough recruits to start commissioning officers by early May 1862. Keeping the words "black" and "contraband" out of his correspondence, he solicited "the most intelligent and energetic of our non-commissioned officers" to apply, "men who will go into it with all their hearts."[9]

The first white man to accept the call to duty was Hunter's own orderly, Sergeant Charles Tyler Trowbridge, a budding Radical Republican from Brooklyn, New York. With the sergeant and his brother John Trowbridge signing on as captain and lieutenant, respectively, Company A of the First South Carolina Volunteers was formally mustered into the service.

Determined to establish fifty regiments, General Hunter pressed forward hastily with two controversial sets of orders. All black men of military age in the region were subject to conscription, he declared. Consistent with these duties and in keeping with martial law, he observed, in his General Order Number 11, issued on May 9, 1862, the black population of three states—Georgia, South Carolina, and Florida—"heretofore held as slaves, are therefore declared forever free."[10]

The Hunter Emancipation did not inspire the same enthusiasm among Radicals and abolitionists as the 1861 edict issued by John C. Fremont. As part of an off-the-books scheme with administration sponsors, it was far less publicized. Alongside Secretary Stanton and his requisitions, support for the orders also materialized from the Treasury Department. Secretary Salmon Chase saw control of the fifteen-thousand-strong black population of the Sea Islands region as a boon to the Union and an avenue to fame and good fortune for himself, as a master of the increasingly inevitable transition from slavery to freedom. With his encouragement, missionaries calling themselves Gideonites arrived to supply and educate the formerly enslaved population. Their ranks included a number of individuals reporting directly to Chase on their work: an associate from Ohio, the Reverend Mansfield French; Laura Towne, a Philadelphia Quaker; and Edward L. Pierce—of the Boston Bird Club Pierces—acting on special assignment from the Treasury Department. Chase also arranged to send his own sweetheart, the reformer and government mathematician Susan Walker, whom the secretary, a three-time widower, did not dare to marry.[11]

Chase's contacts reported favorably on Hunter's emancipation edict but complained about the orders requiring compulsory military service. The War Department, seeking cover after the detection of the operation by members of Congress, formally dissolved the First South Carolina Volunteers. The regiment entered into a guerrilla stage during which the Trowbridge brothers drilled their hard-cores and kept their spirits up with speeches about the rights of citizens.

Lincoln weighed in on the Hunter controversy in May 1862, but his instructions carried none of the sting that had attended the Fremont Emancipation. Though the president took the trouble to publicly disavow the Hunter Emancipation in a formal declaration, he admitted (in lines stricken from the original text before publication) only that he had not "expressly" or "implicitly" authorized Hunter's actions. Lincoln cast no aspersions on General Hunter; in fact, he used the occasion to speculate in public for the first time that the abolition of slavery in the South might "become a necessity indispensable to the maintenance of government." Lincoln drew attention to recent legislation to aid states initiating gradual emancipation, suggesting that the Hunter Emancipation served as a likely alternative where the rebellion persisted.

"You can not if you would, be blind to the sign of the times," wrote Lincoln, in more lines stricken from the text. Like Hunter, Lincoln had come to see the hand of God in the mix, an emotional and spiritual perception heightened by the tragic death of eleven-year-old Willie Lincoln in February 1862. The events of the day required considerations, wrote Lincoln, "ranging, if it may be far above personal and partisan politics."[12]

Even the palliated edition of the president's renunciation rang with muted applause for General Hunter, an impression reinforced by Hunter's perpetuation in command of the Department of the South. "We shall need all the anti-slavery feeling in the country and more," Lincoln had told Moncure Conway and other Boston abolitionists that winter, urging them to fight harder for public awareness. He welcomed controversy even at the expense of his own standing among passionate observers. "Don't spare me!" he said laughingly to Conway. "You may say anything you like about me, if that will help."[13] The president took pleasure in the example of the Hunter Emancipation for the proslavery party, North and South. He may even have welcomed the ensuing controversy among Radical Republicans.

On June 9, Democrats in the House of Representatives resolved to learn the truth about rumors of black troops making their way out of the Sea Islands, demanding information and copies of all correspondence in a formal summons to the secretary of war. Stanton responded by denying all knowledge and refusing to submit communications, noting that the president considered such disclosures to be "improper and incompatible with the public interest." After a considerable delay, Hunter submitted a lengthy response that was read aloud in the House of Representatives.

Hunter denied that a regiment of fugitive slaves had been assembled under his command, citing from the text of a congressional resolution condemning his acts. He went on,

There is however a fine regiment of persons whose former masters are "fugitive rebels"—men who everywhere fly before the appearance of the national flag . . . So far, indeed, are the loyal persons composing this regiment from seeking to avoid the presence of their late owners, that they are now, one and all, working with remarkable industry to place themselves in a position to go in full and effective pursuit of their fugacious and traitorous proprietors.[14]

Some Republicans in the House laughed audibly as the reading continued. On the topic of authorization, Hunter cited his instructions from former secretary of war Simon Cameron to the effect that loyal persons would be put at the service of the United States, a text that failed to specify eligibility by race.

As to his authority to issue uniforms and weapons to recruits, Hunter admitted he had none:

> Neither have I had any specific authority for supplying these persons with shovels, spades, and pickaxes, when employing them as laborers, nor with boats and oars when using them as lightermen; but these are not points included in [the congressional] resolution. To me it seemed that liberty to employ men in any particular capacity implied with it liberty, also, to supply them with the necessary tools; and acting upon that faith I have clothed, equipped, and armed the only loyal regiment yet raised in South Carolina.

If their goal had been to find a "smoking gun" linking the Lincoln War Department to Hunter's actions in the field, the members of Congress had asked the general the wrong question. It was not a matter of whether the would-be troops had been supplied with pants, as it were, but whether the pants provided happened to be red.

Congress had not asked Hunter for his estimation of the success of the initiative, but the general was happy to report:

> The experiment of arming the blacks, so far as I have made it, has been a complete and even marvelous success. They are sober, docile, attentive, and enthusiastic; displaying great natural capacities for acquiring the duties of

the soldier. They are eager, beyond all things, to take the field and be led into action.

In conclusion, Hunter indicated his hope "to have organized by the end of next fall, and to be able to present to government, from forty-eight to fifty thousand of these hardy and devoted soldiers"—in short, to have launched a revolution in a little less than six months.[15]

While Stanton was doing his best to put the Hunter controversy to rest, generals in other theaters of the war were assailing Washington with a flood of communications on the same explosive subject.

The capture of New Orleans was strictly speaking a Democratic Party idea, executed by a Democratic regiment with officers selected for their Democratic views by a prominent Democrat, himself driven by a lifelong reverence to pay homage to the Father of the Democracy, Andrew Jackson, by ensuring that "the Union must and shall be preserved" at New Orleans, the site of Jackson's famous victory in the War of 1812. Never mind that the man who captured the city, General Benjamin Franklin Butler, was in nearly all respects Republican by 1862 and that he offered Lincoln his Democrat recruitment scheme with a wink and a smile: the nation needed Democrats and Republicans alike to press for victory. And New Orleans was a prize in its own right: the second city of the South and second-largest port in the United States, set at the endpoint of more than two thousand miles of Mississippi River traffic.

Best of all, it could be had without the firing of a shot—by Butler, anyway, as his army needed merely to be transported across the muddy, surging theater of war.

White people comprised the most numerous proportion of the population of New Orleans in the Civil War era, however distinctly creole and African American culture may have marked its institutions. In capturing its first Southern city, Huntsville, Alabama (Beaufort in the Sea Islands being only a port), the Union Army had encountered at least some gestures of support. Most famously, a white Huntsville attorney and native-born Deep South Republican, George Lane, displayed an American flag at his home as soon as Yankee troops came into view. Not so in New Orleans, where an apparently united front greeted Butler on the wharves. No armed rebels were present, but the crowd shouted for Jefferson Davis and General P.T.G. Beauregard, who made his home nearby in a quiet nook of the city's French Quarter. The crowd cheered for William P. Mumford, a middle-aged man who climbed up to remove a U.S. flag newly raised above the Customs House.

Establishing his headquarters at the city's finest hotel, General Butler ordered Mumford's arrest and warned the population about attacks on U.S. dignity. "They shall fear the *stripes* if they do not reverence the *stars* of our banner," he wrote.[16]

Between April and December 1862, Benjamin Butler's occupation of New Orleans produced comparisons to the Spanish Conquest and the Haitian Revolution. The general was distinctive in appearance: large-headed, cross-eyed, and magnetic. He reveled in the role of conquering antihero, staging ostentatious military parades, removing the mayor and police chief from their offices, closing newspapers, arresting women and clergymen who refused to pray for the Union, and cracking down on rebel expression of all kinds, holding up William Mumford as an example in a public hanging on June 7.

The commander brought a devilish humor to his work. After incidents in which women ostentatiously turned their backs on U.S. soldiers, Butler cracked that New Orleans women "evidently know which end of them looks best" and threatened their arrest for solicitation. To the famous statue of his hero Andrew Jackson in the city square he added a quotation on the base that summarized the politics of the military occupation: THE UNION MUST AND SHALL BE PRESERVED.[17]

Butler's picaresque made good news copy, but New Orleans beefs were picayune in the context of the looming question of the Slave Power and the war. The real Radical bastion lay upriver from the city, within the portion of plantation country secured by the farthest Union advance. Here a controversial Union leasing program allowed loyal planters to make use of the partially intact slave labor force. Alongside these commercial enterprises, swelling ranks of refugee camps testified to the crack-up of the traditional order.

Assigned to hardship duty in this sweaty district was General John W.

Phelps, a Vermonter and veteran of the Seminole and Mexican Wars. In a division assembled by Butler as a Democratic Party auxiliary, Phelps was notably a Radical Republican, a close associate and friend of Vermont's Republican governor, Frederick Holbrooke. Phelps could be numbered among those Republicans eager for the Lincoln administration to make up its mind about slavery and black soldiers. "Instead of taking a strong hold of the question and of the country we are using policy," Phelps complained in his diary on May 15. "What we are doing it is not possible to tell."[18]

His command at Fort Parapet in Carrollton, Louisiana, gave Phelps an opportunity to spur the national debate. The first sign of conflict emerged with the onset of the rainy season late in May 1862. Butler's orders were to roust up "contrabands" to reinforce a number of levees north of the city—a flood control measure local whites had recommended urgently. Phelps responded with what eventually turned out to be a flat refusal, complaining in his diary that the assignment was immoral.

> Hence, negroes who flee from their masters a hundred miles off, and seek protection from the United States are—what?—not formed into Regiments to oppose the wicked rebellion . . . but are set to work by United States authority to protect those masters against the threatening of nature made doubly formidable by the crimes of their masters who, neglecting their levees, turn their attention to the destroying of our government.[19]

Instead, Phelps set about to organize eligible black men into military companies for a proposed assault upon Baton Rouge. To ensure an adequate enlistment, he employed his regular troops to investigate conditions on surrounding plantations, delivering to the base any persons who complained of ill treatment.

White elites were appalled to hear about a Yankee general personally drilling black recruits in the hot sun. When Phelps sent a crew of five hundred for artillery training at the Gulf Coast Fort Jackson and St. Philip naval stations, the news generated controversy far beyond Louisiana.[20]

Butler viewed Phelps and his new soldiers with pointed interest. For all the bluster, Butler's "Department of the Gulf" consisted only of his thirteen thousand troops, hard pressed to defend the city or extend their conquests far beyond its limits. Stretching troops along this thin line, Butler may have imagined the military advantages to be gained from black recruitment.

The political dimensions of the move also caught Butler's attention. In June 1862, just as he had started to address Phelps and his initiative—rewarding the Vermonter with a promotion and a gift of shoulder straps, which Phelps refused—the controversy surrounding David Hunter's emancipation and enlistment program in the Department of the South made headlines. Secretary Stanton pleaded with Butler to use his well-known political wiles to keep the Phelps issue out of the newspapers, suggesting in a letter to Butler that Lincoln did not wish to interfere with Phelps's enterprise.

Butler did not remain quiet, leaking his own communications with Phelps to the newspapers before July 4. He considered it a measure of success that his enemies had offered $10,000 for his assassination, Butler told reporters. Go ahead, he let it be known: Phelps would succeed him.[21]

Back in Washington, pressures mounted in favor of more Radical policies. The Radical Republican contingent in Congress pressed the issue in a flurry of proposed bills addressing both the status of refugees from slavery and the authority for recruiting black troops. The omnibus of legislation passed as the Second Confiscation Act, for example, stipulated that all slaves of rebels reaching Union lines obtained their freedom. The act also authorized the president to enlist "persons of African descent" for any service he deemed "necessary and proper." A Militia Act—championed by Henry Wilson of Massachusetts—passed in Congress on July 17, explicitly providing for the recruitment of black troops and offering freedom to their families.

Northern conservatives hastened the pace of change by their insistence on remaining "blind to the times." The antislavery thrust of the Hunter and Phelps occupations had produced a backlash against U.S. military policy. A satirical summary of complaints appeared in a Republican newspaper: "[The Army] must be further weeded of abolitionists. Hunter must follow Fremont; Democratic Butler, even, cannot be trusted; and Secretary Stanton, though of the same political school, is assailed with every epithet of abuse because he is supposed to wink at the employment of blacks in the army."[22]

Speaking for conservatives (and as the supreme commander of U.S. forces), General McClellan presented Lincoln with a letter demanding the protection of private property, including the enslaved, during a pained meeting at McClellan's headquarters at Harrison's Landing, Virginia. On the heels of the failure of the Army of the Potomac in the Peninsula Campaign, the McClellan's insistence on limited war proved especially galling. Representatives of the Border States, summoned to the White House on July 12, refused pointedly to take action on the president's proposal for compensated emancipation.[23]

Abraham Lincoln confronted these pressures amid wrenching emotional times. The whole North mourned the failures of the war in Virginia that summer, with no news from the western front to enliven the public mood. The young child of Edwin Stanton passed away, roiling the president's experience of Willie's death only months before. In the days surrounding Stanton's memorial services on July 13, Lincoln explained to Secretary of State Seward and Secretary of the Navy Gideon Welles that he had resolved to abolish slavery in the rebellious states. "He said that he had given it much thought and had about come to the conclusion that it was a military necessity absolutely essential to the salvation of the Union," Welles recorded in his diary, "that we would free the slaves or be ourselves subdued."[24]

On July 22, 1862, President Lincoln read aloud to his cabinet from a document two paragraphs long, including the following statement:

> As a fit and necessary military measure for effecting [the restoration of the Union], I, as Commander-in-Chief of the Army and Navy of the United States, do order and declare that on the first day of January in the Year of Our Lord one thousand, eight hundred and sixty three, all persons held as slaves within any state or states wherein the constitutional authority of the United States shall not then be practically recognized, submitted to, and maintained, shall then, thenceforward, and forever, be free.[25]

Lincoln's draft included a plea for federally compensated voluntary emancipation in the loyal slave states, and a justification of his action on the authority created by the Second Confiscation Act passed by Congress only on July 17. He was determined to issue the proclamation but solicited the thoughts of his advisers, in the end accepting Seward's suggestion that he wait for a military victory to make the pronouncement.

Awaiting the right moment to unveil the Emancipation Proclamation—at the outset of a series of disappointments for the Union war effort—Lincoln fed the suspicions of Radicals and abolitionists who thought he would never move against slavery. Radicals who supported the Hunter and Phelps Emancipations—led by Treasury Secretary Chase—were disappointed that Lincoln would not consider military service as a gateway to freedom, a "better and quieter" policy than a proclamation, in Chase's opinion.[26] More troubling still were the president's gestures in support of colonizing freed African Americans at an overseas location. Lincoln met with Samuel Pomeroy, the Kansas filibusterer and senator, to organize a U.S. colony for blacks on the Central American isthmus. He also hosted a disastrous meeting with black District of Columbia ministers in which he disparaged their prospects for attaining equality in the United States, called their expectations "selfish," and proposed that they organize to leave the country.[27] William Lloyd Garrison—appalled and embarrassed—called the president a cynic and a liar, and Frederick Douglass called Lincoln the tool of Border State racists.[28]

Lincoln, a master of misdirection, concealment, and shaping public opinion, may well have been continuing his strategy of stimulating public discussion of emancipation and its significance. If so, he was more straightforward in preparing conservatives to accept the new policy, a goal abetted by the continuing apostasy of John W. Phelps.

Phelps's recruitment and training of black troops produced more and more controversy as the summer progressed, emerging as a topic of national discussions by the end of July. In answer to a complaint by Maryland senator Reverdy S. Johnson, Lincoln referred specifically to Phelps in the context of the emerging emancipation policy. Summarizing Johnson, Lincoln observed that Southerners were short-sighted to complain of being "annoyed by General Phelps."

If they can conceive of anything worse than General Phelps, within my power, would they not better be looking out for it? They very well know the way to avert all this is simply to take their place in the Union upon the old terms. If they will not do this, should they not receive harder blows rather than lighter ones?

Johnson should know better than to underestimate the possibility of an escalation, Lincoln said. His letter served notice that "it may as well be understood, once and for all, that I shall not surrender this game leaving any available card unplayed."[29]

To abolish slavery was to kill the wolf that had endangered the survival of the American experiment. Abolitionists girded for combat like Generals Hunter and Phelps operated in accordance with natural law, transcending the requirements of mere military regulations. They embodied the spiritual and philosophical imperatives at the center of the Radical Republican movement. Their advocacy proved a valuable foil for Lincoln's outwardly conservative campaign to build a consensus around military emancipation. Beyond the control of government policy and tangled up with matters of military necessity and expedience, the Radicals had moved from the margins to the center of debate.

12

ARMING AFRICAN AMERICANS

The announcement on an autumn night in 1862 was received with "deafening cheers" at Shiloh Church on Prince Street in Manhattan. Robert Smalls of Charleston Harbor, South Carolina, was in the house, he who had "with his comrades, seized a rebel gunboat, rescued his family and those of his companions from Slavery, pass[ed] six forts, reach[ed] the Union squadron, and present[ed] the Government with the trophies of his achievement," as organizers of the occasion described him. Smalls had come to tell his incredible story—and to beat the drum for black military enlistment, object of his semiofficial visit to the North as the representative of the occupied Department of the South. The patrons persisted in "wild and prolonged cheering," presented Smalls with a gold medal, and passed five congratulatory resolutions.

While they were crazy about Smalls, black New Yorkers could scarcely summon a single kind word about the other big event of the fortnight—Abraham Lincoln's Preliminary Emancipation Proclamation, issued after the victory of Union forces at Antietam Creek in Maryland late in September.

The Reverend James N. Gloucester—the militant Brooklyn minister—said he "regretted the ninety days' delay" before the freedom edict took effect, which he considered "as merely a day of grace for the rebels." The Reverend Henry Highland Garnet denounced the Preliminary Proclamation's references to colonization, insisting that freedmen should be free to remain in place. In resolutions voted by acclamation, the crowd excoriated the Lincoln administration for disregarding the capacity and patriotism of what they called "four million black Unionists now living in the rebel or semi-rebel states."[1]

The preliminary proclamation reiterated the claim, tiresome to black people, that the primary aim of the war was restoring the Union. It urged Congress to compensate loyal states that adopted legal emancipation and to provide funds for the colonization of freedmen overseas. The only part of the decree that was truly "preliminary," moreover, was its failure to take effect immediately, with the roughly ninety-day grace period expiring on January 1, 1863, affecting only the areas still in rebellion on that date. Black Americans such as those on Prince Street may have been the first to perceive—as revisionists later liked to claim—that the promised proclamation would result in the emancipation of essentially no one.

On the positive side, two other elements were apparently intended to take effect right away: to enforce the Confiscation Act's prohibition on the return of fugitives to purported owners, and to prohibit members of the armed forces from cooperating in the restoration of fugitives. An unspoken new commitment, moreover, brought the Lincoln administration into alignment with the work of Robert Smalls and the Radical sponsors of his mission.

If anyone in America could make the case for black military service it was Smalls, then serving as a seaman in the U.S. Navy and a special emissary of the army high command in his district. Admiral Samuel Francis Du Pont considered Smalls "superior to any [man] that has yet come into the lines," and he relied on the ensign to conceive the 1862 naval campaign against Charleston.[2] Small's store of knowledge included Confederate signals and code, the location of mines in Charleston Harbor, the location of military strongpoints, and strategic alignments—most notably the relative scarcity of rebel forces in certain districts.[3] Within weeks of his defection, he had helped to orchestrate movements that resulted in the capture of the Stono River region of South Carolina. It was a step toward meeting the Lincoln administration's high expectations for the Charleston campaign, a doomed enterprise but one that carried a heavy burden of symbolism.

The renegade pilot had also proved adept at negotiating political differences in the Sea Islands, where military officials, white missionaries, and

Treasury officials had a hard time making themselves understood among local people. Though he was only twenty-three years old, illiterate, and subject to the doubts of a racist society, Smalls assumed an oversized role in shaping U.S. policy in a high-profile theater of the war.

The idea of sending Smalls to Washington and New York originated with the agitator General David Hunter, then in his final weeks in command of the Department of the South. Hunter's dream had been consistently bound up with the idea of forming black regiments, a goal that seemed to be unraveling that summer in the aftermath of the forced disbandment of his own First South Carolina Volunteers. Hunter had learned all about Smalls from Admiral Du Pont; he believed that Smalls was just the man to make the case for black recruitment in the War Department. On August 9, Smalls had been summoned to a meeting with Hunter, Du Pont, and the incoming military governor of the Sea Islands, a Massachusetts Radical named Rufus K. Saxton. He accepted an assignment to represent the cause of black enlistment in the army.

Accompanied by the Republican missionary Mansfield French, he met extensively with Secretary Stanton, Salmon Chase, and Lincoln himself. At the White House, he spent more than an hour with the president, who asked Smalls just how he summoned the courage for his heroic act. Smalls would also hit the fund-raising and publicity circuit, traveling with French to New York City for his church appearance in October.

Smalls returned to headquarters at Hilton Head carrying a letter signed by Stanton and the president, providing the first official authorization to initiate the formation of black regiments.[4] The document that he delivered in person to General Saxton, commander of the Department of the South, bore the imprint of the former bondsman's discussions with the high and mighty. Secretary Stanton wrote Saxton that he approved the enlistment of up to five thousand soldiers of African descent, a necessary limit in light of "the small force under your command, and the inability of the Government at this time to increase it." In exchange for their service, "the wives, mothers, and children" of enlisted men were declared "forever free." Black soldiers would receive "the same pay and rations as are allowed by law."

Stanton—considered intemperate, intriguing, and insincere, even by friends—chided Saxton for his hesitancy in taking the same steps toward creating black regiments that had resulted in the eventual removal of his predecessor, General Hunter. "It is considered by this Department that the instructions given at the time of your appointment were sufficient to enable you to do what you have now requested authority for doing." In order to "place your authority beyond all doubt," the secretary wrote, with a hint of triumph, "you are hereby authorized and instructed."[5]

Stanton's instructions made no reference to the race or previous experience of the new regiments' officers. By instinct, Saxton sought white men, including the persistent Brooklynites Charles and John A. Trowbridge, who had remained with the "First South Carolina" during the months when it was officially disbanded. The Trowbridges were fighters—even scrappers. At a time when black men feared being assigned only menial tasks in the armed forces, no soldiers under their instruction could be mistaken for a merely ceremonial guard or work detail. All were combat veterans, having participated off the books in skirmishes on St. Simon's Island.[6]

To send a message of the deadly earnestness of the new force, General Hunter hoped also to commission a commanding officer of impeccably militant antislavery credentials. One name above all others invoked the John Brown spirit. The appointment of Thomas Wentworth Higginson, should he accept it, would send the message that the first official regiments of black troops would be used in combat. If they were not, his sponsors understood, Higginson would be the best man to make his objections heard in Radical circles.

Higginson had been slow to join the war, not because he lacked the physical courage, of course, but because he had been sidelined by one of his many passions. In 1861 and 1862, the Worcester minister had come into his own as a writer, publishing articles on a number of topics in the *Atlantic Monthly* and other journals. His reputation grew at such a rate that he attracted a following and gained a reputation as a mentor and critic of other work. Earlier in 1862, he had received unsolicited the first examples of the poetry of Emily Dickinson, who shyly inquired if Higginson considered her verses to have any merit. Struck by her genius, he had devoted himself to editing and publicizing Dickinson's work alongside his own.[7]

Higginson may have also delayed on the grounds that the Union-only war policy of the Lincoln administration fell far short of Radical goals. He could hardly present himself as "non-resistant," in any case. On the occasion of his first commitment to raise a regiment—early in September 1862—*The Liberator* was at pains to point out that the minister had never been "technically, a 'Garrisonian abolitionist,'" as many readers assumed him to be. Instead, *The Liberator* corrected, "[he] has always acted with the Republican party."[8] On the eve of the Emancipation Proclamation, Higginson may have perceived the revolutionary trajectory of army policy overwhelming the hesitancy within the Lincoln administration. If so, Higginson would have been one of the few Radicals to see the truth behind President Lincoln's consensus-building obfuscation and feints to the right in the weeks leading up to the proclamation of September 22.

In any case, Higginson was serving as a captain in a Massachusetts camp when he received the summons to South Carolina. He could scarcely resist the enticements of the offer: to fight for emancipation; to rise in the officers' ranks; and to go down in history as the first commander of black troops. "I had been an abolitionist too long and had known and loved John Brown too well," he wrote, "not to feel a thrill of joy on finding myself in the position where he only wished to be."

Commissioned as a colonel, Higginson steamed toward Port Royal, going to the South for the first time in his life. He wrote in his diary about his first view of the "universal Southern panorama" of live oaks and Spanish moss. Alongside it, he saw a sight "so un-Southern that the whole Southern coast at this moment trembles at the suggestion of such a thing—the camp of a regiment of freed slaves."[9]

Higginson's account of being present in the Sea Islands for the Department of the South celebration of January 1, 1863, has become a classic of Civil War literature. After a reading of the Emancipation Proclamation, he stood upon a platform and received the regimental colors for the first time. A spontaneous rendition by a trio of African American voices of "My Country, 'Tis of Thee" stirred the crowd to religious and patriotic ecstasy. "I never saw anything so electric," Higginson wrote in his journal: "It made all other words cheap; it seemed the choked voice of a race, at last unloosed . . . Art could not have dreamed of a tribute to the day of jubilee that could be so affecting; history will not believe it; and when I came to speak of it, after it was silent, tears were everywhere." In the ceremony in occupied territory, the abolitionist and writer found his two callings joined.[10]

The final version of the Emancipation Proclamation published on January 1, 1863, gave Radicals everywhere cause to celebrate. The document revealed the president's gravitation toward their side of the political spectrum, specifying terms more Radical than those envisioned in the preliminary version. For example, the January proclamation asserted that the army and navy would "recognize and maintain" the freedom of persons liberated by the act. Freedmen were enjoined from violence but encouraged to engage in self-defense. The Emancipation Proclamation also formally initiated the enlistment of African Americans everywhere in the armed forces—a measure that moved black recruitment beyond its disputed origins into the mainstream of military policy.[11]

Emancipation under the proclamation represented a kind of opening rather than an end result. Its promise could only be realized by ongoing and expanded action. Thus the most effective Radical Republicans saw its issuance as a call to renewed action. Among those set in motion by the opportunity, none responded more immediately than the dedicated George L. Stearns.

Stearns made haste to visit Washington in January 1863 in the company of like-minded men: Dr. Howe, F. W. Bird, Wendell Phillips, a Virginia-born and Kansas-tested Radical minister, Moncure Conway, and Oakes Ames of Easton, Massachusetts, a shovel magnate, feminist, and former pacifist recently elected to the House of Representatives. The group had military business to address with Secretary Stanton and the president, particularly a recommendation that their standard-bearer John C. Fremont be established as military governor of North Carolina, where the current commander was seen as lukewarm on emancipation.

Radicals had remained steadfast in support of Fremont, celebrating his September 1861 emancipation decree as a game changer and proposing his name for a number of commands. A rumor that Fremont had been appointed "commander in chief" to replace the faltering McClellan was shouted across the picket lines during the proclamation ceremony Higginson described. The news, which turned out to be false, "was received with great enthusiasm." Fremont himself maintained his nearly complete silence on the subjects of slavery and black soldiers, excusing his inaction as an officer's gesture of restraint.

Enthusiasm for the general in antislavery circles reflected no small measure of respect for the general's wife, who managed to keep her name and her husband's in the spotlight in 1862 and 1863. Jessie Benton Fremont's *The Story of the Guard*, a romantic profile of the largely foreign-born honor guard that had surrounded Fremont in St. Louis, offered the family point of view on the events of 1861. The book also made claims for an expanded sphere of women's influence during wartime, including a shout-out to the emerging corps of professional nurses such as those employed in the Western Sanitary Commission, which she had helped to create during her time in St. Louis. The book celebrated "the new positions in which women are finding themselves during this strange phase of our national life," noting that "the restraints of ordinary times do not apply now." The slim volume was also "made spicy," a reviewer noted, by the publication of more of Fremont's strained 1861 communications with the actual commander in chief.[12]

Lincoln was happy to help Stearns and the others jump-start recruiting in occupied North Carolina. As regards the idea of Fremont as military governor, however, he parted ways with the Massachusetts delegation. Unmoved by Wendell Phillips's clumsy argument that it would "help him gain another four years of power," the president dismissed the proposal outright without so much as a humorous story.

Lincoln gained some personal experience with recruiting black troops in the region opened up by naval victories at New Bern, North Carolina, and the other outer reaches north of Charleston. Here a large and passionate population of African American allies had managed to catch the eye of military officials. General Ambrose Burnside, for one, had not been insensitive to the value of a regiment of coastal Carolina locals who had formed themselves under the leadership of William H. Singleton.

Burnside had cut a heroic profile in the capture of New Bern and the Carolina coast, distinguished in no small part by his wonderfully distinctive mustache and "sideburns" and his dapper presentation in uniform. His stint as the top commander of U.S. forces would prove disastrous, culminating in the horrific carnage at Fredericksburg in December 1862. But his tenure in office overlapped with the last fertile stage of the black enlistment initiative, placing a Republican of firm antislavery values in a position to make a difference. With a simple act of advocacy, Burnside forged a personal link between the black grassroots and the president of the United States.

William Henry Singleton was born enslaved but destined for something bigger. By the time of his adulthood he had learned the magic names Wendell Phillips, William Lloyd Garrison, and Canada. In 1861 he had obtained permission to march with Confederates and to study their procedures and military drill in his master's company. At the earliest approach of Union forces to North Carolina's Eastern Shore, in March 1862, Singleton stole away and presented himself at Burnside's headquarters, taking work as a scout and also as a servant to a colonel in the 19th Connecticut Infantry.

Singleton could not be satisfied with pay, particularly after his horse was shot beneath him and his life had flashed before him during a reconnaissance mission. He demanded a weapon of the colonel, who informed him that black men could not be armed. Singleton corrected him: "The war will not be over before I have a chance to spill my blood. If that is your feeling toward me, pay me what you owe me and I will take it and go."[13]

Collecting the substantial sum of $5, Singleton "hired out" the building that would soon become the New Bern African Methodist Episcopal Church and began recruiting black men for a Union regiment under his command. General Burnside encouraged the recruits but did not arm them, permitting Singleton and others to drill them using cornstalks instead of guns and looking out for opportunities to advance the aspiring officer's cause.

In a memoir published in 1922, William Henry Singleton remembered a day in November 1862 at Aquia Creek, Virginia:

> [Burnside's] adjutant pointed to a man who was talking to the general in an inner room and said, "Do you know that man in there?" I said, "No." He said, "That is our President, Mr. Lincoln." In a few minutes, the conference in the inner room ended and Mr. Lincoln and General Burnside came out. I do not know whether they had told President Lincoln about me before or not, but the General pointed to me and said, "This is the little fellow who got

up a colored regiment." President Lincoln shook hands with me and said, "It is a good thing. What do you want?" I said, "I have a thousand men. We want to help fight to free our race. We want to know if you will take us in the service?"[14]

The president told Singleton to keep on drilling. "Hold on to your society," said Lincoln, "and there may be a chance for you." Within sixty days of their encounter, the War Department would recognize the New Bern unit as the First North Carolina Volunteers.

At Stearns's request, Lincoln authorized a pass to New Bern for Edward W. Kinsley, an associate of Massachusetts governor Andrew's. On the scene, Kinsley led negotiations with local African American leaders, trying to enlist fighting men in a volunteer regiment being assembled by the state of Massachusetts. In the end, few North Carolinians enrolled as members of what became the Massachusetts 54th, being strongly committed to the military organization they had built on their own.[15]

Glory rained on the Massachusetts 54th, the first black regiment to be recruited at the state level, as authorized by the January 1 Emancipation Proclamation. Stearns and his network had assessed the number of eligible African American men in Massachusetts and decided that the regiment must be recruited from among all the black communities in the North and in the occupied territories of the South. They rapidly established operations in Rhode Island, New York, and Ohio, with Stearns riding the rails as Andrew's noncommissioned agent. The manufacturer used his address book of famous names in black and abolitionist circles to spread the reach of his recruitment. Within weeks he had persuaded so many men (including two of the sons of Frederick Douglass) that he filled the 54th with enough recruits left over to form a second regiment, the Massachusetts 55th. An aristocratic young Bostonian was tapped to lead the more famous 54th Regiment. Robert Gould Shaw, the son of wealthy abolitionists, took command as a colonel attended by other white commissioned officers.

Stearns also played godfather to two other budding black regiments, both with ties to his old schemes in Kansas. A group led by Jim Lane sought recognition as the First Kansas Colored Volunteer Infantry. Its officer corps gathered "fifty sixers and antislavery men" from the Old Free State: James

Montgomery; Richard Hinton, now an army lieutenant; and James W. Blunt, like Lane a brigadier general. It also featured men of color as commissioned officers, including Captain William D. Matthews, later commissioned as an army first lieutenant, and Second Lieutenant Patrick Minor, a black graduate of Oberlin College. Martin Stowell, the Worcester, Massachusetts, and Peru, Nebraska, veteran of the antislavery fight, did not participate, having already signed on with an Iowa regiment and met his death in the fighting near Fort Henry in Tennessee. Two sons of the Shawnee Charles Bluejacket served, while a daughter, Eliza Silverheels, tomahawked to death a Confederate raider but did not enlist.

Lane's African American recruiting was an outgrowth of his independent efforts to win Native Americans in Kansas and vicinity to the Union cause. Indians displaced from the Deep South in the Andrew Jackson era—including such "Civilized Tribes" as the Creek and Cherokee—were longtime practitioners of slavery, many of whom had taken sides with the Confederacy at the outset of the war.[16] Kansas regiments had made a special project of inducing rebel Indians to change sides in 1862, employing violence and incentives and also benefiting from Confederate blunders. The campaign climaxed with the defection of the great septuagenarian Cherokee chief John Ross, who journeyed from Tahlequa, Oklahoma, to the federals at Fort Gibson, bringing hundreds of warriors, family members, and enslaved African Americans in his company.

Ross had never sympathized with the rebellion; he was glad to put his resources at the disposal of the United States, including his nephew William Potter Ross, a turncoat Confederate colonel. Despite the red record of U.S. abuses of the Cherokee and Ross himself, whose wife had died upon the Trail of Tears a quarter century before, the Cherokees' principal chief saw nothing in Confederates to give them a greater claim to Indian loyalties.

The defection of John Ross to the Union opened the latest in a series of violent schisms within the Cherokee Nation, as pro-Confederates concentrated under the leadership of Stand Watie. For Lane and other U.S. commanders in Kansas, however, the changing loyalties of the Cherokee proved fruitful, resulting in the enlistment of more than fifteen hundred warriors and their slaves.[17]

Buoyed by the Shawnee, Cherokee, Creek, and other Unionist Indians,

Lane reported that his recruitment mission had "open[ed] up beautifully." In addition to Indian and white divisions, he enrolled what amounted to two black regiments from the large number of war refugees from Indian territory, Arkansas, and Missouri. "I have not arms for you," Lane told recruits, confessing to highly informal relations with the War Department, "but if it is in your power to obtain arms from rebels, take them, and I will use you as soldiers against traitors."[18]

Lane's mixed-race militia headed west into Missouri, engaging with Confederates in October 1862 at Toothman's Mound and Island Mound, in what proved to be the first fight for African American troops in the Civil War. Newspapers reported that "the colored soldiers fought like tigers" and credited them with a victory over rebel forces two or three times more numerous.[19]

Lacking both the formal recognition of the Lincoln War Department and a paymaster, the First and Second Kansas Colored Infantries, which coalesced around the same time as the several other black regiments described in this chapter, nonetheless broke the boundaries of black enlistment in decisive local ways. Authorities in Washington affirmed their appreciation of the mixed-race jayhawking model by elevating Colonel James Montgomery to a national assignment.

Since the days of John Brown, jayhawkers had sown chaos and aimed to benefit from it, whether by the seizure of arms and destruction of enemy assets, as in the 1850s, or in the contraband recruitment opportunities of the Civil War years. Fighters willing to strike in enemy territory in small numbers could expect to create maximum chaos in dense slave districts, such as those in the South Carolina interior, where for months a campaign to create a black army division had been under way.

Once again David Hunter stirred the pot, appearing at Hilton Head amid the series of temporary posts that took his instigator tactics to the different theaters of war, and repeatedly to the Department of the South. Hunter had obtained a meeting with Harriet Tubman, who joined forces with the Union Army on her own initiative in 1863, and who named James Montgomery as the best choice of army officers to command slave-raiding expeditions in the interior. As a mixed pair, Colonel Montgomery and the quasi-civilian Tubman, who later drew the pension of an army major, were tasked to mount a John Brown attack backed by the Army and Navy of the United States.[20]

Though she'd conducted many missions into Maryland and other Border States, Tubman had no store of knowledge of pathways and safe houses on the Combahee River. The Department of the South also lacked accurate maps that took into account the substantial reorganization of the coastal region created by the withdrawal of plantation owners and their dependents during the Union occupation. To succeed, the mission had to locate the remaining plantations with large numbers of the enslaved and evacuate them safely to Union lines without encountering the large bodies of Confederate troops operating in the area. Tubman operated a small fund from the general's office to pay spies and orderlies, and she struggled to maintain her anonymity among Low Country blacks with distinctive cultural practices. She cooked and brewed root beer to raise money, and she negotiated long distance with Secretary of State William Seward about delaying payments on her parents' farm in Auburn, New York.

Montgomery's task was to raise an official army regiment, the Second South Carolina Volunteers. At the urging of Secretary Seward and the governor of Massachusetts, John A. Andrew, from whom Tubman carried letters of recommendation, Montgomery was to depart Kansas and meet officials in New York City before leaving for Key West, Florida, a toehold of Union control. Key West held interest insofar as it was home to black people, a population certified to be an asset in the military confrontations of the emancipation era.

The arrival of Colonel Montgomery on January 24, 1863, brought news of the Emancipation Proclamation to the town of Key West for the first time. By January 30, Montgomery and the residents had organized a grand jubilee celebration and recruiting event. Local freedmen dressed in their finest clothes paraded through the streets of the town, past colorful homes and the impressive Customs House and church spires to the wharves. They had food and music at the Barracoon—a large tropical stockade only recently employed as a slave trade pen—hearing speeches from Montgomery and from the local black impresario Sandy Cornish on the great opportunities of emancipation and military service.

Cornish himself would not enlist—having years before cut off his fingers and severed his leg muscles to avoid being sold into slavery after a fire destroyed his free papers. Galvanized by his example, more than one hundred locals signed on as the embryo of Colonel Montgomery's South Carolina force.[21]

Sailing north toward Port Royal, Montgomery's transport intercepted a vessel in which a number of enslaved persons were being "refugeed" out of areas near the Georgia coast, where Colonel Higginson's soldiers had conducted a number of February raids. Declaring the inmates to be free, Montgomery brought on board a man known as Big Dave, whom he later promoted to color sergeant.[22]

Before the end of February, Montgomery delivered his Key West recruits to General Hunter's command, making camp alongside Colonel T. W. Higginson and the First South Carolina Volunteers.[23] Higginson had been failing at slave raiding but making progress as a raider of enemy stores such as lumber and sheep. Higginson bragged that his colored troops had exercised tremendous discipline regarding personal theft from civilians (amid a raid in which a black corporal had come face-to-face with the woman who had claimed him as a slave). He himself set a more mixed example, as the literary colonel recorded in his published account of his experiences, *Army Life in a Black Regiment*, in an incident involving a piano and a packing crate left outside a house designated to be burned.

> With such a receptacle all ready, even to the cover, it would have seemed like flying in the face of Providence not to put the piano in. I ordered it removed, and afterwards presented it to a school for colored children at Fernandina. This I mention because it was the only piece of property I ever took, or knowingly suffered to be taken, in the enemy's country, save for legitimate military uses, from first to last; nor would I have taken this, but for the thought of the school, and, as aforesaid, the temptation of the box. If any other officer has been more rigid, with equal opportunities, let him cast the first stone.

Having seized his highbrow booty, Higginson and his black regiment took pains to cover their retreat, consigning the town of St. Mary and several outlying plantations to the flames.[24]

Montgomery would also loot and burn, scandalizing the upright Bostonian Colonel Shaw when leading the Massachusetts 54th and his own troops against the town of Darien, Georgia, in June 1863. In company with Tubman, however, the Kansas veteran would execute some of the most exalted military emancipations of the war.

On the longest day of the year, June 21, the steamer USS *John Adams* bearing Tubman and James Montgomery (remembered by an eyewitness as two women sitting on an upper deck in chairs) appeared on a quiet stretch of the Combahee (called Cumby) River. They anchored at a dock adjacent to the plantation house of Joshua Nichols. Being quiet enough to be mistaken for a pleasure outing taking in the early sunrise, the mission advertised its intentions by sending out black men in uniform to spread the word by setting fire to barns and watercraft at Nichols's and all the neighboring plantations. Laying anchor for six hours, the *John Adams* and a second steamer offered refuge to any in the area who cared to escape.

As the number of escapees mounted into the hundreds, the pandemonium of the flight and loading somehow tickled the funny bone of Harriet Tubman, who related to her friend and collaborator Sarah H. Bradford a memory of the event to transcribe for her autobiography, an account of a woman carrying upon her person three small children, live pigs in a sack, and a steaming pot of cooking rice.

In his own account, Colonel Montgomery emphasized the tragic dimensions of the mission, which ended with far more slaves awaiting transport than could be loaded on the little fleet. The grip of those not taken, actually, had nearly exposed the *John Adams* and company to capture with the approach of Confederates by land. When exhortations to let go of the boats had failed, the colonel turned to Tubman and requested that she sing. Raising her voice and her hands in a rendition of "Uncle Sam's Farm," a Hutchinson Family favorite, she inspired a wave of praise and emulation that freed the boats to dash away:

> Of all the mighty nations in the East or in the West
> This glorious Yankee nation is the greatest and the best
> We have room for all creation and our banner is unfurled
> It's a general invitation to the people of the world.

So come along, come along
Make no delay.
Come from every nation, come from every way.
This land is broad enough so don't be alarmed.
For Uncle Sam is rich enough to buy us all a farm.

Though Tubman thought it was funny, Montgomery remembered the raising of hands and betrayal as "the saddest sight of the whole expedition, so many souls within sight of freedom, and yet unable to attain it."[25]

Tubman's regret was tempered by the victory in numbers of the Combahee raid, in which the Union captured seven hundred persons and more than a million dollars in stores. She had also encountered personal, practical complications on the mission. Going ashore to assist some of the earlier arrivals, the humble liberator had torn her skirt and soaked what was left of it up to the waist. Her parcel holding extra clothing had been lost. Upon return to camp, she sent word via newspaper to sympathetic ladies in Boston that she had nothing to wear. On all of her subsequent antislaving expeditions, she indicated, she would wear the Bloomer pants and not a dress.[26]

13

TURNING THE MISSISSIPPI

White Americans of the nineteenth century did not perceive the state of nature with the awe that subsequent generations would accord it. In the name of progress, harbors had been dredged, logjams dynamited, and the switchbacks of rivers plowed through without regard for broader geological and ecological effects. In the name of bypassing Confederate defenses at Vicksburg, for example, soldiers under the command of U. S. Grant spent months digging a great canal network that aimed to redirect the Mississippi River (though it would not come close to the achievement of its monumental goal). Likewise, the U.S. armies of the western theater would seek to turn the tide of human energy that had nurtured the Confederacy to serve the Union interest. Encountering hundreds of thousands fleeing bondage, whose arrivals were described as "the oncoming of cities," Union organizers seized the opportunity to serve justice and the gods of war by the same means.

Officers such as James Montgomery and Thomas Wentworth Higginson had long been incendiaries. The true measure of the transformative politics of the Civil War were the changes experienced by moderates such as U. S. Grant, the commander of the armies in the West.

Grant had been a mildly antislavery man since the time when he and his Border State bride, Julia Dent Grant, had come into possession of a human being presented as a gift. Though he had been broke since practically the day

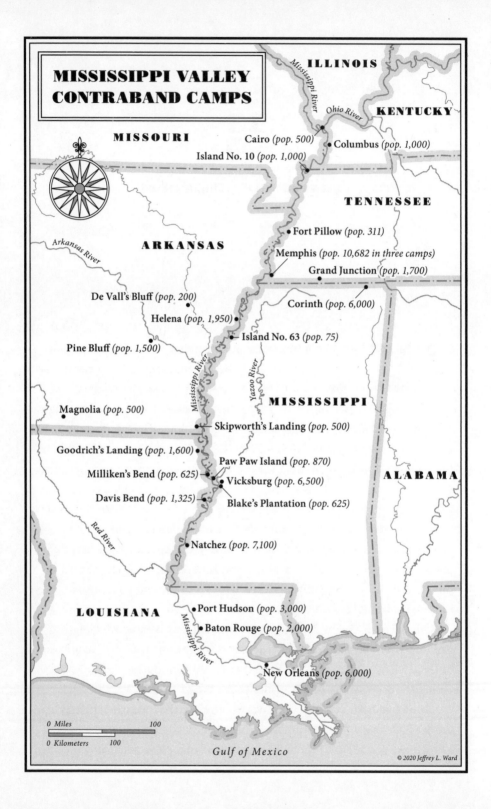

MISSISSIPPI VALLEY
CONTRABAND CAMPS

ILLINOIS

Mississippi River

Ohio River

KENTUCKY

MISSOURI

Cairo *(pop. 500)*

Columbus *(pop. 1,000)*

Island No. 10 *(pop. 1,000)*

TENNESSEE

Arkansas River

ARKANSAS

Fort Pillow *(pop. 311)*

Memphis *(pop. 10,682 in three camps)*

Grand Junction *(pop. 1,700)*

De Vall's Bluff *(pop. 200)*

Corinth *(pop. 6,000)*

Helena *(pop. 1,950)*

Island No. 63 *(pop. 75)*

Pine Bluff *(pop. 1,500)*

Mississippi River

Yazoo River

Magnolia *(pop. 500)*

MISSISSIPPI

Skipworth's Landing *(pop. 500)*

Goodrich's Landing *(pop. 1,600)*

Paw Paw Island *(pop. 870)*

Milliken's Bend *(pop. 625)*

Vicksburg *(pop. 6,500)*

ALABAMA

Davis Bend *(pop. 1,325)*

Blake's Plantation *(pop. 625)*

Red River

Natchez *(pop. 7,100)*

Port Hudson *(pop. 3,000)*

LOUISIANA

Mississippi River

Baton Rouge *(pop. 2,000)*

New Orleans *(pop. 6,000)*

0 Miles 100

0 Kilometers 100

Gulf of Mexico

© 2020 Jeffrey L. Ward

that he became an adult, the future president found the means to liberate the man immediately and help establish him in independence. Grant had been the kind of man whom Lincoln had dismissed as immorally indifferent to the institution in 1860, when he preferred Stephen Douglas and the Democrats, but not with so much conviction that he did not agree to help a group of St. Louis Republican Wide Awakes with their drill. By his own admission, he did not vote in the most momentous election in U.S. history.

Grant had always struggled, and the first months of the Civil War had been no different, as he confronted indifference, backstabbing, and mean-spirited gossip in the Western Army. Even after he began to win, Grant still had to jockey for his job amid complaints (legitimate and otherwise) about his abuse of alcohol. He did not seek to engage the slavery issue in his work as Hunter and other commanders had done, and yet his victories on the Tennessee, Cumberland, and Mississippi Rivers in 1861 and 1862 had opened the dark heart of Dixie to his command. Encountering refugees by the tens and hundreds of thousands as he entered the Mississippi River Delta, and administering large occupied districts where slavery relationships remained intact, the rising commander confronted the problem of slavery and its dissolution more concretely than did any other influential party in the nation.

To feed the needy was difficult enough for commanders sensitive to army regulations, which specified the distribution of rations only to laborers employed on official business. The extremity of the need for medical services for civilians overwhelmed everything the army could offer, particularly as many refugees had sustained injuries in the course of their escape, and others succumbed to diseases that thrived on chaos and displacement.[1] Worst of all, for most of 1862, Grant could scarcely determine his legal obligations regarding persons entering the Union lines, including whether he was required to accept and defend them, allowed to entice them to run away, or obligated to cooperate in their return to those claiming ownership. The release of the Preliminary Emancipation Proclamation in late September offered clarity on the latter point, reiterating that laws passed during the summer guaranteed freedom to all who made it to Union lines.[2] The problem of sick, injured, hungry, and destitute arrivals remained.

Meanwhile, rebel armies ranged dangerously around Grant's armies and the clusters of refugees at Helena, Arkansas; Memphis, Tennessee; and Corinth, Mississippi.

Grant remained characteristically silent as his officers expressed a range of views on the collapse of slavery and the creation of experimental African American regiments. Without consulting anyone, he dispatched instructions in November 1862 to the Reverend John Eaton, an army chaplain, commissioning him superintendent of contrabands and directing him to organize the harvest of the standing crop of cotton.

Eaton was so shocked by the appointment that he took to his cot, pulling his blanket over his head. Summoned to headquarters, he discovered "in the course of my first conversation with General Grant [that] his mind had already grappled with the problem, and had far outstripped [such] meager instructions [as had been drafted by the army], which, indeed, he had not as yet received."

Eaton reported that Grant said of freedmen that "their interests were identical . . . with the needs of our armies." Black refugees would be sheltered, fed, clothed, and cared for as a matter of military necessity. In return, refugees would be put to work at wages bringing in the Mississippi, Arkansas, and West Tennessee cotton crop. Men among them could assist in all aspects of army life in camp. They would speed the work of river engineering, earthworks, and the construction of bridges and roads, while women served the army's unlimited needs for cooking, sewing, and laundry.[3]

> He then went on to say that when it had been made clear that the Negro,
> as an independent laborer—for he was not yet a freedman—could do these
> things well, it would be very easy to put a musket in his hands and make
> a soldier of [him], and if he fought well, eventually to put the ballot in his
> hand and make him a citizen.

Meanwhile the problem of the darkies, as Grant called them, rested on Chaplain Eaton's shoulders. It would prove to be as daunting as the fight for any asset in the State of Mississippi.[4]

Grant had chosen Eaton from his subordinates to carry out his orders. Beginning in the spring of 1863 he would obtain additional assistance from the Lincoln administration, which recognized the special challenge and opportunity of the Mississippi emancipation. As the president and his advisers understood it, the preparation of the army for the wholesale enrollment of black troops was the most urgent task confronting the Union, and they properly reckoned the matter of black enlistment as being tied to the government's ability to provide for the security and comfort of the families of enlisted men. They dispatched a plenipotentiary emissary of the administration charged with managing the humanitarian and military dimensions of the war in Grant's command. It was his task to reverse the momentum of the Mississippi Valley's human tide.

For more than four decades, Lorenzo Thomas had been part of the army: at West Point in the era of James Monroe and Quincy Adams, as part of the Florida Indian wars and the invasion of Mexico, and for more than thirty years in the Office of the Adjutant General in Washington, where he had held the top job for as long as anyone there could remember.

The Civil War had created a great deal of work for General Thomas, who was ably supported by Assistant Adjutant General E. D. Townsend. Encouraged by Lincoln's first war secretary and General Winfield Scott to hype the ceremonial aspects of mustering state volunteers into the service, and formally charged with the designation of rank and promotions, he was highly visible as a gold-braid-and-dress-sword type of general, the epitome of a desk man and a fixture of high society in Washington. The overlap of his role's elevation with the explosive growth of the army under the command of Major General George McClellan, that other spit-and-polish master of the army parade ground, did little to enhance Thomas's standing among Radicals and rough-and-ready men. Edwin Stanton did not like him, favoring the younger Colonel Townsend and letting it be heard that he considered Thomas "only fit for presiding over a crypt of Egyptian mummies like himself."[5]

Lincoln saw something different in Thomas, apparently, and together with Stanton, he recognized an advantage in applying a strong dose of pageantry and military hierarchy to the challenge of integrating black regiments into the partly recalcitrant army. Given only one day to pack and take his leave, the fifty-nine-year-old Thomas was dispatched to the Mississippi

River war corridor on March 26, on an assignment that would keep him there for most of the next two years. His instructions from Stanton designated him as the chief administrative officer of the race revolution of 1863.

The old soldier did not complain, though he would later concede that he found his responsibilities "at first distasteful."[6] He recognized his special qualifications for the role, both as a matter of rank and also as a representative of the antebellum slaveholding society. For all his travels in his long career, Lorenzo Thomas had never lived where slavery did not. Only while he was in Mexico—fighting with his country to expand the dominion of a slave state—and in the months since the 1862 emancipation in Washington, D.C., had he breathed the air that made men and women free. Born in Delaware to a family of slaveholders, he had experienced the troubling intimacies of the system, including personally owning and selling human beings. Thomas thought he understood the nature of the challenge that he faced, and his strong Christian faith helped to gird him for the physical and professional discomforts of the work.

Stanton's letter outlined a great body of responsibilities vis-à-vis black people. In his ceremonial and human resources role, the adjutant general was to recruit and muster in as many regiments of men as could be raised and to designate officers from sympathetic and qualified whites. A key to his success in this regard, however, required that he allay the fears of would-be soldiers and their families about physical security. Thus he was authorized to requisition arms and supplies of every kind for distribution to the "contraband camps."

The administration gave Thomas authority to organize free labor and the leasing of plantations to loyalists in the vicinity of the river, instructions in keeping with General Grant's recent order that the strategic waterways be cleared of rebel households.[7] Arriving just before the close of the planting season, the adjutant general was asked to do his best to generate a cotton crop for 1863. To defend this work, Thomas had orders to distribute weapons to able-bodied freedmen, including some who did not enlist formally as soldiers.

Thomas also carried the administration's message to army whites, that "none is in discharge of his duties who fails to employ to the utmost extent the aid and cooperation of the loyal colored population." His instructions charged him to identify and punish "any obstacle thrown in the way" of black recruitment and adherence to the army. Moving particularly to fore-stall the noncompliance of army quartermasters and commissary chiefs, Thomas must see that black units were equipped "in the same manner as other troops in the service."

A number of less sweeping obligations burdened Thomas with respon-sibilities that no one would entrust to an Egyptian mummy. He would halt the practice of using transport ships as barracks, ensure that no one in the army was trafficking in cotton, and investigate anything else that Thomas deemed "material to the service."[8] Thomas embraced his executive role (as well as his emerging Republican Party identification) by referring to himself as the representative of "this administration."

Unspoken in Stanton's instructions was a request for Thomas's evalu-ation of the leadership of U. S. Grant, a matter of tremendous speculation among army officers, the press, and the Lincoln administration. The gen-eral's lifelong struggle with alcohol abuse, coupled with the outrageous gossiping and competition among Union officers, had left Washington con-fused about Grant's competence to lead. General Thomas would file reports with his superiors alongside contemporaneous observations by Representa-tive Elihu Washburne, Grant's sponsor in Congress, and Charles A. Dana, the journalist and assistant secretary of war. All found Grant to be in deadly earnest, though Dana had the misfortune to be with him during what was likely an episode of drunkenness in June 1863. General Grant's record of sober days in combat stood as a testament to the determination that would soon make him the master of Vicksburg.[9]

On April 1, the day he arrived in Memphis, Thomas delivered dishonor-able discharges to thirty officers and a chaplain from the 128th Illinois, a Democratic or "Copperhead" regiment that had virtually disintegrated in protest against emancipation and black troops. He disbanded the unit along with what was left of the 109th Illinois, a regiment that Grant had seen fit to arrest en masse for desertion and insubordination.[10] Beginning a series of public rebukes, the adjutant general had troops assemble in formation for brief addresses in which he outlined the new practices regarding emancipa-tion and black recruitment. He asked soldiers who did not approve of the policy to step out of ranks—and when they did, the dissenters were arrested and hauled to the stockade, a practice one observer described as having "a sort of grim humor."[11]

In part because he seemed draconian in such confrontations, Thomas encountered a cool reception from the white rank and file. Some complained in letters that he was a weak and ineffective public speaker, while others called him vain, intemperate, and radical. His speeches made it clear that he had arrived "clothed with the fullest power" to manage emancipation and black enlistment, authorized to act "as if the President of the United States were present." Thomas said, "What I have to do, [I have] to do at once—to strike down the unworthy and to elevate the deserving."

> This, fellow soldiers, is the determined policy of the Administration. You all know full well when the President of the United States, ([t]hough he is said to be slow in coming to a determination,) when he once puts his foot down, it is there, and he is not going to take it up. He has put his foot down. I am here to assure you that my official influence will be given, that he shall not raise it.[12]

Thomas succeeded most when commanding officers endorsed his views in their own remarks. Among the most sensational addresses of his early tour was heartfelt commentary from Brigadier General John A. "Black Jack" Logan, a former Democratic congressman who would be reelected as a Radical Republican after the war. After listing the advantages of black enlistment, he declared, "we'll unite on this policy," to the loud approval of his troops.[13]

With such support—and in light of opportunities for promotion, even for enlisted personnel—Thomas was able to commission officer corps for ten African American regiments in his first weeks on the scene. To do so, he maintained a furious pace of appearances, traveling from camp to camp along the river and giving as many as seven speeches a day.[14]

U. S. Grant offered his warmest endorsement to the Thomas mission, in keeping with the vision of black service he had outlined for Reverend Eaton some six months earlier. He saluted the arrival of the adjutant general at his headquarters on April 10 with the firing of big guns.

Thomas had come just in time to participate in major events. For months

Grant had set his troops to the impossible task of redirecting the Mississippi River by means of canals, a strategy that seemed to offer an alternative to confrontation with Vicksburg's fortifications. Now he had set his mind on a new strategy and brought together most of his top generals to discuss the idea of sending troops loaded onto Admiral David Porter's flotilla past the Vicksburg defenses at night. Within hours of Thomas's arrival, Grant's army had abandoned its quarters at Milliken's Bend north of Vicksburg, cut the nearby levees to flood their works, and moved back toward Memphis by land and water to hide. A simultaneous move by General McClernand's forces south of the city succeeded in confusing the enemy.

The Confederate commander at Vicksburg, General John A. Pemberton, mistakenly credited Lorenzo Thomas with ordering the change in strategy. Thomas was well known among Confederates who had formerly served in the U.S. Army—as adjutant general and also as the man who had called General Robert E. Lee a traitor to his face back in 1861.[15]

In Grant's company, General Thomas would participate in the most thrilling and dangerous work of the Vicksburg campaign. He rode with the greatly augmented Union fleet in its nighttime charge past the fortifications at Vicksburg, passed through the gauntlet of fires and artillery that Confederates lit along the riverbanks, and reconnoitered with divisions under Sherman and McClernand at an improvised headquarters near Grand Gulf. In command of the USS *General Price*, a rescued Confederate ram, Thomas observed the all-day bombardment of Confederate defenses at Grand Gulf, a battle in which, he later said, half the guns were manned by African American seamen. Also present was an unnamed freedman who told Porter and Grant about a landing some thirty miles below Davis Bend, where Union troops could be ferried across from Louisiana to the Mississippi bank of the river.[16]

Onboard the *General Price*, Thomas must have wondered if he had grown too old for this kind of work. He was already sick with the typical intestinal maladies of camp life. Like the rest, he was plagued by mosquitoes and the torrential rains that began on May 1. Grant had asked him to babysit, leaving twelve-year-old Fred Grant onboard the *General Price* while everyone but the children and old men marched without tents toward Port Gibson and Jackson in the rain.[17] The old bureaucrat maintained his dignity, however, carrying his nightshirt in a carpetbag and letting it be known that he had arrived with full authority to demote General Grant, if he saw fit, and put his rival General John S. McClernand in his place.[18]

Having survived the first part of the adventure, General Thomas got back to work recruiting black troops, making camp with some two hundred white Iowa volunteers at Grant's former headquarters in Milliken's Bend, Louisiana. Equipped with a small steamboat from Porter's eclectic fleet, the USS *Rocket*, the adjutant general resumed his wide-ranging appearances, now taking the administration's message to what were still known as contraband camps. At a number of locations, the black regiments initiated on paper early in April had developed into actual troops, complete with uniforms and weaponry, by May.

Thomas's practice (with whites as well as blacks) was to assemble soldiers in what was known as the hollow square, a Napoleonic-era military formation adapted for ceremonial occasions. In contraband camps he supervised a demonstration of soldierly maneuvers by new recruits, calling out the "presenting of arms" himself, greeting teachers and schoolchildren, and clapping time to lead the assemblies in the singing of hymns. Tall, white-haired, and handsome, impeccably dressed, the adjutant general only looked the part of representative of the ancien régime. When he called for silence to speak to them formally as Abraham Lincoln's emissary, Lorenzo Thomas showed himself to be Jacobin and beyond.

Thomas for one had long had faith in black soldiers. "When he shipped on a man-of-war in Florida [in the 1830s] two of the largest guns were manned by blacks," a reporter who heard Thomas speak in Memphis late in May wrote. "He visited Havana, where he had seen two regiments of black soldiers, well-drilled and orderly, and the Spanish people relied upon them as soldiers."

> Will you fight soldiers? Yes I know you will. I have seen many black soldiers.
> Half the guns at the late great battle of Grand Gulf were manned by blacks.
> I have ten thousand black soldiers down the river. I want two regiments or
> more here.

And Thomas wanted more than that. "I came here to tell you what the President expects you to do," said Thomas. "He wishes every one of you who can, to work. You used to work for masters: now you are free—free as I am, good as I am. We are all men; the only difference between us is—I have had more advantages than you."

Freedom entailed obligations. The people must be literate, he advised: "Learn to write. You can, I know you can. Hold up your heads, be men. When you meet white men be polite, courteous; but be men."

"I tell you these things not only because I am commanded to do so by the President," Thomas insisted, "but because I feel them. I was raised by a slave, I once owned slaves, I know what all the prejudices are upon this subject, but I have overcome them."[19]

Among those most charged by the adjutant general's advocacy was John A. Eaton, Grant's superintendent of contrabands, who spread the word of the great significance of Thomas's tour:

> You should see him at his work. For forty years his business has been to deliver military orders, write them. Now that he speaks them tis not so much his oratory as his orders that tell, they are clearly, pointedly, delivered, no one can misunderstand the will of the government of the nation.[20]

Prior to May 1863, Eaton's program had operated on the authority of U. S. Grant alone. "[Thomas] has come and put the broad responsible seal of his government upon us by authority of the President," he reported. The experience for both men transcended politics and army policy to the realm of religious ecstasy. Eaton wrote of Thomas finishing a speech at the battlements in Corinth, Mississippi:

> Vociferous cheers rolled up from the depths of their hearts for the President, for the good news, for the General, cheer following cheer, their echoes flying among the defences erected by Beauregard and over the field red with the blood of friends and foes of liberty and union.
>
> . . . the General then turned to me and said now I am prepared to die, no one can know how much he had endured to attain this success.[21]

Thomas was merely a soldier serving in the most dangerous theater of that phase of the war, prepared to die for his country and his belief. He asked nothing of the Mississippi Valley recruits that he was not willing to offer himself.

Sooner rather than later they would face the test.

By June the adjutant general had succumbed to his war zone ailments. After three weeks in a Louisville hospital, he returned to Washington in July in the company of medical attendants. While still bedridden, he gave a two-day interview to a reporter for *The New York Times*, the subject of an article that proved to be the opening of a personal campaign to return to the scene of the action. "The nation has reason to be grateful for the mercy that has saved the life of the Adjutant-General of the army," wrote the *Times* reporter, who called Thomas "one of the purest and most devoted patriots in the country," and "one of the ablest, and in all respects the most valuable officer in the Army."

Thomas confronted the likelihood that his mission would be assigned to a younger officer or one more amenable to Secretary Stanton. News in July had speculated that General David Hunter might be transferred from the Sea Islands to take his place. Restored to health, Thomas lobbied President Lincoln, granted more interviews, and made long speeches about "the prejudices and discouragements that were at first thrown in his way but had now disappeared before the success which attended the policy."[22]

The president took note, telling Stanton that he thought Thomas "one of the best, if not the very best" officer to lead the administration's fledgling African American program. At a dinner hosted by the publisher John Forney just before his departure, Lincoln saluted Thomas with his observant personal secretary, John Hay, at his side. "General!" said Lincoln. "You are going about a most important work. There is a draft down there [a reference to the recent riots in New York City] that can be enforced." Hay wrote in his diary,

> A few moments afterward at the lunch at Forney's quarters [Thomas] used the President's expression as his own & was cheered for it. I regard his attitude as most significant. He is a man accustomed through a long lifetime to watch with eager interest the intentions of power and the course of events; till he has acquired an instinct of expediency that answers to him the place of sagacity & principle. He is a straw which shows whither the wind is blow-

ing. The tendency of the country is toward universal freedom, when men like Thomas make abolition speeches at public dinners.[23]

Among his themes in the East was the need for a stronger national mandate to manage the transition from slavery to freedom. Questions attending on race had "outgrown the power of States to deal with them harmoniously and safely," said Thomas. "The heterogeneous and disgraceful legislation of several of the Free States, to say nothing of the Slave States, is proof of this." Going beyond the Lincoln administration's piecemeal encouragement of emancipation in the Border States, Thomas proposed to "let Congress take possession of the whole subject of legislation with respect to the black race in the United States at its next session," to settle the question permanently and universally "upon equitable and just principles."[24]

The political importance of the Thomas mission became apparent in a scheme engaging Frederick Douglass as a partner for the adjutant general's work in Mississippi. After years on the outside—as a critic, editor, and Liberty Party candidate and speaker—Frederick Douglass was ready to come into the Republican Party. In an ironic twist, his pathway toward the mainstream had been opened by the irreconcilable Radical George L. Stearns. Stearns had made Frederick Douglass's house in Rochester, New York, the first stop on his out-of-state recruitment tour on behalf of the Massachusetts 54th. Two Douglass sons—Charles and Lewis—had been among the first to enlist. But Stearns was hunting for bigger game, hoping that the father himself would sign on to the staff of the newly created Bureau of Colored Troops.

General Order Number 143 had established the bureau on Stearns's recommendation and also to forestall what appeared to be a competition among states to recruit African Americans in conquered areas other than Mississippi to fill their federal quotas for state troops (a contest in which Massachusetts—with personnel on the ground in North Carolina, South Carolina, and much of the North—ran strongly in the lead). Under the auspices of Adjutant General Thomas, the new office claimed exclusive authority for enlistment in black-only military companies, now redesignated—from the patchwork of Corps d'Afriques and African Descents—as numbered regiments of United States Colored Troops. The orders designated that "three or more field officers" would assist the adjutant general by serving as administrators in areas with large concentrations of eligible men.[25] George L. Stearns had already accepted one of these positions and a commission as a U.S. Army major.

Stearns had made his headquarters in Philadelphia, where he was rapidly recruited as a member of the upper-crust Republican Union League Club. Wearing a uniform but keeping his beard quite long, he secured property to establish a camp for colored troops. He wrote to his wife, "We have a camp at Chelten Hills, nine miles from the Continental; a beautiful location I am told. I named it Camp Wm. Penn. The Quakers wince, but I tell them it is established on peace principles; that is, to conquer a lasting peace."[26]

Stearns remained at work all summer, even as others in the Union League Club deserted the city for vacation locales. One of his compatriots in the struggle was Frederick Douglass, who had accepted a position as a recruiter in Stearns's operation.

Both men wanted a bigger role for Frederick Douglass in the war. At forty-three, the editor and orator retained the strength and will that had led him to attack and subdue the last man who had ever used the whip against him as a slave. Douglass's stature made him a natural candidate for an officer's commission. Recognized by the administration, moreover, he could apply his mighty voice to the challenges that faced black recruitment in the present—including the recently announced pay differential that reduced the pay of black troops and the problem of the Confederate promise to execute captured black soldiers. He could also look out for the long-term goals of African Americans as soldiers and as citizens.

On Stearns's suggestion, the black leader made a "flying visit" to Washington on August 10, 1863, seeking interviews with "heads of departments," including his fellow New Yorker, Secretary of State William Seward. Making his case in the War Department and the White House, Douglass proffered his unique services to the government—and not incidentally also to the Republican Party.

Douglass obtained a thirty-minute interview with the secretary of war during which Stanton by extreme effort managed to avoid being loud or discourteous, as he usually was. It was a measure of the War Department's eagerness to ramp up its black recruitment program that Stanton allowed Douglass—a civilian and political figure—to state his views on a number of issues without interruption. Stanton indicated strong agreement with Douglass's arguments in favor of equal pay and assured him of his "readiness to grant commissions to any reported to him by their superior officers for their capacity or bravery."

Stanton wanted Douglass to join General Lorenzo Thomas in the Mississippi Valley recruiting project. While he was not specific about an offer of rank, Stanton did refer to a commission for Douglass—a departure from the official policy that blacks would serve only in enlisted ranks. The secretary offered Douglass a position as assistant adjutant general, asking him to "report to" Thomas in Mississippi immediately.[27]

Douglass also held a bracing interview with the commander in chief, petitioning for an audience in the company of Stearns's friend, the Kansas senator Samuel C. Pomeroy. "No man who had not worn the yoke of bondage and been scourged and driven beyond the beneficent range of brotherhood of man by popular prejudice," Douglass later wrote, "can understand the tumult of feeling with which I entered the White House."[28] Lincoln's friendliness and sustained attention put Douglass at ease and laid the foundation for the black man's enduring admiration.

The president countered most of Douglass's suggestions, counseling patience and reminding Douglass that "the country needed talking up to" on the issue of black soldiers' pay. Lincoln showed Douglass his humanitarian side, shuddering at Douglass's suggestion that the United States retaliate for the execution of black prisoners with executions of Confederate prisoners. The president smiled but did not joke: the only funny aspects Douglass noted in their talk were the gangly particulars of Lincoln's posture.[29]

At the close of their discussion, Senator Pomeroy raised the subject of Douglass's assignment with the War Department. "Mr. President, Mr. Stanton is going to make Douglass Adjutant-General to General Thomas, and is going to send him down the Mississippi to recruit."

Mr. Lincoln said in answer to this: "I will sign any commission that Mr. Stanton will give Mr. Douglass."

Stanton had not offered a commission for any signature, though he had assured Douglass that "the paperwork" would be expedited and sent. As if to fill the gap, Senator Pomeroy presented a document that he had signed himself along with the hitherto unremarkably Radical secretary of the Interior

John Usher, stating that Douglass was "a loyal, free man, entitled to travel."
Lincoln signed and wrote, "I concur," beneath the statement. "We trust that he
will be recognized everywhere, as a free man, and as a gentleman."[30]

Douglass sped home to Rochester and published his last edition of *Douglass' Monthly*—too soon, as it turned out, except insofar as he had been
looking for a chance to exit from the publishers' life. Regrettably, the historic paper's final columns included the erroneous statement that he would
soon depart for Mississippi and General Thomas's command. It was "natural and consistent" with his life's work, Douglass assured his readers, that "I
should take some humble part in the physical as well as the moral struggle
against slavery."[31]

There were limits to Douglass's humility, however, and when Stanton's
commission failed to arrive, he declined to rush toward the barricades.
Douglass knew "the value of shoulder straps" in army life; he would not
proceed into its midst "without some visible mark of my rank."[32] Another
eighteen months would pass before the Lincoln administration recognized
a black man as a commissioned officer, a conservatism that forestalled the
military participation of Douglass, the Langston brothers of Ohio, Octavius
Catto of Philadelphia, and other distinguished African American men.

The offended Douglass could not know the large number of private
citizens—including journalists and members of Congress—circulating in
the various army commands in unofficial capacities, but later he would
recognize the difficulty of assigning him a rank that was consistent with
his stature and symbolic role. Parting company with Major Stearns—
who received orders relocating his offices to Nashville, Tennessee, on
August 13—Douglass considered his next move, allowing another son,
Frederick, Jr., to enlist in the army. His disappointing debut as a Republican
foreshadowed the difficulties that black participation would soon present to
the party and the nation.

14

REVOLUTION BY CONFISCATION

The mansion known as Arlington House had not sustained damage during its capture by Union forces: its eight massive columns remained unscarred and its open view of the city of Washington was uninterrupted. The lawn and gardens were so beautiful in the summer of 1862 that it seemed "as if the master had given his orders every morning," reported Harriet Jacobs, on assignment from *The Liberator* to report on emancipation in the District of Columbia. The row of cabins that had formerly been home to nearly two hundred slaves was still populated by black people—a number approaching fifteen hundred by July 1862—and as in slavery times, everyone was hard at work.

"They seem very happy," Jacobs observed, noting a significant change. Now they lived amid the camps of the Army of the Potomac, packed into the eleven hundred acres of the old estate by the tens of thousands. "It is a delightful place for both the soldier and the contraband," wrote Jacobs. Enjoying its vistas, she admitted, "I was much inclined to say," on the subject of its former owners, that "although the wicked may prosper for a season, the way of the transgressor is hard."[1]

Arlington House remained officially in the possession of Confederate General Robert E. Lee and his wife during Harriet Jacobs's visit, and yet its occupation by the government of the United States was already more than a matter of military expediency. "Lee" had been the unwritten syllable in the

Confiscation Act passed by Congress on July 17, 1862. His name and estate shadowed the list of types of rebels forfeiting their worldly goods that began with "an officer of the army." To "insure the speedy termination of the present rebellion," as the new law put it, the property of those who swore loyalty to the "so-called confederate states of America" was to be employed "for the support of the army of the United States."

Arlington House fit the army's need for an encampment in defense of the capital city, and its elevation provided high ground for military operations and healthful quarters for the soldiers and their growing ranks of African American crews. Its confiscation served necessary and proper army operations and also satisfied the impulse of Republicans in control of government to punish their enemies.

Confiscation and the use of eminent domain were political acts for Radical Republicans, however much they might be justified by military ends. Below the surface of such policies lay more than one political goal. To begin, as was said by Andrew Johnson, the native-born military governor of occupied Tennessee, treason must be made odious. The propertied class that had foisted secession and war upon the world would be made to know the cost. In what seemed to some to be a transcendent bend toward justice, moreover, the seizure of rebel estates created conditions to redress an even greater wrong, the sin of slavery, and to offer a path forward for the millions formerly held in bondage. The most radical of Radicals imagined confiscation and redistribution as the culmination of the Civil War's clash of cultures. Seizing the moment of opportunity in 1862 and 1863, they touched the levers of class warfare and the race relations revolution.

Unlike future manifestations of the same trends, the assault on white privilege in the South did not initiate in the margins, but instead at the center of the supercharged U.S. government of the war years. Led by the ultras Thaddeus Stevens in Congress, Salmon Chase in the executive branch, and Benjamin Butler in the army Department of the Gulf, a campaign to seize the property of rebels gained momentum alongside the unfinished business of emancipation and black military service. The participation of prominent African American reformers and local chiefs heightened the stakes and prolonged the expectation among blacks that their independence would be assured by gaining access to an acreage to call their own.

The new Confiscation Act included the moderately Radical proposition that slaves of rebels would become "forever free" wherever federal forces could ensure their liberation, a clause that became active after the formal Emancipation Proclamation in January 1963. The act also permitted the permanent seizure of real estate such as General Lee's Arlington House and other property in land. For Lincoln and the mainstream, such provisions violated the Constitution in a way that slavery emancipation did not. The president signed the bill, making it law, but attached a nonbinding message along with his signature, explaining that the Constitution banned bills of attainder, the designation of particular categories of individuals as criminals, and arguing that legal tradition shielded property in land from permanent seizure.

Such reservations would be valid, argued Thaddeus Stevens, the major spokesperson for confiscation in the 38th Congress, if Southern rebels remained citizens of the United States. Stevens argued that rebels had forfeited the benefits of constitutional protection when they took up arms against the constitutional government. By war's end and in Reconstruction, the crusty Pennsylvanian would develop an elaborate theory around the lost standing of Southern aristocrats and their disgraced political institutions. Stevens's "State Suicide" and "Conquered Provinces" argument would become the dominant justification for a campaign for redistributive land reform in the South that outlived Stevens himself, who died in 1868. The language he contributed to the Confiscation Act—never amended despite Lincoln's objections—remained part of the text that guided U.S. policy during Lincoln's term and afterward.

The zeal for seizing rebel estates also animated the "Direct Tax to Be Charged in Insurrectionary Districts," a provision of the 1862 tax code passed during the same session. States in the North and West had drained their treasuries to meet their obligations to provide regiments of troops to the war effort, sponsors of the legislation argued. The Direct Tax took note of the failure of Southern property owners to pay their fair share alongside citizens of loyal states. In what might be seen as a theoretical proposition, families deemed to be in arrears on their individual tax obligations risked the forfeiture of their estates as an in-kind contribution toward their debts. Paired with the actions of administrators in the Treasury and War

Departments who shared in the Ultras' revolutionary goals, the confiscation regulations had the potential to upend property relations in the South.[2]

Benjamin Butler had come to recognize a new standard of high living
during his tenure as head of the occupation of New Orleans. The opulent
mansions of St. Charles Avenue and the Uptown District had no counterpart in the stolid New England cities of the day. The policing of uptown
property had occupied much of his energy and time, especially in light of
pro-Confederate smuggling across Union lines. Portable valuables such as
silverware and jewelry still made their way across Union lines, often in the
charge of women, who may have hoped to escape the scrutiny undergone
by men.

The effrontery of Union guards during inspections resulted in a number
of high-profile seizures and arrests and saddled the general with a lifelong
reputation (among critics) for stealing silverware. A new pejorative nick-
name, Spoons Butler, was added to a growing list—"the Beast," "the Devil,"
"Old Strabismus" (a reference to his vision problem), "Picayune," and "the
Bluebeard of New Orleans."[3]

Banks stood at the top of Butler's list of institutional enemies. They had
played a central role in the distribution of Confederate currency and bonds.
A secondary line of service saw the banks extending credit for individual
and family contributions to the Confederate cause. The Record of Mortgages, seized by U.S. officials at the outset of the occupation, showed deep
leveraging of plantations, town houses, artwork, jewelry, and personal silver
services. The ledgers allowed Union officials to distinguish between loans
incurred for household use and funds transferred to Confederate accounts.
The most striking mortgages allowed slaveholders to draw up to $1,000 per
individual held in bondage. In a scandalous case adjudicated during the occupation, the white New Orleans father of an enslaved teenager took a loan
of $600 on her person, only to see her auctioned with the threat of sexual
predation when he defaulted on his debt.[4]

Deeming the banks rebel institutions, Butler imposed harsh requirements to avoid the total forfeiture of bank assets in late summer 1862, using
the authority of the new Confiscation Act. The first—but hardly the last—
required a transfer to the general's occupation accounts of a U.S. dollar
amount equal to each bank's investment in Confederate bonds.

Butler also took aim at individuals making contributions to the rebel state. Simply to look at the values on the Record of Mortgages, he wrote to Salmon Chase, enclosing a copy, "speaks more for a sequestration [or seizure] act than any argument."[5] On August 4, his General Orders No. 55 published a list of contributors to a Confederate fund, noting the dollar value of each donation and assessing 25 percent of the amount to create an account for poor relief.

The Butler sequestration was one part vengeance, three parts humanitarian concern. As a longtime philanthropist from the progressive state of Massachusetts, Butler was appalled by the condition of the poor, including black refugees and New Orleans families now reduced to poverty by the exigencies of war. The public infrastructure in the city—as elsewhere in the South—had been inadequate even in peacetime. Indulging the idea that "treason must be made odious," Butler established a protocol for the distribution of the new fund that emphasized the politics of occupation uplift. He would scrub the sordid city in a public works campaign. Those who served the Union, including "contraband" laborers of both sexes, partook first, destitute women and children second. Confederate soldiers and other undesirables were eligible for jobs and aid only after others had been served.

Butler planned yet more radical applications of the confiscation doctrine for the fall and winter. In August he assessed all local merchants—including high-flying cotton brokers—a payment equal to their contributions to the Confederate-era New Orleans Committee of Safety, an action that deepened their resistance against federal authority.

In September, he required all New Orleans residents who had not taken an oath of loyalty to the United States to register with his office a list of assets. In October, he declared that tenants should cease paying rent to disloyal landlords. In December, his provosts initiated a series of daily public auctions of rebel property, including sugar, cotton, teams, wagons, and carriages, the inventory of warehouses and shops, and the contents of magnificent homes. Butler ordered a Great Sale of Blooded Stock and advertised the names of five stallions and the white men to whom they had formerly belonged, noting that the proceeds would go "for the benefit of the United States Government."

Individuals who could not abide the terms of the occupation would not be spared sequestration, but they were invited to leave the city if they preferred to live among the rebels. The provost marshal ordered all such individuals to present themselves in his office bringing "personal clothing only, not exceeding $50 in value for each adult."[6]

The Radical display expanded Butler's national political profile. Unfortunately for the general, it also drew unfavorable attention from governments representing their expatriates in cosmopolitan New Orleans. Foreign nationals and even official consular representatives of sovereign states had found their names on Butler's list of Confederate sponsors. Efforts to reverse General Butler's seizures of foreign assets created such headaches for the State Department that Secretary Seward successfully lobbied for Butler's removal from his post in December 1862.

He would not go quietly. Addressing citizens before his departure—in a speech that was published in order to reach those who refused to attend in person—the Radical general observed that he had been considered harsh, and yet things could have been worse. Reminding listeners that "treason persisted in is *death*," he noted:

> You might have been smoked to death in caverns . . . or roasted, like the inhabitants of Algiers during the French campaign; your wives and daughters might have been given over to the ravisher as were the unfortunate dames of Spain in the Peninsular war [*sic*]; or you might have been scalped and tomahawked . . .

By world historical standards, New Orleans had had it easy under Benjamin Butler. Never motivated by "personal animosity," he had merely treated its disloyal element with what he considered "merited severity."[7]

If anyone deserved severe treatment it was Jefferson Davis, president of the illegal Confederacy. With less fanfare than Butler in New Orleans, military officials moved to expropriate Davis's family estate in Davis Bend, Mississippi, a slip of land at a sharp turn of the river south of Vicksburg. The adjoining plantations of Jefferson Davis and his brother Joseph Davis had formed a model community in the years before the war, practicing experimental agricultural techniques and offering enslaved residents an unusual degree of self-government, education, and leadership opportunities, in keeping with Joseph Davis's advanced ideas.

Despite these advantages, relatively few of the enslaved on the Davis estate elected to "refugee" with Joseph Davis to more protected terrain as Union forces threatened the region in 1862. The plantations had been home to some 350 slaves in their prime, but after the fall of New Orleans only seven boarded the boat that their masters had sent to carry them away to safekeeping. In the care of overseers, Davis family bondsmen witnessed the sack of Hurricane and Brierfield—the residences of the two estates—when troops in the command of Admiral David Farragut dispatched a raiding party on June 24, 1862.

The Yankees found little of immediate value in the interior of the Davis mansions. Though they smashed china and portraits and burned books, useful furnishings and supplies had been previously removed by the slave population of the island, still in residence, and as it turned out, fully in control of the Davis estates.

A key indicator of black control was the fate of Jefferson Davis's cotton. Unlike other lots within the zone jeopardized by federal operations, 1861 crops belonging to the Davis brothers had not been burned, in keeping with Confederate regulations, which aimed to keep the valuable commodity out of the hands of the enemy. A neighbor taking note of this inconsistency in a June 7 letter informed Jefferson Davis that all of the local planters knew that his slaves had become "seriously demoralized" since the departure of his brother to Vicksburg, and speculated that the slaves withheld the cotton in anticipation of delivering it to federal troops. The laborers had put in the spring crops but refused to be directed by the white plantation overseers, who tried to no avail to expel recalcitrant blacks from the premises. They "declared that on no conditions would they agree to leave the places," reported the neighbor. Davis Bend residents would employ the Davis estates and its stores of salable goods at their own discretion—to enrich themselves or to aid their allies as they saw fit. "I am sorry to say," the letter continued, "that I think the Yankees would be offered any facilities in the power of the negroes to grant on your place and the Hurricane."[8]

The mastermind of the seizure of the Davises' assets was Benjamin

Montgomery, a bondsman of such conspicuous talent and intelligence that Joseph Davis had facilitated his education and established him in a supervisory role. After the evacuation of the masters, Montgomery remained on friendly terms with the Davises, but he conducted business on the estates in the interest of his own people. For example, he nonchalantly took possession of his own son, one of the few enslaved persons who had retreated with Joseph Davis, when young Isaiah Montgomery came to Hurricane to deliver a message.

On Benjamin Montgomery's instructions, the workforce put its own subsistence and security first. As wartime shortages and high water on the Mississippi threatened, the Montgomerys (father and son) concentrated on subsistence and security, directing the planting of food crops and the slaughtering of Davis cattle and setting up a tannery and shoemaking enterprise with the hides. When circumstances permitted—in keeping with the fortunes of the new campaign against Vicksburg—they would assist and cooperate with federal armed forces, initiating their transition up from slavery to Radical Republicanism.[9]

Practicing careful diplomacy, the Montgomerys maintained a friendly correspondence with the Confederate president's brother, reporting to him on events at Davis Bend as if the property relations that had prevailed before the war remained intact. They were quick to seek the protection of United States armed forces once the war began to penetrate the river below Vicksburg, however, sending word that young Isaiah had been witness to the clash between Confederate rams and the USS *Indianola*, an 1862 model ironclad battleship.

Even before he interviewed Montgomery, Admiral Porter knew in his heart that the *Indianola* had been sunk. The ship had not made its way back to the Union fleet above Vicksburg on schedule. Porter had been counting on the ironclad to close the line of supply to Confederate forces at Port Hudson, Louisiana, but from the outset its performance had been disappointing. The vessel's vulnerabilities were many: an exposed undercarriage, weak propulsion, design flaws that limited the range of action of its guns, and paddlewheels on either side that could scarcely be protected in close fighting.[10] All of these weaknesses had combined to assure its defeat in its final engagement, in which the Confederate rams overtook the *Indianola* by stealth, moved so close that the crews exchanged pistol fire, and sheared the sidewheel from the starboard side, disabling the monitor and opening its hold to the river.

It sank so quickly that the rebels could not safely tow the ironclad to a secure location. Its prize crews cut the ropes to save their tugboats, allowing the hulk of the *Indianola* and its four big guns to come to rest upon a deep-water sandbar directly offshore from Davis Bend.

Isaiah Montgomery knew what had happened, and more important, where it had all taken place. The boy's report that the crew had not destroyed the vessel prior to its capture caused Admiral Porter to lose his composure. Apprised of its location, Porter had to decide whether to risk an effort to raise the *Indianola* in an area where Confederates operated freely on the river. He also had to take responsibility for the defeat, which he called "the most humiliating affair that has occurred during this rebellion." If any rescue effort would be mounted, the admiral concluded, he would have to supervise the undertaking in person, and Isaiah Montgomery would have to go with him whether he wanted to or not.[11]

Montgomery was not intimidated by the admiral's temper or by the luxurious appointments of the flagship *Black Hawk*, which the Navy had converted from a cruise ship to a tinclad gunner. Unlike Robert Smalls and many other refugees from slavery who collaborated with the Union in the war, Montgomery had experience of personal dealings with commanding whites, having grown up at the knee of one of the most powerful men in the Confederacy. Joseph Davis had made a point of educating Isaiah to be fluent in both speech and perception, giving him full access to the family library that Union forces destroyed in 1862. It had been his duty to be the first in the household to read newspapers and letters, reporting on their contents in order to save his master's time.[12]

The young man answered Porter's questions with an aplomb that must have been astounding, and though he did not formally enlist in the U.S. Navy until April 1863, Montgomery signed on as Porter's personal assistant that day in late February. He observed and probably advised on the hasty construction of a dummy ironclad to assist in the raising of the *Indianola*, perhaps suggesting where to find the black clay that Navy engineers employed to mock up smokestacks on a barge. Upon dummy sidewheels the mocking Northerners transcribed a message to the people who had staked their all on the system justified by the idea that all whites were superior to individuals such as Isaiah Montgomery. "Deluded people," they had painted, "cave in."[13]

Davis Bend became a stronghold of Union operations as the epic final Mississippi River campaigns got under way. Ulysses Grant loved the idea—proposed by Admiral Porter—that the properties on Davis Bend could be converted to a "negro paradise."[14] While the Montgomery family evacuated temporarily to safer environs, other former vassals of the Davis family would remain in place, encouraged to sell beef and firewood to the navy and to cultivate food and cotton for their own use.

Freedmen on Davis Bend obtained fifteen formal leases from the army in the spring of 1863, along with firearms to be distributed for self-defense. Confederates probing the peninsula that summer were surprised to encounter armed African American irregulars on Davis Bend, and they fled the scene after executing a mentally disabled hostage. By year's end, the army had detailed two companies of the 64th U.S. Colored Troops to defend a growing population of more than one thousand refugees from slavery.[15] By order of Adjutant General Lorenzo Thomas, officers of the 64th were the only white men permitted on the plantations without a pass.

The 1863 harvest was a partial success, wrested from a plague of army worms that destroyed much of the cotton crop in the region and diminished by the disruption of repeated Confederate incursions on the Davis estates. A *New York Times* reporter touring the government farms pronounced the yields on the plots managed by the black lessees at Davis Bend and Helena, Arkansas, to be "more abundant than on any of the others."[16]

In addition to individual leases, Reverend Eaton's Freedmen's Department (and later the Freedmen's Bureau) operated a "Home Colony" for the support of former slaves who were elderly, orphaned, or disabled. The 1864 cotton crop raised $160,000 for the Home Colony, making it one of the most profitable enterprises in the South.[17]

Except for a brief interlude in the spring of 1864, the Davis Bend colony operated under the auspices of the U.S. Army. As part of a bid to put the management of Mississippi Valley plantations in the hands of the Treasury Department, an abortive reorganization saw the extension of leases to loyal whites on the peninsula, including relatives of the Confederate raider John A. Quitman. The failure of the Treasury plan to cope with the ongoing security crisis in the region, however, resulted in the rapid reestablishment of army control. In a directive of January 1865, General Thomas ordered all white leaseholders to vacate Davis Bend, putting control of its five thousand acres once again in the hands of the formerly enslaved.[18]

The leasing fiasco resulted from the ambitious political machinations of Treasury Secretary Salmon Chase. Chase dreamed of the presidency and saw himself as having the greatest antislavery credentials of any likely candidate, including his boss. Lincoln tolerated the large number of offenses arising from this conflict out of personal generosity—and also because he believed that Chase's ambition would inspire him to make the most of his executive responsibilities. In his homey language, Lincoln compared the secretary to a plow horse motivated by the agitation of a biting insect: "If Mr. [Salmon] Chase has a presidential chin fly biting him," Lincoln told a friend, "I'm not going to knock him off, if it will only make his department go."[19]

Chase pursued authority in Mississippi because the region was home to the largest number of African Americans in the South, a population he was already reckoning to be a political asset of great potential power. From the Radical perspective, moreover, Treasury was the right branch of government to address the confiscation and redistribution of rebel estates. Though his schemes crashed against the military realities of the western theater, the secretary of the treasury developed a more ambitious and successful confiscation program in the Sea Islands of South Carolina, Georgia, and Florida.

The question of confiscation and redistribution in the Sea Islands was linked to the subject of Reconstruction, which became a formal proposition in December 1863 as President Lincoln introduced his plan for reestablishing loyal governments in the South. Both Lincoln and Chase, as it happened, considered the restoration of states in relation to the coming presidential election. If states such as Louisiana, Arkansas, or Florida could be reestablished in time, they could send delegations to the 1864 party nominating conventions or to the Electoral College. Their example might inspire the cessation of hostilities in other rebellious states. The key to success in such an initiative was to attract residents of occupied areas who were willing to sign the oath of loyalty in sufficient numbers to meet the president's terms.

Secretary Chase endorsed Lincoln's Reconstruction plan but noted privately in correspondence with the president that he did not endorse Lincoln's formula, which initiated the restoration process after 10 percent of the 1860 voting population had sworn a loyalty oath. Chase preferred to say that when "all loyal citizens" thought it proper, they could hold a constitutional convention and address the other key requirements of the plan. Under Chase's proposal, the road to restored statehood could be initiated by a smaller population. Uncoupled from 1860, moreover, the less formal standard might be construed to include a large proportion of new arrivals among the loyalists. More radical still, Chase advocated for the recognition of loyalists "of whatever physical complexion." By defining popular sovereignty in terms that considered the political will of the formerly enslaved, Chase argued, the Lincoln administration could hope "to mark the two civilizations"—freedom and barbarism—"by distinctly recognizable limits."[20]

Chase had written in his journal in August 1862 that "the blacks were really the only loyal population worth counting." Black military service— still officially prohibited during Chase's musings—"might be made the basis of the necessary measures for their ultimate enfranchisement."[21] By December 1863, as President Lincoln's plans for Reconstruction approached implementation, Chase had resolved on black male suffrage as a key means of advancement—for the cause of Union and for African American men as well as for himself.

Chase spent the last days of 1863 in a campaign of letter writing in an effort to put his personal stamp on the new political entities envisioned for occupied parts of the South. Regarding Louisiana, Chase engaged in a flurry of correspondence with Thomas Jefferson Durant, a philosophically Radical member of the Unionist Free-State movement in New Orleans, in which he advocated "the universal suffrage of all men, unconvicted of crime, who can read & write and have a fair knowledge of the Constitution of the State & of the United States." The move would be "a glory for Louisiana," Chase predicted, despite "a little hard working of the machinery at first."[22] Though Durant and other Louisiana Radicals did their best to maintain good relations with the secretary, the proposal to expand suffrage at the upcoming constitutional convention in the state elicited little enthusiasm.

At the same time, Secretary Chase pursued votes as part of a more comprehensive strategy in partially occupied Florida. He had proven himself to be the most important participant in the visionary scheme launched early in the war to colonize the southernmost state, casting his lot with some of the old New England emigrationists, led by Eli Thayer. Florida was envisioned as the latest and greatest target for a paramilitary filibuster expedition. Armed homesteaders using the Kansas model could hope to secure a region that had proven inhospitable to direct military attack. Relocating on the promise of securing grants of land, the colonizers would be the beneficiaries of the Treasury Department, making use of properties seized under the Confiscation and Direct Tax Acts.

Sometimes such mechanisms worked to further the interests traditionally associated with Radical Republicanism. To aid in the establishment of a school for black children in the vicinity of Fernandina, Florida, for example, Treasury officials obtained the deed to a 165-acre farm with orange trees for a missionary schoolmaster, the Reverend James D. Lynch of the African Methodist Episcopal Church.[23]

Since 1863, the army and Treasury had collaborated in an effort to dislodge congregations of the Methodist Episcopal Church, South, an organization born of the sectional conflict before the war that fiercely resisted federal authority during the war. In far-flung locations such as Memphis, Tennessee, and Huntsville, Alabama, commanders had seized control of MECS church buildings and authorized their use by the Methodist Church, North, and the African Methodist Episcopals. Other times they made other public buildings available for use as black churches, such as when they offered the use of the Brunswick County Courthouse in coastal North Carolina to a black congregation.[24] Though commanders offered the facilities, all captured properties were technically under the supervision of agents of the Treasury Department. Therefore black missionaries such as Lynch or the North Carolina–based Reverend Henry McNeal Turner became the beneficiaries of Chase's Direct Tax and Treasury commissioners.

Lynch saw the Treasury largesse as a boost to the mission of uplift initiated by the mostly white Gideonite teachers and ministers, and as an inspiration to African Americans in the North. "No one should find fault with it," he wrote; "everyone should rejoice at it, and be fired thereby with an heroic, self-sacrificing zeal to go and do likewise." Lynch himself—supported by the national churches as well as the federal government—oversaw the establishment of seventy schools for pupils of color in the Sea Islands vicinity by 1864.[25]

Alongside such exemplary uses, Direct Tax commissioners completed a number of more self-serving transactions. More than one of Chase's agents seized properties for the enrichment of himself or of his friends and family, as indictments in 1865 and 1866 would reveal. Disregarding the moral imperative, moreover, the redistributors made sales based on dubious titles that could not be guaranteed in U.S. courts.

The lure of Florida real estate was a new force in American history in the 1860s, having attracted small colonies of transplants from the Caribbean and the Northern states to centers such as Key West, St. Augustine, and Jacksonville. These settlers established a commercial-minded culture that was distinct from the Old South pattern in the state's sparsely populated interior and panhandle regions, where cotton, sugar, and cattle raising predominated. Tourism had introduced itself by the 1850s, alongside extractive enterprises such as sponge harvesting, salt, lumber (particularly from the hardy cypress), and marine salvage. Most exotic of all was the nascent traffic in oranges, delicacies that could be cultivated from the wild descendants of Spanish groves, harvested without slavery, shipped without spoilage, and sold at high prices in any market in the Western Hemisphere.[26]

Orange cultivation—which began in earnest in the 1870s with a surge of Northern investment—offered a perfumed temptation to the early speculators who were targeted as champions of Reconstruction in Florida. Among those taking a bite of the Treasury offerings was John Hay, President Lincoln's personal secretary and protégé.

The fresh-faced Hay—not yet twenty-five years old—had first visited St. Augustine in the company of his brother, who had contracted pneumonia and obtained leave from the Department of the South for convalescence. Arriving in April 1863, the young man was struck by East Florida's beauty and economic prospects. "I wish I could buy the State for taxes & keep it as a Castle of Indolence," he wrote to his White House partner, John G. Nicolay.

As it happened, he would have the chance to take advantage of an investment opportunity: an orange grove foreclosed for failure to pay the federal
Direct Tax and was offered at the bargain price of $500 by a close associate
of Salmon Chase, a faux Floridian, grifter, and Direct Tax commissioner
named Lyman D. Stickney.[27]

Stickney had been goading Chase to push for the greater conquest of
Florida within the Lincoln administration. Unbeknownst to the president,
in fact, the treasury secretary established a direct line of communication
with General John Quincy Adams Gillmore, commander of the Department
of the South.

Gillmore had been the antihero of the (Second) Battle of Fort Wagner,
July 18, 1863, in which the celebrated white colonel Robert Gould Shaw
had been killed in what turned out to be a futile assault using the high-
profile black regiment the Massachusetts 54th Volunteers. Union armed
forces would never abandon the effort to take the fort, a defense of the city
of Charleston, which finally fell to troops still serving under Gillmore in
February 1864.

Chase told Gillmore that he had urged the greater conquest of Florida
on Lincoln and Secretary Stanton for more than a year. He outlined what he
saw as a superior grand strategy of the war—that the seizure of the coast-
lines could form the basis of a gradual reorganization of the rebel states,
starting with the Deep South. He conceded that Gillmore's current orders
from the top were "not . . . based on this idea," and yet Chase thought it was
possible to "drive the enemy in a very few weeks from every part of Florida"
and to ensure its early readmission to the Union "on a permanently safe
basis."

Lest the general think that Chase was speaking out of turn, he insisted,
"I feel a special anxiety for prompt and efficient action, arising from my responsibilities as Head of the Treasury Department." He knew better than
anyone that "the possibility of crippled finances & deranged payments &
greater evils is not as remote as one could wish." Besides, he wrote, "I am an
Ohio man and so are you. May I not look for your sympathy and trust that
the motives that have such power with me will not fail to influence you?"

Chase's main request was that the general meet with Lyman Stickney
to discuss the prospects for prompt military action in Florida. Already, he

said, the tax commissioner had held a meeting in St. Augustine, collecting signatures on loyalty proclamations that Chase himself had helped to draft. According to Stickney's report on the meeting, General Gillmore not only endorsed the military plan but expressed confidence in Chase as an 1864 presidential candidate.[28]

Chase imagined reconstructed Florida as a point of origin for pro-Chase presidential politics. As a founding father of the new state, he could hope to win the loyalty of its delegates at the nominating convention less than six months in the future.

President Lincoln immediately perceived the same opportunity, not only to secure the Republican nomination but as a step toward a victory in November and other goals. Moreover, he shared the treasury secretary's sense of the importance of enlisting new states in the Union cause. Rather than standing aside to let Chase put his stamp on Florida Unionism, he dispatched a loyal personal representative. Returning to Florida in the uniform of an army major in January, John Hay took responsibility for reconstructing the state on the president's terms.

Hay carried Lincoln's own version of the loyalty oath in printed "blanks" for distribution to Florida citizens and a book of printed forms for the official record (in fact, the delivery of Hay's papers was delayed). The president wrote his own letter to General Gillmore requesting courtesies and assistance for his aide.[29]

Starting in Fernandina, a beach town just south of the Georgia border, Hay solicited oaths inside a general store owned by Lyman Stickney. He needed only fourteen hundred to meet the requirements of the Ten Percent Plan, and yet he encountered only a few who were willing to swear for the United States. He moved on to Jacksonville in the company of the Massachusetts 54th, who had been summoned to the area in preparation for a new offensive. The coastal city—occupying the mouth of the navigable St. Johns River—had been subject to a number of raids and invasions, most of which resulted in little more than local destruction. Thomas Wentworth Higginson (who burned a number of city blocks before retreating early in 1863) described Jacksonville as something like "the proverbial elephant in the lottery"—an asset nobody really wanted. The city was simple enough to capture, but useless without the force to push farther into the interior.

Among its liabilities was its nearly depopulated condition—there were no African Americans for Higginson to recruit, and practically no white civilians ready to sign John Hay's record book. Introduced to a few dozen Confederate prisoners, however, the president's aide managed to collect loyalty oaths among the ex-soldiers.[30]

Hay was not present two weeks later when the commander of Union forces (appointed when Gillmore returned to Port Royal and Beaufort a few days before) launched an ill-considered offensive into the interior. The operations included troops under the Kansas Radical James Montgomery, still trying to fill the ranks of his 2nd South Carolina Regiment. George Stearns's brainchildren, the Massachusetts 54th and 55th, also participated. A total of six thousand took the field against about as many Confederates, squaring off on February 20 in a major battle known later as Olustee.

The Battle of Olustee (about which we will hear more later) epitomized certain trends in the experience of black military units in the Civil War. Union observers remarked upon the pronounced bravery and tenacity of the men. Confederates demonstrated their resolve to protest against the use of black troops by refusing to follow procedures regarding wounded and captured soldiers. "Let's teach them a lesson," one commander, Colonel Abner McCormick, told his cavalrymen: "I shall not take any negro prisoners in this fight." The Union commander, for his part, employed his troops recklessly. Hay noted the day after that General Truman Seymour "seemed very unsteady and queer" and "subject to violent alterations of timidity & rashness."

In fact, Gillmore's subordinate had acted in accordance with the commander's wishes. In a telegram to the War Department, Gillmore had described a set of Radical Republican and administration-friendly goals for wider action in Florida: to recruit slaves for combat, to seize lumber, turpentine, and other military stores, and to advance "the speedy restoration of Florida to her allegiance." In a pattern soon to be repeated, the white commander took risks with black soldiers that he might have hesitated to take with other troops. The result was a rout for the Union, with one of the most shocking fatality ratios of the war.[31] Apart from the scandal, the battle proved insignificant from a military point of view. The Florida theater, such as it was, remained peripheral to the overall war.

Politically it exacted a sharper toll. Democratic newspapers in the North denounced the expedition as an Electoral College ploy, seeing through the plot to restore Florida to the Union in time to vote for Lincoln's reelection. Secretary of War Edwin Stanton and General in Chief Henry Halleck publicly questioned Gillmore's authority to act. When the general answered lamely that he was acting on the president's own orders, Lincoln denied "distinctly, especially, and emphatically" that he had given "any instructions or orders to Gen. Gillmore, requiring directly or impliedly any movement of his command into Florida with either military or political objects." Indeed, friends of the administration observed, Gillmore's movement in advance of Olustee had taken place before the arrival of Major Hay, whose presence was the only piece of evidence suggesting a White House role in the affair.

The aide returned to Washington with his reputation somewhat battered, implicated in both a military defeat and an effort to create a "rotten borough" for the 1864 Republicans. In a series of gleeful reports on his experiences in the opposition press, Hay took heat for his association with the unsavory Direct Tax commissioner (with whom the young man had invested another $4,000 in confiscated properties later deemed nontransferable). He also stood accused of "junketeering" in the Sunshine State with a number of "feminine female women."[32]

Secretary Chase's hand in the Florida mishap remained hidden, even as he confronted embarrassments closer to home. Since December, the secretary had spoken openly with Radical Republicans about his aspirations to replace Lincoln at the head of the ticket. By January, as many as two dozen conspirators—mostly Radical members of Congress—were actively campaigning in the shadows for Chase. On February 20, the same day as the Olustee debacle, a pro-Chase document that had been making the rounds in Washington surfaced in the newspapers. Called the Pomeroy Circular because the only man bold enough to sign his name to it was the ultra-left Kansas senator, the printed document chided Lincoln for his "manifest tendency toward compromise and temporary expedients" and found in Chase "more of the qualities needed in a President." Few commentators on the news seemed to agree. The treasury secretary pled ignorance of the movement (though his daughter Kate Chase Sprague had bankrolled the printing of the subversive materials). He offered Lincoln his resignation, but the president declined. The dashing of his presidential hopes was punishment enough for Salmon Chase.[33]

Republicans were quick to jettison Chase as an alternative to Lincoln. Diehards had not forgotten his lack of action in the case of Margaret Garner, and speakers such as Wendell Phillips made sure that winter audiences heard regular reminders. Initiatives on black enfranchisement quieted in Congress and the cabinet, and at least for an interlude, complaints about the leniency of Lincoln's terms of restoration stayed out of the headlines. Lincoln himself made private overtures on behalf of black voting rights, suggesting that Louisiana's restoration governor-elect consider extending the suffrage to "highly intelligent" black men and soldiers, a suggestion that exceeded the sweep of Chase's call for enfranchising literate men, but his advice was ignored and hardly discussed.

A highlight of the season was the relatively smooth compliance of occupied Arkansas, a territory equal to about half of the state, with the restoration plan. Counting only white voters, more than ten thousand took the loyalty oath in elections in March, joining Restored Tennessee in sending representatives to the United States Congress.[34]

The Union girded itself for major spring offensives, with U. S. Grant taking command of U.S. forces as the first lieutenant general since George Washington.

Failing to acknowledge the landmarks abounding in administration policy, Radicals were acting nasty (as John Hay complained to his diary). The substance of their insubordination was the ongoing pursuit of an alternative to Lincoln at the head of the Republican ticket.

15
☙✺❧

REPUBLICAN NATION-BUILDING

Despite the prospect of Southern delegations to the 1864 party conventions, the long run-up to the contest took place primarily in the North. Starting in 1863, patriotic Philadelphia made a bid to be the center of the Republican presidential contest and a model of civilian engagement in the war. The Union League, a gentlemen's club of the city—created to address the emergency of sharing the old-line Philadelphia Club with Southern-loving Copperheads in wartime—burst into action with a number of resourceful projects to support the Union effort. Union Leaguing became a fast-growing regional craze, with ward-level clubs by the dozens around Philadelphia and branches in Trenton, Atlantic City, and farther reaches.

The flagship Union League rooms on Chestnut Street—soon to be supplanted by an architecturally ambitious house on Broad—served as the epicenter of high-level social, financial, and political transactions for Philadelphia's elite. And while they swore off labels in deference to sentimental former Democrats in their ranks, the clubmen quickly came to function as a supercharged version of the Boston Bird Club, complete with a cadre of Philadelphia litterateurs. Union Leaguers embraced abolition, black soldiers, and other Radical precepts, and as the 1864 elections got under way, its advocacy grew partisan. Invited to visit the rooms at the Union League Club, for example, a national Presbyterian delegation hesitated: "The question arose whether the Union League was a political organization or otherwise, when Otis Allen, of this city, remarked that the 'gentleman who does not know that this "Union League" is as emphatically political as a "Wide Awake," has a great deal to learn.'[1]

In the summer of 1863, Union Leaguers bustled with plans for a great Fourth of July celebration. Committees of the various branches were hard at work organizing speeches, resolutions, military parades, and banquets—and glowing with anticipation of President Lincoln's appearance as the keynote speaker. A discordant note, however, began to cloud the prospects for the event in late June, when a Macon, Georgia, newspaper disclosed,

> We are informed that private letters as long ago as the 13th state that all Lee's army was on the move except for General A. P. Hill's corps. Of course nobody knew where they were going. Some say that General Lee has received an invitation to attend the Great Union League Meeting in Philadelphia on the Fourth of July next. Lincoln, it is well known, is to be there, and the great Black Republican party is to be largely represented. Under these circumstances Gen. Lee aspires to take with him as strong a deputation as possible.[2]

The Emergency of 1863—as Lee's invasion was known in Pennsylvania—stirred the Union League to more direct action. Canceling their festivities, they redirected many of their gentlemanly drill clubs to a pair of new Union League army regiments.[3] By the Fourth, they were ready to march in defense of Philadelphia and the Union itself.

The real action was in Gettysburg, Pennsylvania, and on the Mississippi River, where slaves deserted by the millions and enlisted by the thousands in what had recently been designated the United States Colored Troops. Those contested districts produced the news of the season in the days after the mostly unacknowledged national holiday.

President Lincoln had been thinking about July 4—almost certainly in preparation for his remarks at the canceled Philadelphia Union League event. Twin victories at Gettysburg and Vicksburg—both announced on the Fourth of July—seemed suddenly to shift the momentum of the war decisively toward the Union for the first time. Greeting serenaders from a White

House balcony on July 7, the president may have made use of remarks he had prepared for the aborted Union League event. His words also anticipated some of the language of his immortal address at Gettysburg National Cemetery, still some months in the future:

> How long ago is it?—eighty odd years—since on the Fourth of July for the first time in the history of the world a nation by its representatives, assembled and declared as a self-evident truth that "all men are created equal." [Cheers.] That was the birthday of the United States of America.

The four score and seven, as he saw it, had seen more than one unhappy commemoration of the original event. Three presidents had died on July 4, a coincidence not lost on the superstitious Lincoln:

> And now, on this last Fourth of July just passed, when we have a gigantic Rebellion, at the bottom of which is an effort to overthrow the principle that all men were created equal, we have the surrender of a most powerful position and army on that very day, [cheers] and not only so, but in a succession of battles in Pennsylvania, near to us, through three days, so rapidly fought that they might be called one great battle on the 1st, 2d and 3d of the month of July; and on the 4th the cohorts of those who opposed the declaration that all men are created equal, "turned tail" and run. [Long and continued cheers.][4]

For Lincoln, the remarkable events associated with the day manifested a divine engagement with the experiment initiated in 1776 and recently rededicated to its original promise of equality.

To celebrate the Declaration of Independence in 1863 and 1864 was conservative—insofar as it exalted the American tradition—and Radical—intending to expand the definition of liberty to include all people. Only three years after it was disavowed by some Republicans in deliberations on their presidential platform, the founding text had come to occupy the center of political discourse in Lincoln's thinking. He declined to comment further than his quizzical introduction, telling the serenaders, "Having said this much, I will now take the music." It was too soon to say whether a nation dedicated to the radical July 4 proposition could long endure.

Frederick Douglass, the Ebenezer Scrooge of July 4, marked the eleventh anniversary of his famous speech "What, to the Slave, Is the Fourth?" in Philadelphia, a city he had long described as the most racist place in the country.[5] In fact, he would not favor its white audiences with a lecture hall appearance. Appearing, like Lincoln, just after the holiday, he addressed his appeal directly to black men on the recruiting ground at Fort William Penn. "Men of Color, to Arms!"—Douglass's appeal for black enlistment in the army—opened with an acknowledgment that the speaker had not always embraced his status as an American. "[There] were dark and terrible days for the republic," he acknowledged, but he had set aside the "dead past" in favor of embracing the "living present." While Lincoln sought to reclaim the unfulfilled promise of the Declaration in his thinking, Douglass considered the potential of the other founding text, in keeping with his longtime view as a political abolitionist.

> I hold that the Federal Government was never, in its essence, anything but an anti-slavery government. Abolish slavery tomorrow, and not a sentence or syllable of the Constitution need be altered . . . There is in the Constitution no East, no West, no North, no South, no black, no white, no slave, no slaveholder, but all are citizens who are of American birth.

The view of the Supreme Court, where ancient Taney still held sway, had been overtaken by events, and now the attorney general of the United States, Edward Bates, had emphatically argued in favor of citizenship for all African Americans. And "so far from their being any opposition" to the fulfillment of their obligations as citizens to serve in the armed forces, Douglass said,

> the President at Washington, the Cabinet and the Congress, the generals commanding and the whole army of the nation unite in giving us one thunderous welcome to share with them in the honor and glory of suppressing treason and upholding the star-spangled banner. The revolution is

tremendous, and it becomes us as wise men to recognize the change, and to shape our action accordingly. [Cheers and cries of "We will!"]

Douglass acknowledged that much remained to be done to achieve fairness even in the midst of revolution. "Do you say you want the same pay that white men get?" he queried. "Don't you work for less every day than white men get?" he answered. "Do I hear you say you want black officers?" So did Douglass, and he anticipated officers, colonels, and even generals before the war was done. "Once let the black man get upon his person the brass letters U.S.," he predicted, and all the unfinished business of securing equal rights could be addressed from a position more powerful than "mere parchment guarantees."

In your hands that musket means liberty; and should your constitutional rights at the close of this war be denied . . . your brethren are safe while you have a Constitution which proclaims your right to keep and bear arms. [Immense applause.][6]

Black men would fight for their claim to freedom, Douglass suggested, whether they did so in unity with white America or against it.

For African Americans and their allies, the main fight was for voting rights. The idea of suffrage for black men as an electoral advantage for Republicans had tended to trickle up toward the party leadership from activists in the field, particularly in the occupied parts of the Confederacy. Black voters could be counted toward the totals required by the Ten Percent Plan for reconstructing the states. Polling that included black voters in the Sea Islands had resulted in the election of two delegates to the Republican convention in Baltimore, and a group from a U.S.-sponsored black settlement on Roanoke Island in North Carolina met with Lincoln in the spring of 1864 in search of similar recognition. Starting in December 1863, the leading congressional alternative to Lincoln's Reconstruction plans had been a bill submitted by Ohio representative James Ashley that embraced voting rights for black Union veterans.

James Ashley was a large man—"physically, intellectually, and morally," as he would be remembered. An abolitionist since childhood, he became a leader of the Radical faction in the House. Without attracting the public scorn attached to more famous colleagues such as Thaddeus Stevens, Ashley asserted the ethical stakes of Reconstruction in a bid for a congressional role in the process.[7]

"Sir," said Ashley, in introducing the legislation, "I know that the loyal people of this nation will never be guilty of the infamy of inviting the loyal blacks to unite with them in fighting our battles, and after our triumph . . . deny these loyal blacks political rights while consenting that pardoned but unrepentant rebels shall again be clothed with the entire political power of these States." Ashley sought

> the declaration here, on the part of the Congress of the United States, that the people of no rebel States shall hold a convention and frame a constitution which does not contain a provision securing the civil rights of these people. And even if the word "white" is not stricken . . . I secure by the provision of the seventh section to every colored citizen who is or who has been in the military or naval service of the United States, the right to vote for delegates to a convention, and then upon the constitution that that convention may adopt and submit to the people for their ratification or rejection.[8]

Alongside Representative Ashley's proposed constitutional amendment to ban slavery, also submitted to the House in December 1863, the bill to reorganize the states under terms dictated by Congress languished through the spring of 1864, even as the president endorsed its contents in a series of discussions with its author. "Come again, Ashley," the president enjoined after a tense discussion, "and we will take up reconstruction again."

Having embraced the idea of voting rights for soldiers and educated blacks in his private correspondence, Lincoln was open to the terms that Ashley had proposed. Committed to the success of his Louisiana reboot first and foremost, however, he rejected the proposal to abolish the state government created under the president's procedures. Lincoln wanted Congress to approve Louisiana's readmission regardless of any standards established for future readmissions of Confederate states. His progressive views on black suffrage remained unreported, allowing Radicals to speculate ungenerously about Lincoln's character and motivations.

Radicals in Congress and the party councils wanted less deference to the popular will and a chief executive willing to act forcefully in support of principles. While they had disparaged Chase as a replacement candidate for 1864, they had not yet extended their endorsement to the unloved incumbent. Another candidate—propelled by an ambition no less sweeping than that of the treasury secretary—had been working the rounds in anticipation of a second chance.

John C. Fremont had endured a tough season since his failed emancipation edict back in 1861. He had been roundly ridiculed for putting on airs as commander in the Western District, and members of his vaunted bodyguard of European elites had found it difficult to get commissions in other units after his dismissal. Fremont himself had secured an 1862 appointment in the Virginia theater only to be soundly bested by the talented Confederate general Thomas "Stonewall" Jackson after refusing to comply with the War Department's elaborate battle plans. Facing censure, Fremont was relieved of command at his own request. Since that time he had called himself a general while he waited for new orders month after month.

The War Department had added injury to insult in the fall of 1863 when it confiscated and destroyed his home on San Francisco's Golden Gate, practically the only structure on what was then a brilliant wild promontory, saying that the site was necessary for national defense and notifying Fremont after the fact. Except for the national German American community, which idolized Fremont for his antislavery gesture and his open door for U.S.-based Forty-Eighters and other Europeans, the Pathfinder spent 1862 and most of 1863 in the political wilderness.

But Fremont was hardly friendless, being blessed with the support of his dynamic wife. Described by an admirer, the Reverend Thomas Starr King, as "a she-Merrimac" carrying "guns enough to be formidable to a whole Cabinet," Jessie Benton Fremont moved to resuscitate the career that she shared with her husband as "the secretary and other-self."[9] She scored an unlikely coup with her purchase of a cottage on the beach in the summer of 1863.

Nahant, Massachusetts, was not just any beach, but the vacation epicenter of New England Radicalism. And the house that Jessie called the Anchorage was not just any cottage, but a property sold by Wendell Phillips, adjacent to his summer estate, adjoined on the other side by the beach home of the abolitionist poet Henry Wadsworth Longfellow and just down the bluff from the home of the Boston Brahmin brothers John Ellerton and Henry Cabot Lodge, where Senator Charles Sumner spent his summer recess. The Fremonts made a splash in Nahant, tenting on the beachfront in a suite of canvas rooms complete with carpets and exotic birds and entertaining lavishly. Jessie made a special project of winning Phillips over to the cause, and the normally reticent John C. even appeared on a speakers' platform in Boston at the orator's request, traveling overland from the peninsula because Nahant's only ferry had been pressed into wartime service in the navy.[10] The most dazzling of their conquests, however, was the Quaker poet and politico John Greenleaf Whittier, who lived in family seclusion in the town of Amesbury, some thirty-five miles to the north.

Jessie made the journey to Amesbury uninvited in the company of Charles Zagonyi, the Hungarian count and revolutionary who became briefly famous as the captain of Fremont's bodyguard back in St. Louis. Noting the arrival of strangers, Whittier retreated to his peach orchard, leaving instructions with his housekeeper that he should not be disturbed. Mrs. Fremont chose to wait until the reluctant poet finally faced his guests. Even then she refused to introduce herself or identify her companion:

> "Thy speech is Southern; what is thy name?" [Whittier asked.]
> "Not yet," I said. "I am Southern; but let me tell you more first."

She proceeded to quote to Whittier lines from his poem "To John C. Fremont," sent to the general's headquarters in St. Louis in 1861: "Who would recall [his emancipation orders] now must first arrest / The winds that blow down from the free North-west / Ruffling the Gulf; or like a scroll roll back / The Mississippi to its upper springs."

> Whittier had grasped my arm, and his eyes blazed. "What is thy name?"
> "Fremont."
> Without a word he swung out of the room, to return, infolding in his helping embrace a frail little woman, tenderly saying to the invalid he was bringing from her seclusion,—

"Elizabeth, this is Jessie Fremont—under our roof. Our mother would have been glad to see this day."

After this we came down (with our hearts still in our throats all the same) to everyday talk; but the everyday of the war time was a sublimated life in itself, a grand epoch to have lived in, and taken part in.[11]

Repeating this story ever afterward to feminists and admirers of the poet, Jessie Fremont leveraged its social capital in the circles most inclined to favor her husband's political prospects.

She followed up her season at the beach with a smashing social success in New York City. In command of a peerless address book of associates, Jessie Fremont obtained valuable curiosities for the New York Sanitary Commission's fund-raising auction: a poem written and signed in Whittier's hand, the painting *Valley of the Yosemite* by Albert Bierstadt, and a commemorative object fashioned from the hair of John C. Fremont and George Washington. She also raised $2,842 for the cause with her children's production of *Cinderella*, which made use of two hundred child dancers and a carriage pulled by six matching Shetland ponies and featured ten-year-old John Charles Fremont, Jr., as the prince.[12]

The "Fremont and Jessie" ticket for 1864 made New York City its major hub of operations. Though the support of New Englanders such as Wendell Phillips (the "Golden Trumpet" of abolitionism) was decisive, New Yorkers provided the publicity and organization required to mount a challenge to the Republican mainstream. A key event in John C.'s emergence as a candidate was his appearance at a lecture by the English abolitionist George Thompson at the city's Cooper Institute, later known as Cooper Union. In formally presiding over the assembly, Fremont offered a speech in which he made general observations about the success of abolitionism in the United States and the diplomatic obstacles created by the Civil War—a subject he considered a specialty. The Englishman offered words of praise for the Pathfinder, while the young Radical Theodore Tilton praised him as the man who "[taught] statesmanship to Abraham Lincoln."

A few weeks later, in a meeting room of the same venue, a platform of resolutions endorsing Fremont for the presidency was adopted. The crowd of Germans and lesser-known abolitionists endorsed the principles of single-term presidencies and of equal rights before the law without regard for race. They heard remarks from Horace Greeley, who welcomed Fremont but indicated that he would support the nominee of the national convention.[13]

New York feminists rallied for the Fremont candidacy, buoyed by memories of his wife's historic role in the 1856 canvass. The slogans "Fremont and Our Jessie," "Jessie's Choice," and "Jessie for the White House" still carried weight with activists such as Susan B. Anthony and Elizabeth Cady Stanton. The two signed an early call for an alternative Republican convention, and they put the New York City offices of the Women's Loyal National League, an organization dedicated to expanding suffrage to include women and African American men, at the disposal of the Fremont candidacy. Anthony also gained the signature of her Rochester neighbor and ally Frederick Douglass on the Radical convention petition.[14]

By April a pro-Fremont newspaper appeared on New York newsstands, financed by the Fremonts at a cost of $20,000 and distributed to readers at no cost. Calling itself the *New Nation*, the sheet denounced the decision of the Republicans (temporarily acting under the name National Union Party) to move their nominating convention to June from the original proposed date in September. "We advise everyone at once to give up all idea of taking part in the Baltimore Convention," its editors urged. The scheduled assembly was a "nonentity." In early May, a "Bolters' Convention" of anti-Lincoln Republicans was scheduled to take place in Cleveland by the end of the month.

Attended by Stephen Foster and Parker Pillsbury of Massachusetts, the Reverend Henry T. Cheever of New York, some well-known Missouri Radicals, and 150 assorted individuals without a national reputation, the Cleveland convention moved to nominate Fremont (and for vice president a Democratic New Yorker, John Cochrane). Though they heard a few speeches, the only words deemed fit to print in most newspapers were those of Wendell Phillips, who did not attend.

In his letter, Phillips outlined the 1864 Radical agenda: a rejection of Lincoln's terms for Reconstruction; the confiscation and distribution of rebel estates, with "every loyal man, white or black, sharing in the land and the ballot"; and a constitutional amendment banning slavery and extending equal protection of the laws to African Americans. He was open in acknowledging that the convention might not approve the Radical measures for its platform. "But if some of these points are not covered," he wrote, "I shall still support its action with all my heart, if it puts the name of Fremont or Butler on its flag."[15]

Despite the participation of antislavery extremists, the Cleveland convention did not convincingly present itself as a Republican Party affair. One clue was the repeated shout-out to Benjamin F. Butler and others from the 1860-era Democratic Party, including the vice presidential nominee, John F. Cochrane. A central message of the Cleveland convention was that Radicals and Democrats could make common cause against Lincoln. The proposed alliance was forecast in the very name Radical Democracy, in which, as one newspaper described it, "the extremes meet."

John C. Fremont seemed to acknowledge as much in his strategically vague letter accepting the Radical Democracy nomination. The specifics he saw fit to include in his comments were pet topics of the Democratic Party opposition: Lincoln's suppression of the constitutional liberties of Northern dissidents; the unlawfulness of confiscation; and the recklessness of the administration's finance plans. Slavery was deemed to be "practically destroyed," and "with this extinction of Slavery the party divisions created by it have disappeared." We were all Democrats and all Republicans, he suggested, who saw the dangers in the present course of the executive and sought to check them.[16]

With the Fremont movement at risk of "Copperheadism," a pro-Confederate stance, true Radicals turned their attention to the two conventions yet on the calendar for June: Democrats and the real Republicans. The choice of Baltimore as a venue for the National Union / Republicans proved to be an inspired choice when Maryland convened a constitutional convention in April to act at last to terminate slavery within its borders. Lincoln's reverence for this development lent a special poignancy to an appearance by the president at the Baltimore Sanitary Fair. His remarks struck a philosophical note:

> The world has never had a good definition of the word liberty, and the American people, just now, are much in want of one. We all declare for liberty; but in using the same word we do not all mean the same thing . . .

The shepherd drives the wolf from the sheep's throat, for which the sheep thanks the shepherd as a liberator, while the wolf denounces him for the same act as the destroyer of liberty, especially as the sheep was a black one. Plainly the sheep and the wolf are not agreed upon a definition of the word liberty; and precisely the same difference prevails to-day among us human creatures, even in the North, and all professing to love liberty . . .

Recently, as it seems, the people of Maryland have been doing something to define liberty; and thanks to them that, in what they have done, the wolf's dictionary, has been repudiated.[17]

To convene Republicans in a slave state was in itself a revolutionary act. The work of the convention, however, did not go far beyond this significant gesture. The most progressive element of the Republican Platform of 1864 was its call for a constitutional amendment to abolish slavery—a possibility that was not yet officially recognized as a mechanism for restoring the status of Confederate states that were willing to ratify it. The platform also cheered for black soldiers and condemned the rebel no-quarter policies that had prevailed at the Battle of Olustee, and more recently in the massacre of black troops at Fort Pillow in Tennessee. Otherwise it omitted the main points of the Radical agenda, slighting the subjects of confiscation and land reform, black suffrage and civil rights, officers' commissions and equal pay for black soldiers.

Despite these omissions, some among the small number of eligible black voters in the North expressed support for the Republicans' Baltimore platform. "There was a kind and wise Providence in bringing Mr. Lincoln into the Presidential chair," wrote John Brown's New York ally James W. C. Pennington. "I say OUR president because he is the only American President who has ever given any attention to colored men as citizens."[18]

In choosing Andrew Johnson as Lincoln's running mate, the Baltimore convention deftly nodded to conservatives and Radicals at the same time— choosing a Southerner and Democrat whose deep personal antipathy for rebel aristocrats led him to the belief that "treason must be made odious" by the punishment of traitors.

The recognition of William Lloyd Garrison from the podium, and the crowd's raucous chanting of his name, lent a Radical slant to the meeting's

228 WHEN IT WAS GRAND

tone. The editor's attendance also represented his personal apotheosis as a Republican partisan.[19]

In admitting delegations from the restored states of Virginia, Louisiana, Tennessee, and Arkansas (though rejecting those from fragmentary Florida and South Carolina), the convention offered tacit recognition of the legitimacy of Lincoln's Reconstruction policies. In the weeks to come, the Radicals would dispute this issue in the fiercest condemnations of the president they had yet unleashed.[20]

May, June, and July 1864 found the president and Radicals more than usually at odds. The Cleveland and Baltimore conventions had produced rival Republican tickets (though Fremont proved an immediate disappointment to the Radicals as he sought to win the middle ground and Northern Democrats). A dispute over patronage resulted in a final confrontation between Lincoln and Treasury Secretary Salmon Chase. Lincoln's acceptance of Chase's resignation on June 29 brought the full Senate Finance Committee to protest in the president's office. A new Reconstruction bill added to the tension. Setting aside James Ashley's December proposal, House members led by Henry Winter Davis of Maryland and Thaddeus Stevens of Pennsylvania and a Senate faction under Benjamin Wade, Zachary Chandler, and Charles Sumner adopted a new Reconstruction program that became known as the Wade-Davis bill.

Wade-Davis differed from presidential Reconstruction in particular ways. It included a requirement that seceded states repudiate Confederate debts as a precursor to reorganization—a penalty imposed on Southern aristocrats and other creditors of the illegal regime. In place of Lincoln's amnesty plan, the bill denied voting rights to all men who could not swear an "ironclad oath" that they had not supported the rebellion. The proposal also withheld recognition until 50 percent of the 1860 electorate had sworn the oath, a proportion that could not be achieved without enfranchising black voters. Like Lincoln's own arrangements, Wade-Davis also required states to pass constitutions that banned slavery. Its adoption threatened to set aside the progress toward establishing a government in Louisiana, to the president's chagrin.

While Wade-Davis was more Radical than the Ten Percent Plan, it disappointed the most progressive members of the party in its failure to provide directly for black suffrage. Last-minute maneuvers on July 2 saw the word "white" struck from Winter Davis's original language about the electorate and then restored in the name of political expediency. The revised version, endorsed by all the top Republicans, passed the House and the Senate on July 4—the last day until December that the 38th Congress was in session. Legislators were shocked when the president refused to sign it, executing a pocket veto of the bill.

Lincoln offered purely practical objections to the Wade-Davis bill, explaining first in person and a few days later in a written message that he was unwilling to accept the derailment of Louisiana statehood and that he wanted more flexibility rather than a single formula when admitting other states. Radicals were not mollified by his suggestion in the July 8 message that he was "fully satisfied with the system for restoration contained in the bill" and his invitation to recognize "any State choosing to adopt it." A "Wade-Davis Manifesto" published by the authors of the bill during the recess reminded Lincoln that "the authority of Congress is paramount" and that the president's action regarding the restoration of states was "rash and unconstitutional." The text obliquely referenced impeachment as "the remedy for these usurpations," lining up its authors with the conspiracy to replace Lincoln at the top of the 1864 party ticket. All through August, the breach within the establishment rivaled the poor results of the Union military effort that summer as the subject of antiadministration gossip. "We have Lee and his [bastards] on one side, and Henry Winter Davis & Ben Wade and all such hell-cats on the other," complained Montgomery Blair, Lincoln's controversial conservative postmaster general.

"They have never been friendly to me," Lincoln observed of the Radicals. In the end their threats of impeachment—which foreshadowed the crisis of the Johnson presidency in the coming years—did little to win the support of the party or the public. Lincoln may have been unpopular in the awful month of August 1864, but if anything, the congressional Jacobins led by Wade and Davis proved more unlikable still.[21]

16

NEVER SURRENDER THE FLAG

Political leaders considered the changes wrought by the Civil War mainly in abstract terms, but black soldiers and their commanders experienced the revolution firsthand. In a literal sense, their participation in official capacities altered the complexion of the state. Black enlistments had surged in 1863, with more than twenty thousand mustered in by Lorenzo Thomas and his agents in the Southern states, and thousands more enrolled in Northern volunteer regiments created in Massachusetts, Michigan, Ohio, and Rhode Island. They had proved their mettle as soldiers at Milliken's Bend, Port Hudson, and Fort Wagner, and fears that they would be consigned to fatigue duties had proved unfounded. Indeed, as 1864 progressed, the rapidly expanding ranks of the U.S. Colored Troops played a vital part in the most horrific fighting in the war. Their valor did not guarantee equal treatment, however, either at the hands of the enemy or by the government they were sacrificing to defend. Their fight on two fronts would summon the Radical Republicans to the barricades as allies and, increasingly, as partisans willing to open their ranks to include African American men.

Much remained to be done. An incident on January 1, 1864, revealed the extent to which race prejudice persisted in the U.S. Army—by then, among the most egalitarian institutions in the country. Officers of the occupation army had organized a New Year's celebration at a fine Nashville hotel. Like the ranks of commissioned officers nationwide (North and South), all par-

ticipants in the gala affair were Caucasian American. In an unpleasant incident, a lieutenant colonel from Ohio refused the extended hand of a USCT
officer, Colonel Thomas J. Morgan, explaining in an aside to his companions
that he "did not recognize these [Negro] officers."

Unfortunately for the offending officer (unnamed in Morgan's reminiscences), news of the slight circulated and quickly reached the ears of Adjutant General Lorenzo Thomas, who happened to be in Nashville at the
time. Within hours, General Thomas had dismissed the lieutenant colonel
from the army—a reminder that the Lincoln administration had taken aim
at army racism as a hindrance to military operations.[1]

The disgraced Ohioan made a show of his disdain for colored troops by
his gesture and his use of rude language, but his behavior may well have
reflected class prejudice alongside his racism. Officers in U.S. volunteer regiments were drawn mostly from educated local elites, but the colored troops
relied on promotions of individuals from a variety of backgrounds. Whereas
some (like Colonel Morgan, whom Thomas would make a brigadier general the following month) had been commissioned officers of lower rank,
others were promoted from the ranks of noncommissioned officers and
enlisted men.

Starting in May 1863, a War Department Board of Examiners evaluated
USCT officer candidates for their knowledge of army tactics, geography,
history, and arithmetic. When too many proposed officers fell short in these
categories, the War Department turned to the Union League of Philadelphia
for assistance. A "Free School" for USCT officers offered basic literacy and
instruction in the designated subjects to working-class applicants, including
a large number of veterans from the rank and file.[2]

The policy of reserving officers' commissions for white men stood at
odds with the progressive elements of army life. Already, the limitation had
cost the Union the services of famous African Americans who chose to serve
as recruiters rather than enlist and fight. After serving for a trial period as
enlisted men, the elite officers of the reconstituted Louisiana Native Guards
(a Unionized elite Confederate militia based in New Orleans) had resigned
en masse in protest. One consequence was an ongoing shortage of qualified
USCT officers.[3] Another was the perpetuation of the gulf of mistrust that
separated qualified blacks from their allies in the Republican Party.

White Radical Republicans sometimes considered the inequity of officers' commissions, but other USCT issues figured more prominently on their political agenda. Since the announcement by Jefferson Davis in 1862 that Confederates would deliver captured African Americans to state officials with authority to enslave them, Radicals had led in pressing the Lincoln administration to ensure that black troops benefited from the protections extended to other prisoners of war. Influential whites such as Francis Shaw, the father of the late Robert Gould Shaw, and African Americans such as Frederick Douglass, urged retaliatory measures, including the execution of Confederate soldiers, man for man, upon confirmed assassinations in contravention of military law. Because the management of prisoners fell firmly under the jurisdiction of the kindly head of the executive branch, whose sensibilities could barely tolerate the execution of deserters and other criminals, proposals for retaliatory measures fell short of being concrete policy proposals for Radicals in Congress. Radicals of the 1860s model did not pursue a progressive outlook on Indian affairs, and mostly had forgotten or entirely disregarded the disruptions surrounding the tragic Sioux Uprising of 1862, so no one reminded the president of his readiness to execute 38 of 303 Dakota men convicted of rebellion by a military court.[4] The protection of black troops from draconian Confederate practices remained a constant subject of Radical political agitation, a policy matter that Douglass saw fit to press during his August 1863 interview with Lincoln in his White House office.

Another Radical initiative addressed the ongoing problem of unequal pay. This inequity originated in Congress, which authorized a differential pay scale in the original legislation enabling the creation of black units. Allotted only $7 per month versus $10 for whites, and given 50 cents less per month for clothing, black soldiers earned less than 58 percent of the going rate for white counterparts.[5] Lincoln and the War Department were slow to correct the disparity, believing, in the president's words, that the country needed "talking up to" on the subject of blacks in military service generally before truly equal terms could be established. In fact, resistance to equal terms proved resilient, particularly because of the irregular intervals of nineteenth-century congressional sessions. The indifference of Congress in March and July 1863 allowed the problem to persist until December. Even then, the Thirty-Eighth Congress did not include a raise and the restoration of back pay on its agenda for early consideration.

Soldiers and their advocates protested the injustice. Most prominently, the Massachusetts 54th and 55th Regiments refused to accept the partial wage, with officers and enlisted men forgoing their pay for more than a year. When Governor John Andrew proposed to offset the differential using Massachusetts funds, the most famous black soldiers in the country rejected the offer, taking a stand on principle. An African American corporal (who, like other noncommissioned black officers, was paid at the same rate as a black private), wrote the governor with a gentle rebuke.

[We are] not surprised at the solicitude of the Governor to have us paid that we have so dearly earned, nor would we be surprised if the State would cheerfully assume the burden; but the Governor's recommendation clearly shows that the General Government don't mean to pay us, so long as there is a loophole to get out of it . . .

To accept the reduced rate, he wrote, "would rob a whole race of its title to manhood."[6]

Frederick Douglass complained that his sons were fighting for the United States "with halters about their necks," and abolitionist officers from Massachusetts such as Wentworth Higginson and Colonel James Beecher protested the policy in letters to the president and the War Department.[7] Governor Andrew pressed the case with his Radical Republican allies in Congress, writing to Charles Sumner that the discrepancy meant that "the government means to disgrace and demean" by denying equal pay, "so that [the black soldier] may always be in his own eyes, and the eyes of all men 'only a [Negro].'"[8]

Massachusetts also took the lead in pushing for equal pay in Congress. In January 1864, Senator Henry Wilson introduced legislation discreetly titled "A bill to promote the enlistment of colored troops." The bill provided for equal pay and also for the payment of a federal bounty to black enlistees—an effort to offset the difference between white soldiers enrolled in Northern states that offered bounties and black soldiers enrolled directly from slave plantations in the South. Wilson's bill occasioned little discussion in the

Senate and did not inspire a companion bill in the House of Representatives. "The people of Maryland did not believe that colored troops could do the duty of white men," another senator insisted, noting that the recruitment of African American troops in his home state had resulted in a loss for Republicans in his state's House delegations.[9] The session adjourned without action to address the discrepancy in pay.

Meanwhile, black soldiers found new opportunities to demonstrate their fitness and commitment. As we've seen, the Battle of Olustee on February 20, 1864, took place in a theater of interest mostly to Radical colonizationists and restorationists, and yet the sacrifices of its mostly black legions did not pass unnoticed. A noncommissioned officer of the Massachusetts 54th, Sergeant Stephen Swails, marched to the battlefield under protest, having requested an honorable discharge from the service on the grounds that the pay policy constituted a breach of the contract he agreed to upon enlistment. Swails was a veteran of the parapet of Fort Wagner, and after taking a heroic part at Olustee, the sergeant was shot in the head during the Union retreat. He recovered to be recommended by his commander for promotion to 2nd lieutenant, a promotion approved by Governor Andrew but later denied by the War Department on the grounds of his African descent. In the interim, under orders from his company colonel, Swails dressed in the uniform of a commissioned officer. His pay remained a meager $7 a month.[10]

Black soldiers at Olustee understood they faced greater risks than the white troops fighting at their sides. Fearful of reenslavement by Confederates, wounded men staggered and crawled to get to safety, and a white surgeon refused to take men of his own race onto Union ambulances, insisting that wounded blacks faced more danger. When a train taking wounded African Americans from the scene became stalled, exhausted members of the 54th lashed it with ropes and pulled it to safety using their own strength.

Despite these efforts, an estimated fifty captured colored troops were shot or clubbed to death by rifles as Confederates continued the fight after the retreat of the Union army. Some units acted on the direct orders of their commanders. "General Seamore's [sic] army is made up largely of negroes . . . who have come to steal, pillage, run all over the state, and murder, kill, rape, and pillage our wives, daughters, and sweethearts," a Confederate colonel instructed. "I shall not take any negro prisoners in this fight." Other troops were restrained from greater destruction: "I tell you our men slayed the Ne-grows & if it had not been for the officers their would not one of them be spared," a Virginian wrote.[11]

Black soldiers were willing to respond in kind, whether Confederate actions were official policy or not. "Should Jeff Davis enforce his threat of treating us as servile insurgents, there will be but little quarter shown to rebels who fall into our hands," wrote a 55ther. "Every man shall die who has not the power to defend himself, and then we will hear what Jeff Davis had to say about enslaving or butchering black soldiers."[12] In pursuit of what later generations of African American activists would call the "Double V" of victory in war and against oppression at home, black soldiers of the Civil War recognized Confederates as their truest enemy.

By 1864, a rough pattern had emerged in the distribution and use of the U.S. Colored Troops. Black soldiers figured prominently in the assignment of garrison duty in captured territory, including a concentration of black ar-tillery units in fortified locations. Assignments such as these were common in the occupation of the Mississippi Valley, stretching primarily between Port Hudson, Louisiana, and Helena, Arkansas. The West Tennessee riv-ers captured early in the war—and subsidiary occupations stretching into Athens and Huntsville, Alabama—employed a mix of white and African American troops. Before and after Olustee, the Department of the South and nearby Department of North Carolina dedicated themselves to liberat-ing slaves, seizing Confederate assets, and recruiting new black troops in low-level skirmishes and raids.

In spring 1864, black soldiers played a crucial role as four major Union offensives got under way: the far-west Red River Campaign; Sherman versus Georgia and South Carolina; Philip Sheridan's destruction expedition in the strategic Shenandoah Valley agricultural corridor; and Grant's two-pronged attack on Richmond and General Lee, the Overland and James River Campaigns.

The U.S. Colored Troops in Virginia prepared to participate in the bloodiest fighting yet in world history, in which the technology of war and the numbers of troops would produce astronomical casualty counts, re-peated over the course of twelve months of pitted fighting. But black soldiers assigned to U.S. forts in the Southern states also operated at tremendous risk, in which their relatively small numbers exposed them to attacks by Confederate irregulars. An incident at Fort Pillow, in West Tennessee, illustrated the terrible possibilities for black troops not afforded the status of legal combatants by the rebels.

The Union Army took control of Fort Pillow on the Mississippi River near Arkansas in 1862 and employed the old Confederate fortifications as part of their outer defenses of the city of Memphis, forty miles to the south. Success in the western theater had created a far-flung set of such Union assets, including railroads, telegraph lines, supply depots, and new and reconstituted forts such as Pillow, which was named for Confederate General Gideon Pillow, thought to have been the richest slaveholder in Tennessee. Pillow's defenders included some of the region's rawest recruits—both black and white Union soldiers recruited in the still contested arc stretching between Fort Donelson in the northwest and Chattanooga in the southeast, an area equal to roughly half of the state, including Nashville, the capital of Restored Tennessee. Confederate commanders had withdrawn their infantry units from the area after the Union victory at Chattanooga late in 1863, but cavalry continued to harass Union positions across the river delta. The most formidable of these was the intrepid mobile unit led by Major General Nathan Bedford Forrest.

Union commanders and the press liked to call Forrest and his mounted partisans guerrillas, and yet they operated with the formal sanction of the Confederate government, which had recognized the legitimacy of armies raised by private citizens such as Forrest, who had initially recruited and mounted his own men, with special legislation in 1862. Moreover, his cavalry operated under the military command of Braxton Bragg's Army of the Tennessee, however much its movements created geographical distance from the whole. Forrest was a guerrilla (a term born in Spanish resistance to Napoleon's invasion of the Iberian Peninsula early in the nineteenth century) by virtue of his tactics, which were mobile, independent of centralized strategic planning, and focused on destruction and the seizure of moveable assets. The general himself seemed more like a warlord or knight errant than a modern commander. "COME ON BOYS, IF YOU WANT A HEAP OF FUN AND TO KILL SOME YANKEES," he exhorted, in capital letters, in a newspaper recruitment.[13]

The Forrest cult of personality—destined to outlive the Civil War and Reconstruction—was still in the emerging stages in the spring of 1864, but the cavalryman had already linked his name to bloodletting and racial hierarchy.

Forrest's early 1864 operations in Mississippi, Arkansas, and West Tennessee had everything to do with Georgia, where Forrest and others could see General Sherman's concentration of troops in the making. The Confederates aimed to make it difficult for Sherman to move forward by keeping up the pressure at the rear. The assault on Fort Pillow was one of a half dozen moves after January that tested the firmness of Union control. It was an asset with both military and political significance. Commanding a high point on the river above Memphis, it secured a checkpoint that could be leveraged should Arkansas be redeemed by Confederates Kirby Smith and Sterling Price. Garrisoned by black and white Tennessee recruits, moreover, the outpost stood as a symbol of Southern Unionism, of racial uplift, and of defiance of the way of life that Nathan Bedford Forrest and his troops were trying to defend.[14]

Commanding at Fort Pillow was Major Lionel Booth of the 6th Alabama Heavy Artillery, a USCT. He was a fitting symbol of the leadership practices of the U.S. Colored Troops, having risen to his post from the rank of private. In contrast to the aristocratic Forrest, the major was more than humble, having enlisted in the army under the nom de guerre of Lionel Booth when in fact his name was George Lanning, an identity that he discarded under anguished unknown circumstances for which he obsessively apologized in letters to his relatives, compiled later in his widow's U.S. Army pension file. Perhaps the rupture had something to do with his wife, an unconventional woman who had attracted the scrutiny of newspapers and police in a pair of incidents involving theft in 1859, and whom he may have married without his family's consent.[15]

Lanning *alias* Booth would not live long enough to tell his story or to overcome his past. Struck by a sniper's bullet, he was practically the first man to die during Forrest's attack on the fort on April 12, 1864.

Another major, William Bradford of the 13th Tennessee Cavalry, assumed command. Bradford and his 235 white unionists (backed by another five hundred colored troops) were mostly local boys, freshly recruited in

West Tennessee and experiencing their first assignment. Despite their in-experience they gave Forrest's cavalry a good fight, lasting four hours under assault by a force of six thousand, and shooting three horses out from under General Forrest himself. Bradford demonstrated unjustified confidence and courage, rejecting Forrest's demand for terms in a note he signed under the deadly alias Lionel Booth that said, "I will not surrender." He was quickly overrun, his fortress captured, and his soldiers thrown haphazardly upon the mercy of their enemies.

Bradford/Booth had not surrendered, but his troops laid down their weapons when confronted with the rush of Confederates into the fort. Many fled the structure for the riverbank or nearby cabins. According to a Min-nesota participant, the assailants refused to stop the fight, resulting in what he called "the most horrible slaughter that could possibly be conceived." A veteran named Charley Robinson wrote,

> Our boys when they saw that they were overpowered threw down their arms and held up, some their hankerchiefs & some their hands in token of surrender, but no sooner were they seen than they were shot down & if one shot failed to kill them the bayonet or the revolver did not. I lay behind a high log & could see our poor fellows bleeding and hear them cry surrender I surrender but they surrendered in vain for the rebels now ran down the bank and putting their revolvers right to their heads would blow out their brains or lift them up on their bayonets and throw them headlong into the river below.

The racially charged motivation of Confederates was not disguised. When a cavalryman detected Robinson (a white man) behind the log, he made his racism explicit. "You'll fight with the [Negroes] again will you? You d___d Yankee," and "he snapped his revolver [against Robinson's chest], but she wouldn't go off as he had shot the last load." Another witness heard a cav-alryman ask, "Do you fight with these God-damned [Negroes]?" and say, "I would not kill you, but you fight with these God-damned [Negroes], and we will kill you," before shooting a man point-blank. "Damn you, you are fight-ing against your master," said one, holding on to a black soldier. He shot the black man in the mouth, but the soldier lived to testify about what happened to a committee of Congress. Major Bradford was taken prisoner and later shot, and his unburied body was abandoned fifty feet from a road.[16]

The Fort Pillow Massacre took the Confederate no-quarter policy to new extremes. In actions supposedly authorized by General Forrest himself, both black and white detainees were killed, leaving fewer than 150 of the original 600 to 800 alive. The incident provided new fodder for Radical Republican agitation on the subject, especially after two members of the ultra-left Joint Congressional Committee on the Conduct of the War traveled to Tennessee to investigate. In keeping with the failed campaign of previous months, information about the outrages did not lead directly to changes in War Department policy on Confederate captives. The killings at Fort Pillow did, however, lead to Radical Republican action—not on the part of Congress or the Lincoln administration, as it happened, but with the agency of an unlikely politician.

Elizabeth Wayt, aka Lizzie Wayt Lanning, aka Mrs. Major Lionel Booth, was not the kind of woman typically associated with high-level politics or even humanitarian causes. Since sometime early in her adulthood she had scrambled mainly to protect her own self-interest—as a public speaker on "household arts" at a time when the public frowned on women speakers; as a woman who traveled alone; as a suspect in the disappearance of a large sum of money from a boardinghouse guestroom, who was not charged but was nonetheless ordered to stay away from Pittsburgh back in 1859; as the bride of a man on the run from his own mother, a man enrolled in the army under a false name; as a widow drawn to a war zone in search of her husband's body, combing the wreckage of one of the war's worst atrocities without success.

She made a difference. Traveling by steamboat and on horseback (a practice widely condemned at the time as inappropriate for women), she interviewed all the survivors of the Fort Pillow Massacre she could find, well before the arrival in Memphis of investigating members of Congress Daniel Gooch and Benjamin F. Wade. She interviewed black soldiers as well as whites, and sought out the wounded as well as the able-bodied. Visiting a hospital for black soldiers in Mound City, Illinois (160 miles upriver from Memphis), Wayt encountered Private Eli Cothel of her husband's Company B. "[A]s soon a[s] Private Cothel learned who she was, he drew [a] flag from his bosom and with tears in his eyes present[ed] the same to her telling that the Major had told him never to give up the flag and here it is."

Cothel explained that he had lain near the flagpole at Fort Pillow, shot three times but conscious enough to see that he was unobserved. He crawled to the pole, hauled down the flag, and used it to bandage his wounds before fainting. The banner he gave the major's wife was stained and stiff with Cothel's blood.

A white officer who observed the encounter was awed. "Such bravery in a white man would promote," he reported, in introducing Mrs. Booth to the commander of Fort Pickering in Memphis. "I think I can truly say[,] Captain[,] that men never fought more brave than did the colored soldiers at, [sic] Fort Pillow on the morning of April 12, 1864."[17]

Lizzie Wayt Booth did not take the flag of Fort Pillow as a personal remembrance. Backed by the officers who facilitated her interviews with survivors of her husband's command, she returned it to Memphis for a formal presentation and display. The coordinated effort reflected the importance of battle flags and regimental colors in the Civil War—banners that served a practical as well as politically symbolic role. "The Colors" offered a visual signal on the battlefield that helped soldiers orient their actions in the fog of war, but black soldiers in the Civil War saw more than just the physical manifestation. Starting with the doomed assault on Fort Wagner in 1863—after which a wounded man presented the regimental colors, saying, "Boys, the old flag never touched the ground," and later won a Medal of Honor—stories of heroic acts to keep the colors waving became staples of black combat narratives.[18]

Association with the flag reinforced black claims to citizenship, and their efforts on its behalf illustrated their commitment to the cause it represented. Starting in wartime, and continuing for many decades afterward, Radical Republicans sought to honor black soldiers who protected the regimental colors with formal recognition, including the award of the newly established Medal of Honor. Such commendations not only boosted African American soldiers collectively and as individuals, but also left a record of heroic acts in their citations and supporting documents, preserving stories of Civil War blacks in combat.

The bloody flag of Fort Pillow found its way into one of the most dramatic—if lesser known—narratives of the genre. The commander of the 6th Alabama Heavy Artillery, working with the commanders of the other survivors of Fort Pillow units, organized a formal presentation of the regimental colors at Fort Pickering, the post in urban Memphis that was home to a number of companies charged with the city's defense. Colonels of all three of the decimated regiments assembled their men in the hollow square, with the small number of active-duty members of Major Booth's company in the center. Lieutenant Colonel Jackson of the 6th escorted Elizabeth Wayt Booth to the center of the formation. In what may have been the only incident of its kind in the war, Mrs. Booth addressed the soldiers and their officers with the flag of Fort Pillow in her hand. Her remarks were captured by a sympathetic journalist:

> The ranks before her observed a silence that was full of solemnity. Many a hardy face showed by twitching lips and humid eyes how the sight of the bereaved lady touched bosoms that could meet steel . . . Turning toward to the men before her, she said: 'Boys, I have just come from a visit to the hospital at Mound City . . . There I found this flag; you recognize it! One of your comrades saved it from the insulting touch of traitors at Fort Pillow!
>
> I have given all I have to give—my husband, such a gift! Yet I have freely given him for freedom and my country.
>
> . . . Soldiers! this flag I give to you, knowing that you will ever remember the last words of my noble husband—'Never surrender the flag to traitors'" [sic].

The widow presented the flag to Lt. Colonel Jackson, who made a single searing remark:

> He called upon the regiment to receive it as such a gift ought to be received. At that call he and every man in the regiment fell upon their knees, and, solemnly invoking the God of battles, each one swore to avenge their brave and fallen comrades, and never—*never to surrender the flag to traitors!*
>
> The scene was one never surpassed in emotional incident, [the newspaper report continued]. Beside the swift rolling waters of the Mississippi, within the enclosure that bristled with the death-dealing cannon, knelt

242 WHEN IT WAS GRAND

these rough soldiers, whose bosoms were heaving with emotion, and on many of whose cheeks quivered with a tear they tried to hide, though it did credit to their manly natures. Beside them stood in grief the widow of the loved officer they had lost, and above them was held the bloody flag—that eloquent record of crime . . .

A second colonel stepped forward, speaking forcefully, and finally a third commander, a German American, who connected the bathos of the flag presentation to policy. "Colonel Kappan followed him, expressing himself in favor of such retaliatory acts of justice as the laws of warfare required, in a case of such fiendish and wicked cruelty."

The 1864 army constituted a society in itself, male and ceremonial. The portion created by the arming of the former slaves took a vow at Fort Pickering, sanctioned by the arresting figure of the standing widow: Remember Fort Pillow; *never surrender the flag to traitors*; let the black flag prevail on both sides; "Woe to the unlucky Reb who falls into the hands" of the Sixth (Alabama) U.S. Artillery, African Descent; the Thirteenth Tennessee Cavalry; the 2nd U.S. Colored Light Artillery; and any other regiment inspired by their example.[19] The colored troops and their commanders would act to fill the vacuum in U.S. policy created by the president's hesitation to execute Confederate prisoners in retaliation for attacks on black prisoners of war. As necessary, and in the interest of the nation, the army would go where even Radical Republicans were loath to tread.

The politics of solidarity articulated by the white speakers at the Fort Pickering event—three men and one woman—had been only implicit. Fort Pillow Revolutionists, like John Brown, transcended the ordinary workings of government. To connect this militant spirit of the battlefield to the organs of the state, one of their number left Memphis for Washington. Within weeks of the ceremony, the flag bearer had made her way to the office of the president of the United States.

Abraham Lincoln was not a fan of women politicians, as he suggested in remarks to Jessie Fremont back in 1861. No woman but Mary Lincoln shared his inner circle, an isolation compounded by the lack of female progeny to inspire him. He did not, however, discriminate against women when receiving public petitioners at the White House. "He said that as a republican government all men & women & Children had a right to see the Presdt [sic] and state his grievances," an adviser remembered.[20] The needs of widows in particular occupied him in his office and in correspondence, and a caller such as Lizzie Booth would be sure to gain his full attention. In those days of elaborate mourning rituals and dress, Mrs. Booth's attire revealed her status as a person in the most immediate stages of bereavement. Also, there was something about the way she spoke and carried herself that made people meeting her perceive her in extreme terms, characteristics that generated warmth but also led observers to describe her as odd, abrasive, or a disgrace to womanhood. Her message to Lincoln was unconventional, but it was only Radical in the broadest, most humanitarian sense.

Speaking for the widows of Fort Pillow, Booth informed the president about an unintentional injustice of War Department policy, which offered pensions only to the legal wives of soldiers killed in action. Because marriages in slavery were extralegal, and because the facilities to legalize existing unions lagged behind recruiting in the conquered districts, large numbers of survivors of black soldiers who had lost their lives were experiencing destitution. It was a lesson learned in her search for witnesses to the final hours of Lionel Booth, during which she came to see the need for a more accommodating government policy.

Lincoln agreed, taking pen and paper and addressing a letter to the Radical Republican senator Charles Sumner. "She makes a point which I think very worthy of consideration which is, widows and children in fact, of Colored soldiers who fell in our service, be placed in the law, the same as if their marriages are legal," he wrote.

Senator Sumner was not the kind of man to respond enthusiastically to political proposals from a striking woman; a thoroughgoing bachelor, he was the idol of an all-male intellectual circle. He could recognize a good idea when he heard one, however, and he immediately steered legislation to good effect. Sumner gave the petitioner a full interview, soliciting her views on the welfare of black dependents of active-duty servicemen as well as those killed in the service. He publicized her data in the Senate and summarized his interview for *The Liberator*, renewing the campaign for equal pay for black soldiers. The pay bill passed on June 14, and included provisions for collecting back pay to the date of enrollment for soldiers who had been free and to January 1864 for liberated slaves. The matter of widows' pensions also percolated with dispatch, adopted as clause of an omnibus appropriations act passed as H.R. 406 on July 2.[21]

After launching her policy initiative, Lizzie Wayt Booth/Lanning returned to Memphis and accepted work in the federal hospitals. She became friendly with district commander Stephen Hurlbut, who made plans to appoint her superintendent of the federal hospital at Cairo, Illinois. Her speechmaking and Radical politics were not forgotten, by citizens of Memphis or by unsympathetic army observers in Fort Pickering. Such behavior was deemed unacceptable in a nineteenth-century woman, particularly one without social connections.

> I regret very much that the rediculous [*sic*] farce enacted here by the Woman, *calling* herself Mrs. Booth . . . should be republished at the North under the title "An Affecting Scene at Fort Pickering" [wrote a conservative Illinois officer to his brother]. This woman has evinced, by her conduct, that she cares no more for the sad fate of the man whose name she dishonors, than she does for a stuck *pig*.[22]

Mrs. Booth was an early feminist and also a social outcast perhaps for reasons connected to a lack of personal integrity. She may have acted unwisely, or perhaps she became the target of a campaign of retribution. Within weeks, in any case, she encountered serious trouble—accused of taking a cut of contraband gold coins that she had intercepted while searching (on the Union payroll) Southern women crossing army lines in occupied Memphis.

Found guilty in a court-martial, Lizzie Wayt Booth would have gone to prison had not a freak of fate or other great irregularity intervened. Less than one hour after pronouncing her guilty, the officer presiding in her trial presented himself in Mrs. Booth's boardinghouse bedroom, thrust his hand into her blouse, and clutched her to his lap until her screams alarmed the neighbors. General Hurlbut sanctioned the judge and summarily vacated the conviction of Lizzie Booth, who retreated to Kansas and later drew a widow's pension of her own.[23] Her engagement in black army politics proved to be her last foray as a public figure.

The curse of the flag of Fort Pillow, however, haunted Memphis even after the widow was gone. An exchange of letters revealed the repercussion of the story of the kneeling oath among Confederate listeners. Among those rebels taking offense at the colored regiments' affirmed "no quarter" policy was Nathan Bedford Forrest, who directed a complaint to Major General Cadwallader C. Washburn, the commander of the Memphis occupation, a former Republican congressman from Wisconsin.

> It has been reported to me that all your colored troops stationed at Memphis took, on their knees, in the presence of Major Gen. Hurlbut [commander of the Mississippi Department] and other officers of your army, an oath to avenge Fort Pillow, and that they would show my troops no quarter. [And also that] as they were moved into action on the 11th [of June] they were exhorted by their officers to remember Fort Pillow.

Forrest complained that a recent skirmish (at Tishamingo Creek in West Tennessee) had produced far more fatalities than necessary because both sides had "acted as though neither felt safe in surrendering, even when farther resistance was useless." Did laws of war prevail or not? Forrest wanted to know, protesting his own innocence (in keeping with the new Confederate party line, that rebels did not execute Union prisoners) and proposing terms for a prisoner exchange.[24]

Washburn waited five days to respond to Forrest's letter. The founder of what became the General Mills Corporation, Washburn had grown stout in his middle age, but he was no less intrepid than athletic-in-the-saddle Forrest. He had resigned his seat in Congress in 1860 and signed on as an officer in U. S. Grant's command, helping to win Vicksburg, and participating in the fall of 1863 in a doomed amphibious assault on coastal Texas.

The commander asked for more specifics about Forrest's policy toward black soldiers. "If you contemplate their slaughter or return to slavery please state that, so we may have no misunderstanding hereafter," he wrote. Given assurances, he would urge the troops to recall their bloody oath, which Washburn insisted was "not influenced by any white officer, but [as] the result of their own sense of what was due to themselves," Hurlbut having not been present. If Confederates would not adhere to rules of war regarding the colored troops, however, "then let the oath stand, and upon those who have aroused this spirit by their atrocities, and upon the Government and people who sanction it be the consequences."[25]

Forrest responded by taking aim at Cadwallader Washburn personally (and going after General Hurlbut while he was at it). What Confederates called the Second Battle of Memphis was in fact a raid by Forrest's horsemen that lasted about two hours. The Confederates failed in an attempt to liberate war prisoners, but managed to roust the targeted officers in bold initiatives. Forrest himself charged the stairs to Washburn's bedroom, but the general escaped in his nightshirt to Fort Pickering, leading his nemesis to take Washburn's uniform prisoner and waggishly return it later under flag of truce. The city later marked the route of his flight by renaming it "General Washburn's Escape Alley." Forrest's brother led the search for Stephen Hurlbut, filling the lobby of the Gayoso Hotel with mounted men in a display of force but departing Memphis empty-handed.[26]

Less entertaining was Abraham Lincoln's response to the no-quarter drama. The Frontiersman Who Could Not Hunt had been oppressed by the issue for nearly a year. While Radical Republicans and others dogged him to take retaliatory measures on Confederate prisoners, his humane nature had pushed just as relentlessly to forestall such a resort. Two days before he met with Elizabeth Wayt Booth the president had arrived at a personal threshold for changing his policy, drafting a memorandum in which he announced his intention to "set aside" a designated number of rebel prisoners as hostages. Emphasizing his belief that "blood cannot restore blood," he demanded nonetheless an accounting from Confederates for all African American troops declared missing-in-action, setting July 1 as his deadline for deeming that "they shall have been murdered, or subjected to slavery." Upon making "said assumption," he would "take such action" regarding the hostages "as may then appear expedient and just."

The retaliation memorandum may not have been sent to the War Department, and it did not result in new procedures. Secretaries Nicolay and Hay would later explain unconvincingly that the response to Fort Pillow had been "crowded out" by the mounting distractions of the war.[27] In any case the Army of the United States had taken the no-prisoners policy into its own hands, ready to act where their kindhearted commander in chief had hesitated. "Remember Fort Pillow" emerged as an enduring battle cry for black soldiers, and even sometimes for whites—perhaps the only Union shout to approach the fame and ubiquity of the Rebel Yell. Fighting under its banner, units displayed a take-no-prisoners ferocity, as one described it, that "give[s] the Provost Marshal nothing to do."[28]

17

WEARING THE BRASS LETTER

The summer of 1864 would be the worst in American history, and black people fighting for the Union experienced the most terrible parts. Black men enlisted (and also acted as recruiters, whose words survived, if in fragments, for the consideration of future generations) in the name of both the love of nation and their own self-interest. Those fighting on the front lines participated in a battle to the death with the Slave Power. Black men's heroism would inspire their white contemporaries in military and political circles, helping to hasten the progressive direction of Radical Republican government. Bringing energy and manpower to a decisive effect in Virginia and the Mississippi River Valley, the colored troops secured an outsized share of the ultimate success of the Union effort, however much all-white commands such as W. T. Sherman's and Phil Sheridan's became more celebrated. Fighting under progressive white officers, and amassing particularly in a pair of controversial commands, the USCT had to be twice as good while incurring a greater risk of death or dismemberment.

The experience of two regiments of United States Colored Troops in the Virginia theater best illustrated the confluence of the war and Radical Republican politics. The 5th USCT—formerly the 127th Ohio Volunteer Infantry—had its roots in the Oberlin community of educated refugees and local blacks. Its organizers included John Mercer Langston and his doughty brother-in-law, the Oberlin rescuer O.S.B. Wall, who accompanied the troops in the uniform of an enlisted man while the War Department considered the recommendation of Ohio's Republican governor that he receive an officer's commission. Langston and his associates remained open partisans of the Republican Party (hailing from a state that allowed men of mixed race to vote at the discretion of registrars).

In recruiting for the 127th, as the only black elected official in the country, Langston had led a convention of black men that resolved:

> That we stand as ever on the side of the government, and pledge to it our lives, our property, and sacred honor, in its effort to subdue the rebellion of the slave oligarchy [and] to establish freedom in the District of Columbia and the national territories [and] to recognize the citizenship of native born colored Americas . . . and to protect the colored soldiers who are taking the American musket.

Wall (having set aside his 1858 top hat for a noncommissioned officer's cap) marched to "join in the work of elevation of the race from degradation to equality."[1]

Among enlisted men in the 5th was Milton Holland, an eighteen-year-old of light complexion who served with the distinction of taking the field against an army in which his white Southern father was a general, at least until April 1864, when the elder Holland died leading Texans to victory at the Battle of Mansfield, Louisiana. Holland and the 5th did not see service in the western districts, however, but deployed immediately to coastal North Carolina and Virginia, into what was shaping up to be a Radical Republican enclave of colored troops and sympathetic commissioned officers. Young Holland was not a voter yet and might never have qualified by the standards of 1863 Ohio, but as a member of the 5th USCT, he cast his lot among once and future partisans and officeholders, some of whom would use their influence in Holland's favor. In his future—along with dozens of gravely dangerous engagements with the enemy—lay an encounter with a president, a government-issued Medal of Honor, and a job in the Treasury Department.[2]

In the upper tier of the Atlantic South, where the states adjoined the ocean amid piles of sand and tidal rivers, another unit, the 1st Regiment of

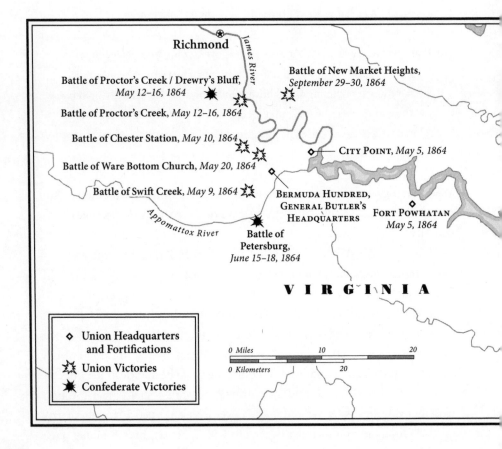

Richmond

James River

Battle of Proctor's Creek / Drewry's Bluff, *May 12–16, 1864*

Battle of New Market Heights, *September 29–30, 1864*

Battle of Proctor's Creek, *May 12–16, 1864*

Battle of Chester Station, *May 10, 1864*

CITY POINT, *May 5, 1864*

Battle of Ware Bottom Church, *May 20, 1864*

Battle of Swift Creek, *May 9, 1864*

BERMUDA HUNDRED, GENERAL BUTLER'S HEADQUARTERS

FORT POWHATAN *May 5, 1864*

Appomattox River

Battle of Petersburg, *June 15–18, 1864*

VIRGINIA

◇ Union Headquarters and Fortifications

✸ Union Victories

✹ Confederate Victories

0 Miles   10   20

0 Kilometers   20

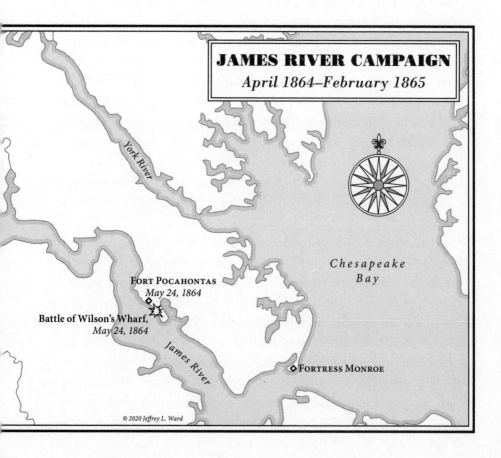

JAMES RIVER CAMPAIGN
April 1864–February 1865

York River

Chesapeake Bay

FORT POCAHONTAS
May 24, 1864

Battle of Wilson's Wharf,
May 24, 1864

James River

◆FORTRESS MONROE

© 2020 Jeffrey L. Ward

North Carolina Volunteers—later the 1st USCT—obtained its designation with a push from George L. Stearns and John Andrew. It traced its pedigree to 1862 and the cornstalk regiment led by William Henry Singleton and others.

The 1st USCT did not fall into step with the federal war effort without due consideration of the risks. All were willing, as a group dominated by refugees from slavery, to take up arms in self-defense, but key organizers of the original group, including Abraham Galloway, a military operative and community organizer, balked at the prospect of doing so under army auspices. In 1863, Galloway headed a series of negotiations with Governor Andrew's representative in New Bern, Edward W. Kinsley. According to Kinsley's dramatic memoir of the event, the recruits blindfolded the envoy and Galloway held a pistol to Kinsley's ear. They demanded equal pay and the protection and education of members of their families and said they mistrusted the Lincoln administration policy on the abuse of prisoners by Confederates, insisting on the full protection of the U.S. government. The regiment remained active in the service for a year before securing any of the promises they sought.[3]

In addition to their material concerns, the North Carolina volunteers also illustrated the injustice of the War Department policy on commissioning officers for black troops. Neither William Henry Singleton nor Galloway attained rank when their recruits mustered in as USCT. Singleton took the opportunity to enlist in the part of the North Carolina Volunteers that became the 35th U.S. Colored Infantry and served in Florida before moving to Virginia in early 1864. He was promoted to sergeant.

Abraham Galloway refused to enter on the same terms, working closely with the army and yet charting an independent path as a speaker for hire and political organizer in New Bern and in the freedmen's colony on Roanoke Island. Galloway had escaped from slavery on the North Carolina coast only in 1857; from his base in Canada, he had played a role in the John Brownism that had helped to create the war. Though he did not enlist, he continued his work as a spy and active recruiter in the region of his upbringing, risking his life in dozens of missions into hostile territory.

For Galloway, the war had created opportunities for the advancement of the colored race, but he believed that only lobbying and black participation in politics could deliver on the promise. His willingness to lay his pistol alongside the head of the Republican Kinsley in the New Bern attic was merely symbolic of his broad understanding of the links between force and political power. In January 1864 he told a crowd that African Americans "would not have only their personal freedom, but political equality [as well]." Military service lay the best claim upon such an elevation, he insisted, not only in a moral sense but also as an acquisition of material strength. If equal accommodations "should be refused them at the ballot box," he said, echoing the Kansas Fifty-Sixers, African Americans "would have it at the cartridge box!"

Galloway led his audience to resolutions demanding black male suffrage in the reconstruction and restoration of North Carolina, promoting the state's prospects under Lincoln's Ten Percent Plan. Though he could scarcely read and write, the North Carolinian would take his message directly to the government as embodied by Abraham Lincoln. On April 29, 1864, Galloway led a citizens' delegation of black men that met the president and told him that they deserved equal rights and access to the vote.[4]

Galloway was a talented native of coastal North Carolina who rose above the hardships of his upbringing to make a difference there as an agent of a revolutionary conspiracy. Other African American influentials arrived in New Bern and Virginia only by the happenstance of war. One such notable was Henry McNeal Turner, born a free man in South Carolina, but risen to prominence as a minister of the African Methodist Episcopal Church in the Northeast. Along with James Lynch and other missionaries, Turner had been charged by A.M.E. Bishop Daniel Payne to join with the army to bring a form of liberation theology to those enslaved in the South.

Early in the war Turner had served that purpose from his pulpit in Washington, D.C., where he became associated with such Radical Republicans as Committee on the Conduct of the War cochairman Benjamin Wade. His assignment to the 1st USCT was a straightforward political appointment, organized by the War Department, which arranged Reverend Turner's transportation down to New Bern. In a first, he would hold the rank of chaplain, an informal but honorific title that roughly corresponded to an officer's rank.[5]

While the regiment accumulated the full number of recruits, Turner and the white officers had time and opportunity to transform practices in seaside New Bern and its vicinity. Turner's religious mission kept him in constant motion, founding churches. Church-founding in the occupied South had become an exercise of martial law, as Union commanders cracked down on disloyalty among local white denominations. Starting as early as 1862, these officers supervised the transfer of physical church assets to ministers willing to preach loyalty to the Union. With help from provost marshals and Treasury Department agents, Turner and other missionaries obtained facilities for church services around New Bern and in scattered hamlets and towns around the coast, preaching one day in an abandoned plantation house and another in a church or the courthouse of a county seat.

His Methodist circuit riding produced what he jokingly called "a greater slaughter among the fowls, if nothing else," as families eager to establish independent black churches invited him to dinner, he wrote in a newspaper column. "Somehow these North Carolina chickens will get in my way at every invited meal."[6] His travels also established a more enduring legacy, in an emerging network of institutions with spiritual and political weight.

Turner participated firsthand in some of the cultural changes wrought by emancipation, particularly among the white women of New Bern and vicinity. In one instance he intervened in uniform to disrupt a group offering "impudence" to a woman of color who was badly outnumbered, identifying himself as "a United States officer."

> "We want you to know we are white and your superiors. You are our inferior, much less she." "Well," said I, "All of you put together would not make the equal of my wife, and I haven't yet to hear her claim superiority over me." After that I don't know what was said, for that remark was received as such an aggravated insult, that I can only compare the noise that followed, to a gang of fice [fierce] dogs holding at bay a large cur dog, with a bow-wow-wow-wow. Finally, becoming tired of their annoying music, I told them to leave or I would imprison the whole party.

Later, in a more unsettling incident, Turner saw white women crowd the sidewalks and windowsills of Smithville to observe silently as naked men of the 1st USCT emerged from fording the Neuse River, holding their clothing high on bayonets.

"Yes, though naked we are your masters," Turner mused as he dried himself and dressed. Passing Jamestown, Virginia, he remembered it as the site of the first sale of Africans in the old colonies, and made note of the way the war had turned the world around.[7]

The experiences of the 5th and 1st USCT Regiments became joined to Ulysses S. Grant's attack on Richmond and the pursuit of Lee's army, with black soldiers especially concentrated under the command of Major General Benjamin Butler. The Army of the James, assembled in the winter of 1863–64, cut its teeth as a military organization in jayhawker formation: slave raiding, seizing rebel supplies, and taking action to thwart smuggling and guerrilla activity along the coast.

The leadership of Benjamin Butler introduced more Massachusetts hard-cores to the mix. Brigadier General Edward A. Wild was no ordinary Boston abolitionist, even if his correspondents list included such notable antislavery Republicans as Governor John Andrew and Senator Henry Wilson. He was the only one in the circle of Bay State philanthropists to have dedicated his muscle to the Crimean War, the biggest global conflict of the 1850s, in which he fought as an officer of the army of the Ottoman Empire. He had signed on early in the Civil War, serving in the Army of the Potomac and seeing action in Virginia and Maryland. A physician by training, Wild had supervised the amputation of his own arm after being wounded at the Battle of South Mountain in 1862. Returned to service in 1863, he had worked with George Luther Stearns and Governor Andrew to maximize the recruiting potential of the North Carolina coast.

Wild wore his abolitionist fervor on his empty sleeve, coaxing into his officer corps other Massachusetts Radicals, including James C. Beecher of the famous antislavery family, who became the colonel of the portion of the 1st North Carolina Volunteers designated as the 35th USCT. Beecher presented his unit with regimental colors designed by his sister, Harriet Beecher Stowe, and sewn by sympathetic Massachusetts women. He and Wild dedicated themselves to the well-being of the soldiers and their dependents, soliciting materials to boost literacy among the troops and charitable giving to help to close the pay gap that persisted until June 1864. The most philanthropic initiative was the establishment of a freedmen's colony on Roanoke Island near the mouth of the Albemarle Sound, an ancient site that organizers promoted as the nucleus of a new social order in the South.[8]

Who better than Yankees to plan a strategic hamlet for Carolina freedmen? General Wild and the Department of North Carolina and Virginia command could put the benefits of years of philanthropic and commercial experience at the service of the colony. Establishing a superintendent of freedmen and assigning to the duty Horace James, a Boston-area minister and abolitionist turned army chaplain, the department created a forerunner of the Freedmen's Bureau, which was established by an act of Congress in March 1864. The effort relied on substantial subsidies from charitable giving in Massachusetts and New England. An early tour by James (later appointed a captain of the U.S. Colored Troops) secured more than $8,000 in donations. The Massachusetts men also made the most of their quartermasters' and requisition authority to supply the colony with means of economic advancement, delivering a steam engine with grist and sawmill equipment, mules and horses, rations, and much of the local fleet of skiffs and fishing boats—seized as contraband from Confederate operators. When ropes and nets proved hard to find in wartime, the occupiers collaborated with North Carolina unionists to raid the decks and fishing piers of rebel-minded locals.[9]

With special urgency, Wild sought teachers and church missionaries to join the occupation, a call answered with enthusiasm by the enterprising Methodists. The church paper *Zion's Herald and Wesleyan Messenger* predicted, "When the dangers of our present social revolution have passed, and the American Nation is fully delivered from its internal dangers, the credit thereof will be due in great measure to those who have devoted themselves or their treasures to the work of teaching the freedman properly to improve and enjoy the liberty and exercise the power that belongs to him under our democratic institutions."

North Carolina colonizers looked to the examples in Kansas and the state of West Virginia, where an Eli Thayer acolyte, Zophar D. Ramsdell, founded the emigrationist town of Ceredo in the 1850s and helped to organize secession from the Old Dominion and statehood without slavery by early 1863. In

West Virginia—and in Kansas—the establishment of Free-State electoral districts by filibustering and colonization had already delivered electoral advantages for Republicans in 1864. Radical programs to restore government in the Carolinas and in Florida were bold enough to consider black political participation in an early bid for restoration under the presidential plan.

Agitation on behalf of black voting rights for North Carolina simmered among Roanoke Island residents and the Northern missionaries who worked with them. Advocates cited the opinion of the late William Gaston, the white New Bern–born justice of the North Carolina Supreme Court and delegate to the constitutional convention, who had nearly secured votes for free blacks in the state back in 1835. Roanoke Island residents nominated a delegation to present an argument to the president about the use of black votes to meet the standards of the Ten Percent Plan—the same delegation that took Abraham Galloway to meet Abraham Lincoln at the White House. With military officials such as Galloway participating—and commanders facilitating transportation for the group to Washington across the war zone—the North Carolina campaign for black suffrage bore a stamp of army approval.[10]

In addition to its humanitarian functions, Wild's African Brigade assumed its war responsibilities with alacrity. The one-armed general became notorious for his harsh measures versus coastal guerrillas and smuggling operations. Wild's response to the threat of execution or enslavement for his black soldiers was to seize the wives of two wanted white men as hostages. "I still hold in custody Mrs. Munsen and Mrs. Weeks as hostages for the colored soldier taken by you," he wrote to a Confederate officer. "As he is treated, so shall they be, even unto hanging." When relatives of the two captives appealed to General Butler at Fortress Monroe, the Bluebeard of New Orleans assured them he would spare the lives of the two women detained by his North Carolina subordinate. Butler would not intervene, however, to prevent the women being held in an open room with male prisoners and guarded by African American troops.

Relying on local slave recruits for strategic and topographical advice, Wild was drawn into their personal experiences of enslavement and abuse. He did not hesitate to apply the weight of the armed forces to remedy the grievances of local refugees from slavery. In an early incident he detached a military company to liberate the son of a member of a colored regiment. Wild's career as an official avenger of slavery's wrongs, however, reached its climax as he joined his command to the newly created Army of the James in April 1864.

In support of the Overland Campaign, General Grant directed thirty-three thousand troops to General Butler, the beneficiary of Radical Republican congressional lobbying, whom Grant considered ineffective as a military leader. While Grant and General George Meade led the Army of the Potomac against Richmond from the North, Butler's troops were to strike new forward positions on the James River, supported by the U.S. Navy.

Where the James opened wide to meet the Chesapeake Bay, the Union could strike rapidly into Confederate territory using its Atlantic fleet to move troops and equipment in the navigable stretches. Well before May 1864, Confederates had withdrawn defenses from the first of the witchy switchbacks that marked the river's inland course, and Butler's troops encountered only slight resistance from fortified positions at Wilson's Wharf, Fort Powhatan, City Point, and Bermuda Hundred, taking the rebels by surprise. Richmond slept only miles from these fronts, maintained in security from naval assault by the rock-bottomed Falls of the James and on land by the maze of entrenchments that circled the city and its satellites in successive waves of earth and timber. The arrival of Butler, taking the field in person with eighteen thousand troops, found the city at a disadvantage as Grant massed more than a hundred thousand troops in its vicinity. Awaiting further instructions, however, or hamstrung, in Butler's account, by the hesitation of other division commanders, the Army of the James did not push forward into a direct assault.

Instead they effected the occupation of the river districts, an enterprise freighted with a widely shared awareness of the historical context—thanks to Northern education and the fascination of enlisted men with black history. Sergeant George W. Hatton of the 1st USCT, for example, made note of a historic site at the first new river bend of the James invasion, the peninsula where the Jamestown colony had stood and "the very spot where the first sons of Africa were landed," a reference to the first sale of Africans in England's North American colonies, in 1619. Passing Jamestown without landing, the 1st USCT and a cavalry detachment from the 10th USCT came ashore at Wilson's Wharf or Wilson's Landing, a steamboat station in better times, and overwhelmed a minor Confederate defense. "I knew that they would fight more desperately than any white troops," Butler later wrote, because "if captured they would be returned to slavery [or killed] and the officers commanding them might be murdered." Wild and his soldiers commemorated the ancient and alternative history of Virginia in their choice of a name for the embankments they constructed on the site: Fort Pocahontas.[11]

The Army of the James operated among the remnants of core American experiences, including the origins of American slavery, and their memoirs and letters showed their appreciation of the irony of their encounter with historic sites: Pocahontas; the captured Confederate redoubt called Fort Powhatan at Jamestown; City Point, established 1613; and Bermuda Hundred, named for the island where the appointed governor of Virginia and his crew had shipwrecked in 1609. Lest their own knowledge fail, they found themselves schooled by the remainder of the class of masters of the James River waterway, including those who called themselves the FFV—the First Families of Virginia—descendants of the original colonial elite.

The war had depleted the ranks of the FFV as age-eligible men joined the Confederate armed services or government agencies in Richmond. Others had fled the destruction of their stately homes during naval bombardment in 1862. A core remained at the center of an active web of communications, petitions, and appeals to legal, military, and political authorities, and the Army of the James confronted these notables with a full understanding of just how important they were. New England officers such as Butler, Beecher, and Wild had been taught to revere their own colonial forebears, and they showed their scholarly engagement with Virginia's origins and ruling class by their references in letters and the designation of military place-names. The colored troops carried firsthand associations among individuals enlisted from the Virginia and North Carolina coasts. Disembarking at Wilson's Wharf for an easy victory on May 7, Wild's African Brigade carried a list of the most important rebel civilians in the vicinity of the new fort. By May 8, the 1st USCT had detained and transported to Fortress Monroe nearly a dozen FFVs and their friends, including prominent women.

The management of the estate and family of former president John Tyler manifested the occupiers' vengeful spirit and political sense. The Tyler family attracted the scorn of Union officials in light of President Tyler's high-profile betrayal of the United States by his participation in Virginia's secession convention and the Confederate Congress (Tyler had died shortly before taking his seat in early 1862). Sherwood Forest, the Tyler plantation, also had the misfortune to stand immediately adjacent to Wilson's Wharf and Fort Pocahontas. Wild's thirteen May 8 detainees included Tyler's nephew J. C. Tyler, sent away for thirty days as part of an effort to suppress rebel communications. The manor house at Sherwood Forest, meanwhile, fell into the possession of the African Brigade and its local allies, who followed the lead of a Tyler family house slave in seizing valuables and documents, destroying furniture, and depleting the stores of food and forage. Taking note of the mansion's grand oblong ballroom—a tribute to the former first couple's role in introducing dancing to polite society—Wild made plans to convert the confiscated property into a school for black children. Tyler's second wife and small children scattered into exile, inspiring outraged volleys of letters to U.S. and Confederate officials.

Also instructive was the fate of William H. Clopton, a descendant of seventeenth-century grandees. Omitted from Wild's original roundup, Clopton probably came to the general's attention after Tyler's niece fled Sherwood Forest for Selwood, Clopton's Charles City County estate. While most of the detainees were seen as fellow travelers of the rebellion and its armies, Clopton attracted additional scrutiny due to his reputation as a harsh slaveholder. Viewing the scars on women of the estate and interviewing a soldier under his command who had run away from Clopton to enlist, Wild learned of the ready use of corporal punishment at Selwood, and of the master's cruelty when applying the whip with his own hand. Taking Clopton into custody on May 10, Wild decided on "the administration of Poetical justice" to accompany his standard security operations, as described by Sergeant Hatton:

> On the arrival of Mr. C. in camp, the commanding officer determined to let the women have their revenge, and ordered Mr. C. to be tied to a tree in front of headquarters, and William Harris, a soldier in our regiment, and a member of Co. E, who was acquainted with the gentleman, and who used to belong to him, was called upon to undress him, and introduce him to the

ladies I mentioned before. Mr. Harris played his part conspicuously, bringing the blood from his loins at every stroke, and not forgetting to remind
the gentleman of days gone by.

After giving him some fifteen or twenty well-directed strokes, the ladies, one after another, came up and gave him a like number, to remind
him that they were no longer his, but safely housed in Abraham's bosom,
and under the protection of the Star Spangled Banner, and guarded by their
own patriotic, though once down-trodden race.

Oh, that I had the tongue to express my feelings while standing upon
the banks of the James river, on the soil of Virginia, the mother state of
slavery, as a witness of such a sudden reverse!

Wild expressed dissatisfaction in his official report on the incident. "I
wish[ed] that his back had been as deeply scarred as those of the women."
He confessed to wanting to take the whip into his single hand. "But I ab-
stained," he wrote, "and left it to them"—the better to reward Clopton with
his just desserts.

William Clopton, for his part, understood that his Tidewater world was
upside down. "Truly these are terrible times," he wrote upon his release
from confinement some weeks afterward, and yet "the loss of my negroes
[as slaves] gives me no concern up to the present." He was happy to be alive,
"blessed so far above thousands languishing in prison, where I should have
died." And as for black folk: "My feelings have been so changed in regard to
them that I don't feel that I ever care to see another."

The flogging of William Clopton changed his political perspective, forc-
ing him to recognize African Americans as his resourceful adversaries.
Black participants experienced a similar shift in outlook, though the political lessons of the event were more ambiguous. For one thing, they recognized the need to fight to defend their freedom and that of emancipated
persons in the vicinity of the army. Moved in part by the complaints of the
Tylers and Cloptons and their friends, the Army of Northern Virginia detached cavalry under General Fitzhugh Lee (of the FFV Lees), the nephew
of the rebel commander. In a pitched battle lasting five hours, Wild's eleven
hundred held off twenty-five hundred attackers, inflicting heavy casualties.

The Confederates retired upon the arrival of reinforcements by gunboat, executing a handful of prisoners, supposedly, and shipping to Richmond a captured infantryman claimed to be a slave.

The colored troops could take pride in their victory while still complaining about their terms of service. As Sergeant Hatton described it afterward in a letter to the *Christian Messenger*, the engagement epitomized the dual experience of black men:

> When marching to the field of battle, by the side of my captain, who is one of the brave sons of old Massachusetts, I feel that I am a man, fighting for a Government that recognizes me as such; but, behold, when I call my wandering mind to view facts, and the ground upon which I stand, I find that the leaders of the Government are still keeping us far behind the times. I appeal to the leaders of this great Republic to know the reason why they hesitate to give us our God-given rights.

The matter of $7 a month still stuck in Hatton's craw: for a free man like himself, having signed on in Washington, the bill pending in Congress offered back pay to the date of enlistment, but the formely enslaved in Hatton's company could collect only back to January 1864. Such men would fight for the flag "until the last drop of blood be drawn from our veins," and they had, Hatton said. "I want to know if the star spangled banner represents such unjust deeds."[12]

Hatton had become a soldier of the republic but not yet a Black Republican. Nonetheless his advocacy and the military action prosecuted with his aid served to advance the black cause within the Republican Party and beyond.

In June 1864, the 1st and 5th USCT were transferred from the command of General Butler to divisions working directly under Ulysses Grant. The time of tending quarters, making music, and passing stories about great men in camp had passed. In movements coordinated by Lt. General Grant, the black brigades invaded the Confederate entrenchments around Petersburg, Virginia, with terrifying results, as described in the surviving diary of an 8th USCT musician and infantryman, William Woodlin.

11th We got Steam up about daylight and got underweigh [*sic*] before sunrise. the Verona which brought up the 7th MD & Gen been in our wake and then passing us as well as a great [number] of other boats. The scenery is very good but the Gen' character is Southern quite so . . . We soon after took up the line of march for Gen. Butler's Hed Qur's about 7 miles distant through Virginia dust, which is terrible indeed. Water was very scarce and the evening was enlivened by the bombardment of Petersburg.

13th The morning was ushered in by the [Navy] Monitors shelling the woods. things very uncertain about our future destiny. the Guns soon opened on us and some 8 or 9 shells were thrown in on our camp before we could get out of the way our Srgt. Major was wounded and several in the 7th U.S.C.T. We fell back about half a mile and left our dress clothes [79] and knapsacks and moved in. height marching order we started about 11 P.M. and moved across the river on a pontoon bridge and haversacks for the night. Sunrise was ushered in by sharp skirmishing.

Woodlin moved through a natural landscape transformed, the green in the scenery replaced by bare mounds and tunnels and the stripped wood spikes of the abatis. Bullets flew thick enough to cut down an oak tree two feet in diameter, and the fog of war lay thick around the Army of the James, obstructing the unhappy town from its sights. Though Woodlin had survived the Battle of Olustee, he had not seen any fighting as all-encompassing as the mature assault on Richmond's outer defense. In fact, there had never been anything like it in the world.

Woodlin's regiment marched under Major General William F. Smith in an army corps briefly known as Butler's Black Brigade, a configuration that also included the 1st and 5th USCT under Brigadier General Wild and a few white regiments. A Massachusetts private recorded the climax of the Petersburg campaign:

About 1 o'clock a.m. Wednesday, the 15th. We heard the bugle, and sprang to our arms, and with two days rations, we started toward Petersburg . . . Our Major and Col. [Henry S.] Russell were wounded, and several men fell— to advance seemed almost impossible; but we rallied, and after a terrible charge, amidst pieces of barbarous iron, solid shot, and shell, we drove the desperate graybacks from their fortifications, and gave three cheers for our victory. But few whites were with us . . .

The colored troops here have received a great deal of praise. The sensations I had in the battle were, coolness and interest in the boys' fighting. They shouted, "Fort Pillow," and the rebs were shown no mercy.[13]

Butler's troops had achieved one of the first victories in the Virginia Theater, while Grant's massive lines became locked in place after swinging to encircle more than 180 degrees around Petersburg and Richmond.

The heroes of the First Petersburg Campaign made a striking addition to the polished divisions of the Army of the Potomac as they filed in reduced numbers onto navy transports and an ingenious set of pontoon bridges. "Everything bore the terrible imprint of a month's hard fighting, and made sad contrast to the hopeful men who in new uniforms who had so recently started out . . . under the great commander, Grant," remembered a witness, the artist Edwin Forbes. With his eye for visual effect, Forbes observed that veterans were "ragged and footsore, their faces much discolored by powder-stain and dust." Indeed, the faces of the white officers were so blackened, Forbes recorded, that they were "scarcely discernible from the privates."[14] Accompanying Grant to City Point, the black brigades helped to establish the new logistical and command center of the Petersburg Siege.

Thanks to the Army of the James (which never received the appreciation Butler felt it deserved), the river and its landmarks offered a secure corridor for the movement of men and matériel. Only days after his arrival, the general in chief felt so much confidence in its security that he invited the president of the United States to visit in person at City Point to plan with Grant the next phase of the campaign. In 1865, only weeks before the president's death, Grant would invite Lincoln and his family and other couples for the fresh air and entertainment at City Point, once victory had been nearly assured. Lincoln's visit to Grant's headquarters on June 21, 1864, however, was all urgent business and rearguard-of-the-battlefield accommodations.[15] Arriving by steamer, Lincoln mounted a horse to review the troops, braving the dust raised by the transit of thousands of soldiers and mounts and by the work of the United States Military Rail Road Construction Corps, laying tracks and building wharves, a hospital, a bakery, and dozens of other necessary structures. His familiar black clothing and hat took on a coating of gray as the president received the cheers of members of the Army of the Potomac.

Grant took Lincoln to see the black veterans of the James and Petersburg. The president had "read with the greatest delight," he explained, the newspaper descriptions of "how gallantly they behaved." He happily took credit for the success of the experiment with black enlistment, he told Grant, for which he had been "opposed on nearly every side." They "had proven their efficiency," said Lincoln, "and I am glad that they have kept pace with the white troops in the recent assaults."

Riding to their lines, Grant and the president initiated another parade review, in which Lincoln rode holding his top hat in his lap. The men were quick to break formation, however, when they perceived the identity of their mounted guest. Surging forward and around him, the colored troops laid their hands on Lincoln's horse and its tack, touching and kissing the president's hands and clothing and shouting words of gratitude and admiration. An officer, General Horace Porter, recorded his reaction:

> The President rode with bared head; tears had started to his eyes, and his voice was so broken by emotion that he could scarcely articulate the words of thanks and congratulation which he tried to speak to the humble and devoted men through whose ranks he rode. The scene was affecting in the extreme, and no one could have witnessed it unmoved.

Lincoln had been known to weep—while visiting wounded troops; while writing letters; in the company of orphans and old friends; upon hearing "John Brown's Body" and the "Battle Hymn of the Republic." He had wept to the point of heaving with sobs over the fate of emaciated Confederate prisoners on a railway platform. He would weep again at City Point on that longest day of the year, exclaiming, "You must live! You must!" upon meeting a horribly wounded soldier. "Oh, this awful, awful war!" the president had said. The achievements of the black troops offered an opportunity to weep for joy, even as the high price of their participation came more clearly into view.

How high the price had now become the central question of the war. Lincoln had arrived at City Point burdened with a new awareness of the sacrifices at the heart of General Grant's strategic plan. "I begin to see it. You will succeed," he cabled Grant on June 15, the high point of the forward movements. A war of attrition perpetuated at the expense of thousands of lives would inevitably favor the inexhaustibly resourceful USA. "His whole conversation during his visit showed the deep anxiety he felt and the weight of responsibility resting on him," remembered Porter.

Reprising John Brown's last words, Lincoln repeated his wish "that all may be accomplished with as little bloodshed as possible." Yet he did not "pretend to advise" U. S. Grant that his strategy was not the best.[16]

18

BLACK REPUBLICANS

The Reverend James N. Gloucester of Brooklyn had collected donations for more than a year as president of the American Freedman's Friend Association, a mixed-race group headed by some of New York City's best-known philanthropists. Gloucester directed the thousands of dollars in clothing, books, and cash contributions to the attention of the Western Sanitary Commission in St. Louis. Western Sanitary (founded with help from Jessie Fremont in 1861) had made itself known as the single greatest program of outreach and assistance to refugees from slavery, seeking to ease the suffering of the largest concentration of freedmen in the country in the Mississippi River Valley. The minister had come to feel as if he played a role in the organization, taking pride in its success. As a mark of his participation in its endeavor, Gloucester traveled to St. Louis to take part in the Western Sanitary Fair of May 1864.

Traveling with a friend—who was also of African American descent—Reverend Gloucester wanted more than simply to attend the event. As a benefactor of the effort, he hoped to partake in the mutual congratulations of the organizers of the fair, to meet like-minded patriots, and to celebrate with them the yawning opportunity to lift up the oppressed race in the South and Southwest. Gloucester was an older man and a veteran of the antislavery struggle. He had learned from John Brown, his friend, houseguest, and coconspirator, that it paid to put the body at the service of the best cause,

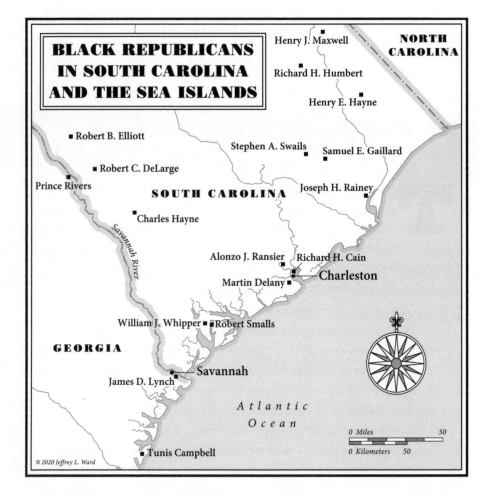

BLACK REPUBLICANS
IN SOUTH CAROLINA
AND THE SEA ISLANDS

NORTH
CAROLINA

Henry J. Maxwell

Richard H. Humbert

Henry E. Hayne

Robert B. Elliott

Stephen A. Swails   Samuel E. Gaillard

Robert C. DeLarge

Prince Rivers

SOUTH CAROLINA   Joseph H. Rainey

Charles Hayne

Savannah River

Alonzo J. Ransier   Richard H. Cain

Martin Delany   Charleston

William J. Whipper ■ ■Robert Smalls

GEORGIA

James D. Lynch   Savannah

Atlantic
Ocean

Tunis Campbell

0 Miles   50
0 Kilometers   50

© 2020 Jeffrey L. Ward

and therefore he presented his person and that of his unnamed friend on the doorstep of the top Sanitary man of St. Louis, the kindly Radical Republican James E. Yeatman.

Yeatman and the others had done their best to make African Americans at home in their experience of the patriotic spirit of the fair, opening its doors to visitors of both races and selecting a sharp-dressed unit of the United States Colored Troops to guard it.[1] Freedmen's Aid comprised a special part of its mission, being the object of its own subscription booth at the center of the hall, near a towering display of flowers. Organizers hoped the close association of the effort with the plight of former slaves would help to overcome ennui, three years into the war, with giving in the name of logistical support for soldiers. "Here is a new charity, never before included in Fairs," wrote Lydia Maria Child in a publicity column published in *The Liberator*. "For the Union refugees and freedmen, now suffering for food and clothing, they can and will give a little more."[2]

Sincere in his dedication to the cause of freedmen, and welcoming to black ticket holders and subscribers, Yeatman nonetheless failed to show perfect courtesy to his guests, being flummoxed by the protocols of receiving black visitors as colleagues and equals. The awkwardness of the encounter was recorded in a newspaper report that circulated nationally:

> They first saw James E. Yeatman, President of the Sanitary Commission, who referred them to Mr. [E. W.] Fox [a commission trustee]. By Mr. Fox they were referred to someone else, who procured season tickets for their use. This third party did not like the embarrassment and responsibility of dealing with the visitors, and rid himself of them by turning them over to the Rev. Dr. Nelson, pastor of the First Presbyterian Church of this city, who is in an official position at the Fair, as Chairman of the Freedmen and Refugee Department. Here their wanderings ended.

Nelson, the minister of gospel to Yeatman himself as well as other prominent Radicals in the city, thought he knew what Jesus would do when confronted with such a dilemma. Heading toward Twelfth Street and passing USCT sentinels on the way, he escorted his guests to the social heart of the fair, a table at the Café Laclede, where he pulled up a chair for himself and joined them.

Had Radical Republicans envisioned true equality and the integration of public accommodations? The ordeal of James N. Gloucester and his guest suggested otherwise. While embracing the cause of black soldiers and suffering freedmen, organizers of the Sanitary Fair showed themselves to have limited vision about the prospects for the advancement and recognition of the race. At least they were more advanced in their views than the society women operating the Café Laclede (named for the founder of the city of St. Louis). The managers rebuked Nelson sternly. Some of the young white women acting as servers—photographed amid the bunting in their colored hoops, in a happier moment—broke into tears at the affront. Only one of their number deigned to offer Gloucester and his friend some food and drink, approaching the table while people shouted around her. Though she was disenfranchised and uncredited by name in the newspaper accounts, the volunteer was a political woman.

Scorned by Radical elites as uncouth and uneducated, Abraham Lincoln showed a better command of race relations etiquette, as in his inviting Frederick Douglass to the White House for a one-on-one meeting in August. It was a historic first that passed without fanfare amid the painful military exigencies of the season. The bloody summer of 1864 had slogged on without hope of victory in Virginia, while troops and gunboats in the Red River Campaign had been defeated and forced into a breakneck retreat. The near-invasion of Washington, D.C., and the death of General James McPherson in the previous weeks had deepened the sense that the Union war effort was losing ground.

Arriving at the White House, Douglass found the president musing on the possibility of losing the election. What did it mean for the war, with Democrats clamoring for peace at any price? His proposal to Douglass was to draw upon the George Stearns and John Brown playbook. Would he lead a covert operation after a U.S. surrender to "hive the bees," as Brown had called it? Would Douglass direct black men of the South into an extended guerrilla operation?

The president also showed his appreciation of Douglass as an informal adviser on political subjects (a view Lincoln had shared with Freedmen's

Department chief John Eaton, calling the orator "one of the most meritorious men in America"). He showed Douglass a letter in which he suggested he might agree to end the war with slavery partially intact, a move that Douglass protested could do "serious damage" to Lincoln's reputation and the cause. Douglass kept the contents of his conversation with the president confidential, despite his early support for the Fremont candidacy and his persistent reservations about the Republican Party as a champion for black America.

On August 29, Douglass wrote describing his plan to create a "band of scouts" to serve as emancipation agents in the aftermath of a military or political defeat. The president, meanwhile, had his cabinet sign an oath intended to reinforce their commitment to the war in the event that Lincoln's bid for reelection failed.[3]

Events in September lightened the atmosphere for Republicans of all types. General Sherman's capture of Atlanta broke through the Union military impasse and the Democrats nominated George B. McClellan on a pro-peace platform at their national convention. The victory cheered the outlook for Lincoln's military strategy and the juxtaposition of McClellan's essentially proslavery views with the president's finally solidified the party behind the incumbent for the general election. Radicals who had been openly agitating to replace Lincoln at the head of the ticket in August (including George Stearns, who launched *The Nation* magazine to air his extreme views that summer, and who had published an open letter calling on both Lincoln and General Fremont to step aside in favor of an unnamed replacement) now brought the intraparty insurgency to an end. Stearns himself, assisted by the poet John Greenleaf Whittier, traveled to Nahant to pressure Fremont to resign from the race in order to prevent the disaster of a McClellan and Peace Democrat presidency, a request that gained the reluctant acquiescence of John C. and Jessie B.

United for Lincoln, Republicans now acted to mobilize the electorate, applying themselves with special vigor to delivering the votes of soldiers in the field. They successfully lobbied in some states to permit soldiers to vote by absentee ballot, and when Indiana refused to modify traditional balloting, the Lincoln administration urged commanders to offer leave so that troops could travel home to Indiana to vote. Military transportation passes were provided even to Republican voters not serving in the armed forces.

For example, Walt Whitman, who was caring for wounded soldiers as a hospital volunteer and drawing a Treasury Department salary thanks to his Republican friends, obtained a railway ticket home to New York in exchange for assurances that he would vote.

The Union League of Philadelphia took on the mission of capturing soldiers' votes in Pennsylvania, going so far as to instruct its membership to supervise the registration and the payment of poll taxes for absentee voters. The drive to enlarge the Republican electorate, however, stopped short of agitating for expanded voting rights for African American men. One measure of this oversight was the disappointing result of Louisiana's newly created state government, which convened in early October to write laws that limited the franchise in the state to white men. The move disregarded a suffrage petition to the legislature signed by five thousand black Louisianans, including men in military service as well as New Orleans elites. "It will be time enough to grant this petition when all the other free states grant it and set us the example," insisted an official, who added, "When this state grants it, I shall go to China."[4]

Simultaneous with this disappointment, a convention of black men gathered in Syracuse, New York, to assess the prospects for raising the status of African Americans in the North as well as the South. Colored conventions had been a staple of African American organizing since 1830, when the first national convention took place in Philadelphia. The onset of the war had interrupted the pattern of holding national or at least regional conventions every year, creating an interlude during which divisions within the black community had become more pronounced. For many years, opinion had been divided between emigrationists (such as Martin Delany and the New York minister Henry Highland Garnet) and those who preferred to struggle to improve the standing of the race at home by legal, economic, and political means. Emancipation and the enrollment of African American troops had swelled the fortunes of the latter group, empowering patriotic activists such as Frederick Douglass within the movement. A signal of the success of the antiemigrationists was the election of John Mercer Langston, the recognized Republican officeholder, to preside over the convention and its successor organization, the National Equal Rights League, which established headquarters in Philadelphia. Despite this recognition for one who worked within the system, however, the convention refused to embrace voting Republican as the means of ascent for blacks in the United States.

The most famous names in black America attended the Syracuse convention, including a number strongly associated with the Republican Party. In addition to Langston, the partisan delegates included John S. Rock representing Massachusetts (who organized and printed the proceedings), Frederick Douglass, Robert Hamilton, and J.W.C. Pennington of New York, Rhode Island and NYC's George Downing, and the spy and organizer Abraham Galloway and others representing the Southern states. Douglass made a strong argument in favor of voting rights and political participation, calling the franchise "the keystone in the arch of human liberty." Langston introduced himself as "a voter in Ohio, under the law as construed, which enables men to vote who are more white than black," who had "supported the Republican party, and he expected to do it again."

Other delegates questioned whether the political parties offered any policies worthy of the black man's vote. "The Democratic party belongs to slavery," delegates concluded in the official statement of the convention, "and the Republican party is largely under the power of prejudice against color."

> While gratefully recognizing a vast difference in our favor in the character and composition of the Republican party, and regarding the accession to power of the Democratic party as the heaviest calamity that could befall us in the present juncture of affairs, it cannot, be disguised, that, while that party is our bitterest enemy, and is positively and actively re-actionary, the Republican party is negatively and passively so in its tendency.

Not all Republicans were Radicals on race relations, and even among Radicals the commitment to black rights was seen as whimsical and shallow.

> However antislavery in sentiment the President may be, and however disposed he may be to continue the war till slavery is abolished, it is plain that in this he would not be sustained by his party. A single reverse to our arms, in such a war, would raise the hands of the party in opposition to their chief. The hope of the speedy and complete abolition of slavery, hangs, therefore, not upon the disposition of the Republican party, not upon the disposition

of President Lincoln; but upon the slender thread of Rebel power, pride, and persistence.

Embracing what the statement conceded was "a somewhat gloomy view of the condition of affairs," the convention disbanded without endorsing Lincoln in the pending election.[5]

In fact, the antiwar and proslavery extremism of the Democratic Party left Republicans ample room to maneuver in the run-up to November without seeking the enthusiasm of the party's Radical wing. Lincoln continued to call on Radicals, however, as reliable—if thorny and ungrateful—allies in important public tasks. In this spirit he asked Benjamin Butler, the unofficial leading man of the faction in the aftermath of Fremont's withdrawal, to take on a delicate task in support of the ticket on the eve of the election itself.

New York City remained the most reactionary city in the Union less than eighteen months after the deadly draft riots of 1863. Apprised of a plot to derail balloting with a new round of civil unrest in the city, the War Department called on Butler to make a show of force in New York, directing him to leave his post at Fortress Monroe for a last-minute trip to the city. The call was so urgent that Secretary Stanton denied the general's request for time to pack clothing suitable for city use. Sent to New York in his battlefield flannel shirt, Butler later sent the War Department the bill for a tailored new uniform "in full feather."

Butler's experiences in Baltimore and New Orleans made him the ideal candidate to impose order on an unruly city. The War Department and General Grant may have also valued the new assignment as a step toward removing Butler from his troublesome battlefield command. The general made the most of his role, engaging in behavior that was sure to capture headlines. He appeared at the opera to public applause, rode his "camp rig" rawhide saddle on a battle-scarred horse in the weekend promenade, and threatened to encamp his squadron of thirty-five hundred troops (housed on naval transports) on the broad lawns of Central Park at the first sign of trouble.

Butler also saw to critical tasks. He cut short a speculation in gold organized to undermine confidence on Election Day by calling the perpetrators to his headquarters and telling them that he had plans to confiscate bullion suspected of belonging to Confederates. By the day of the election, Butler had put in place a network of telegraphing centers, assigned soldiers to polling places, and positioned gunboats strategically around the city. As an added bonus, the Massachusetts general had managed to magnify his stature as a statesman and a Cossack-like figure of fun. *The New York Times* opined,

> So far as we have heard he has not yet erected a single gallows or hung anybody; he has shot nobody; he has knouted nobody; he has hamstrung nobody; he has crucified nobody; he has impaled nobody on a poker, or bastinadoed nobody. He has sent nobody to Fort Lafayette, and put nobody in chains or irons. He has suppressed no newspapers, and insulted no women. But he took the most active and admirable measures to secure the peace of the city and State during the election yesterday; and the peace has been undisturbed.

While Butler did not deliver a majority for Lincoln in New York City, he had helped to ensure an outcome that was indisputable.[6] Indeed, the National Union ticket with Andrew Johnson as vice president had won the election by four hundred thousand popular votes and a landslide in the Electoral College. Republicans gained fifty seats in the House and two in the Senate, for a total of more than 70 percent of the votes in each house. The era of the Republican supermajority in Congress had begun.

Radical Republican voices had not penetrated the judiciary branch with the same effect. Much of the truly radical policy of the Civil War years took place in military settings where civil law had been suspended, exaggerating the power of the executive branch, and compelling Congress often to follow up on military policy with legislation. While Lincoln appointed a total of five justices to the Supreme Court, moreover, he did not impose a particular judicial interpretation on the court. If anything, Lincoln's high court jurisprudence might be said to be dismissive of the weight of the authority of the Supreme Court versus other branches. Beginning with *Dred Scott*, the lawyerly president had argued against the idea of judicial review of acts of Congress and the executive branch.

A pair of operative federal courts in proximity to war districts had provided the most to Union jurisprudence. The District Court judge William Marvin in Key West had used his post to manage the large number of cases of ships and cargoes seized in the waters around Confederate states, delivering a substantial financial and military boost to the union cause. The former emigrationist John C. Underwood, business partner to Eli Thayer, took up a lifetime appointment to the federal bench in the Eastern District of Virginia in 1864. He made headlines shortly after the election by ruling in favor of the right of African Americans to testify in court.[7]

The death of Chief Justice Roger Taney in October 1864 had opened a door for the radicalization of the Supreme Court of the United States, a transformation initiated (though never completed) by the appointment of Salmon P. Chase to Taney's seat. Though he had not known it, the man goaded by the "presidential chin fly" during his important years of service in other high offices had been born to be chief justice. The war had rendered obsolete much of the content of the Freedom National antislavery agenda that Chase had pioneered, but much remained to be done to advance Chase's life work as a humanitarian and advocate of African American rights.

Chase believed in not only the equal standing of African Americans before the law, but also the derivative principle that their race should not provide an obstacle to their political participation. He had championed black voting rights at length in a late 1863 letter written to the president, in which he outlined Radical objections to Restored Louisiana. The chief justice now delivered his opinions from the height of the highest bench, with little regard for the separation of powers or illegitimate precedents. He had not surrendered his campaign for the presidency, and therefore felt free to comment and engage on the political issues of the day. In a letter that articulated his broad sense of judicial leadership, delivered later in 1865, Chase took Lieutenant General William T. Sherman privately to task for racist statements on the status of African Americans, reminding Sherman of his grave responsibility to the public.[8]

Chase's most Radical act as chief justice, similarly, took place outside the purview of judicial rulings and court opinions. Presiding in the Senate Chamber—at a time when the high court met in Congress and lacked an independent facility—Chase recognized a motion from Senator Charles Sumner, who stood upon the very spot where he had been beaten unconscious in 1856. Sumner did not make a speech, but merely asked "that John S. Rock, a member of the Supreme Court of the State of Massachusetts, be admitted to practice as a member of this Court [known in legal circles as the Bar of the United States]." When Chase replied laconically in the affirmative and directed the administration of the oath, a precedent of broad significance became established.

Without returning to the despised doctrines laid out by Justice Taney in the *Dred Scott* decision, the new Radical Republican chief repudiated the old standard by his recognition of Rock's standing in the court—a privilege extended only to citizens. The chief justice could have cited the recent opinion of new federal district judge John Underwood, but he did not, allowing the naturalness of the gesture to speak for itself.

Having been admitted to the bar of the United States, Rock stood eligible by extension to participate in any institution in American life. Sumner, for his part, understood this status to include equal access to education and to public accommodations, and the senator would devote the remaining years of his life to fighting for what became the Civil Rights Act of 1875, as well as other causes.

John S. Rock considered his ascent to citizenship as a good place to begin. The move added to the momentum of his own wartime emergence as a regional and national orator of note. Appearing now on the platform with Garrison and Douglass and the like, Rock professed to being pleased and "thankful" for the progress so far. As a trained doctor as well as a lawyer, the forty-year-old consumptive may well have known how little time he had to live (eighteen months). Nonetheless he described himself before the Union League of Philadelphia as ready to wait before declaring victory against oppression.

When . . . all proscriptive laws [are] abolished, and the right of suffrage extended to his race throughout the broad extent of this great Republic [said Rock], his cup of pleasure would be full. (Applause.) He would then be able to say, as the old maid was reported to have said on the eve of her marriage: "This is the day I long have sought / And mourned because I found it not."

The unmarried Rock claimed to be holding out for a fuller embrace from the American establishment, and yet he had already bedded down with the Republicans, for whom he had been one of the few black speakers taking the stump in the great campaign events of late 1864.[9]

Another African American working in partnership with Republicans was John Jones of Chicago, the friend of John Brown and Allan Pinkerton who with his wife had procured the suit of clothes in which the old revolutionary was hanged. The results of the election had emboldened Jones to ask more of Illinois Republicans, who were slated to assume a majority of seats in the state legislature early in 1865. Jones reasoned with the incoming members of the new assembly to consider the unacceptable conditions in which black individuals stood in relation to the state.

The Black Laws of Illinois—adopted serially over decades, and reflecting the divided sentiments of a state with both pro- and antislavery constituencies—asked that African Americans carry proof of their free condition; denied trial by jury; and prohibited blacks to testify against whites in court. The consummation of all of them denied the equal citizenship of African Americans in Illinois, a status that Jones attacked in a pamphlet of some thirty pages.

> Now it may be said by our enemies, that we are not citizens, and therefore have no rights as above mentioned. If being natives, and born on the soil, of parents belonging to no other nation or tribe, does not constitute citizenship in this country, under the theory and genius of our government, I am at a loss to know in what manner citizenship is attained by birth. Fellow citizens, I declare unto you, view it as you may, we are American citizens; by the principles of the Declaration of Independence, we are citizens; within the meaning of the U.S. Constitution, we are citizens; by the facts of history, and by the admission of American statesmen, we are American citizens; by the hardships and trials endured; by the courage and fidelity of our ancestors in defending the liberties and achieving the independence of our land, we are American citizens.

Republicans adopted Jones's initiative with alacrity, inviting the author of the pamphlet to appear in the assembly hall of the legislature and publishing the text in its entirety in a local paper. In a party-line vote taken shortly after the first session of the new state legislature, on February 7, 1865, the legislature repealed all the laws creating special conditions for African Americans in Illinois, rendering the laws of the state officially blind to color (though not taking steps to ensure the enrollment of African American voters).

Once access to the ballot had been obtained by means of the Fifteenth Amendment, John Jones made a point of voting Republican until his death in 1879, serving two terms as a Republican member of the Cook County Commission.[10]

"My colored countrymen," Jones said on the eve of casting his first ballot, in 1870, "the Republican Party has lifted us up from the degradation of slavery and put us upon an equal footing with themselves."[11] As such they were worthy of Jones's devotion, even when they failed to overcome the prejudices and limitations of their age.

More skeptical about the Republicans was Jones's partner in what had shaped up to be an effective army recruiting enterprise, contracting with the Northern states for black enlistments to meet federal quotas. Martin Delany had lived with Jones for a time in Chicago, in what proved to be a waylay in a peripatetic life. Delany had been born in Charles Town, (West) Virginia; moved with his mother to Chambersburg and Pittsburgh, PA; lived on the road as a correspondent of Garrison's *North Star* in the 1840s; enrolled briefly at Harvard Medical School, and retreated after his expulsion on racial grounds to the black expatriate community in Chatham, Ontario. He explored Abeokuta, Liberia, in 1859 and 1860 and promoted it as a destination for U.S. black nationalists even after the onset of the war. Intrigued by the Emancipation Proclamation and black enlistment, Delany chose to linger in his native land in 1863 and 1864, working with Jones to recruit for (and around) Rhode Island, Connecticut, and Ohio. Early in 1865, he and his family relocated to Wilberforce, Ohio, to align with the newly founded African Methodist Episcopal college there and immerse themselves in its educated African American community.

Could the talented Delany (author, doctor, orator, organizer) be recruited as a Radical Republican? The party that could win his heart must needs be Radical in the extreme. No African American of the nineteenth century spoke more forcefully of the wrongdoing of whites, the superiority of Africans and their descendants, and the necessity for violence and revolution. In his family's move to Wilberforce, however, Delany drew within the orbit of one of the most practical and resourceful African American leaders in the country, Bishop Daniel Payne of the African Methodist Episcopal Church. Payne had envisioned a nonviolent victory in the South, making a crusade of sending black ministers and missionaries in the wake of armies, having sponsored the 1863 initiative that sent James D. Lynch to the Sea Islands and Savannah. Late in 1864, Martin Delany addressed a letter to the secretary of war in Washington, outlining a plan for accelerating the assembly of black regiments among former slaves.

The plan called on the government to assist in the creation and deployment of a streamlined military force commanded by African American officers. Like Lynch—who had been assisted by the navy in reaching his new post, by the army's seizure of churches and other buildings for his services, and by the Treasury Department's distribution of confiscated properties to support his churches and schools—Delany saw the Radicalized U.S. government as a tool to advance the interests of his race. He would collaborate with the Lincoln administration as part of an any-means-necessary bid for black advancement.

For the moment, Delany explained to Secretary of War Stanton in his letter, his vision for racial uplift worked "in perfect harmony with the course of the President and your own enlightened views." Delany and Jones had "associated themselves permanently together," he explained, "in an Agency for raising Black troops for all parts of the Country," including "any of the Southern or seceded states." At the earliest order they were ready to depart and able to deliver "a Regiment, or Brigade if required, in a shorter time than can otherwise be effected." The letter made plain the insistence of Delany and Jones on having command of such an operation without white officers present. The writer expressed the belief "that this is one of the measures in which the claims of the Black Man may be officially recognised without seemingly infringing upon those of other citizens."[12]

Delany traveled from Wilberforce to Washington in February 1865 and obtained an interview not with Stanton but with Lincoln himself, as described in an autobiographical account:

"What can I do for you, sir?" he inquired.

"Nothing, Mr. President," I replied; "but I've come to propose something to you, which I think will be beneficial for the nation in this critical hour of her peril." I shall never forget the expression of his countenance and the inquiring look which he gave me when I answered him.

Delany must serve as an officer, Lincoln told him, addressing instructions to Stanton to confer "with this extraordinary and intelligent black man."

Just as he began writing, the cannon commenced booming.

"Stanton is firing! listen! he is in his glory, noble man!" he exclaimed.

"What is it, Mr. President" I asked . . .

"Why, you don't know? Haven't you heard the news? Charleston is ours!"

The partnership was struck—and not for strictly military reasons. In January, General Lorenzo Thomas (who had personally enrolled more than seventy thousand soldiers) had acknowledged that the drive for black enlistment was winding down in response to the diminishing demand for troops. Though Lincoln had been desperate to incite slave rebellion in the interior as a last resort back in August 1864, he probably did not foresee the need for new regiments at the time of his meeting with Delany. Instead he could hope to recruit resourceful black men of the North to assist in meeting the immediate and long-term challenges of Reconstruction. He wanted a black officer as an ally and as a precedent—and this time there was no delay in the delivery of paperwork and the arrangement of transportation. Within two weeks of the meeting, during which he obtained a uniform and delivered speeches in Wilberforce and nearby Xenia, Martin Delany had reported to the newly enlarged Department of the South as a major of U.S. volunteers.[13]

In partnership with two Radical institutions—the U.S. Army and the African Methodist Episcopal Church—Major Delany set out to transform the South in the final weeks of the war. Delany joined a coterie of notable African Americans serving in official capacities in the vicinity of Charleston,

Savannah, the Sea Islands, and Wilmington, North Carolina, which fell to
the Union on February 22. The capture of the last significant Confederate
port featured the arrival in triumph of the 1st United States Colored Troops,
descendants of the original North Carolina all–African American cornstalk regiment. Included in their company was Chaplain Henry McNeal
Turner, the survivor of thirteen battles and twenty-six skirmishes, and prior
to Delany's appointment, the only African American receiving an officer's
salary.[14] Orindatus Simon Bolivar Wall was present, though debilitated by
illness in the early months of 1865. In addition to Lynch, Richard Cain, another of Bishop Payne's African Methodist Episcopal circuit riders and a
future member of Congress, had arrived in Charleston. Cain worked with
local African Americans to resurrect the long-suppressed but not forgotten
antebellum congregation that became known as the Mother Emanuel AME
Church.

Except for Delany, assigned to an infantry unit under the command
of Rufus Saxton, most of the distinguished Northern black men in the area
found their way into the Freedmen's Bureau, which sprang into operation in
the final six weeks of the war. The encouragement and direction of the freed
persons in their districts proved to be the bulk of the responsibilities in the
early phases, resulting in the delivery of a number of black-to-black addresses with few or no whites in attendance. In his first encounters with the
locals, the New York caterer Tunis Campbell (serving with the Gideonites
since 1863) urged them to cultivate food rather than cash crops and helped
them obtain seed potatoes and other essentials in time for the growing season. Campbell also imported three black New York teachers at his own expense to establish schools. Martin Delany wowed his audiences with his
references to African greatness and the Haitian Revolution. He told them
that black was beautiful and condemned the "infernal white women" of the
South, "arousing . . . the wonder and exciting the uproarious applause of
the recently freed slaves around him," as a newspaper recorded it.

Delany warned of corrupt and exploitative whites, including some who
arrived under the guise of humanitarianism:

> Believe none but those who are sent out by Government, to enlighten and
> guide you. I am an officer in the service of the U.S. Government, and or-

dered to aid Gen'l Saxton, who has been only lately appointed [commander] for South Carolina. So is Gen'l [Edward A.] Wild [Assistant Commander] for Georgia . . . I shall not be intimidated whether by threats or imprisonment, and no power will keep me from telling you the truth. So I expressed myself even at Charleston, the hotbed of those scoundrels, your old masters, without fear or reluctance.[15]

Delany described himself as working with the government and yet not constrained by its policies in case of conflict with his core beliefs. The same held true for the Republicans, whom the major embraced only partially and for expediency. In 1874—still in the vicinity—Delany challenged the Radical candidate for lieutenant governor of South Carolina. Two years later he supported the white Democratic Party candidate, Wade Hampton, for governor, securing Hampton's support for his continuation as a (Republican) trial judge in Charleston. Delany organized a new Liberian migration company based in Charleston, and moved back to Ohio after the end of Reconstruction.

Southern blacks expressed grave concerns about the prospects for working with white people, even as some Republicans among them urged collaboration. A case in point was the participation of James D. Lynch in the most important integrated policy talk of the war. Lynch had remained on the move in the conquered coastal districts, establishing churches and schools and encouraging black congregations to stand up for their rights. Almost immediately after the surrender of Savannah to General Sherman in December 1864, the missionary made his way to the city to continue his work. He launched a school for a hundred pupils at Andrew's Chapel, an established African Methodist Episcopal Church, and made connections in the black community. When Sherman sent an invitation, Reverend Lynch found his way onto a list of twenty black leaders selected to confer with the commanding general and visiting Radical Republicans.

Sherman's "colloquy"—as it became known in the press—convened at the request of the secretary of war, Edwin Stanton, who arrived in Savannah in the company of the assistant adjutant general and the quartermaster general of the United States. The high-level delegation indicated the Lincoln administration's anxiety about the orientation of the victorious general toward the black population of the South. Sherman had proven hostile to the creation of black military units, amassing an all-white army for his famous campaign and confounding the work of army recruiters brave enough to enter his lines. In orders issued upon his arrival in Savannah, the commander had complained about the encumbrances of "surplus negroes, mules, and horses" to military operations—the remark that had prompted the objections of Salmon Chase, who regretted "that an expression classing men with cattle found place in a paper, which cannot fail to be historical." Radicals also responded to reports of the abuse of black refugees during Sherman's March, particularly an incident in which civilians had been trapped on an exploding bridge. At the suggestion of General Grant, Stanton intended to assess Sherman's attitudes and to convey the importance of establishing goodwill among the formerly enslaved. No group could be expected to speak more clearly than African Americans themselves, summoned on Stanton's orders for an unprecedented meeting of the minds.

Participants were quick to indicate their confidence in General Sherman. "It is probable that he would not meet the Secretary with more courtesy than he met us," a spokesman assured Stanton. Asked what they understood the end of slavery to mean, the speaker, a retired Baptist minister, answered that it was to "reap the fruit of our own labor, take care of ourselves and assist the Government in maintaining our freedom." All but Lynch expressed a wish to live apart from white people on land that they could someday hope to own. Only the Northerner thought that they would be better off if integrated into white society. Similarly, Reverend Lynch refused to offer an endorsement of Sherman's leadership, citing his "limited acquaintance" while tacitly comparing the general's ideas about race to the more progressive officers he had worked with since 1863.

The Republicans had underestimated Sherman, whose racist views did not preclude his participation in formulating the most Radical policy of the war. In Congress and the Treasury Department—and in conquered districts such as the Sea Islands, Florida, and Davis Bend—the redistribution of rebel estates to former slaves had been seen as the definitive step toward achieving equality and justice in the Confederate States.

Acting in the immediate aftermath of the Savannah Colloquy, the general wrote the famous Field Order No. 15, prohibiting the residence of white people within thirty miles of the coast on land stretching from South Carolina to Jacksonville, Florida, and establishing procedures for settling black families on forty-acre plots. Though Secretary Stanton played a role in editing the document (in yet another instance of his machinations behind the scenes of great events), the order served Sherman's goals of decoupling the refugee population from his army, soon to head north on a final push toward total victory. Confiscation was the just desert of Confederate traitors, he believed, and as always, Sherman would leave it to politicians to sort the details.[16]

James D. Lynch moved on from the Sea Islands district to Mississippi, where he opened churches and practiced politics with equal relish, serving in the state legislature during Radical Reconstruction and running unsuccessfully for Congress. He died suddenly of natural causes in 1872, just before the unraveling of the Republican order in Mississippi, and the resultant spike in the mortality of politically active black men, and was buried in Greenwood Cemetery in Jackson alongside white former governors and senators. The legislature appropriated $1,000 to erect a moving monument with Lynch's face in bas-relief above the motto "True to the Public Trust."

Other Black Republicans prospered and experienced disappointments in turn. Tunis Campbell was elected to the Georgia legislature, but was barred from serving in what amounted to a Democratic Party coup. Campbell served a year in a state prison and became a cause célèbre among Radical Republicans, meeting personally with Presidents U. S. Grant and Rutherford B. Hayes. Richard Cain built the Mother Emanuel Church into a stronghold of black social and political capital in South Carolina. He also helped to write South Carolina's Reconstruction constitution, and served one term in the United States House of Representatives. O.S.B. Wall served in the assembly of the District of Columbia and as Washington's first black justice of the peace; he enrolled each of his five children at Oberlin College.

The key element in the personal ascent of each of these notables was their engagement with the Radicalized United States government, first as participants in the forced interpenetration of the population and territory of the South by the Union, and later, as the leading men in the Southern locations where black voting rights had the most revolutionary impact. The vision of black voting rights articulated in wartime by Lincoln, Chase, and other Radicals bore fruit rapidly and on a national scale during the period of congressional Reconstruction.

The Black Republicans entered late in the Radical history of the Civil War. Their wartime acts modeled the revolution of coming years heroically. Their participation anticipated the greatness of Reconstruction, and bestowed a glory on the Republican Party that subsequent history could not erase.

꙰

POSTSCRIPT: AGE OF TRANSCENDENCE

The junior senator from Massachusetts, "Natick Cobbler" Henry Wilson, published a study of the antislavery achievements of the Thirty-Eighth Congress, in which he served with distinction alongside Charles Sumner. Wilson had labored between sessions to produce a volume of four-hundred-plus pages, *The History of the Antislavery Measures of the Thirty-Seventh and Thirty-Eighth United States Congresses*, which surveyed the war years 1861 to 1865. Wilson's work commemorated the wartime Radical Republican achievements: the confiscation of slaves as contraband; forfeiture of estates by rebels; emancipation in the District of Columbia; a ban on slave trading and slavery in the territories; and the establishment of black military units, with legislation supporting their pay and protection.

It was an epic story presented by a man of action whose name appeared liberally throughout the text. Indeed, its publication (late in 1864) gave notice of Wilson's bid for greater prominence as an intellectual and leader of the next generation of the Radical faction, a trajectory that would culminate in Wilson's election as the second-term vice president to U. S. Grant in 1872 and ultimately in his tragic early death in his office at the U.S. Capitol on November 22, 1875.[1]

Events of early 1865 forced Wilson to withdraw copies of his book from circulation and put him urgently to work on a revised version. In a surprise addition to its portfolio, the Thirty-Eighth Congress successfully adopted the resolution that became the Thirteenth Amendment to the Constitution in January 1865.[2]

The inspiration for the late addition to the Congress's list of achievements had been Lincoln's. In his December 1864 message to the second session, the president made note of the augmented majority of Republicans in the next Congress and drew the attention of the sitting members to the "proposed amendment to the Constitution abolishing slavery throughout the United States."

> Although the present is the same Congress, and nearly the same members, and without questioning the wisdom or patriotism of those who stood in opposition, I venture to recommend the reconsideration and passage of the measure at the present session. Of course the abstract question is not changed; but an intervening election shows . . . the voice of the people now, for the first time, heard upon the question.

Moreover, "as it is to so go, at all events," argued the president, "may we not agree that the sooner the better?"[3]

That the passage of the Thirteenth Amendment by the House of Representatives in January 1865 was not a victory of Radical Republicanism illustrated the revolutionary success of the movement. In the years preceding the war, the antislavery concept of "Freedom National" had never gone so far as to imagine the Constitution as an agent of the end of slavery. Now the drive to transform the founding document to facilitate a new birth of freedom held sway, commanding every single vote of the Republican members of the House and those of a handful of Democrats besides. Combined with the Senate version of the bill—passed earlier in 1864—the passage of the House bill by the required two-thirds majority sent the proposed Thirteenth Amendment to the states, where legislatures controlled by Republicans ensured its uneventful ratification before the end of 1865.

The Radicals' most important contribution to progress of the Thirteenth Amendment was the conspicuous silence that allowed the public to forget that they had ever agitated for the end of slavery in the first place. Thanks to the near unanimity of Northern states (with only Delaware refusing), the Radical 1863 and 1864 schemes of Lincoln and Chase to rehabilitate

the Southern states in the name of electoral advantages proved unneces-
sary. Only later, when the restoration of representation in Congress became
formally tied to ratification of the Fourteenth and Fifteenth Amendments,
did the strategy of harvesting states for Radical purposes come into play.
As ratification got under way, the Republicans stood accused by William
Lloyd Garrison of transforming the Constitution—formerly a "covenant
with death"—into a revitalized "covenant with life."[4]

The Fourteenth Amendment (passed by Congress in 1868 and ratified
under duress by all of the former Confederate states) created birthright citizenship and guaranteed due process and equal protection under the law. It
also addressed a number of problems arising from the war, such as the status
of Confederate debts, the political rights of former rebels, and the problem
of representation in a region where such a large proportion of the population had formerly enjoyed no voting rights. Voting rights—protected from
discriminatory racial preferences by the letter of the law in the Fifteenth
Amendment, which was ratified in 1870—proved hard to sustain in the long
run. For a period of years during Reconstruction and afterward, however,
black men in the South held real political power in collaboration with national Radical Republicans. Such achievements written into the highest law
proved capable of outlasting and transcending some of the nation's reactionary trends.

The revolution had been telescoped—so said Frederick Douglass, anyway, in a letter to a black political club in Washington, D.C.:

> The work of an age has been suddenly compressed into a single day. Events
> have succeeded each other so rapidly, overlapping and overstepping each
> other so thickly, each rising higher than the other, that we are puzzled to
> separate and estimate at its value any one of all of them. Their variety, veloc-
> ity, and proximity dazzle us and cause us to lose our reckoning. Only after-
> coming generations . . . far remote from this stormy and bewildering hour,
> will be able to describe with accuracy these great events, and to give to each
> its true grandeur and importance.[5]

At that single moment in January 1865, the Radical Republicans stood intact
as they never would again: united, living in the thick of the fight, upon the

very parapet, victorious, and not yet touched by the disasters and divisiveness and lives cut short that the coming weeks and years would bring, beginning with the assassination of Abraham Lincoln on April 14.

The Republican Party had formed at a moment when the Slave Power seemed almost unassailable. In the space of eleven years, white and black and male and female participants in the struggle had achieved a high proportion of their most unlikely goals: physical security in freedom for the formerly enslaved; employment at wages; opportunities for black military service; equal pay and protection in military service; a fledgling black officer corps; and the recognition of citizenship for African Americans. They had already launched the initiatives for black voting rights, equal accommodations, and equal protection under the law that would take shape as legislative and constitutional protections shortly after the conclusion of the war.

But legislating was not achieving. As acknowledged in the texts of the new amendments, the exercise of the new constitutional rights was dependent upon an active commitment to their enforcement by Congress. In the aftermath of the Civil War, the achievement of racial justice remained linked to the military and to martial law, which formed the basis of authority for the Freedmen's Bureau and controls on voting rights in the occupied Confederacy. President Andrew Johnson terminated the "forty acres and a mule" program initiated by Sherman and Stanton. The restoration of the political rights of former rebels and the restoration of Southern states to representation in Congress created opportunities for recalcitrant whites to threaten the progress toward equality for African Americans in the South. The Enforcement Acts of 1870 and 1871 and the establishment of the Department of Justice by the U. S. Grant administration aimed to extend federal protections to thwart such reversals. Violent resistance by white Southerners and the narrow interpretation of the federal mandate in the Supreme Court permitted the gradual contraction of African American freedoms. Starting in the 1870s, and continuing until the mid-twentieth century, much of what had been gained was lost.

Radical Republicans were born into a state of war with slavery and racial oppression. The Kansas 1856 and John Brown spirit suffused their actions in the Civil War era with passionate intensity. Achieving victory, they stood astride what they called conquered provinces, intent on creating a revolutionary new social order. Their aims were not pure, and even during the Civil War the Radicals manifested a venality and love of power that coexisted uneasily with their humanitarian goals. Accused of overreaching and riding roughshod over the rights of whites, they proved vulnerable to repudiation in their own time and in historical perspective.

Though the Republican Party boomed in the post-Reconstruction era, the Radical humanitarian faction lost momentum and influence. It proved easy for white Republicans to turn their backs on their citizenship and voting rights initiatives. All along, only John Brown and Gerrit Smith among the activists had truly engaged in collegial relations with black counterparts, and neither of these men had ever called himself a Republican. The party's uplift project also encountered hard knocks, including the assassination of Abraham Lincoln and the special obstinacy and identity politics of his successor, Andrew Johnson. A number of the most resourceful Radicals died of natural causes in the critical years—George L. Stearns (1867); Thaddeus Stevens (1868); Salmon Chase (1873); and Charles Sumner (1874)—and a rising star with progressive views, James A. Garfield, became the victim of the second presidential assassination in American history in 1881. Nonetheless Republicans and Radicals within the movement prospered, achieving an enduring supermajority in control of Congress and electing a string of Radical Republican presidents and vice presidents, including Ulysses Grant, Schuyler Colfax, and Henry Wilson (Rutherford Hayes having always been a moderate). Rather than losing their positions of influence in the party, however, many Radicals chose to surrender the fight for black civil rights in favor of more certain or more popular objectives. William Seward, Eli Thayer, Allan Pinkerton, and Chester Arthur, who was an almost comically establishment figure by the time he became president in 1881, became conservatives. Senator Benjamin Wade, author of the Wade-Davis Manifesto in 1864, pronounced himself "thoroughly sick of [Negroes]" only three years later, articulating a point of view that became increasingly common among Republican whites in the nineteenth century.

Republicans disengaged from racial politics during the Jim Crow era, decades when they aligned themselves with big business and conservative social values. They prized moderation, coming to view references to racism as more offensive than racism itself. Starting in 1968, the party openly fomented racial divisions in pursuit of partisan advantages. The persistence of racial oppression and the ongoing celebration of the lost Confederate cause stand as sober reflections of the shortfall of Grand Old Party expectations.

Can Americans of the twenty-first century redeem the promise of the Radical Republicans? The sesquicentennial anniversaries of their Reconstruction-era achievements raise the question. As debates ignited about Civil War monuments and the symbolism of the American flag in 2017 and afterward, the role of the Republican Party when it was grand received scant recognition.

The Radicals excelled at envisioning an alternative America, even in the darkest days. Their example instructs the present, illuminating a path to a better world. By commitment, organizing, and relentless activism, they made themselves into the greatest generation of American progressives, despite their reverses. To commemorate their trials and triumphs is to move at last in the direction of a truly post-Confederate United States.

NOTES

1. Filibustering in Kansas

1. Heather Cox Richardson, *To Make Men Free: A History of the Republican Party* (New York: Basic Books, 2014), 7–8; "Appeal of the Independent Democrats, January 19, 1854," http://teachingamericanhistory.org/library/document/appeal-of-the-independent-democrats; "Speech of William H. Seward, on the Kansas and Nebraska Bill" (Washington, DC: Buell and Blanchard, 1854), https://archive.org/details/speechofwilliamh00sewa; "Grand Old Dispute: Where Were the Republicans Born?" *Chicago Tribune*, October 19, 1993; Walter Stahr, *Seward: Lincoln's Indispensable Man* (New York: Simon and Schuster, 2013), 142–43; Eric Foner, *Free Soil, Free Labor, Free Men: The Ideology of the Republican Party Before the Civil War* (New York: Oxford University Press, 1995), 124–27; David Herbert Donald, *Charles Sumner and the Coming of the Civil War* (New York: Sourcebooks, 2009), 209–14; Marc Egnal, *Clash of Extremes: The Economic Origins of the Civil War* (New York: Hill and Wang, 2009), 209–16; Sean Wilentz, *The Rise of American Democracy: Jefferson to Lincoln* (New York: W. W. Norton, 2006), 672–74.
2. Quoted in Elizabeth Varon, *Disunion! The Coming of the American Civil War, 1789–1859* (Chapel Hill: University of North Carolina Press, 2008), 310.
3. Nebraska and Kansas Report of the Massachusetts Emigrant Aid Society with the Act of Incorporation and Other Documents (Boston: Published for the Massachusetts Emigrant Aid Co., 1854), 5, 8, 30.
4. Horace Andrews, Jr., "Kansas Crusade: Eli Thayer and the New England Emigrant Aid Company," *New England Quarterly* 35 (December 1962), 500.
5. "Emigrant Aid Company," *Boston Evening Transcript*, June 20, 1854; "A Plan for Freedom, Squatter Sovereignty," *National Era*, June 8, 1854.
6. [Emigration Meetings], *Albany Journal*, July 14, 1854; Eli Thayer, *A History of the Kansas Crusade: Its Friends and Its Foes* (New York: Harper & Brothers, 1889), 2.

7. "The Devices of Slavery," *Farmer's Cabinet*, August 3, 1854.

8. "Southern Chivalry," *The Liberator*, October 27, 1854.

9. James C. Malin, "Emergency Housing at Lawrence, 1854," *Kansas Historical Quarterly* 21 (Spring 1954), 40–41.

10. "Arms for Kansas," *The Baltimore Sun*, May 28, 1855.

11. Quoted in Wilentz, *Rise of American Democracy*, 678; Foner, *Free Soil, Free Labor, Free Men*, 10.

12. Frederick Law Olmstead to James Burnett Abbott, October 24, 1855, *Biennial Report*, vols. 1 and 2 (Topeka: Kansas State Historical Society, 1879), 224; Richard Lawrence Miller, *Lincoln and His World: The Path to the Presidency, 1854–1860* (Mechanicsburg, PA: Stackpole Books, 2006), 114.

13. James Hoyt, *Seen & Heard by Megagee*, vol. 1, part 4 (Philadelphia: L. N. Megagee, 1901), 17.

14. "Transcript of the Topeka Convention," *Territorial Kansas Online*, n.d.; "Constitutional Conventions of Kansas," www.legendsofkansas.com/constitutionalconventions .html.

15. Theodore Parker to Nathaniel P. Banks, October 23, 1855, in John Weiss, *Life and Correspondence of Theodore Parker*, vol. 2 (New York: D. Appleton, 1864), 207.

16. Gunja SenGupta, *For God and Mammon: Evangelicals and Entrepreneurs, Masters and Slaves in Territorial Kansas, 1854–1860* (Athens: University of Georgia Press, 1996), 103–105.

17. Charles Robinson, "Topeka and Her Constitution," *Transactions of the Kansas State Historical Society*, vol. 6 (Topeka, KS: W. Y. Mogan, 1900), 298.

18. Stanley Harrold, *The Abolitionists and the South, 1831–1861* (Lexington: University Press of Kentucky, 1999), 108.

19. "Brooklyn Taking Kansas Stock," *Milwaukee Daily Sentinel*, February 5, 1856.

20. "Sharp's [sic] Rifles as a Moral Agent," *The Liberator*, February 29, 1856.

21. Clara Holzmark Wolf, "Bibles and Rifles," *Overland Monthly* 55 (January–June 1910), 362.

22. Andrew Delbanco, *The War Before the War: Fugitive Slaves and the Struggle for America's Soul* (New York: Penguin Press, 2018), 269; W. H. Isely, "The Sharps Rifle Episode in Kansas History," *American Historical Review* 12 (April 1907), 552.

23. "Memoir of the Vegetarian Settlement Company," *Kansas Collection Articles, Territorial Kansas Online*, www.kancoll.org/articles/stewart/ws_section04.htm.

24. Theodore Parker, "From the Journal, April 2, 1856," in Weiss, *Life and Correspondence of Theodore Parker*, 160.

25. Weiss, *Life and Correspondence of Theodore Parker*, 212.

26. Elias Nason and Thomas Russell, *The Life and Public Services of Henry Wilson* (Boston: D. Lothrop, 1881), 169, 176, 181–84.

27. Charles Sumner and George Frisbie Hoar, *Charles Sumner: His Complete Works* (Boston: Lee and Shepard, 1900), 128–29.

28. Edward Lillie Pierce and Charles Sumner, *Memoirs and Letters of Charles Sumner*, 2nd ed., vol. 3 (Boston: Roberts Brothers, 1894), 438–39.

29. George Henry Haynes, *Charles Sumner* (Philadelphia: G. W. Jacobs, 1909), 201.

30. *The Crime Against Kansas . . . Speech of Hon. Charles Sumner, in the Senate of the United States, 19 and 20 May, 1856* (Boston: J. P. Jewett, 1856), University of Michigan's Making of America Books online, http://quod.lib.umich.edu/m/moa/ABT5841.0001.001?rgn=main;view=fulltext; Don E. Fehrenbacher, *The South and Three Sectional Crises* (Baton Rouge: Louisiana State University Press, 1980), 52.

31. Sarah Tappan Lawrence Robinson, *Kansas: Its Exterior and Interior Life* (Boston: Crosby, Nichols, 1856), 256–59.

32. "Letter from Charles M. Stearns," *The Liberator*, April 28, 1856.

33. Frank B. Sanborn, ed., *The Life and Letters of John Brown* (Boston: Roberts Brothers, 1891), 208.

34. Pierce and Sumner, *Memoirs and Letters of Charles Sumner*, 455; Douglas quoted in Marion Mills Miller, *Great Debates in American History*, vol. 4: *Slavery from 1790 to 1857* (New York: Current Literature, 1913), 344.

35. Quoted in George Henry Haynes, *Charles Sumner* (Philadelphia: G. W. Jacobs, 1909), 216.

36. "Peace on Earth," *The Liberator*, December 5, 1856.

37. "Anniversary of the American Antislavery Society," *The Liberator*, May 23, 1856.

38. Weiss, *Life and Correspondence of Theodore Parker*, 181–82.

39. Richard J. Hinton, "Wendell Phillips: A Retrospective Study," *Arena* 13 (July 1895), 226.

40. "The Meetings at the Tabernacle," *National Era*, May 8, 1856.

41. Ruth Tenzer Feldman, *Chester Arthur* (New York: Twenty-First Century Books, 2006), 26; Heidi M. D. Elston, *Chester Arthur* (Minneapolis: ABDO, 2009), 12; "Chester Arthur, James Masten, and Henry Haynesworth," www.picturehistory.com/product/id/14731.

42. Howard Atwood Kelly, *A Cyclopedia of American Medical Biography* (Philadelphia: W. B. Saunders, 1920), 274.

43. Quoted in Richard J. Hinton, "Making Kansas a Free State," *Chautauquan* 31 (July 1900), 345.

44. Hoyt, *Seen and Heard by Megargee*, 12.

45. Ralph Crump and Marjorie Crump, *Augusta's Journal*, vol. 4: *From Kansas to Montana via Colorado, 1860–1914* (n.p.: Authorhouse, 2010), 42–48.

46. Ibid., 58–61.

47. Ibid., 84; Hinton, "Making Kansas a Free State."

48. "Martin Stowell, Founder of Peru, NE," *Omaha World Herald*, May 20, 1928, Clippings Collection, Peru State College Library, Peru, NE.

2. The Antislavery Resistance

1. Edward L. Ayers, *In the Presence of Mine Enemies: War in the Heart of America, 1859–1863* (New York: W. W. Norton, 2004), 49; Matthew Pinsker, "The Underground Railroad Reconsidered: Antebellum Politics and the Challenges of Counting

Fugitive Slaves and Their Allies," *The Antislavery Bulwark: The Antislavery Origins of the Civil War*, Graduate Center of the City University of New York, October 17, 2014 (conference).

2. Diane S. Butler, "The Public Life and Private Affairs of Sherman M. Booth," *Wisconsin Magazine of History* 82 (2007), 176; Harry Ellsworth Cole, *A Standard History of Sauk County, Wisconsin*, vol. 1 (Chicago: Lewis, 1918), 336; "Wisconsin Necrology—1880," *Collections of the Wisconsin State Historical Society for the Years 1880, 1881, and 1882* (Madison: David Atwood, 1882), 449; Fugitive Slave Act of 1850, *The Avalon Project: Documents in Law, History, and Diplomacy*, Yale Law School, Yale University, New Haven, CT, http://avalon.law.yale.edu/19th_century/fugitive.asp.

3. C. C. Olin, *A Complete Record of the John Olin Family* (Indianapolis, IN: Baker-Randolph, 1893), liii–lxi; H. Robert Baker, *The Rescue of Joshua Glover: A Fugitive Slave, the Constitution, and the Coming of the Civil War* (Clark: Ohio State University Press, 2006), 75–76; "The Rescue Case at Milwaukee," *The Liberator*, April 7, 1854; "A Fugitive Slave in Milwaukee," *New York Daily News*, March 17, 1854.

4. Thomas Wentworth Higginson, *Cheerful Yesterdays* (Boston: Houghton Mifflin, 1898), 150–53; Mary Potter Higginson, *Thomas Wentworth Higginson: The Story of His Life* (Boston: Ayer, 1914), 143; Albert Von Frank, *The Trials of Anthony Burns: Freedom and Slavery in Emerson's Boston* (Cambridge, MA: Harvard University Press, 1998), 64–65; "The Boston Slave Riot and Trial of Anthony Burns," (Boston: Fetridge, 1854), London School of Economics Pamphlet Collection, London School of Economics Library, www.jstor.org/stable/60221777, 9; David R. Maginnes, "The Case of the Court House Rioters in the Rendition of the Fugitive Slave Anthony Burns," *Journal of Negro History* 56 (January 1971), 33; "Great Meeting in Worcester," *The Liberator*, June 2, 1854; "Mr. Hallett and His Interference with the Purchase of Burns," *Boston Evening Transcript*, June 5, 1854; *Proceedings of the Worcester Society of Antiquity*, vol. 21 (Worcester, MA: Worcester Society of Antiquities, 1907), 10–11; Lawrence Lader, *The Bold Brahmins: New England's War Against Slavery, 1831–1863* (New York: Dutton, 1961), 212; "Hallett Is at Work!" [pamphlet reprint], in Weiss, *Life and Correspondence of Theodore Parker*, 135.

5. Quoted in Weiss, *Life and Correspondence of Theodore Parker*, 141.

5. Sumner to Parker, December 12, 1854, in ibid., 143.

6. John D. Gordan III, *The Fugitive Slave Rescue Trial of Robert Morris: Benjamin Robbins Curtis on the Road to Dred Scott* (Clark, NJ: Lawbook Exchange, 2013), 87–95; Benjamin Robbins Curtis, *A Memoir of Benjamin Robbins Curtis, LL.D.* (Union, NJ: Lawbook Exchange, 2002), 122; Paul Finkelman, *Slavery in the Courtroom: An Annotated Bibliography of American Cases* (Union, NJ: Lawbook Exchange, 1998), 116.

7. Theodore Parker, *The Trial of Theodore Parker for the "Misdemeanor" of Speech* (Boston: Published for the Author, 1855), 17.

8. Theodore Parker, "Transcendentalism [n.d.]," in *Theodore Parker, American Transcendentalist: A Critical Essay and a Collection of His Writings* (Metuchen, NJ: Scarecrow Press, 1973), 66.

9. Parker, "Transcendentalism," 67, 74.

10. Theodore Parker, "Justice and the Conscience," in *The Collected Works of Theodore Parker*, vol. 2: *Prayers, Sermons*, Frances Power Cobb, ed. (London: Treubner, 1879), 48.

3. Transcendental Politics

1. Quoted in Paul Finkelman, "Garrison's Constitution: The Covenant with Death and How It Was Made," *Prologue Magazine* 32 (Winter 2000), www.archives.gov /publications/prologue/2000/winter/garrisons-constitution-1.html.

2. "Incidents of the Boston Riot," *New Orleans Times-Picayune*, June 6, 1854; Madeleine B. Stern, *L. M. Alcott: Signature of Reform* (Boston: Northeastern University Press, 2002), 11.

3. "The Fourth of July at Framingham," *The Liberator*, July 7, 1854; Deak Nabors, *Victory of Law: The Fourteenth Amendment, the Civil War, and American Literature, 1852–1867* (Baltimore: Johns Hopkins University Press, 2006), 1; Owen W. Muelder, *Theodore Dwight Weld and the American Anti-Slavery Society* (Jefferson, NC: McFarland Press, 2011), 27; Junius P. Rodriguez, *The Encyclopedia of Emancipation and Abolition in the Transatlantic World* (New York: Routledge, 2015), 30; Fram Ingham, "Framingham Grove," *Historic Framingham* (blog), http://historicframingham .blogspot.com/2009/09/harmony-grove.html; Donald Yacovone, "A Covenant with Death and an Agreement with Hell": Online Object of the Month, Massachusetts Historical Society, July 2005, www.masshist.org/objects/2005july.cfm; Caleb McDaniel, "The Fourth and the First: Abolitionist Holidays, Respectability, and Radical Interracial Reform," *American Quarterly* 57 (March 2005), 133, 139.

4. Emerson's whiteness and racial consciousness is the subject of a chapter in Nell Irving Painter's book, *The History of White People* (New York: W. W. Norton, 2011), 186, 188.

5. Len Gougeon, *Virtue's Hero: Emerson, Antislavery, and Reform* (Athens: University of Georgia Press, 1990), 238; Henry David Thoreau, "Civil Disobedience," in *The Essays of Henry D. Thoreau*, Lewis Hyde, ed. (New York: Macmillan, 2002), 137.

6. James Oakes, *The Scorpion's Sting: Antislavery and the Coming of the Civil War* (New York: W. W. Norton, 2015), 58–59.

7. Henry David Thoreau, "Slavery in Massachusetts," African Studies Center, University of Pennsylvania, www.africa.upenn.edu/Articles_Gen/Slavery_Massachusetts .html; Sandra Harbert Petrulionis, "Editorial Savoir Faire: Thoreau Transforms His Journal into 'Slavery in Massachusetts,'" https://commons.digitalthoreau .org/docs/petrulionis-editorial-savoir-faire-thoreau-transforms-his-journal-into -slavery-in-massachusetts.

8. William Whiting to Theodore Parker, July 10, 1854, in Weiss, *Life and Correspondence of Theodore Parker*, 142–43.

9. "To the Whigs," in *The Journals and Miscellaneous Notebooks of Ralph Waldo Emerson*, vol. 14: *1854–1861* (Cambridge, MA: Harvard University Press, 1978), 380; "People's Party in Massachusetts," *National Era* (Washington, DC), July 6, 1854; "Worcester Convention," *Pittsfield Sun*, July 27, 1854.

4. Free Soil, Free Men, Fremont

1. James K. Conant, *Wisconsin's Politics and Government: America's Laboratory of Democracy* (Lincoln: University of Nebraska Press, 2006), 62; Heather Cox Richardson, *To Make Men Free: A History of the Republican Party* (New York: Basic Books, 2014), 9.
2. "Liberty or Death," *The Liberator*, February 29, 1856.
3. "From the N. Y. Tribune, the Cincinnati Slave Case," *The Liberator*, April 11, 1856, quoted in Dennis Brindell Fradin, *Bound for the North Star: True Stories of Fugitive Slaves* (New York: Houghton Mifflin Harcourt, 2000), 41.
4. "Scene in a U. States Courtroom—Speech from Lucy Stone," *The Baltimore Sun*, February 18, 1856; Lillie B. Chace Wiley, "Black and White," *Bay State Monthly* (Boston: John N. McClintock, 1892), 479; "The Fugitive Slaves in Cincinnati," *New York Daily News*, March 3, 1856. See also Fergus M. Bordewich, *Bound for Canaan: The Epic Story of the Underground Railroad* (New York: HarperCollins, 2009), 402–403.
5. "Mrs. Lucy Stone," *Vermont Journal*, March 7, 1856; "The Kentucky Slaves," *New York Daily Times*, February 18, 1856.
6. "Liberty or Death," *The Liberator*, February 28, 1856; John Niven, *Salmon P. Chase: A Biography* (New York: Oxford University Press, 1995), 184; Mark Reinhardt, *Who Speaks for Margaret Garner?* (Minneapolis: University of Minnesota Press, 2010), 134.
7. Parker to Chase, July 28, 1856, Papers of Salmon P. Chase, Box 2, Salmon P. Chase Papers, Historical Society of Pennsylvania, Philadelphia, PA.
8. Horace Greeley, *Proceedings of the First Three Republican Party Conventions of 1856, 1860, and 1864* (Minneapolis, MN: C. W. Johnson, 1893), 4–5, 12.
9. ["Anti-Fillmore American Party Nominating Convention"], *New York Herald*, June 14, 1856.
10. ["Republican National Convention"], *National Era*, June 26, 1856.
11. Foner, *Free Soil, Free Labor, Free Men*, 122.
12. Orville J. Victor, *A History of Conspiracies in the United States of America, 1760 to 1860* (Whitefish, MT: Kessinger, 2005), 491.
13. Mark A. Lause, *Race and Radicalism in the Union Army* (Champaign: University of Illinois Press, 2009), 21; John Bicknell, *Lincoln's Pathfinder: John C. Fremont and the Violent Election of 1856* (Chicago: Chicago Review Press, 2017), 193–94.
14. "Politics and Religion," *The Baltimore Sun*, July 7, 1856.
15. Foner, *Free Soil, Free Labor, Free Men*, 43.

5. *Dred Scott* Nullification

1. "The Political Prospects," *Charleston Mercury*, March 14, 1857; Edward E. Baptist, *The Half Has Never Been Told: Slavery and the Making of American Capitalism* (New York: Basic Books, 2014), 378–79.
2. Keith E. Whittington, "The Road Not Taken: *Dred Scott*, Judicial Authority, and Political Questions," *Journal of Politics* 63 (May 2001), 378–79.

3. Wilentz, *Rise of American Democracy*, 712–13; Whittington, "Road Not Taken," 379–80.

4. "Interesting," *Pittsfield Sun*, March 19, 1857; "Dred Scott Owned by a 'Republican' Member of Congress," *Macon Weekly Telegraph*, March 24, 1857.

5. "Chief Justice Taney at School to a Colored Oyster Dealer," *Albany Evening Ledger*, March 25, 1857.

6. "Taking the Benefit of Taney's Decision," *Albany Evening Ledger*, April 23, 1857.

7. "State Disunion Convention at Worcester," *The Liberator*, January 23, 1857.

8. Higginson to Gerrit Smith, November 22, 1856 quoted in Allan Nevins, *The Emergence of Lincoln*, vol. 2: *Prologue to Civil War* (New York: Charles Scribner's Sons, 1950), 21; Parker to Higginson, January 18, 1857, in Weiss, *Life and Correspondence of Theodore Parker*, Vol. 2, 193.

9. "Report on the Dred Scott Decision," *The Liberator*, May 1, 1857.

10. "New York Showing Her Teeth," *Columbus Tri-Weekly Encounter*, May 5, 1857.

11. "The Dred Scott Decision at Albany," *The New York Times*, May 11, 1857.

12. "Twenty-Fourth Annual Meeting of the American Anti-Slavery Society," *The Liberator*, May 22, 1857.

13. Smith to Littlejohn, March 18, 1857, Gerrit Smith Broadside and Pamphlet Collection, Syracuse University, http://library.syr.edu/digital/collections/g/GerritSmith/503.htm.

14. Phyllis F. Field, *The Politics of Race in New York: The Struggle for Black Suffrage in the Civil War Era* (Ithaca, NY: Cornell University Press, 2009), 105; "Domestic Summary," *Independent* (New York), March 19, 1857.

15. Charles M. Snyder, "DeWitt C. Littlejohn: A Study in Leadership in the Nineteenth Century," *Twentieth Publication of the Oswego Historical Society* (Oswego, NY: Palladium-Times, 1957), 6–9; *Freedom in Kansas: Speech of William H. Seward in the Senate of the United States, March 8, 1857* (Washington, D.C.: Buell and Blanchard, 1858), 8.

16. [No headline], *Albany Evening Journal*, April 13, 1857.

17. Eric Foner, *Gateway to Freedom: The Hidden History of the Underground Railroad* (New York: W. W. Norton, 2016), 169–70; "Important from Albany: Rapid and Reckless Legislation," *New York Daily Times*, April 15, 1857; "Interesting from Albany: The Police Commissioners and the Port Wardens," *New York Daily Times*, April 17, 1857; Jerome Mushkat, *Fernando Wood: A Political Biography* (Kent, OH: Kent State University Press, 1990), 69.

18. "The Case of Dred Scott in the Albany Assembly," *The Liberator*, May 8, 1857.

19. Foner, *Gateway to Freedom*, 170; "From Albany," *The New York Times*, May 30, 1857; "The Dred Scott Decision," *The New York Times*, May 11, 1857.

20. "The Legal Rights Association" [reprint of February 26, 1858, article], *Crisis* 75 (June–July 1968), 197–99.

21. Edwin G. Burrows and Mike Wallace, *Gotham: A History of New York City to 1898* (New York: Oxford University Press, 1998), 857; "Superior Court General Term," *New York Herald*, February 22, 1857.

22. Ibid., 198.
23. Ibid., 199.
24. Tunis Campbell, *Never Let People Be Kept Waiting: A Guide to Hotel Management* (New York: D. E. King, 1973), 6.
25. "Houses of Ill-Fame Burnt by a Mob," *New York Daily Times*, June 25, 1857.
26. "Discussion Between Frederick Douglass and Charles Remond," *New York Daily Times*, May 21, 1857; Frederick Douglass, "Speech on the Dred Scott Decision [May 1857]," http://teachingamericanhistory.org/library/document/speech-on-the-dred-scott-decision-2; John Stauffer, *The Black Hearts of Men: Radical Abolitionists and the Transformation of Race* (Cambridge, MA: Harvard University Press, 2009), 298.
27. David Blight, "Admiration and Ambivalence: Frederick Douglass and John Brown," Gilder Lehrman Institute for American History, www.gilderlehrman.org/history-by-era/failure-compromise/essays/admiration-and-ambivalence-frederick-douglass-and-john-brown; *Two Speeches by Frederick Douglass* (Rochester, NY: C. P. Dewey, 1857), 21–22.
28. Brown to F. B. Sanborn, February 26, 1858, in "1858 Letters," FamilyTales.org.
29. Theodore Parker, [pamphlet] *The Present Aspect of Slavery in America and the Immediate Duty of the North: A Speech Delivered in the Hall of the State House Before the Massachusetts Anti-Slavery Convention, on Friday Night, January 29, 1858* (Boston: B. Marsh, 1858), online at Hathi Trust Digital Library, https://catalog.hathitrust.org/Record/000409158, 5.
30. "[Speeches Commemorating the Anniversary of the Boston Massacre]," *The Liberator*, March 12, 1858.
31. Ibid.

6. John Brownism

1. "From St. Louis," *Daily Ohio Statesman*, February 14, 1857; "Arrest of the Kansas Legislature!" *Milwaukee Sentinel*, January 13, 1857.
2. Hinton, "Making Kansas a Free State"; "John Brown Speech to Massachusetts Legislative Committee, February 18, 1857," Boyd B. Stutler Collection, Ms78–1, West Virginia Archives and History, www.wvculture.org/history/jbexhibit/bbsms02-0002.html.
3. "Old Brown's Farewell . . . ," in Weiss, *Life and Correspondence of Theodore Parker*, 162.
4. Philip F. Rose, *John Brown's Virginia Raid* (n.p.: Trafford, 2013).
5. Catherine Clinton, *Harriet Tubman: The Road to Freedom* (n.p.: Lulu.com, 2004).
6. Benjamin Quarles, *Allies for Freedom and Blacks on John Brown* (New York: Da Capo Press, 2001), 79; "Africans in America," www.pbs.org/wgbh/aia/part4/4p1535.html.
7. [Lucy Stone Blackwell], *Trenton State Gazette*, April 15, 1858.
8. Tappan to Higginson, April 7, 1858, "Kansas Memory," Kansas Historical Association, www.kansasmemory.org/item/90780/text.

9. Ibid.

10. Felt to Higginson, June 25, 1858, http://territorialkansasonline.ku.edu/index.php ?SCREEN=show_document&document_id=101936; Thomas W. Higginson, "Saints, and Their Bodies," *Atlantic Monthly*, March 1858, http://en.wikisource.org /wiki/The_Atlantic_Monthly/Volume_1/No._5/Saints,_and_Their_Bodies.

11. Parker to Sumner, May 6, 1858, in Weiss, *Life and Correspondence of Theodore Parker*, 222.

12. "Kansas News," *National Era*, May 13, 1858; Mark Lause, *Race and Radicalism in the Union Army* (Champaign-Urbana: University of Illinois Press, 2009), 39–40.

13. Richard J. Hinton, *John Brown and His Men* (New York: Funk and Wagnalls, 1894), 218.

14. "The New Troubles in Kansas," *The New York Times*, January 6, 1859.

15. Hinton, *John Brown and His Men*, 220–21.

16. Hinton, *John Brown and His Men*, 222–23; "Augustus Wattles," http://kansas boguslegislature.org/free/wattles_a.html.

17. Quoted in Kirstin Tegameier Oertel, *Bleeding Borders: Race, Gender, and Violence in Pre–Civil War Kansas* (Baton Rouge: Louisiana State University Press, 2009), 52.

18. Quoted in "Augustus Wattles," http://kansasboguslegislature.org/free/wattles_a .html.

19. Oertel, *Bleeding Borders*, 45; Evan Carton, *Patriotic Treason: John Brown and the Soul of America* (Lincoln: University of Nebraska Press, 2009), 215.

20. Quoted in Lause, *Race and Radicalism in the Union Army*, 40.

21. Addison Erwin Sheldon, *Nebraska History and Record of Pioneer Days* (Lincoln: Nebraska State Historical Society, 1921), 16.

22. Franklin B. Sanborn, "John Brown and His Friends," *Atlantic Monthly*, July 1872, 59.

23. "A Fugitive Slave in the White House," *The Liberator*, January 28, 1859.

24. David Blight, *Frederick Douglass: Prophet of Freedom* (New York: Simon and Schuster, 2018), 300.

25. Quoted in Dorothy Sterling, *We Are Your Sisters: Black Women in the Nineteenth Century* (New York: W. W. Norton, 1997), 148; Carol E. Mull, *The Underground Railroad in Michigan* (Jefferson, NC: McFarland, 2010), 155.

26. Quoted in Gregory Toledo, *The Hanging of Old Brown: A Story of Slaves, Statesmen, and Redemption* (Westport, CT: Greenwood, 2002), 166.

27. Quoted in ibid., 166.

28. Quoted in Gougeon, *Virtue's Hero*, 237; Carton, *Patriotic Treason*, 279.

29. Jacquelin L. Tobin, *From Midnight to Dawn: The Last Tracks of the Underground Railroad* (New York: Knopf Doubleday, 2008), 52.

30. Roger L. Ransom, "The Economics of the Civil War," *Eh.net Encyclopedia*, Economic History Association, 2001, https://eh.net/encyclopedia/the-economics-of-the-civil -war; David Blight, "Slavery and State Rights, Economies and Ways of Life: What Caused the Civil War? [Lecture 11], *Open Yale: The Civil War and Reconstruction*

Era, 1845–1877, https://oyc.yale.edu/history/hist-119/lecture-11; Ta-Nehisi Coates, "Slavery Made America: The Case for Reparations, A Narrative Bibliography," *The Atlantic*, June 24, 2014; Sven Beckert, "Slavery and Capitalism," *Chronicle of Higher Education*, December 12, 2014.

31. Sanborn, *Life and Letters of John Brown*, 510.
32. *Report of the Senate Select Committee Report on [the Harpers Ferry Invasion]* (Washington, DC: Government Printing Office, 1860), 238.
33. Sanborn, *Life and Letters of John Brown*, 503.
34. Henry Wilson, *The History of the Rise and Fall of the Slave Power in America*, vol. 2 (Boston: J. R. Osgood, 1872), 593.
35. Ibid., 510.
36. Quoted in Sanborn, "John Brown and His Friends," 599; Frank Preston Stearns, *Life and Public Services of George Luther Stearns* (Philadelphia: J. B. Lippincott, 1907), 182.

7. House Divided

1. The "scorpion's sting" strategy of antislavery Northerners is described at length in Oakes, *Scorpion's Sting*. The idea that Lincoln grew as a humanitarian during his presidency is a central claim in Eric Foner, *The Fiery Trial: Abraham Lincoln and American Slavery* (New York: W. W. Norton, 2010).
2. Abraham Lincoln, "House Divided Speech," June 16, 1858, Springfield, IL, www.abrahamlincolnonline.org/lincoln/speeches/house.htm.
3. Don E. Fehrenbacher, "The Origins and Purpose of Lincoln's 'House Divided' Speech," *Mississippi Valley Historical Review* 46 (March), 1960, 618–22.
4. Parker to Herndon, August 28, 1858, in Weiss, *Life and Correspondence of Theodore Parker*, 240.
5. Parker to Herndon, September 9 and 23, 1858, in ibid., 241–42.
6. Quoted in Elbert William Robinson Ewing, *Legal and Historical Status of the Dred Scott Decision* (Cobden, IL: Cobden, 1908), 194.
7. Hans Trefousse, *The Radical Republicans: Lincoln's Vanguard for Racial Justice* (New York: Knopf Doubleday, 2014), iii.
8. "State Convention of the Colored People of Ohio," *Ohio State Journal*, December 3, 1858.
9. Ibid.
10. Bruce Chadwick, *1858: Abraham Lincoln, Jefferson Davis, Robert E. Lee, Ulysses S. Grant, and the War They Failed to See* (Naperville, IL: Sourcebooks, 2008), 143.
11. "Oberlin College Commencement," *Ohio State Journal*, September 1, 1858.
12. Chadwick, *1858*, 145, 154.
13. "The Siege of Oberlin," *The Liberator*, December 17, 1858; Ronald and Nancy Hendrickson, "History of the Hiram A. Pease Property," Electronic Oberlin Group: Oberlin Through History, www.oberlin.edu/external/EOG/Default.html.
14. [Speech of Charles Langston in U.S. District Court], *Friends Intelligencer*, July 23, 1859.

15. Nat Brandt, *The Town That Started the Civil War* (Syracuse, NY: Syracuse University Press, 1990), 121.

16. Quoted in Brandt, *Town That Started the Civil War*, 136. See also "The Slave Rescue Case in Ohio—Letter from Professor Peck," *The Liberator*, January 28, 1859.

17. "Celebration of the Oberlin Recue Affair," *The New York Times*, January 19, 1859.

18. Quoted in Brandt, *Town That Started the Civil War*, 134–35.

19. John Mercer Langston, *From the Virginia Plantation to the National Capitol; or, The First and Only Representative in Congress from the Old Dominion* (Hartford, CT: American, 1894), 191.

20. Daniel J. Scharfstein, *The Invisible Line: Three American Families and the Secret Journey from Black to White* (New York: Penguin, 2012), n.p.

21. Ibid.

22. "The Oberlin Rescuers," *The New York Times*, May 17, 1859.

23. William C. Cochran, *The Western Reserve and the Fugitive Slave Act: A Prelude to the Civil War* (Cleveland, OH: Western Reserve Historical Society, 1920), 186–87.

24. "Governor Chase at the Cleveland Meeting," *The New York Times*, May 28, 1859; "The Hon. J. R. Giddings on the Oberlin Rescue—He Counsels Hanging the Slave-Catchers," *The New York Times*, May 9, 1859; Cochran, *Western Reserve and the Fugitive Slave Act*, 192.

25. "Bushnell at Home: The Oberlin Demonstration," *The Liberator*, July 22, 1859.

26. Laura F. Edwards, *A Legal History of the Civil War and Reconstruction* (Cambridge, UK: Cambridge University Press, 2015), 70.

27. Lincoln to Schuyler Colfax, July 6, 1859, in *The Collected Works of Abraham Lincoln*, vol. 3 (New Brunswick, NJ: Rutgers University Press, 1953), 390–91.

28. Lincoln to Chase, June 20, 1859, in ibid., 386.

29. Lincoln to Nathan Sargent, June 24, 1859, in ibid., 388.

30. "Speech at Columbus, Ohio," September 16, 1859, in ibid., 400–425. See also Walter Stahr, *Seward: Lincoln's Indispensable Man* (New York: Simon and Schuster, 2013), 175.

31. Ibid; "Speech at Beloit, Wisconsin," October 1, 1859, and "Speech in Janesville, Wisconsin," October 1, 1859, in ibid., 482–86. See also Foner, *Free Soil, Free Labor, Free Men*, 215–16.

32. "Speech at Springfield, Illinois," October 15, 1859, in Lincoln, *Collected Works*, vol. 3, 489.

8. Harpers Ferry

1. Leonard J. Ralston, "Governor Ralph P. Lowe and State Aid to Railroads: Iowa Politics in 1859," *Iowa Journal of History* 58 (1960), 207; Nicole Etcheson, "Where Popular Sovereignty Worked: Nebraska and the Kansas-Nebraska Act," in John R. Wunder and Joann M. Ross, eds., *The Kansas-Nebraska Act* (Lincoln: University of Nebraska Press, 2008), 169; Leo Morgan Hauptman, "Martin Stowell" (Peru: Nebraska State Normal School Library, 1929), 35–36.

2. Gougeon, *Virtue's Hero*, 238; Henry David Thoreau, "Civil Disobedience," in *The*

Essays of Henry D. Thoreau, Lewis Hyde, ed. (New York: Macmillan, 2002), 137; Parker to George Ripley, October 29, 1859, in Weiss, *Life and Correspondence of Theodore Parker*, 378.

3. Gougeon, *Virtue's Hero*, 240; Brian McGinty, *John Brown's Trial* (Cambridge, MA: Harvard University Press, 2009), 158; Janet Kemper Beck, *Creating the John Brown Legend: Emerson, Thoreau, Douglass, Child and Higginson in Defense of the Raid on Harpers Ferry* (New York: McFarland, 2009), 128.

4. McGinty, *John Brown's Trial*, 258.

5. Blight, *Douglass*, 305–6.

6. Quoted in Gougeon, *Virtue's Hero*, 239.

7. Sanborn, *Life and Letters of John Brown*, 523.

8. Beck, *Creating the John Brown Legend*, 128.

9. "News and Humor of the Mails," *Ohio State Journal*, November 1, 1859.

10. Quoted in C. Vann Woodward, *The Burden of Southern History* (Baton Rouge: Louisiana State University Press, 2008), 46.

11. Quoted in McGinty, *John Brown's Trial*, 261.

12. "The Virginia Insurrection," *The Liberator*, October 21, 1859.

13. Ralph Waldo Emerson, "Biographical Sketch," in *Thoreau's Excursions with a Biographical "Sketch" by Ralph Waldo Emerson* (Rockville, MD: Arc Manor, 2007), 11.

14. Henry David Thoreau, "A Plea for Captain John Brown," in *Essays: A Fully Annotated Edition* (New Haven, CT: Yale University Press, 2013), 190–215.

15. Gougeon, *Virtue's Hero*, 241.

16. "Selections: Emerson on Courage," *The Liberator*, November 18, 1859.

17. "The Harpers Ferry Outbreak," *New York Herald*, November 5, 1859.

18. "Meeting in Aid of the Family of John Brown," *The Liberator*, November 25, 1859.

19. Henry Clarke Wright, "The Natick Resolution; or, Resistance to Slaveholders the Right and Duty of Southern Slaves and Northern Freemen," Antislavery Literature Project, Arizona State University, http://antislavery.eserver.org/tracts/the_natick _resolution; Wright to John Brown, November 21, 1859, in ibid.

20. "News from Washington: The 'Irrepressible Conflict' in Congress," *New York Herald*, December 7, 1859.

21. Parker to Francis Jackson, November 24, 1859, in Weiss, *Life and Correspondence of Theodore Parker*, 170–78.

22. John Brown to Mary Preston Stearns, November 29, 1859, Boyd B. Stutler Collection, Ms78-1, West Virginia Archives and History, www.wvculture.org/history /jbexhibit/bbsms02-0053.html.

23. Louisa May Alcott, "With a Rose, That Bloomed on the Day of John Brown's Martyrdom," *The Liberator*, January 20, 1860.

24. "[Harpers Ferry Investigation News]," *New York Herald*, January 20, 1860; see also "Miscellaneous Accounts of Conditions Resulting from Drought," in *Kansas's War: The Civil War in Documents*, Pearl T. Ponce, ed. (Columbus: Ohio University Press, 2011), 34.

25. Henry C. Wright, *No Rights, No Duties* (Boston: Private Printing, 1860), 3–29.

26. Blight, *Frederick Douglass*, 315.
27. "News by Telegraph: The Harpers Ferry Affair," *The New York Times*, April 5, 1860; "Sanborn Arrest," *New York Herald*, April 7, 1860; Louisa May Alcott to Alfred Whitman, April 5, 1860, in *Selected Letters of Louisa May Alcott*, Joel Myerson and Daniel Shealy, eds. (Athens: University of Georgia Press, 1995), 53.
28. Quoted in Theodore H. Genoways, "Whitman's Lost War: America's Poet During the Forgotten Years of 1860–1862" (Iowa City: unpublished master's thesis, University of Iowa, 2007), 47.
29. "Sanborn Arrest," *New York Herald*, April 7, 1860.
30. Ibid.; Louisa May Alcott to Whitman; Frank Preston Stearns, *Sketches of Concord and Appledore* (New York: G. P. Putnam's Sons, 1895), 18.
31. Louisa May Alcott to Alfred Whitman, April 5, 1860, *Selected Letters of Louisa May Alcott*, 53.
32. Quoted in Louis A. DeCaro, *John Brown: The Cost of Freedom* (New York: International, 2007), 97.
33. Debby Applegate, *The Most Famous Man in America: The Biography of Henry Ward Beecher* (New York: Random House, 2007), 314.
34. "An Interesting Scene in Plymouth Church—Purchase of a Slave by the Congregation," *Albany Evening Journal*, February 6, 1860; "A White Slave at Mr. Beecher's Church: A True History of the Case," *The New York Times*, February 9, 1860.
35. Harold Holzer, *Lincoln at Cooper Union: The Speech That Made Abraham Lincoln President* (New York: Simon and Schuster, 2004), 106–107; L. A. Pittinger, ed., *Macaulay's Speeches on Copyright and Lincoln's Address at Cooper Union* (New York: American Book, 1914), 60.
36. Pittinger, *Macaulay's Speeches and Lincoln's Cooper Union*, 85.
37. Ibid., 90–91.
38. Ibid., 97.

9. Wide Awake

1. "Speech at New Haven, Connecticut," in Lincoln, *Collected Works*, vol. 3, 14–27; "The Abraham Lincoln Walking Tour," Exeter Historical Society, Exeter, NH, www.exeterhistory.org/lincoln/images/stories/documents/lincoln_walking_tour _booklet-021210.pdf; Holzer, *Lincoln at Cooper Union*, 185–92.
2. Holzer, *Lincoln at Cooper Union*, 186, 193.
3. "The Contest of 1860," *New York Herald*, March 22, 1860; Jon Grinspan, "Young Men for War: The Wide Awakes and Lincoln's 1860 Presidential Campaign," *Journal of American History* 96 (Spring 2009), 361–63; Mark Scroggins, *Hannibal: The Life of Abraham Lincoln's First Vice President* (Washington, DC: University Press of America, 1994), 145.
4. "News from the State Capital," *New York Herald*, March 28, 1860; William M. Evarts, "Slavery in the Free States," *Independent*, March 29, 1860.
5. "News by Telegraph," *New York Herald*, March 3, 1860; [No Headline], *Milwauk*

Sentinel, March 3, 1860; Frederick J. Blue, *No Taint of Compromise: Crusaders of Antislavery Politics* (Baton Rouge: Louisiana State University Press, 2006), 133.

6. *Congressional Globe*, 36th Cong., 1st sess., Appendix, 202–207, online at "His Soul Goes Marching On: The Life and Legacy of John Brown," West Virginia Archives and History Online Exhibit, www.wvculture.org/history/jbexhibit/lovejoyspeech .html; Manisha Sinha, *The Slave's Cause: A History of Abolition* (New Haven, CT: Yale University Press, 2016), 581.

7. "The Pryor and Potter Difficulty," *New York Herald*, April 14, 1860; "Historical Fragments: The Potter-Pryor Duel" *Wisconsin Magazine of History*, vol. 2, issue 4 (1918–1919), 449–51. See also Joanne B. Freeman, *Field of Blood: Violence in Congress and the Road to Civil War* (New York: Farrar, Straus and Giroux, 2018), 253–54.

8. Quoted in Stearns, *Life and Public Services of George Luther Stearns*, 226.

9. "That Bowie Knife," *Wisconsin Daily Patriot*, May 12, 1860; "The Latest: Our Special Chicago Dispatch," *New York Herald*, May 16, 1860.

10. Foner, *Free Soil, Free Labor, Free Men*, 132; "The Chicago Convention," *New York Herald*, May 18, 1860; Richard S. Green, *Lincoln and the Election of 1860* (Carbondale: Southern Illinois University Press, 2011), 51; Sinha, *The Slave's Cause*, 583.

11. "Great Breckinridge Meeting in Milwaukee," *Wisconsin Daily Patriot*, August 6, 1860; "Old Booth Escaped from Jail," *Wisconsin Daily Patriot*, August 1, 1860; Blue, *No Taint of Compromise*, 135; "Keep an Eye on the Little Girls," *Wisconsin Daily Patriot*, August 6, 1860.

12. Quoted in Bob Schuster, "Ripon's Booth War, 1860," Wisconsin Local History Network (December 1999), www.wlhn.org/wisconsonian/dec99/booth_war_milwaukee .htm.

13. "Form Reply to Requests for Political Opinions," c. June 1860, in Lincoln, *Collected Works*, vol. 4 (Ann Arbor: University of Michigan Digital Library Production Services, 2001), 60.

14. "The Case of Sherman Booth," *Barre Gazette*, August 17, 1860; Schuster, "Ripon's Booth War."

15. John B. McMaster, *The History of the People of the United States from the Revolution to the Civil War*, vol. 8 (New York: D. Appleton, 1913), 460.

16. Schuster, "Ripon's Booth War"; "From the Madison (Wis.) Journal," *The Liberator*, August 24, 1860.

17. Hauptman, "Martin Stowell," 34–57; "Political Anti-Slavery Convention," *The Liberator*, June 15, 1860; "The Presidency: Republican Mass Meeting at Cooper Union," *The New York Times*, July 12, 1860.

18. Quoted in Paul Kendrick and Stephen Kendrick, *Douglass and Lincoln: How a Revolutionary Black Leader and a Reluctant Liberator Struggled to End Slavery and Save the Union* (New York: Bloomsbury, 2009), 52; Blight, *Douglass*, 322.

19. Walt Whitman, "The Eighteenth Presidency!" in Justin Kaplan, ed., *Complete Poetry and Collected Prose* (New York: Library of America, 1982), 1307–25.

20. Michael Burlingame, *Abraham Lincoln: A Life* (Baltimore, MD: Johns Hopkins University Press, 2013), 634; Foner, *The Fiery Trial*, 142.

21. Lori D. Ginzberg, *Elizabeth Cady Stanton: An American Life* (New York: Macmillan, 2010).

22. Susan B. Anthony to Henry B. Stanton, Jr., and Gerrit S. Stanton, September 27, 1860, in *The Selected Letters of Elizabeth Cady Stanton and Susan B. Anthony: In the School of Anti-Slavery, 1849–1866* (New Brunswick, NJ: Rutgers University Press, 1997), 443; Elisabeth Griffith, *In Her Own Right: The Life of Elizabeth Cady Stanton* (New York: Oxford University Press, 1984), 105.

23. Julius G. Rathbun, "The Wide Awakes: The Great Political Organization of 1860," *Connecticut Magazine* 1 (1895), 333.

24. Adam Goodheart, *1861: The Civil War Awakening* (New York: Knopf Doubleday, 2011), 52; Douglas R. Egerton, *Year of Meteors: Stephen Douglas, Abraham Lincoln, and the Election That Brought On the Civil War* (New York: Bloomsbury, 2010), 193; "Wide Awake Parade," *The Liberator*, October 19, 1860.

25. Stearns, *Life and Services of George L. Stearns*, 233.

26. Susan B. Martinez, *The Psychic Life of Abraham Lincoln* (Pompton Plains, NJ: Career Press, 2007), 74.

10. Military Emancipation

1. William Roscoe Thayer, ed., *The Life and Letters of John Hay*, Vol. I (Boston: Houghton Mifflin, 1915), 102.

2. "By Telegraph for the Boston Daily Advertiser," *Boston Daily Advertiser*, April 19, 1861; "Visitors from Congress: Jim Lane," www.mrlincolnswhitehouse.org/residents-visitors/visitors-from-congress/visitors-congress-james-h-lane-1814-1866; "The National Capital," *New York Herald*, May 2, 1861.

3. Quoted in "Visitors from Congress."

4. Benjamin F. Butler, *Butler's Book: Autobiography and Personal Reminiscences of Major-General Benjamin F. Butler* (Boston: A. M. Thayer, 1892), 195.

5. "Proclamation of General Butler to the Citizens of Baltimore, May 14, 1861," in Jessie Ames Marshall, ed., *Private and Official Correspondence of Gen. Benjamin F. Butler* (Norwood, MA: Plimpton Press, 1917), 83–84; Michael Burlingame, ed., *Abraham Lincoln: The Observations of John O. Nicolay and John Hay* (Carbondale: Southern Illinois University Press, 2007), 72.

6. "General Butler's Response to a Serenade, Tendered Him Before the National Hotel, Washington, D.C., May 16, 1861," in Marshall, *Correspondence of Gen. Butler*, 89–90.

7. Quoted in "General Butler and the Contraband of War," *The New York Times*, May 30, 1861.

8. Benjamin Quarles, *Lincoln and the Negro* (New York: Da Capo Press, 1991), 69.

9. Stearns, *Life and Public Services of George Luther Stearns*, 252.

10. Ibid., 248; Richard Cordley, *A History of Lawrence, Kansas: From the First Settlement to the Close of the Rebellion* (Lawrence, KS: E. F. Caldwell, 1895), 182.

11. Stearns, *Life and Public Services of George Luther Stearns*, 254.

12. "A Good Argument," *Circular* (Brooklyn), August 1, 1861.

13. "Mr. Lovejoy and His Nigger," *Vanity Fair* 4 (July 27, 1861), 41.

14. Hampton Sides, *Blood and Thunder: The Epic Story of Kit Carson and the Conquest of the American West* (New York: Random House, 2007), 238.

15. Katharine T. Corbett, *In Her Place: A Guide to St. Louis Women's History* (St. Louis: Missouri History Museum, 1999), 84.

16. Sally Denton, *Passion and Principle: John and Jessie Fremont, the Couple Whose Power, Politics, and Love Shaped Nineteenth-Century America* (New York: Bloomsbury, 2007), 329; Jessie Benton Fremont to John Greenleaf Whittier, February 14, 1864, in *The Letters of Jessie Benton Fremont*, Pamela Herr and Mary Lee Spence, eds. (Champaign-Urbana: University of Illinois Press, 1993), 370–71; Axel Nissan, *Bret Harte: The Prince and the Pauper* (Oxford: University Press of Mississippi, 2000), 62; Glenna Matthews, *The Golden State in the Civil War: Thomas Starr King, the Republican Party, and the Birth of Modern California* (Cambridge, UK: Cambridge University Press, 2012), 79.

17. "Letter from St. Louis," *San Francisco Bulletin*, September 6, 1861.

18. Jessie Benton Fremont to Montgomery Blair, July 28, 1861, in Herr and Spence, eds., *Letters of Jessie Benton Fremont*, 256.

19. Ibid.

20. John C. Fremont to Montgomery Blair, July 31, 1861, in ibid., 257–58.

21. Jessie Benton Fremont to Abraham Lincoln, August 5, 1861, in ibid., 262.

22. Salmon Chase to John C. Fremont, August 4, 1861, Collection #0121, vol. 8, Copies of Special Letters, 1861, 1862, 1865, Papers of Salmon P. Chase, Historical Society of Pennsylvania, Philadelphia, PA.

23. *The Last Political Writings of Nathaniel Lyon, U.S.A.* (New York: Rudd and Carlton, 1861), 233.

24. John Thomas Scharf, *History of Saint Louis City and County: From the Earliest Periods to the Present Day: Including Biographical Sketches of Representative Men*, vol. 1 (St. Louis: L. H. Evarts, 1883), 399; "Reports from St. Louis," *The New York Times*, September 24, 1861.

25. Andrew Rolle, *John Charles Fremont: Character as Destiny* (Norman: University of Oklahoma Press, 1999), 201.

26. Carl Schurz, *The Reminiscences of Carl Schurz*, vol. 1 (New York: McClure, 1907), 344.

27. Quoted in "Fremont in Missouri: [Excerpts of Accounts] by John McElroy, Galusha Anderson, W. T. Sherman," www.civilwarstlouis.com/History/Fremont.htm.

28. Frank B. Goodrich, *The Tribute Book: A Record of the Munificence, Self-Sacrifice, and Patriotism of the American People During the War* (New York: Derby and Miller, 1865), 294.

29. [Editorial note], Herr and Spence, eds., *Letters of Jessie Benton Fremont*, 263.

30. Isobel V. Morin, *Women Chosen for Public Office* (Minneapolis, MN: The Oliver Press, 1995), 20–2.

31. Jessie Fremont to William G. Eliot, August 27, 1861, in Herr and Spence, eds., *Letters of Jessie Benton Fremont*, 227; Mary C. Gillett, *The Army Medical Department, 1818–1865* (Washington, DC: Center of Military History, United States Army,

1987), 174–75; James N. Primm, *Lion of the Valley: St. Louis, 1764–1980* (St. Louis: Missouri History Museum, 1998), 251.

32. Denton, *Passion and Principle*, 310–11; Vernon L. Volpe, "The Fremonts and Emancipation in Missouri," *Historian* (Spring 2004), www.questia.com/library /1G1-17312346/the-fremonts-and-emancipation-in-missouri; Emancipation Order (1861) by John C. Fremont, in *Documents of American History*, vol. 1, Henry Steele Commager, ed. (New York: Prentice-Hall, 1973), 397–98.

33. Lincoln to Fremont, September 2, 1861 in *Lincoln's Writings: The Multimedia Edition*, Matthew Pinsker, ed., http://housedivided.dickinson.edu/sites/lincoln/letter -to-john-fremont-september-2-1861.

34. "The Lincoln Interview: Excerpt from *Great Events*," in Herr and Spence, eds., *Letters of Jessie Benton Fremont*, 264. See also Charles M. Segal, ed., *Conversations with Lincoln* (Piscataway, NJ: Transaction Publishers, 2002), 131–34.

11. Wolf Killers

1. "Mr. Garrison's Lecture: The Abolitionists and Their Relations to the War," *The New York Times*, January 15, 1862.

2. "Interesting Correspondence" [Price to Halleck, January 11, 1862], *Albany Evening Journal*, January 24, 1862.

3. "Jayhawker," *Philadelphia Inquirer*, January 13, 1862; "The Manner of Prosecuting War," *Crisis* [of Ohio], January 29, 1862.

4. Oakes, *Scorpion's Sting*, 150.

5. Quoted in "Visitors from Congress: James H. Lane (1814–1866)," www.mrlincolns whitehouse.org/inside.asp?ID=159&subjectID=2; Nicole Etchison, "Jennison's Jayhawkers," *The New York Times*, December 28, 2011.

6. "Jim Lane's Expedition," *Hartford Daily Courant*, January 23, 1862.

7. Benjamin P. Thomas and Harold M. Hyman, *Stanton: The Life and Times of Lincoln's Secretary of War* (New York: Random House, 2013), 138–39; Thomas G. Mitchell, *Antislavery Politics in Antebellum and Civil War America* (Westport, CT: Greenwood, 2006), 192.

8. Quoted in Walter Stahr, *Stanton: Lincoln's War Secretary* (New York: Simon and Schuster, 2017), 202; Doris Kearns Goodwin, *Team of Rivals: The Political Genius of Abraham Lincoln* (New York: Simon and Schuster, 2005), 405; Carl Sandburg, *Lincoln: The War Years* (New York: Sterling, 2007), 181–82; Shelby Foote, *The Civil War: A Narrative, Fort Sumter to Perryville* (New York: Random House, 1986), 558.

9. "David Hunter to General Isaac I. Stevens, May 8, 1862," *The War of the Rebellion: A Compilation of the Official Records of the Union and Confederate Armies, Series III, Volume II* (Washington, D.C.: U.S. Government Printing Office, 1899), 30.

10. General Hunter's Order 11, Headquarters, Department of the South, Hilton Head, SC, May 9, 1862, online at *The Civil War* [original Civil War resources], http:// www.sonofthesouth.net/leefoundation/civil-war/1862/may/hunter-frees-slaves -order-11.htm.

11. Amy Dru Stanley, *From Bondage to Contract: Wage Labor, Marriage, and the Market in*

the Age of Slave Emancipation (Cambridge, UK: Cambridge University Press, 1998), 129; Gordon A. Christenson, "A Tale of Two Lawyers in Antebellum Cincinnati: Timothy Walker's Last Conversation with Salmon P. Chase" (2002), Faculty Articles and Other Publications, Paper 168, http://scholarship.law.uc.edu/fac_pubs/168.

12. [Edited Online Edition] Abraham Lincoln's Response to General David Hunter's Orders No. 11, May 19, 1862, online at *The Civil War* [original Civil War resources], http://www.sonofthesouth.net/leefoundation/civil-war/1862/may/hunter-frees-slaves-order-11.htm.

13. Quoted in Moncure Daniel Conway, *Autobiography: Memories and Experiences of Moncure Daniel Conway*, vol. 1 (Boston: Houghton, Mifflin, 1904), 307.

14. Hunter to Stanton, June 23, 1862, in *United States Congressional Serial Set*, vol. 1138 (Washington, DC: Government Printing Office, 1862), 34.

15. Ibid., 35.

16. Benjamin Butler to Salmon Chase, May 8, 1862, Box 2, Papers of Salmon Chase, Historical Society of Pennsylvania, Philadelphia, PA; Benjamin F. Butler, *Life and Public Services of Major-General Benjamin F. Butler, The Hero of New Orleans* (Philadelphia: T. B. Peterson and Brothers, 1864), 71; Taylor M. Polites, "The Bloody Occupation of Northern Alabama," *The New York Times*, February 28, 2013; Terry L. Jones, "The Beast in the Big Easy," *The New York Times*, May 18, 2012.

17. [Newspaper clipping], n.d., n.p., box 258 [scrapbook], Headquarters Department of the Gulf, New Orleans, Papers of Benjamin F. Butler, Library of Congress, Washington, DC; Special Order No. 179, July 10, 1862, box 187, Subject File: Dispatches, Butler Papers, LC; Gerald M. Capers, *Occupied City: New Orleans Under the Federals* (Lexington: University of Kentucky Press, 2015), 67; Sean A. Scott, "'The Glory of the City Is Gone': Perspectives of Union Soldiers in New Orleans During the Civil War," *Louisiana History* 57 (Winter 2016), 54.

18. Diary entry for May 15, 1862, J. W. Phelps Commonplace Book Number 2, Diary, 1862: February 19–August 2, John W. Phelps Papers, New York Public Library, New York.

19. Diary entry for May 27, 1862, ibid.

20. John D. Winter, *The Civil War in Louisiana* (Baton Rouge: Louisiana State University Press, 1991), 144–45.

21. "The Negro Question in General Butler's Department," *The Liberator*, July 4, 1862; [undated newspaper clippings], Box 187, Butler Papers, LC.

22. "Retreat of General McClellan," *The Liberator*, July 18, 1862.

23. Foner, *Fiery Trial*, 213, 216–17.

24. Quoted in Alan Guelzo, *Lincoln's Emancipation Proclamation: The End of Slavery in America* (New York: Simon and Schuster, 2005), 124. See also *Diary of Gideon Welles, Secretary of the Navy Under Lincoln and Johnson*, vol. 1 (Boston: Houghton Mifflin, 1911), 70.

25. "Preliminary Draft of Emancipation Proclamation," Abraham Lincoln Papers: Series 1. General Correspondence. 1833–1916, online at the Library of Congress, https://www.loc.gov/resource/mal.1723200/?st=text.

26. James Oakes, *Freedom National: The Destruction of Slavery in the United States, 1861–1865* (New York: W. W. Norton, 2013), 304–305; Michael Burlingame, *Abraham Lincoln: A Life*, vol. 2 (Baltimore, MD: Johns Hopkins University Press, 2013), 362.

27. Foner, *Fiery Trial*, 226; Robert E. May, *Slavery, Race, and Conquest in the Tropics: Lincoln, Douglas, and the Future of Latin America* (New York: Cambridge University Press, 2013), 257; Oakes, *Freedom National*, 308–309.

28. David Williams, *I Freed Myself: African American Self-Emancipation in the Civil War Era* (Cambridge, UK: Cambridge University Press, 2014), 110, 183–84; Dorothy Wickenden, "Lincoln and Douglass Dismantling the Peculiar Institution," *Wilson Quarterly* 14 (Autumn 1990), 104.

29. Lincoln to Reverdy Johnson, July 26, 1862, Box 14, General Correspondence, Butler Papers, LC.

12. Arming African Americans

1. "The Hero of the Planter," *The New York Times*, October 3, 1862.

2. Andrew Billingsley, *Yearning to Breathe Free: Robert Smalls of South Carolina and His Families* (Columbia: University of South Carolina Press, 2007), 60.

3. Ibid., 66.

4. Edward A. Miller, *Lincoln's Abolitionist General: The Biography of David Hunter* (Columbia: University of South Carolina Press, 1997), 112–13; Billingsley, *Yearning to Breathe Free*, 69.

5. Edwin Stanton to Rufus K. Saxton, August 25, 1862," *Freedom: A Documentary History of Emancipation, 1861–1867*, vol. 3, Series 1: *The Wartime Genesis of Free Labor* (Cambridge, UK: Cambridge University Press, 1982), 269–70; Billingsley, *Yearning to Breathe Free*, 71.

6. Susie King Taylor, *Reminiscences of My Life in Camp with the 33rd United States Colored Troops* (Boston, MA: Published by the Author, 1902), 11–13.

7. Brenda Wineapple, *White Heat: The Friendship of Thomas Wentworth Higginson and Emily Dickinson* (New York: Random House, 2009), 3–5.

8. "Rev. Mr. Higginson's Company Full and Organized," *The Liberator*, September 5, 1862.

9. Thomas Wentworth Higginson, *Army Life in a Black Regiment* (Boston, MA: Fields, Osgood, 1870), 9.

10. Christopher Looby, ed., *The Complete Civil War Journal and Selected Letters of Thomas Wentworth Higginson*, vol. 53 (Chicago: University of Chicago Press, 2000), 77–78.

11. "A Fireside Chat: Looking at the Emancipation Proclamation," sponsored by the Virginia Sesquicentennial of the American Civil War Commission, September 21, 2012, University of Mary Washington, Fredericksburg, VA, www.youtube.com/watch?v=DjktIx0wiFg.

12. "Review—No Title," *Little's Living Age*, January 17, 1863; "Review No. 8—No Title," *Universalist Quarterly and General Review* 20 (January 1863), 109.

13. William Henry Singleton, *Recollections of My Slavery Days*, introduced and

annotated by Katherine Mellon Charon and David S. Cecelski (Raleigh: Division of Archives and History, North Carolina Department of Cultural Resources, 1999), 46–48.

14. Ibid., 48.

15. "Raising the First North Carolina Colored Regiment," unpublished manuscript, Edward W. Kinsley Papers, Archives and Manuscripts, University of Massachusetts, Amherst Library, Amherst, MA; Singleton, *Recollections*, 50.

16. *Lynch v. State of Alabama*, No. 08-S-450-NE, slip op. at 9 (N.D. Ala. Nov. 7, 2011), www.gpo.gov/fdsys/pkg/USCOURTS-alnd-5_08-cv-00450/pdf/USCOURTS -alnd-5_08-cv-00450-3.pdf.

17. Lause, *Race and Radicalism in the Union Army*, 62; "The Cherokee in the Civil War," *Cherokee Nation*, www.cherokee.org/AboutTheNation/History/Facts/The CherokeeandtheCivilWar.aspx.

18. Quoted in "First Kansas Colored Volunteer Infantry," *Community & Conflict: The Impact of the Civil War in the Ozarks*, www.ozarkscivilwar.org/archives/1192; Lane to Stanton, August 5, 1862, *The War of the Rebellion: A Compilation of the Official Records of the Union and Confederate Armies* (Washington, DC: Government Printing Office, 1891), 295; Richard Cordley, *A History of Lawrence, Kansas, from the First Settlement to the Close of the Rebellion* (Lawrence: E. F. Caldwell, 1895), www.kancoll.org/books/cordley_history/ch_ch13.htm.

19. George Henry Hoyt to George L. Stearns, August 13, 1862, *Civil War on the Western Border*, www.civilwaronthewesternborder.org/content/george-henry-hoyt-george-l -stearns; Lause, *Race and Radicalism in the Union Army*, 71; Robert W. Lull, *James M. Williams: Civil War General and Indian Fighter* (Denton: University of West Texas Press, 2013), 41–44; "Splendid Fighting by Black Regiment," *Independent*, November 13, 1862; Ian Michael Spurgeon, *Soldiers in the Army of Freedom: The First Kansas Colored Volunteers* (Norman: University of Oklahoma Press, 2014), 90–95.

20. "Our Port Royal Correspondence," *The New York Times*, June 19, 1863; Sarah H. Bradford, *Scenes in the Life of Harriet Tubman* (Auburn, NY: W. J. Moses, 1869), 89.

21. Jefferson B. Browne, *Key West: The Old and the New* (Key West, FL: Record Company, 1912), 90–97; Donald Shaffer, "Emancipation Comes to Key West," *Civil War Emancipation* (February 17, 2013), http://cwemancipation.wordpress.com/2013 /02/17/freedom-comes-to-key-west; Tom Hambright, "Tom's Key History Blog," Monroe County Public Library, www.keyslibraries.org/wp-content/uploads/2012 /02/Black-History.pdf.

22. Adam Wasserman, *A People's History of Florida, 1513–1876: How Africans, Seminoles, Women, and Lower-Class Whites Shaped the History of the Sunshine State* (n.p.: CreateSpace Independent Publishing Platform, 2009), 446.

23. Thomas Wentworth Higginson, *Letters and Journals of Thomas Wentworth Higginson, 1846–1906* (Boston: Houghton Mifflin, 1921), 185–86.

24. Higginson, *Army Life in a Black Regiment*, 69–78, 88.

25. "Our South Carolina Letter: Colonel Montgomery's Expedition," *Philadelphia Inquirer*, June 19, 1863.

26. "[Letter Dictated by Harriet Tubman]," *Boston Commonwealth*, June 30, 1863. See also Michelle Diane Wright, *Broken Utterances: A Selected Anthology of Nineteenth-Century Black Women's Social Thought* (Baltimore, MD: Three Sistahs Press, 2007), 260; "Negro Stealing," *New Hampshire Patriot and Gazette*, June 17, 1863; "Important from the South," *Evening Union*, June 8, 1863; "Yankee Raid," *Macon Telegraph*, June 6, 1863.

13. Turning the Mississippi

1. Jim Downs, *Sick from Freedom: African American Illness and Suffering During the Civil War* (New York: Oxford University Press, 2012), 50.

2. Oakes, *Freedom National*, 320, 322.

3. Chandra Manning, *Troubled Refuge: Struggling for Freedom in the Civil War* (New York: Knopf Doubleday, 2017), 213–14.

4. John Eaton, *Grant, Lincoln, and the Freedmen: Reminiscences of the Civil War with Special References to the Work for the Contrabands and Freedmen of the Mississippi Valley* (New York: Longmans, Green, 1907), 14–15.

5. Quoted in Michael A. Eggleston, *President Lincoln's Recruiter: General Lorenzo Thomas and the United States Colored Troops in the Civil War* (Jefferson, NC: McFarland, 2013), 7; "Memoir of Brigadier and Brevet-Major General Lorenzo Thomas," U.S. Army Military History Institute, U.S. Army Heritage and Education Center, Carlisle Barracks, PA.

6. "Memoir of General Thomas," 1.

7. [Grant's General Orders on Riverfront Security, n.d.], Box 1, RG 94, National Archives and Records Administration.

8. Stanton to Thomas, May 25, 1863, Entry 363, RG 94, National Archives and Records Administration.

9. Ron Chernow, *Grant* (New York: Penguin Press, 2017), 274–75.

10. [Editor's Note] *Papers of Ulysses S. Grant*, vol. 8 (Carbondale: Southern Illinois University, 1967), 51–52; Victor Hicken, *Illinois in the Civil War* (Champaign-Urbana: University of Illinois Press, 1991), 140.

11. Eaton, *Grant, Lincoln, and the Freedmen*, 55.

12. "General Thomas's Speech," *Cincinnati Daily Commercial*, April 13, 1863. See also "Lorenzo Thomas Seeks Officers for Colored Troops," www.millikensbend.com /lorenzo-thomas-seeks-officers-for-colored-troops/.

13. James Pickett Jones, *Black Jack: John A. Logan and Southern Illinois in the Civil War* (Carbondale: Southern Illinois University Press, 1995), 155; Christopher Waldrep, *Vicksburg's Long Shadow: The Civil War Legacy of Race and Remembrance* (New York: Rowman and Littlefield, 2005), 29.

14. Thomas to Stanton, October 8, 1865, RG 94, Generals Papers and Books, Gen. Lorenzo Thomas, Letters Sent, July 1864 to April 1865 [sic], National Archives and Records Administration.

15. Edward Davis Thompson, *Anecdotes of the Civil War in the United States* (New York: D. Appleton, 1884), 31; Pemberton to Joseph E. Johnston, April 17, 1863, in

Charles V. Stewart, ed., *Official Records of the Union and Confederate Navies in the War of the Rebellion* (Washington, DC: Department of the Navy, 1895), 89; "By Pony Express," *Houston Tri-Weekly Telegraph*, April 23, 1863.

16. Speech delivered by Isaiah T. Montgomery as reported in the *New York World* under date of September 27, 1890, Benjamin Montgomery Family Papers, Library of Congress.

17. In a 2013 article, the author mistakenly suggested that Thomas had accompanied Grant to Jackson. LeeAnna Keith, "Born Again in Mississippi," *The New York Times*, August 13, 2013.

18. "Report of Adj.-Gen. Lorenzo Thomas, U.S. Army," *War of the Rebellion*, 517; "Battle of Grand Gulf," *The New York Times*, May 11, 1863; Hamlin Garland, "Grant in a Great Campaign: The Investment and Capture of Vicksburg," *McClure's Magazine* 9 (1897), 808; Waldrep, *Vicksburg's Long Shadow*, 31–32; Earl S. Meirs, *Web of Victory: Grant at Vicksburg* (Baton Rouge: Louisiana State University Press, 1955), 146; "Fred Grant's First Land Battle," *Deseret News*, February 16, 1897; Richard Wheeler, *The Siege of Vicksburg* (New York: Thomas Y. Crowell, 1978), 120–21; U. S. Grant, *Personal Memoirs of Ulysses S. Grant* (New York: Konecky and Konecky, n.d.), 288.

19. "Ajt.-Gen. Thomas' Advice to the Negroes," *The New York Times*, June 7, 1863; Eaton to Rev. S. S. Jocelyn, May 18, 1863, Roll 1, Target 1: Office of the General Superintendent of Freedmen, Letters Sent by John Eaton, General Superintendent of Contrabands, vol. 74, Feb.–Dec. 1863, National Archives and Records Administration; Eaton to H. B. Spelman, Esq., May 23, 1863, Roll 1, Target 1: Office of the General Superintendent of Freedmen, Letters Sent by John Eaton, General Superintendent of Contrabands, vol. 74, Feb.–Dec. 1863, National Archives and Records Administration.

20. Eaton to Spelman, May 23, 1863.

21. Eaton to Jocelyn, May 18, 1863.

22. "Conversation with Gen. Thomas," *The New York Times*, July 20, 1863; Lincoln to Stanton, July 21, 1863, in *Abraham Lincoln: Complete Works, Comprising His Speeches, State Papers, and Miscellaneous Writings*, vol. 1 (New York: Century, 1920), 372.

23. Michael Burlingame and John R. Turner Ettinger, eds., *Inside Lincoln's White House: The Complete Civil War Diary of John Hay* (Carbondale: University of Southern Illinois Press, 1999), 69.

24. "Gen. Thomas's Views on the Future of the Black Race," *The New York Times*, July 22, 1863; "Large Colored Army," *Zion's Herald and Wesleyan Journal*, August 12, 1863.

25. War Department General Order 143: Creation of the U.S. Colored Troops, May 22, 1863, Civil War Trust, www.civilwar.org/education/history/primarysources/war-department-general-order.html.

26. Quoted in Stearns, *Life and Public Services of George Luther Stearns*, 302.

27. Frederick Douglass to George L. Stearns, August 10, 1863, in *The Civil War: The*

Third Year; Told by Those Who Lived It, Brooks D. Simpson, ed. (New York: Library of America, 2013), 427–28.

28. Quoted in [editorial remarks] Frederick Douglass, *Selected Speeches and Writings* (Chicago: Chicago Review Press, 2000), 546.

29. Douglass to Stearns, August 10, 1863.

30. "August 10, 1863," *The Lincoln Log*, www.thelincolnlog.org.

31. Frederick Douglass, "Valedictory," *Frederick Douglass: Selected Speeches and Writings*, Philip Foner and Yuval Taylor, eds. (Chicago: Chicago Review Press, 1999), 544.

32. "Douglass' Valedictory," *Pacific Appeal*, October 3, 1863; "Douglass's Valedictory," *Douglass: Selected Speeches*, 545; Frederick Douglass, *The Life and Times of Frederick Douglass* (Mineola, NY: Courier Dover Publications, 2012), 253.

14. Revolution by Confiscation

1. Harriet Jacobs to William Lloyd Garrison, September 9, 1862, in *Civil War 150, Reader #4: From Slavery to Freedom* (New York: Library of America and Gilder Lehrman Institute for American History, 2012), 36; Robert M. Poole, "How Arlington National Cemetery Came to Be," *Smithsonian Magazine* (November 2009), www.smithsonianmag.com/history/how-arlington-national-cemetery-came-to-be-145147007.

2. John Syrett, *The Civil War Confiscation Acts: Failing to Reconstruct the South* (New York: Fordham University Press, 2005), 128; *The U.S. Tax Bill . . . July 1, 1862* (New York: Henry Anstice, 1862), 85.

3. Robert Werlich, *"Beast" Butler: The Incredible Career of Major General Benjamin Franklin Butler* (Washington, DC: Quaker Press, 1962), 28; William Dana Orcutt, "Ben Butler and the 'Stolen Spoons,'" *North American Review* 207 (1918), 66–81.

4. "The Peculiar Institution," *The New York Times*, October 24, 1862.

5. Butler to Chase, July 28, 1862, Box 2, Papers of Salmon P. Chase, Historical Society of Pennsylvania, Philadelphia, PA; Joiner, "Nature of the Beast," 85–86.

6. [Article No. 1—No Title], *The Friend: A Religious and Literary Journal*, August 23, 1862; [newspaper clipping: Timeline of Butler Occupation], box 258 [scrapbook], Butler Papers, LC, Washington, DC; "Latest from New Orleans," *The Baltimore Sun*, December 11, 1862; "General Butler Stirring Up the Rebels," *The New York Times*, December 19, 1862.

7. "Address to the Citizens of New Orleans," Box 258 [scrapbook], Butler Papers, Library of Congress.

8. Charles J. Mitchell to Jefferson Davis, June 7, 1862, *Papers of Jefferson Davis*, vol. 8: *1862*, Linda Lasswell Crist, ed. (Baton Rouge: Louisiana State University Press, 1995), 231; see also David Williams, *I Freed Myself: African American Self-Emancipation in the Civil War Era* (New York: Cambridge University Press, 2014), 88–89.

9. Janet Sharp Hermann, *The Pursuit of a Dream* (Oxford: University of Mississippi Press, 1981), 41.

10. Gary D. Joiner, *Mr. Lincoln's Brown Water Navy: The Mississippi Squadron* (Washington, DC: Rowman and Littlefield, 1997), 93.

11. Chester G. Hearn, *Ellet's Brigade: The Strangest Outfit of Them All* (Baton Rouge: Louisiana State University Press, 2006), 117; Steven M. Mayeux, *Earthen Walls, Iron Men: Fort DeRussy, Louisiana, and the Defense of the Red River* (Knoxville: University of Tennessee Press, 2007), 72; Hermann, *Pursuit of a Dream*, 41.

12. Isaiah T. Montgomery, "He Tells His Own Story," *The American Slave—Mississippi Narratives*, George P. Rawick, ed. (Westport, CT: Greenwood, 1978), 1547.

13. Joiner, *Mr. Lincoln's Brown Water Navy*, 117.

14. Quoted in Eaton, *Grant, Lincoln, and the Freedmen*, 86.

15. Hermann, *Pursuit of a Dream*, 40–46.

16. "The Negroes of the Southwest," *The New York Times*, November 28, 1863; "Abandoned Lands and the Plantation Lease System," http://civilwarhelena.com/history /abandoned-lands.

17. "Register of Freedmen at Home Colony, Davis Bend, MS," http://mappingthe freedmensbureau.com/register-of-freedmen-at-home-colony-davis-bend-ms.

18. Hermann, *Pursuit of a Dream*, 49–50; [Editorial Note], *The Papers of Jefferson Davis*, vol. 10: *January–September 1863*, Linda Lasswell Crist, ed. (Baton Rouge: Louisiana State University Press, 1991), 364.

19. "Daily Story: Chase and the Chin Fly," *Abraham Lincoln's Classroom* by the Lehrman Institute, www.abrahamlincolnsclassroom.org/daily-story-chase-and-the-chin -fly; Goodwin, *Team of Rivals*, 565.

20. Chase to General [John] Quincy Adams Gillmore, December 29, 1863, Chase Papers, 232.

21. [Journal Entry, August 3, 1862], in S. H. Dodson, ed., *Diary and Correspondence of Salmon P. Chase* (Washington, DC: Government Printing Office, 1903), 54; Xi Wang, *The Trial of Democracy: Black Suffrage and Northern Republicans, 1860–1910* (Athens: University of Georgia Press, 1997), 10.

22. Chase to Thomas J. Durant, December 28, 1863, Dodson, *Diary and Correspondence* 230. See also Joseph G. Tregle, Jr., "Thomas J. Durant, Utopian Socialism, and the Failure of Presidential Reconstruction in Louisiana," *Journal of Southern History* 45 (November 1979), 510–11.

23. Alexander Wayman, *My Recollections of African M. E. Ministers: or, Forty Years' Experience in the African Methodist Episcopal Church* (Philadelphia: A.M.E. Book Rooms, 1881), 86; Kathleen Ann Clark, *Defining Moments: African American Commemoration and Political Culture in the South, 1863–1913* (Chapel Hill: University of North Carolina Press, 2006), 46; *Diary of William P. Woodlin*, # GLC06599, Gilder Lehrman Institute for American History.

24. General James C. Veach to Bishop [Edward] Ames, December 23, 1863, *Congressional Globe* 55 (1864), 69; Henry McNeal Turner, *Freedom's Witness: The Civil War Correspondence of Henry McNeal Turner*, Jean Lee Cole, ed. (Morgantown: West Virginia University Press, 2013), 160.

25. Quoted in James McPherson, *The Negro's Civil War: How African Americans Felt*

and Acted During the Civil War (New York: Knopf Doubleday, 2008). See also "Letter to the Editor of the Anglo-African," n.d., Library of Congress [Online], Civil War and Reconstruction, 1861–1877, www.loc.gov/teachers/classroommaterials/pre sentationsandactivities/presentations/timeline/civilwar/freedmen/editor.html.

26. James A. Harris, "The History of Orange Cultivation in Florida," *Proceedings of the Florida State Horticultural Society, 1923,* http://fshs.org/proceedings-o/1923-vol -36/205-215%20(HARRIS).pdf.

27. John Taliaferro, *All the Great Prizes: The Life of John Hay from Lincoln to Roosevelt* (New York: Simon and Schuster, 2013), 67–68.

28. Chase to Gillmore, December 28, 1863; Gregory J. W. Urwin, *Black Flag Over Dixie: Racial Atrocities and Reprisals in the Civil War* (Carbondale: Southern Illinois University Press, 2005), 66; George Winston Smith, "Carpetbag Imperialism in Florida, 1862–1868," *Florida Historical Quarterly* 27 (January 1949), 276.

29. Abraham Lincoln to Q.A. Gillmore, January 13, 1864, *Collected Works,* vol. 7, http://quod.lib.umich.edu/l/lincoln/lincoln7/1:249?rgn=div1;view=fulltext.

30. Higginson, *Army Life with a Black Regiment,* 106–107; Taliaferro, *All the Great Prizes,* 80; William Roscoe Thayer, *The Life and Letters of John Hay,* vol. 1 (New York: Houghton Mifflin, 1913), 161.

31. Higginson, *Army Life with a Black Regiment,* 234; Urwin, *Black Flag over Dixie,* 68–69; Taliaferro, *All the Great Prizes,* 81; Tyler Dennett, ed., *Lincoln and the Civil War in the Diaries and Letters of John Hay* (New York: Da Capo Press, 1988), 164; Q. A. Gillmore to Henry Halleck, January 31, 1864, https://battleofolustee.org /reports/gillmore3.htm.

32. "The Florida Expedition," *The New York Times,* March 4, 1864; William C. Harris, *With Charity for All: Lincoln and the Restoration of the Union* (Lexington: University of Kentucky Press, 2015), 152; [Editorial Note], *Inside Lincoln's White House: The Civil War Diary of John Hay,* Michael Burlingame and John R. Turner Ettinger, ed. (Carbondale: Southern Illinois University Press, 1999), 299.

33. [Letter in Opposition to Renomination of President Lincoln], https://archive .org/stream/letterinopposit00pome#page/n0/mode/2up; Melanie S. Gustafson, *Women and the Republican Party, 1854–1924* (Urbana: University of Illinois Press, 2001), 31.

34. Harris, *With Charity for All,* 201–202.

15. Republican Nation-Building

1. "Presbyterian General Assembly," *Pittsfield Sun,* June 4, 1863.

2. "Public Meeting," *Macon Telegraph,* June 19, 1863.

3. "Pennsylvania Aroused!" *Hartford Daily Courant,* June 29, 1863; "Equalize the Bounties and Consolidate the Skeleton Regiments," *Philadelphia Inquirer,* July 3, 1863.

4. "Response to a Serenade, July 7, 1863," *Collected Works of Abraham Lincoln,* vol. 6, http://quod.lib.umich.edu/cgi/t/text/text-idx?c=lincoln;cc=lincoln;type=simple;rgn =div1;q1=July%207%2C%201863;view=text;subview=detail;sort=occur;idno =lincoln6;node=lincoln6%3A674.

5. Margaret E. Wagner et al., eds., *The Library of Congress Civil War Desk Reference* (New York: Simon and Schuster, 2009), 678–79.
6. "Speech of Frederick Douglass," *The Liberator*, July 24, 1863.
7. Jabez Thomas Sunderland, *A Ministry of Twenty Years in a College Town* (Ann Arbor, MI: Register Publishing, 1895), 7–8.
8. Quoted in *The American Annual Cyclopedia and Register of Important Events of the Year 1865*, vol. 5 (New York: D. Appleton, 1869), 257.
9. Quoted in Rick Beard, "General Frémont's 'She-Merrimac,'" *The New York Times*, September 8, 2011.
10. James B. Stewart, *Wendell Phillips: Liberty's Hero* (Baton Rouge: Louisiana State University Press, 1998), 251; Henry Wadsworth Longfellow to James Thomas Fields, August 12, 1863, in *The Letters of Henry Wadsworth Longfellow*, Andrew Hilen, ed. (Cambridge, MA: Harvard University Press, 1983), 351; Eugene H. Brann, *Sketches of Nahant Showing Many Points of Interest* (Boston, MA: Atlantic, 1911), 12; D. Hamilton Hurd, ed., *Sketches of Essex County, Massachusetts* (Philadelphia, PA: J. W. Lewis, 1888), 1427; Christopher R. Mathias, Kenneth Turino, et al., *Nahant* (Charleston, SC: Arcadia, 1999), 12.
11. Quoted in Samuel T. Pickard, *The Life and Letters of John Greenleaf Whittier*, vol. 2 (New York: Haskell House, 1969), 463–64.
12. John Greenleaf Whittier, "Barbara Frietchie," www.poetryfoundation.org/poems-and-poets/poems/detail/45483; Jessie Fremont to John Greenleaf Whittier, February 14, 1864, in Herr and Spence, eds., *Letters of Jessie Benton Fremont*, 370–71; Jessie Benton Fremont to Horace Greeley, n.d., in ibid., 378; "The Metropolitan Fair," *The New York Times*, April 12, 1864; "Personal," *Round Table*, April 30, 1864; "A Sword Contest," *Prairie Farmer*, April 23, 1864; Herr and Spence, eds., *Letters of Jessie Benton Fremont*, 381; Burton J. Bledstein and Robert C. Johnson, *The Middling Sorts: Explorations in the History of the American Middle Class* (New York: Routledge, 2013).
13. "Welcome to Hon. Geo. Thompson," *The New York Times*, March 1, 1864; "Fremont Meeting at Cooper Institute," *The Liberator*, March 25, 1864.
14. Gustafson, *Women and the Republican Party*, 20–22, 31–32; Mischa Honeck, *We Are the Revolutionists: German-Speaking Immigrants and American Abolitionists After 1848* (Athens: University of Georgia Press, 2011), 164.
15. "The Cleveland Convention," *The Liberator*, June 3, 1864.
16. "The Cleveland Convention: Letter of Acceptance of Fremont," *The New York Times*, June 6, 1864; "The Radicals and Copperheads Convention," *The New York Times*, June 3, 1864; "Extremes Meet," *The Liberator*, June 1, 1864.
17. Abraham Lincoln, "Address at a Sanitary Fair, Baltimore, MD, April 18, 1864," http://teachingamericanhistory.org/library/document/address-at-a-sanitary-fair.
18. Christopher L. Webber, *American to the Backbone: The Life of James W. C. Pennington, the Fugitive Slave Who Became One of the First Abolitionists* (New York: Pegasus Books, 2011).

19. "The Baltimore Convention," *Independent*, June 23, 1864; Foner, *Fiery Trial*, 299–300.

20. Louis P. Masur, *Lincoln's Last Speech: Wartime Reconstruction and the Crisis of Reunion* (New York: Oxford University Press, 2015), 113–14; Thaddeus Stevens to Edward McPherson, July 10, 1864, Furman University: Thaddeus Stevens Papers Online, http://history.furman.edu/benson/hst41/clear/stevens2.htm.

21. Xi, *Trial of Democracy*, 15; "Visitors from Congress: James M. Ashley," www.mrlincolnswhitehouse.org/residents-visitors/visitors-from-congress/visitors-congress-james-m-ashley-1824-1896/; "Wade-Davis Bill," www.mrlincolnandfreedom.org/civil-war/reconstruction/wade-davis-bill; John C. Rodrigue, *Lincoln and Reconstruction* (Carbondale: Southern Illinois University Press, 2013), 86; Masur, *Lincoln's Last Speech*, 110–12; Blair quoted in Edwin S. Grosvenor, *The Best of American Heritage: Lincoln* (Rockville, MD: American Heritage, 2015).

16. Never Surrender the Flag

1. Quoted in Joseph T. Wilson, *The Black Phalanx: A History of the Negro Soldiers of the United States in the Wars of 1775–1812, 1861–1865* (Minneapolis, MN: American, 1890), 186.

2. Rick Beard, "Organizing Black Soldiers," *The New York Times*, May 31, 1863.

3. J. W. Phelps Commonplace Book No. 1, February 17, 1864, J. W. Phelps Papers, New York Public Library.

4. Jon Wiener, "Largest Mass Execution in U.S. History: 150 Years Ago Today," *The Nation*, December 26, 2012.

5. These are the author's calculations based on well-known figures. See also Wilbert L. Jenkins, *Climbing Up to Glory: A Short History of African Americans During the Civil War* (New York: Rowman and Littlefield, 2002), 33–35.

6. Quoted in Lewis Lehrman, ed., *Mr. Lincoln and Freedom: An American History Project of the Lehrman Institute*, www.mrlincolnandfreedom.org/civil-war/black-soldiers/pay-and-promotion.

7. Quoted in David W. Blight, *Frederick Douglass' Civil War: Keeping Faith in Jubilee* (Baton Rouge: Louisiana State University Press, 1989), 167.

8. Quoted in Keith P. Wilson, *Campfires of Freedom: The Camp Life of Black Soldiers During the War* (Kent, OH: Kent State University Press, 2002), 46–48. See also John David Smith, *Lincoln and the U.S. Colored Troops* (Carbondale: Southern Illinois University Press, 2013), 66; Jenkins, *Climbing Up to Glory*, 33.

9. "From Washington: A Discussion of the Enrollment Bill," *The New York Times*, January 17, 1864.

10. Luis F. Emilio, *A Brave Black Regiment: The History of the Fifty-Fourth Regiment of Massachusetts Volunteer Infantry, 1863–1865* (New York: Da Capo Press, 1995) (first published 1894), 91, 169, 176.

11. Glenn David Brasher, "Confusion and Courage at Olustee," *The New York Times*, February 20, 2014; Urwin, *Black Flag over Dixie*, 74–75.

12. Quoted in Jenkins, *Climbing Up to Glory*, 37.

13. Quoted in Eddy W. Davidson, *Nathan Bedford Forrest: In Search of the Enigma* (Gretna, LA: Pelican, 2007), 74.

14. Ibid., 220–24.

15. "The Misfortunes of a Strong-Minded Woman," *The New York Times*, August 1, 1859.

16. Quoted in Al Mackey, "Fort Pillow and Nathan Bedford Forrest, Part I: Was There a Massacre?" November 23, 2013, https://studycivilwar.wordpress.com/2013/11 /28/fort-pillow-and-nathan-bedford-forrest-part-1-was-there-a-massacre; Thirty-Eighth Congress, First Session, Joint Committee on the Conduct of the War, "Fort Pillow Massacre, Report No. 65 [Pamphlet Reprint, Columbia University Library].

17. Report of Lt. Col. Tom I. Jackson to Captain George B. Halstead, April 19, 1864, www.mobile96.com/cw2/Forrest_Pillow.html.

18. Ronald S. Coddington, "The Old Flag Never Touched the Ground," *The New York Times*, July 19, 2013; Glenn David Brasher, "Striking the Blow at Fort Wagner," *The New York Times*, July 18, 2013.

19. "The Bloody Flag of Fort Pillow," *Memphis Bulletin* [April 1864].

20. "Abraham Lincoln and Public Opinion," /www.abrahamlincolnsclassroom.org /abraham-lincoln-in-depth/abraham-lincoln-and-public-opinion.

21. Smith, *Lincoln and the U.S. Colored Troops*, 82; "Justice to Fallen Heroes," *The Liberator*, May 27, 1864.

22. Quoted in Elizabeth Gegenheimer, ed., "Selected Letters of Humphrey Hood, Litchfield Physician, Part II: 1862–1867," *Journal of the Illinois State Historical Society* 72 (November 1979), 248.

23. "Head-Quarters Cavalry Corps, Dist. of West Tennessee, Memphis, TN, June 30, 1865, General Orders No. 4" [Court-Martial of Thomas P. Hepburn], Box 753, RG 153 Records of the Office of the Judge Advocate General (Army), Court-Martial Case Files, 1809–1894, LL2593–LL2598, National Archives and Records Administration.

24. "Gen. Forrest to Gen. Washburn," n.p., June 14, 1864. See also R. R. Hancock, *Hancock's Diary, with Sketches of the First and Seventh Battalions* (Nashville, TN: Brandon, 1904), 403; Bruce Tap, *The Fort Pillow Massacre: North, South, and the Status of African Americans During the Civil War* (New York: Routledge, 2013), 76.

25. "General Washburn to General Forrest" n.p., n.d.; see also Wilson, *Black Phalanx*, 348; General Thomas Jordan and J. P. Pryor, *The Campaigns of Lieut.-Gen. N. B. Forrest, and of Forrest's Cavalry* (New Orleans, LA: Blelock, 1868), 488.

26. John Allan Wyeth, *The Life of General Nathan Bedford Forrest* (New York: Harper and Bros., 1899), 474; Michael Weeks, *The Complete Civil War Road Trip Guide* (New York: Countryman Press, 2009), 59.

27. Abraham Lincoln to Edwin Stanton, May 17, 1864, and editor's note, *Collected Works of Lincoln*, vol. 7, 345–47.

28. George Templeton Strong, quoted in Tap, *Fort Pillow Massacre*, 81–83.

17. Wearing the Brass Letter

1. Versalle F. Washington, *Eagles on Their Buttons: A Black Infantry Regiment in the Civil War* (Columbia: University of Missouri Press, 1999), 10, 13.

2. Richard F. Miller, ed., *The States at War*, vol. 5: *A Reference Guide for Ohio in the Civil War* (Lebanon, NH: University Press of New England, 2015), 428.

3. Albert W. Mann, *The History of the Forty-Fifth Regiment Massachusetts Volunteer Militia* (Jamaica Plain, MA: Brookside Print, 1908), 301–302. See also David S. Cecelski, *The Fire of Freedom: Abraham Galloway and the Slaves' Civil War* (Chapel Hill: University of North Carolina Press, 2012), 77–78.

4. Cecelski, *Fire of Freedom*, 84–85; [Article 1, no title], *The Liberator*, January 15, 1864; Julie Franck, "Galloway, Abraham," *NCPedia*, State Library of North Carolina, http://ncpedia.org/abraham-galloway.

5. Clarence Spigner, "Turner, Henry McNeal," www.blackpast.org/aah/turner-henry-mcneal-1834–1915; James T. Campbell, *Songs of Zion: The African Methodist Episcopal Church in the United States and South Africa* (New York: Oxford University Press, 1995), 54.

6. Jean Lee Cole, *Freedom's Witness: The Civil War Correspondence of Henry McNeal Turner* (Morgantown: West Virginia University Press, 2013), 200–204; Stephen W. Angell, *Bishop Henry McNeal Turner and African American Religion in the South* (Knoxville: University of Tennessee Press, 1992), 65.

7. Cole, *Freedom's Witness*, 199; David Blight, *Race and Reunion: The Civil War in American Memory* (Cambridge, MA: Harvard University Press, 2009), 147; Jean Lee Cole, "Absent from the Roll Call of History?" *Think.Do: Literature, Life, and How It All Fits Together*, https://jeanleecole.wordpress.com/tag/henry-mcneal-turner.

8. Horace James to the Public, June 27, 1863, www.roanokefreedmenscolony.com/james27.pdf; "Col. Wild's African Brigade," *The Liberator*, June 12, 1863.

9. Patricia C. Click, *Time Full of Trial: The Roanoke Island Freedmen's Colony, 1862–1867* (Chapel Hill: University of North Carolina Press, 2001), 46; Horace James to Benjamin F. Butler, February 20, 1864, www.roanokefreedmenscolony.com/techlet3.pdf.

10. "Letter from Rev. J. E. Round: The General Conference and the Colored Work," *Zion's Herald and Wesleyan Journal*, July 20, 1864.

11. "Civil War Fort at Jamestown Is Dug Up to Get at 1607 Site," *Washington Post*, May 7, 2012. See also *Lynch v. State of Alabama*, slip op., at 55.

12. Andy Hall, "George W. Hatton, Soldier," *Atlantic Monthly*, January 18, 2011, www.theatlantic.com/national/archive/2011/01/george-w-hatton-soldier/69659; Ta-Nehisi Coates, "The Very Spot Where the First Sons of Africa Were Landed," *Atlantic*, December 9, 2010, www.theatlantic.com/entertainment/archive/2010/12/the-very-spot-where-the-first-sons-of-africa-were-landed/67717.

13. Steven M. LaBarre, *The Fifth Massachusetts Cavalry in the Civil War* (Jefferson, NC: McFarland, 2016), 87.

14. Edwin Forbes, *An Artist's Story of the Great War* (New York: Fords, Howard and Hulbert, 1890), 189.

15. Elizabeth Varon, "City Point, Virginia: Nerve Center of the Union War Effort," in *Lens of War*, Gary Gallagher and J. Matthew Gallman, eds. (Athens: University of Georgia Press, 2014), 207.

16. Horace Porter, *Campaigning with Grant* (New York: Century, 1897), 220–21.

18. Black Republicans

1. William E. Parrish, *A History of Missouri, 1860–1875* (Columbia: University of Missouri Press, 2001), 76.

2. L. Maria Child, "The Mississippi Valley Sanitary Fair," *The Liberator*, May 13, 1864.

3. Eaton, *Grant, Lincoln, and the Freedmen*; Blight, *Frederick Douglass' Civil War*, 182–83; Masur, *Lincoln's Last Speech*, 118.

4. Quoted in W. E. B. DuBois, *Black Reconstruction in America: An Essay Toward a History of the Part Which Black Folk Played in the Attempt to Reconstruct Democracy in America, 1860–1880* (New York: Oxford University Press, 2014), vi.

5. Proceedings of the National Convention of Colored Men Held in the City of Syracuse, New York, October 4, 5, 6 & 7, 1864 (Boston: J. S. Rock and Geo. L. Ruffin, 1864), http://coloredconventions.org/items/show/282.

6. "Gen. Butler," *The New York Times*, November 9, 1864. See also Butler, *Autobiography and Personal Reminiscences*, 757–67; "The Public Peace/Butler in Command," *The New York Times*, November 7, 1864; Bill Morgan, "Why New York City Opposed Abraham Lincoln," *The New York Times*, September 1, 2014.

7. "Decision of Judge Underwood," *The Liberator*, November 25, 1864; "Testimony of Colored Witnesses in Virginia," *The Liberator*, November 11, 1864.

8. Chase to Sherman, September 2, 1865, Chase Collection #0121, vol. 8, Copies of Special Letters, Chase Papers, Library of Congress.

9. "Caste in North and South," *Spectator*, February 25, 1865; "Domestic," *Zion's Herald and Wesleyan Journal*, February 8, 1865; "Jubilee Meeting of the Colored Citizens of Boston," *The Liberator*, February 10, 1865; "A Colored Man's Views," *Hartford Courant*, March 25, 1865.

10. John Jones, "The Black Laws of Illinois, and a Few Reasons Why They Should Be Repealed" [Appendix A], in Arnie Bernstein, *The Hoofs and Guns of the Storm: Chicago's Civil War Connections* (Chicago: Lake Claremont Press, 2003), 213; Julia Mikuva, "John Jones and the Illinois Black Laws," http://clarkehousemuseum.blogspot.com/2012/02/john-jones-and-illinois-black-laws.html; Robert L. McCaul, *The Black Struggles for Public Schooling in Nineteenth-Century Illinois* (Carbondale: Southern Illinois University Press, 2009), 41–42.

11. Quoted in Richard Guzman, *Black Writing from Chicago: In the World, Not of It?* (Carbondale: Southern Illinois University Press, 2006), 8.

12. "Martin R. Delany to Edwin M. Stanton, 15 December 1863," in *The Black Abolitionist Papers*, vol. 5: *The United States, 1859–1865*, C. Peter Ripley, et al., eds. (Chapel Hill: University of North Carolina Press, 1992), 261–62.

13. Robert S. Levine, ed., *Martin R. Delany: A Documentary Reader* (Chapel Hill: University of North Carolina Press, 1992), 385–88; "Lorenzo Thomas to Major General [illegible], January 24, 1865," Folio 4: Thomas Letters and Special Orders, Thomas Papers, National Archives and Records Administration.

14. "Supplementary Report to the Commissioner of Pensions, June 13, 1901," Pension File 2544939, Henry McNeal Turner, National Archives and Records Administration.

15. Quoted in Edward Magdol, "Martin R. Delany Counsels Freedmen [Edward M.

Stoeber to S. M. Taylor, July 24, 1865]," *Journal of Negro History* 56 (October 1971), 303–309.

16. Jacqueline Jones, *Soldiers of Light and Love: Northern Teachers and Georgia Blacks, 1865–1873* (Athens: University of Georgia Press, 1992), 112; "Minutes of an Interview Between the Colored Ministers and Church Officers at Savannah with the Secretary of War and Major-Gen. Sherman," Freedmen and Southern Society Project, www.freedmen.umd.edu/savmtg.htm; Joseph Wheeler, *Their Last Full Measure: The Final Days of the Civil War* (New York: Da Capo Press, 2015), 32–33; Brooks D. Simpson and Jean V. Berlin, eds., *Sherman's Civil War: Selected Correspondence of William T. Sherman, 1860–1865* (Chapel Hill: University of North Carolina Press, 2014), 795; William Marvel, *Lincoln's Autocrat: The Life of Edwin Stanton* (Chapel Hill: University of North Carolina Press, 2015), 359; Walter Stahr, *Stanton: Lincoln's War Secretary* (New York: Simon and Schuster, 2017), 393; Josef C. James, "Sherman at Savannah," *The Journal of Negro History* 39 (April 1954), 137.

Postscript: Age of Transcendence

1. "Miscellaneous," *Christian Examiner* 33 (November 1864), 381; "Literary Notices," *Zion's Herald and Wesleyan Journal*, November 9, 1864; "History of the Antislavery Measures of the Thirty-Seventh and Thirty-Eighth United States Congresses," *North American Review* 100 (January 1865), 238.

2. In fact, the date 1865 appeared only in the title and on the copyright page, and the historic vote on the Thirteenth Amendment did not appear in the narrative. Henry Wilson, *History of the Antislavery Measures of the Thirty-Seventh and Thirty-Eighth United States Congresses, 1861–1865* (Boston: Walker, Fuller, 1865).

3. "President's Annual Message to Congress, December 6, 1864," in *Collected Works of Abraham Lincoln*, vol. 8, 137, http://quod.lib.umich.edu/l/lincoln/lincoln8/1:298.1?rgn=div2;view=fulltext.

4. Michael Vorenberg, *Final Freedom: The Civil War, the Abolition of Slavery, and the Thirteenth Amendment* (Cambridge, UK: Cambridge University Press, 2001), 8.

5. "Celebration of the Emancipation Proclamation," *The Liberator*, January 20, 1865.

ACKNOWLEDGMENTS

The first debt of any spouse and parent who writes a book over the course of ten years is to the family. I will always be grateful to Brian Plane, who helped to establish the best circumstances for all my summer and holiday work sessions, and to my children, whose patience and interest in history gave me strength.

I am thankful for the support of Collegiate School, without which I could not have completed this work, and to Bill Bullard, Ryland Clarke, Michael Herzig, Peter Herzig, Melanie Hutchison, Lee Levison, and Roger Murray, who facilitated financial support for leave time and research through the Van Horne Foundation for Excellence in Teaching and the Gwen Herzig Academic Enrichment Fund. The book reflects the contributions of student researchers at Collegiate, including Nathan Ashany, Raynor Bond-Ashpole, Jeffrey Chung, Denis Fedin, William Janover, Alexander McDonald, George Mellgard, Easton Orbe, Joshua Peter, Mahir Riaz, Matt Roth, Daniel Ryu, Elliott Snyder, Joseph Tisch, and Henry Wilson. Thanks also to Stephanie Russell for assistance with Latin and classical references.

The Gilder Lehrman Institute of American History offered a fellowship and abundant encouragement, and I am thankful to James Basker and Susan Saidenberg for research support. I also benefited from the generosity of university professors, including David Anderson, David Blight, Mark Elliott, Eric Foner, Timothy McCarthy, Kent Newmyer, and Manisha Sinha.

For help with legal research and reasoning I am grateful to family members Rebekah McKinney, Margaret Plane, and Jake Watson, to Judge Lynwood C. Smith of the United States District Court, and to Maeva Marcus of the Institute for Constitutional History.

I would not be a writer without the support of Andrew Stuart, my literary agent, and of my mentors David Callahan, Thomas Paterson, and Janet Watson. Thomas LeBien offered me the chance to write for Hill and Wang, where I received the assistance of Daniel Gerstle and Ian Van Wye, among others. Alex Star worked patiently on my drafts and taught me a lot. The book is much improved by his efforts.

The best part about writing history is having the opportunity to work in libraries and archives and with specialists in state and local history, and I am grateful for the assistance of staffers at the American Antiquarian Society, the Brooklyn Historical Society, the Cammie G. Henry Research Center at Northwestern State University of Louisiana, Columbia University's Rare Book and Manuscript Library, the Historic New Orleans Collection, the Kansas Historical Society, the Library of Congress, the Library of Virginia, the Mississippi Department of Archives and History, the State Historical Association of Missouri, the Nahant Historical Society, the National Archives and Record Administration (where I benefited from the assistance of a professional researcher, Jon Deiss of Webb Deiss Research), the New-York Historical Society, the Pennsylvania Historical Society, the Peru State College Library in Nebraska, the Texas State Archives, the University of Alabama Library, the University of Virginia, the U.S. Army Heritage and Education Center, West Virginia Archives and History, and the Wisconsin Historical Society. The New York Public Library provided research materials and lovely space for working at the Schomburg Center for Research in Black Culture and the Stephen A. Schwarzman building on Fifth Avenue. I am also grateful to have been accommodated while traveling with family at the Madison County Library in Huntsville, Alabama, and the Volusia County Library in New Smyrna Beach, Florida.

INDEX

A Note About the Author

LeeAnna Keith teaches history at the Collegiate School in New York City. She is the author of *The Colfax Massacre: The Untold Story of Black Power, White Terror, and the Death of Reconstruction* (2009), and a recipient of a Gilder Lehrman Institute fellowship. Her articles have appeared in *The Dictionary of American History* and *The Journal of Southern History*.